Calcutta

Geoffrey Moorhouse's books, which have been translated into several languages, cover a variety of topics, from history to travel. They include *The Other England* (1964); *Against All Reason* (1969), a study of monastic life in the twentieth century; *The Missionaries* (1973); *The Fearful Void* (1974, Penguin 1986), an account of his 2,000 mile journey by camel through the Sahara, the longest solo passage of that desert by a European; *The Diplomats* (1977); *The Best Loved Game* (1979), a prize-winning collection of essays on cricket; *The Boat and the Town* (1979), about a deep-sea fishing community in North America; *India Britannica* (1983), a history of the British in India; *To the Frontier*, which won the Thomas Cook Award for the best travel book in 1984; and *Imperial City* (1988), a study of New York. His most recent work is *Hell's Foundations*, which examines the mythology of heroism in war, in the light of Gallipoli and its effect on one English town.

Geoffrey Moorhouse is a Fellow of the Royal Society of Literature and a Fellow of the Royal Geographical Society. He lives in a hill village in North Yorkshire.

CALCUTTA

GEOFFREY MOORHOUSE

══

PENGUIN BOOKS

PENGUIN BOOKS

Published by the Penguin Group
Penguin Books Ltd, 27 Wrights Lane, London W8 5TZ, England
Penguin Books USA Inc., 375 Hudson Street, New York, New York 10014, USA
Penguin Books Australia Ltd, Ringwood, Victoria, Australia
Penguin Books Canada Ltd, 10 Alcorn Avenue, Toronto, Ontario, Canada M4V 3B2
Penguin Books (NZ) Ltd, 182–190 Wairau Road, Auckland 10, New Zealand

Penguin Books Ltd, Registered Offices: Harmondsworth, Middlesex, England

First published by Weidenfeld and Nicolson 1971
Published in Penguin Books 1974
Reprinted with an Introduction 1983
7 9 10 8

Printed in England by Clays Ltd, St Ives plc
Set in Intertype Plantin

To the men of the CMPO who are incorruptibly there and to E. P. RICHARDS, sometime Chief Engineer of the Calcutta Improvement Trust, who restored some of my national pride

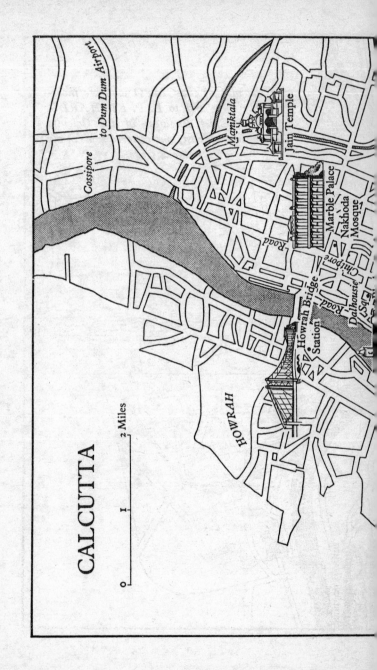

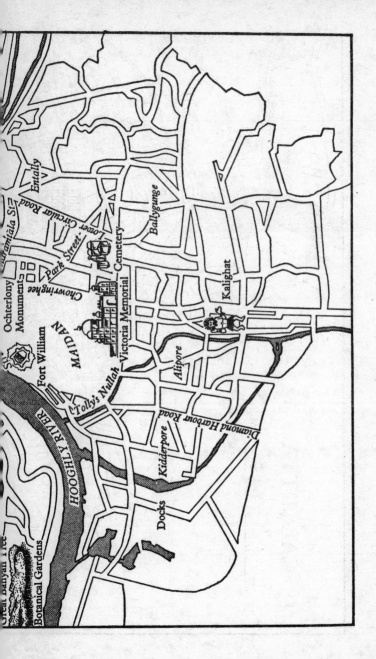

CONTENTS

ACKNOWLEDGEMENTS   5

FOREWORD   7

INTRODUCTION   9

1 Ultimate Experience   15

2 Imperial City   27

3 Poverty   91

4 Wealth   132

5 Migrants   169

6 Bengalis   186

7 People, People   208

8 Faded Glory   224

9 The Petrifying Jungle   265

10 The Road to Revolution   308

11 Zindabad   348

BIBLIOGRAPHY   358

SOURCE NOTES   361

INDEX   373

ILLUSTRATIONS

1 Calcutta 1971 – A crossing along Chowringhee (*Keystone Press*)

2 Two of the most impressive monuments to British rule – the domed Victoria Memorial and St Paul's Cathedral (*Photo: Mark Edwards*)

3 Rabindranath Tagore (*Camera Press; Photo: R. J. Chinwalla*)

4 Jyoti Basu (*Camera Press; Photo: Sunil Dutt*)

5 The Tollygunge Club (*Photo: Mark Edwards*)

6 Ochterlony Monument, on the edge of the Maidan (*Photo: Mark Edwards*)

7 A few of the homeless, asleep outside the Great Eastern Hotel (*Photo: Mark Edwards*)

8 A slum of makeshift shanties by a suburban railway line (*Photo: Mark Edwards*)

9 Bathing and washing clothes at the side of the road (*Picturepoint*)

10 Park Street Cemetery (*Photo: Geoffrey Moorhouse*)

11 The ultimate poverty – the Hooghly as a grave (*Photo: Mark Edwards*)

12 The voice – and the mood – of Calcutta in 1971 (*Photo: Mark Edwards*)

The author and publishers are grateful to the copyright owners for permission to reproduce the pictures.

ACKNOWLEDGEMENTS

A GREAT deal of this book is the product of my own observations in Calcutta. I hope the extent of this will be obvious from a comparison of the text with the source notes at the end. I spent a couple of months there on two visits in 1969 and 1970 and many people helped me while I was in the city. I would certainly have been lost without the guidance and friendship of Prasun Majumdar, who shared a great deal with me, including one of my two gheraos. I would have missed a great deal without the kindness and help of Professor and Mrs Arthur Row Jr and their family. I was also much assisted by Inder Malhotra, Ragau Banerjee, Niranjan Sen, Mr and Mrs S. Sircar, Mr and Mrs D. L. Bannister, Lindsay Emmerson, Tim Scott and Ken MacPherson. My thanks to all of them, as well as to Mr D. R. Kalia and his staff at the National Library, who were extremely helpful during my researches among their bookwormed records. I am similarly indebted to Mr S. C. Sutton and his assistants at the India Office Library in London, on whom I relied heavily for much of the documentation in this book; and I'd like to salute Mr D. W. King of the War Office Library, who dug out a paper on the origins of the Dum Dum bullet. My thanks, too, to my old colleague Peter Preston, who twice smoothed my passage to India. My biggest debt, however, is to John Rosselli, student of Bentinck and Bengal, who presented me with the idea of this book. Without him it would not have been written. I hope it doesn't disappoint him.

It would be as well to say something here about my spelling of local names. There is absolutely no consistency, I'm afraid, either in Calcutta or in this book. When Jamshedpur is spelt with a final 'pur' the same ought to go for one of Calcutta's main thoroughfares, but here it is rendered as Chitpore Road; I apologize in advance to any readers who are accustomed to the other version and I can only plead that the one I have used seemed to be the most popular in the city. People who know Calcutta and India better than I do will probably find other examples of a similar kind. Where possible I have used the local telephone directory as arbiter of style; otherwise I have simply tried to be clear. I have thus failed to call Benares by its now customary title of Varanasi and I hope my Indian friends will forgive me this wilful howler; but I have dared to call the River Ganges by its proper name of Ganga on the assumption that even foreigners can absorb the translation without being confused. If anyone needs convincing further of the difficulty in accurate spelling of proper names, it is worth remarking that in September 1969, one of Calcutta's chief newspapers was publicly asking whether the Ochterlony Monument must now be rendered as Sahid Minar, Saheed Minar or Shaheed Minar.

This is perhaps the place to say to anyone who may still be in doubt that Calcutta has nothing at all to do with the revue that bears its name. According to Kenneth Tynan, whose brainchild that was, 'Oh! Calcutta!' is the title of a painting by an elderly French surrealist named Clovis Trouille. It is a pun on the French Oh! Quel Cul T'as, meaning 'Oh what an arse you have'. The reference is to the fact that the model in the picture is displaying her bottom to the painter. I'm obliged to him for that information.

FOREWORD

I CAN offer no bigger or better excuse for writing a book about Calcutta than something on the lines of the old Mallory quotation about Everest; it is there. It is strange, though, that no one has attempted anything like a portrait of the city since Montague Massey published his recollections in 1918. Since then there has been an excellent but highly technical social survey by N. K. Bose and two or three books on Bengali politics, all written by scholars for other scholars; nothing else except occasional memoirs with fleeting references. Yet this was the second city in the British Empire and, for what the computation is worth, it remains the second city of the Commonwealth. It is also the fourth city in the world. Our failure to take much notice of it maybe tells us more about ourselves than it has not told us about Calcutta.

In a sense, the story of Calcutta is the story of India and the story of the so-called Third World in miniature. It is the story of how and why Empire was created and what happened when Empire finished. It is the story of people turning violently to Communism for salvation. It is also the story of Industrial Revolution. The imperial residue of Calcutta, a generation after Empire ended, is both a monstrous and a marvellous city. Journalism and television have given us a rough idea of the monstrosities but none at all of the marvels. I can only hope to define the first more clearly and to persuade anyone interested that the second is to be found there too.

INTRODUCTION

A hazard facing any writer who attempts to bring history up to date – as I did in the last few pages of this book a dozen years ago – is that events shortly afterwards may make his perspective and his conclusions seem comically inappropriate. It may already be thought that the apocalyptic vision with which I finished *Calcutta* fell rather heavily into this trap for the unwary author; and I shall be very happy if someone in the next century is able to confirm that this was indeed the case. Certainly no cataclysmic plague has visited the city since I first studied it, nor have the pavement poor risen with ferocity to dispose of the rich in angry bloodshed. Yet I would not wish to change a word that I wrote then. I was expressing as best I could what Calcutta made me feel. Those paragraphs were much less prophecy than speculation. Above all, they were my effort to convey a spirit that seemed to be abroad in a dark night of the city's soul.

In fact, there was a moment soon after the book was published when it seemed that my imaginings might be given dreadful substance. In 1971 there occurred the revolt in what was then East Pakistan ·against Yahya Khan's military government in Islamabad, which led to the establishment of Bangladesh. Inevitably this produced, as every other terrible conflict on the subcontinent has always done, uncountable masses of refugees streaming away from the centre of violence. With Calcutta only a short distance from the border, the majority of them headed for the city, whose outskirts were soon swollen by many encampments of what the international jargon refers to abstractly (and abstractedly) as 'displaced persons'. Multitudes, who would have starved to death without the charity of the Indian government and the aid that came from further afield, lived for a long time in great drainpipes, which were lying in readiness for some half-executed municipal enterprise, and in a new spread of shanty towns. In those first few months after their arrival, until Calcutta had yet again adapted itself enough to demonstrate its resilience in the face of difficult odds, the already overloaded city must have been perilously close to breakdown, urban collapse or whatever we choose to call the ultimate metropolitan nightmare. After a couple of years, by which time even Islamabad had been forced to recognize the independence of Dacca, many of the refugees staggered back whence they had come; but some stayed behind to compound, as refugees always do, Calcutta's everlasting problems.

There have been other critical moments in the past decade or so. The political machinations of West Bengal have continued in the fashion of the sixties, always tortuously, often incoherently, sometimes violently. The period of president's rule ended with a state election in 1971 which produced a coalition government of eight parties led by a Congress man. Twelve months later the Corporation of Calcutta was effectively suspended, its elected representatives removed, its functions henceforth discharged by the state government. In 1975 the political life of the whole country was thrown into turmoil as a result of the emergency powers adopted by Mrs Gandhi's government in Delhi, and insurrection against those powers was as great in Calcutta as it was anywhere; likewise the Delhi government's response to insurrection. The prisons of West Bengal became as crowded as ever they had been during the most repressive days of the British Raj. But when, in 1977, the Prime Minister submitted herself to general election (a democratic act which her adversaries, axe-grinding opportunists almost to a man, had insisted beforehand to be quite beyond her), she paid the price for her authoritarian regime in West Bengal as elsewhere in India. Not only did the state return its tally of her opponents to the New Delhi parliament; in its own domestic elections it handed power, with a colossal majority, to a Left Front government – yet another medley of parties, but one dominated by the CPI(M). And so Jyoti Basu, whom I had last seen as the power behind the throne on which sat a bewildered Ajoy Mukherjee, came into his own as Chief Minister of West Bengal.

It was his Calcutta, in most senses, to which I returned in the spring of 1981. I had flown down from Patna to a Dum Dum airport which was cut off from the city, with no buses or taxis plying for hire, because a strike had been incited by the Basu government in protest against a faction which had just been demonstrating roughly against its rule. Some citizens had been killed and, that weekend, a dozen tramcars were displayed on the Esplanade, to show what the enemies of the people were capable of in their resentment of the people's willed administration. The smashed windows of the trams and the bodywork scorched by firebombs were testimony enough to the vicious course anybody's resentment may take in Calcutta. To that extent, nothing had changed while I was away. Provocations, reprisals, politicians playing extravagantly to the gallery, consequential strikes and attendant uproar were still the order of the day. So, thank God, were all the things that have always redeemed the nasty facts of life in Calcutta. The warmth of people and their astonishing vitality were also as I remembered them.

As was their ability to charm the outsider with some idiosyncrasy of their own which can make him giggle and be moved at one and the same time. My old lodgings on Wood Street having disappeared in favour of some flats, I stayed at the Great Eastern Hotel – as Kipling stayed when he was in town – one of the great social landmarks of British rule. It has long since been transferred from private hands to those of the government of West Bengal; which means, at the moment, that it is run by Communists. I chose the Great Eastern not because of the imperial connection *per se*, but because I have a taste for bygones which have survived unexpectedly in the modern world. There is much in the Great Eastern that qualifies for my custom in this respect, from the old-fashioned plumbing to the little mosque which Muslim members of the staff have created in an annexe to the boiler room. Above all, there is the inscription which decorates the window of a textile shop near the hotel's reception desk. There, in gilded letters curving in low-relief above the imperial crown, are the words 'By appointment

to HM the King Emperor and HM the Queen Empress', which
the employees of communism were still polishing assiduously
every day, thirty-four years after independence had been
achieved. I beg the government of West Bengal never to discon-
tinue this eccentric task. The act of preserving that fragment
of history is much more their glory than ever the inscription
itself referred to ours.

But, as I found out in the next few days, changes *had* been
wrought to the Calcutta I had fondly but anxiously left in 1970.
The entire length of Chowringhee was sorely disfigured by a
deep trench, whose outcrops also made a mess of Park Street
and other adjacent thoroughfares. This was the excavation for
the underground railway which, one of these days, will run
beneath the city all the way from Dum Dum to Tollygunge,
the first thing of its kind on the sub-continent. Calcutta's desperate need for better systems of transport had been tackled in
other forms, too. Those poor old Leyland double-deckers, which
in their rattletrap way may yet outlast the company that made
them, had been reinforced in my absence by a fleet of smart-
looking minibuses, splendid additions in every respect apart
from the fact that tall passengers who must stand are obliged
to do so in a prehensile stoop. On the Hooghly I found diesel-
engined ferryboats rumbling back and forth where there had
been nothing like them before. A mile or so below Howrah
Bridge, what's more, two concrete arcs were springing towards
each other from either bank, due to join up in a magnificent new
suspension bridge for road traffic in 1985.

A degree of salvation – and one dare not hope for an improvement of Calcutta by more than degrees across long periods
of time – has come to the city by way of its river, which always
was the key to its fortunes. In 1975 the great barrage at Farakka
was completed, a few miles from the border with Bangladesh,
in up-country Bengal. There have been periodic wrangles
since about the proportion of Ganga water which shall be
allowed to flow past Farakka into Bangladesh, and what may
run down into the Indian Hooghly. But Calcutta has certainly
been well served by the engineering up there, as the accumulated

silt of half a century and more has been flushed downstream towards the Bay of Bengal by the increased flow. The depth of navigable water is greater now between Kidderpore Docks and the sea, though the Hooghly will always be a treacherous river for ocean-going ships. Nevertheless, in the twelve months before my latest visit, some 700 vessels had brought their trade right into the heart of the city, a figure that hadn't been heard of for donkey's years. And that is quite apart from the numbers which dock at Halida, fifty-six miles nearer the sea, where the new port would be flourishing at last if international commerce weren't in such a bad way, for it can accommodate the largest merchantmen afloat. Not only has Farakka caused those who forecast the death of Calcutta as a port to brighten it up; it has also done its bit to improve (just a little) the local drinking-water supply. The pumping station at Palta was in a state of collapse when I first saw it, corroding under the high salinity of the Hooghly's sluggish ebb and flow, but now it has been fettled, and fresher water is going through to the taps and stand-pipes of the city beyond.

It would be crass to assume that such advances as these mean that a great new dawn is coming Calcutta's way. The plight of most of its millions remains much as it was when I tried to describe it in the pages that follow. The Calcutta Metropolitan Development Authority, which has evolved from the gallant CMPO, has tinkered with some bustee defects, but its resources are overstretched and a third of the population still live in bustees. Until these are gone, if ever they do go, there is no excuse for anyone to make a song and dance about the basic living conditions of Calcutta. But obviously the deepest pessimisms of 1970 have been lightened a shade or two by what has happened since. I myself underrated Calcutta's enduring capacity for survival in the face of difficulties that might destroy the will to survive in a civilized fashion in any western community of size that I have known. This is a variation of the most common failing of the westerner when contemplating India, based on the assumption that what is valid in his part of the world is or ought to be equally true on the sub-continent. It infrequently is.

I should have known better. I rejoice that Calcutta persists in ways that make us, its devotees, grateful always to refresh ourselves at its sometimes stained fountains. I am glad I picked the right word to symbolize what I felt then, what I feel still. Again . . . Zindabad!

Gayle, 1983

I

ULTIMATE EXPERIENCE

No traveller from the West is completely prepared for his first experience of India. Whether he flies into the fiery dawn of Bombay or Delhi, as he frequently does, his senses will at once be shocked and stimulated and confused by the strangeness of his new landfall. He may have inklings of what to expect but he can never have more than that, for everything that is about to happen to him is on such a scale and of such magnitude as to defy and almost to dissolve all his careful anticipation. He may have been entranced once by the queer and exotic doings of snake charmers, fire eaters and gulli-gulli men at sundown in the great square of Marrakesh, which will have seemed a marvellous spectacle especially organized for the benefit of tourists. In India the traveller discovers that such things can be customary processes of living. He may believe that he has sighted the utmost poverty in the cave dwellings and hovels of Southern Italy or Spain. In India he realizes that this was not so, and that something infinitely worse goes on and on, hopelessly and terribly. The traveller's confusion and the sick feeling he begins to detect in the pit of his sensitive stomach is liable to be increased, moreover, if he happens to be British. For in all this confusion and this riveting strangeness he becomes aware of things as faintly familiar as an old coat of varnish, or a forgotten diary discovered one traumatic day under the dust in the box room. These consist of ways some people have of doing and saying things, of a sign manual casually observed upon a building, of a lingering and homely style inextricably mixed up with all the oddness. They make the traveller fairly blink with recollection as he struggles with some fresh encounter that he suspects he has had some place before. And then one day, while he is still astonished by his landfall, he takes plane again and flies on to the East; for there, he has heard, lies the ultimate in this weird and marvellous and awful experience.

If he has disdained the services of Indian Airlines and boarded someone else's Boeing, he finds that some of his reflexes have disturbingly changed. He spends much of the next three hours pondering the comforts of travel by international jet-propelled aviation. He toys with his glossified meal, complete with dainty salt and pepper shakers and real quill toothpicks wrapped in cellophane; and he catches himself wondering just how many thousands (possibly millions?) of dollars were spent in devising and developing the plastic sheet whose frictional surface is intended to stop his share of hors d'oeuvre sliding off the tray and into his neighbour's lap. He relieves himself of a few uncomfortable thoughts in the lavatory aft, where Pan American have thoughtfully provided handcream and soap (both by Morny) and aftershave lotion (by Onyx); all done up in small attractive packages which invite the traveller to pocket them, for there are plenty more where they came from and he's welcome. He chooses, perhaps, the mouth-wash instead, for a bitter little flavour has been coming on and he likes to make his landfalls nice and clean. Thus revitalized and refreshed, he takes his aerial passage across India, until the warning lights go on and the stewardess hopes he has enjoyed his flight and he knows he is coming to earth again.

As the Boeing flexes its wings in descent, the traveller begins to observe the details of a landscape which has changed somewhat since his taste of Bombay or Delhi. There the ground seemed barren and burnt from the sky but here it looks wonderfully fertile. The predominant colour is green, sometimes vivid and deep, sometimes nearly yellow, but always the promise of growth. And there is water: water in craters, water in canals, water in lakes and, just over there, a great gleaming swamp of saturated fields with what looks like chickweed floating on the top between the dykes. A city appears, enormous and sprawling around a wide brown river which has shaped itself in a dog-leg and which has ships hanging at anchor. Silver oil tanks sparkle in the piercing light but there is a haze of smoke over the city which renders a range of high dockside cranes as an indistinct thicket of industry and a vast row of factory roofs as a rusty sheet of corrugated iron. It could almost be Liverpool on a sensational summer's day. But as the Boeing cants over and skims even lower above the gleaming swamp and past the lunar grey of some gigantic reclamation from the waters, the traveller knows it is no such thing. For there are palm trees here and a brown man coaxing a black bullock along a straggling road and, gracious me, a dazzlingly white Early English church tower poking up from jungle. Then the plane is down, and as it bounds and sways along the runway, the traveller notices that he is about to disembark at a spanking international airport, as new as Prague's, as inviting as Rome's. He blinks yet again, and wonders whether rumour has lied once more. For he has come to Calcutta. And everything he has heard about it sounds quite remarkably unpleasant.

This, he has been told, is the problem city of the world, with problems that not only seem insoluble but which grow every day at a galloping and fantastic rate. This is where nearly eight million people exist, who will have become more than twelve millions by 1986 if the estimates of population experts are correct. Only Tokyo, London and New York contain more people than this and scarcely any of them have a conception of how things really are in the thirty-mile length of Greater Calcutta alongside the Hooghly River. Calcutta is merely said to be the place where thousands (or is it millions?) sleep on the streets at night. Where the poverty is so dreadful that everyone who knows it throws up his hands in horror and turns his back on it. Where there is violence and anarchy and raging Maoist Communism. All this is true. It is also true that Calcutta is not only the largest city in India but commercially, industrially and intellectually the most important. It is the richest city in India. And, paradoxically, set in one of the most ancient cultures known to man, it is one of the youngest cities in the world. Henry Hudson had dropped anchor off Manhattan and begun the history of New York eighty-one years before Job Charnock pitched his tents on the East bank of the Hooghly and made a start on Calcutta; Maisonneuve founded Montreal half a century earlier. What the traveller finds there today is therefore the creation and the legacy of the British.

Very few people have ever said anything nice about Calcutta, unless they were Bengali. Writing in 1863, Sir George Trevelyan was asking us to 'find, if you can, a more uninviting spot than Calcutta ... it unites every condition of a perfectly unhealthy situation ... The place is so bad by nature that human efforts could do little to make it worse; but that little has been done faithfully and assiduously.' Rudyard Kipling, who was there only for a short visit as a newspaper correspondent down from the Punjab, loathed the place and composed a rambling series of essays about it which he called *The City of Dreadful Night* (a title he also bestowed upon a verse epic about Lahore, for he was a repetitive man). A century and more before that, Robert Clive decided that it was 'the most wicked place in the Universe' though, admittedly, he had only England and Madras to compare it with. All these were stock responses of a kind Calcutta has generated from the start. There have been exceptions, though. A junior contemporary of Trevelyan was bowled over by the city when he came to it as a new recruit to the Indian Civil Service. 'Imagine,' William Hunter wrote home to his fiancée, 'Imagine everything that is glorious in nature combined with all that is beautiful in architecture, and you can faintly picture to yourself what Calcutta is.' He was, of course, in love and he'd just arrived from Peckham. But William Bentinck, who was much more sophisticated, and who was to rule India from Government House there, had decided in 1805 as soon as he discovered it that Calcutta was the richest city he had seen after London and 'the spectacle is altogether the most curious and magnificent I have met with'. At the other end of the nineteenth century Winston Churchill told his mother that 'I shall always be glad to have seen it – for the same reason Papa gave for being glad to have seen Lisbon – namely, that it will be unnecessary for me ever to see it again'. But he granted that it was a very great city and then made an unexpected comparison for 'at night, with a grey fog and cold wind, it almost allows one to imagine that it is London'. It put Reginald Heber, the second Bishop of Calcutta, in mind of Moscow. It put Mark Twain, who lectured there in 1896, in mind of very little but a vivid metaphor; he thought the weather of Calcutta 'enough to make a brass doorknob mushy', stayed only a day or two, and recalled the city years later merely as the place where he met an old girl friend, with whom he had a conversation which centred on the peculiarity of dried herring. But the most memorable observation of all was made by some anonymous fellow in a sentence which is usually, but incorrectly, attributed to Lenin. 'The road to world revolution,' wrote this unknown epigrammist one day, 'lies through Peking, Shanghai and Calcutta.'

The truth is that almost everything popularly associated with Calcutta is highly unpleasant and sometimes very nasty indeed. It is bracketed in the Western mind with distant rumours of appalling disaster, riot and degradation. The one incident in its history with which every schoolchild has always been familiar has been called the Black Hole of Calcutta, and nobody who knows the place can ever have been surprised to learn that one of the most vicious weapons ever devised by man, the Dum Dum bullet, was invented and first produced in a small arms factory within a rifle shot of that splendid new airport.

The very name of Calcutta is derived from a symbol of fear and evil. There is no religion in the world richer than Hinduism in the number and variety of its gods. It enshrines a bewildering pantheon of figures who together are venerated for every conceivable reflex and incident in the human condition and philosophy. There are gods as jolly-looking as Ganesh, sitting comfortably with his elephant's head, who is invoked by writers to bring them success. There are goddesses as elegant as Sarasvati, riding upon her gorgeous peacock, patron of music and inventor of Sanskrit. And there are scores of godlings with more unfortunate connotations like Manasa, who is worshipped in Bengal as an antidote to snake bites, and Sitala, who is particularly idolized by people along the Hooghly during outbreaks of smallpox. There is no one at all more respected and feared than the goddess Kali who, like every other Hindu divine, has other names and forms as well; in Bengal she is more commonly known as Durga, in South India they sometimes call her Bhawani. All the representations of Kali are designed to frighten an illiterate and superstitious mind more thoroughly than anything else in creation. She appears with devilish eyes, or with a tongue drip-

ping blood, with snakes entwined round her neck, or with a garland of skulls. She is Kali the Terrible and she is propitiated
with daily sacrifice, as well as with flowers. When the Thugs
strangled a traveller, they knotted in one corner of the handkerchief a silver coin consecrated to Kali, to give them a better
grip.

Kali, says the mythology, was the wife of Siva the Destroyer;
and Siva, together with Brahma the Creator and Vishnu the
Preserver, stands in a divine triumvirate at the head of the
Hindu religion. When Kali died, Siva was both grief-stricken
and angry. He placed her corpse on his shoulders and went
stamping round the world in a dervish dance of mourning
which became more furious the longer it lasted. The other gods
realized that unless Siva was stopped the whole world would be
destroyed by his rage, which was unlikely to end as long as he
had his wife's body on his shoulders. So Vishnu took up a knife
and flung it at the corpse, dismembering it into fifty-two pieces
which were scattered across the face of the earth. By the side of
a great river in Bengal the little toe of the right foot landed, and a
temple was built there, with an attendant village, and the people
called this place Kalikata.

Calcutta, indeed, is a mighty terrible and frightening place today. But there is another side to it, almost unheard of, rarely
figuring in its reputation, sorely neglected by travellers from
other parts of India as well as from farther afield, who dash in
and transact their business, observe the miseries, then turn tail
and run for it before they are totally overcome by violent claustrophobia. They go home and cry woe unto the city, take its
taste out of their mouths with a gin and tonic or a Pepsi, and
recall it thereafter only as an emblem of experience, to show that
they now know the worst that Life has to offer. Yet to balance
(just a little) this conventional rumour of Calcutta, the traveller
can do no better than to spare himself a couple of hours from
the commercial and social horrors of the city and take himself
down to the Marble Palace. This, indisputably, is the richest,
the quaintest, the eeriest, the most haphazard and the most
ridiculous, the most astonishing and the most lovable and almost
the saddest relic in what, by about the start of the nineteenth

century, was beginning to be called the City of Palaces. You trace it – with some difficulty, no doubt, for the taxi-drivers of Calcutta are not very strong on navigation – down a side street among the pullulating alleys off Chittaranjan Avenue. The air reeks down here, like so many of the central thoroughfares, of worn-out engine fumes mixed up with half a dozen varieties of decay. The pushing and shoving and sidestepping past rickshaws and cows and people is almost as concentrated as anywhere. The noise is Calcutta's usual symphony of honks and clatters and clangs and rumbles and shouts, with transistored obligatos on the sitar. It feels and looks and is just about as unsavoury as its past; for this area was once called Chor Bagan, or the thieves' garden. But in the middle of this towering mess you find, unbelievably, a real garden of maybe an acre with a Palladian mansion set square in the centre. This could easily be a luxurious pocket in Rome, not Calcutta, and there is a fountain in the garden that would not be out of place in the Piazza Navona or at the bottom of the Spanish Steps; it has Neptune figures brandishing conch shells, with indeterminate water beasts gaping at them from the surrounding pool and four nubile naiads upholding a classical urn on top of the central column. The adjacent paths are bordered with a galaxy of busts that never quite add up to a rhythmic theme – a Caesar here, a Chinaman there, a Redskin over by the shrubbery – as though someone with a bent for sculpture couldn't make up his mind whether he was also a student of history or phrenology.

There are greater surprises inside the house. You enter a courtyard first, which is topped by a high gallery. The floor is patterned with diamond-shapes and lozenges of multi-coloured marble, the white walls are embellished with swagging in Wedgwood blue, there are wonderfully cool-looking maidens and men cut in stone, wrapped in togas and standing high on plinths. There are a couple of urns with a variety of aspidistra growing from the bowls. And there is a menagerie. Out in the garden, pelicans and peacocks, mallard and teal have been poking and prodding at the lawns or ducking and dozing in the pool. In this courtyard there are scarlet macaws from Burma tethered to perches, albino mynahs from the back of Bihar whistling in cages, and pinioned parakeets from Northern Australia making a mess on the statues.

Beyond lie apartments and galleries, and in these the Marble Palace becomes a fantasy brought to earth. They are full, as no building was ever filled before, with art and objects from Bangkok to Bristol and back, though almost everything seems to have been picked up from the auctions and markets and dispossessed households of Europe. There is a very old Queen Victoria in plaster standing large as life by the main stairway and a very young Queen Victoria in oak, somewhat larger, dominating a red marble room where another squadron of busts glare at her from the shadows. There is marble everywhere, in ninety different varieties it is said, transported across the seas by the ton to provide floors and wall panels and table tops. There are great swathes of satin hanging round windows and enormous follies of crystal glass hanging in chandeliers from ceilings. There are mirrors from Venice and vases from Sèvres and goblets from Bohemia and stags' heads from the Trossachs and figures from Dresden and swords from Toledo and ormolu clocks from Paris and carvings from Bavaria and vast quantities of Victorian bric-à-brac that look as if they were scavenged in job lots from the Portobello Road on a series of damp Saturday afternoons in October; bronze boys on chargers all blackened with age, plaster fruit and stuffed kingfishers presented under glass domes, gewgaws in papier-maché and firedogs in cast-iron. A long gallery is so cluttered with these things upon, between, under and around its marble table-tops, that there is scarcely room to lay a finger between the bits and pieces; all collecting a patina of dust and cobwebs in a creepy half light.

And then there are the pictures. They stagger up the stairways unevenly and they hang lopsided round all the rooms; the gilt of their frames is tarnished and flaked; they are desperate for restoration and some of the oil paint is beginning to slide from the canvases in the terrible humidity of Calcutta. This is catastrophe, for many of them are masterpieces. Reynolds is here and so is Murillo, and Titian is said to be lurking somewhere. The guide books reckon there are four paintings by Rubens in this house: *The Marriage of St Catherine, The Martyrdom of St*

Sebastian, Minerva giving the loving cup to Apollo and *The Return of Ulysses*. But when you stop before an aged and indistinct possibility and ask the old gentleman in the dhoti, who is taking you round, whether that is one, he just says 'Oh, yers. That's a priceless painting. Came from Europe. Oh yers. A priceless painting.' Then he cocks his head on one side and looks at you keenly; and you simply can't tell whether he is pulling your leg or wondering whether you are pulling his.

This is not a museum. It is a home, though you are very welcome to wander around it freely between the hours of ten and five for nothing more than your signature in the visitor's book. It belongs to the Mullick family, who had long service and good conduct under the Mogul Emperors of India and were eventually granted the zamindar title to farm taxes, which made them as rich and landed as any British grandee was to become. It was built in 1835 by Raja Rajendra Mullick Bahadur, who had been orphaned at three and given an English guardian, Sir James Hogg, by the Supreme Court. Sir James presented his ward with a few birds to go with the Marble Palace (which wealthy young Rajendra started making at the age of sixteen) and that was the beginning of the menagerie. The Mullicks have been there ever since, collecting their treasures and their trifles when abroad, establishing a legend of charity when at home. For at noon every day their durwans at the gate begin to hand food and paise, a little gruffly, to a long column of destitutes who have been waiting with clamour and patience since the dawn; and the donation, it is said, continues until the limit of four thousand people has been reached. Meanwhile, the Mullicks themselves count their investments and cultivate their thoughts and are occasionally discovered playing Chopin on a grand piano in a corner of the marble ballroom; while the heat bears down and causes a little more stucco to peel from the buff front of the Marble Palace, and the great wooden blinds are drawn deep between the classical pilasters, and even the figures on the pedimented roof seem to droop in the sun. And if it were not for that burning sun, that queue of beggars, that noise and that smell, that air of being trapped, it could very easily be 7,000 miles away to the West. It is a Chatsworth of a place, muddled up with scenes from an

Indian *Great Expectations*; and it would be no surprise at all to
encounter Miss Havisham reclining in a corner among the bric-
à-brac, the shadows and the cobwebs.

This is Calcutta, too.

It was, all the same, lunacy for anyone not born and bred in
Bengal (or, at least, in India) to settle down here and make an
Empire from it. Everything in Nature was against it, the climate
most of all. Calcutta is tolerable in winter, when the temperature is often in the 70s and when it can become even cooler in
the evening; there was a freakish day in January 1899 when it
dropped to 44·2 degrees, though it is hard to imagine the cold
winds and foggy nights that made Winston Churchill think of
London. But by the middle of March the heat is beginning to
sear the city to the bone. Between then and the start of the
monsoon it can rise to 120 degrees in this part of the world, the
thermometer can stick over 100 for days on end, and it rarely
falls below 80 even in the middle of the night. It becomes so hot
that the tar liquefies on the roads and goes oozing down the
drains, and the colossal steel mesh of the Howrah Bridge is
habitually four feet longer by day than by night. People go out
with black umbrellas for shade, including the policemen trying to
sort out the chaos of traffic at the top of Chowringhee, who have
umbrellas with special handles that slot into the holsters at
their belts so that their arms can remain free; and people without umbrellas are apt to hold briefcases and newspapers, books
and letters and folds of saris between their heads and the sun;
and men walk holding the hems of their dhotis out like sails,
to catch any trace of breeze. When Calcutta has a heat wave –
which means something well over 100 degrees – the cinemas are
packed, like the libraries and reading rooms, because they are
almost the only public places in the city which run to air-conditioning. On top of the blistering heat comes the humidity, and it
is commonplace for that to register 100 per cent.

There is occasional relief from this awful combination. There
are odd evenings in April that bring a shower with blue electric
flashes in the sky. You can get a storm that has the thermometer down and up again through 30 degrees in half an hour

while the city is bombarded with hailstones an inch and a half across; and the crows caught in mid-flight twist and dodge like fighters in anti-aircraft fire to avoid them, while small boys alternately squeal with pain and yelp with delight as they try to catch the pieces of ice before they land. But, generally, Calcutta before the monsoon means being soaked with sweat after walking a slow fifty yards; it means not having an inch of dry skin except in air-conditioning; it means shivering with the shock as you walk off the street into a highly-equipped restaurant that feels like a refrigerator for the first few minutes.

And then, about the middle of May, the occasional puffs of cloud that have been in the sky for a week or two begin to roll up more thickly. This is the worst time of all unless the monsoon fails and anyone in his senses who could possibly get away would do so then. The monsoon breaks in the first week of June, unless there is to be calamity. It comes down in a torrent to a smashing of thunder. It rains for several hours in solid straight shafts of water. Then it stops and the city steams like a laundry in the sun. Then it rains again as before. It goes on like this for four months, while Calcutta collects almost all its annual quota of 64 inches rainfall. It comes down so fiercely and in such quantity, and Calcutta is so ill-equipped to bear this sudden blessing, that the streets are awash, the motor traffic is stalled, the trams can no longer move and only the rickshaw-pullers keep going through the floods, up to their knees and axles in water. This, too, is an awful time and the air is stickier than ever when the rain is not actually pouring. But without it Calcutta would be utterly lost. If the monsoon is delayed the city becomes insane with the tension of waiting in that smothering atmosphere; for it knows that if the monsoon failed, terrible things would happen to its people.

This is probably the filthiest climate on earth, then. But apart from the balmy uplands to the North around Darjeeling, it is much the same wherever you go in Bengal, which sits sodden astride the Tropic of Cancer. The thing that makes this the most impossible place of all in this part of India for metropolitan and imperial ambitions, is the structure of the landscape here. Calcutta lies within the wide flat wedge of delta country containing the outflows of both the Ganga and the Brahmaputra. The Hooghly is a diversion from the Ganga (which only the English-speaking have known as the Ganges) as it plunges towards the Bay of Bengal, eighty-odd miles to the South; and the Mother of the World finds her way to the sea through a hundred smaller channels besides. The whole area, thousands of square miles, is simply untamed tropical fen; 'new mud, old mud and marsh', as a geographer has called it. The only firm ground is by the river banks, so that villages straggle along the watercourses, surrounded by mangoes, palms, bamboos and endless expanses of swamp. When the rains come and the rivers flood, this delta becomes a gigantic inland sea. At any time, it is a perfect breeding ground for malaria and any other disease that thrives on moisture; some of Charnock's sailors found it so unhealthy that they christened their landing place Golgotha. Yet on this bog the British created their capital in India. Nothing but commercial greed could possibly have led to such an idiotic decision.

2

IMPERIAL CITY

THE British were not the first Europeans to come nosing round here. The Portuguese preceded them in Bengal, just as they preceded them in India at large. By the start of the seventeenth century they had their powerful stronghold at Goa in the West, and on this side of the sub-continent they had been in and out of favour with local Nawabs for the better part of a hundred years. In favour, they conducted themselves as merchant seamen, and another early visitor, the Venetian Cesare Federici, who was in the river in 1578, notes that trade was in 'rice, cloth of Bombast of diverse sorts, Lacca, great abundance of sugar, mirabolans, dried and preserved, long pepper, oyle of zerzeline, and many other sorts of merchandise'. Out of favour, they resorted to piracy in the mouth of the Ganga, from bases on the farther side of the Bay.

The erratic history of the Portuguese in Bengal is more or less summarized by what happened to them in the last few years of their dominance there. In 1630 the Muslim rulers of this country had defeated Sebastian Gonzales, in spite of the fact that he commanded 1,000 Portuguese, 2,000 Indians, 200 cavalry and 80 vessels, and had seen him flying in disgrace to Goa. Not all of his compatriots retreated with him, though. Many stayed behind and they were allowed to resettle their old trading post on the west bank, twenty-seven miles upstream of Kalikata, with Michael Rodriguez as governor. For a couple of years there was peace, until the Mogul Emperor appointed a new Governor of Bengal, Cossim Khan, who at once accused the Portuguese of exacting payment from all boats passing their factory and drawing off commerce from the ancient port of Satgaon. For three and a half months Cossim Khan besieged the Portuguese, who repeatedly offered to surrender and pay 100,000 rupees in tribute, but kept firing on the enemy at the same time. Eventually, their fortifications were mined and there was much slaughter; the Portuguese skipper of a boat carrying men, women and children blew up his magazine and sank with all hands rather than fall into Muslim hands. Some young people were spared, however, and packed off to the Imperial court in Agra; the girls to the Emperor's harem, the boys for circumcision and indoctrination into the true faith. And there, presumably, they were incorporated into the life of a disconsolate Shah Jehan, and watched him building the Taj Mahal as a shrine for his beloved Mumtaz.

The British had been on the move for a generation by now. Eight businessmen of London had met in Founders' Hall on 24 September 1599, petitioning their Queen for a charter that would enable them to enjoy 'a quiet trade' in the East. She had been pleased to grant their request in fine Elizabethan tones: 'Whereas our most dear and loving cousin, George Earl of Cumberland and other our well-beloved subjects ... have of our certain knowledge been petitioners unto us for our Royal assent and license to be granted unto them, that they, of their own Adventures, costs and charges, as well for the honour of this our realm of England as for the increase of our navigation and advancement of trade merchandise ... might adventure and set forth one or more voyages, with convenient number of Ships and Pinnaces, by way of traffic and merchandise to the East Indies ...' The East India Company had thus been launched and by the time the Portuguese had been thrashed from the village of Hooghly, the British had a secure foothold of warehouses at Surat in the West; elsewhere, they were still probing for opportunity.

They found it in Bengal when yet another misfortune befell Shah Jehan. In 1636 one of his daughters was badly burned but she was successfully treated by Mr Gabriel Boughton, surgeon of the ship *Hopewell*, which was trading in the Deccan. He was asked to name his reward by a grateful Emperor and 'with that liberality which characterizes Britons, sought not for any private emolument, but solicited that his nation might have liberty to trade, free of all duties, in Bengal, and to establish factories in that country'. The comment is by Charles Stewart, writing loyally after enjoying a majority in Calcutta and a professorship at Haileybury, over a century later. Nevertheless, Boughton's characteristic request was granted and when, in the following year, he treated a lady in the harem of the Emperor's son (we are not told what the complaint was this time) the British were permitted to open more factories at Ballasore and Hooghly. And although the indispensable Dr Boughton died soon afterwards, his countrymen were now at liberty to export vast quantities of saltpetre, apart from other local merchandise, which was profitably much in demand in their Civil War at home.

The scenery was being assembled for Job Charnock's entry. He arrived in India in 1655 and at the start of 1657 appears on the Company's registers as a junior member of the Council of the Bay of Bengal at a salary of £20 a year. For a man who started so much we know disappointingly little of him; the trading registers and the diaries that he kept are merely log books, giving nothing away of the man himself. We are left with a series of observed impressions which, more than not, sound more like gossip than precise reporting. But they are all very colourful. He is first up at Patna as chief of the factory and it is there, in 1663, that he picks his wife; the beautiful widow Maria, who has been condemned by suttee to perish in flames alongside her husband's corpse; but Charnock, who has simply gone to gape at a heathen practice, is smitten by her appearance and snatches her from the pyre. They move down to Hooghly, to more factory management. For the next twenty years they are domestically preoccupied with raising a family of four in a variety of Company posts in Bengal, and it seems to have been a love match; after Maria died, Charnock is said to have sacrificed a cock each year on the anniversary at her tomb.

Otherwise, life is difficult. Charnock is involved in Company arguments about precedence but there are more serious disputes with the local Muslim rulers, after one of which Charnock is flogged. The Muslims become more belligerent, which calls for retribution and Admiral Nicholson is summoned to provide it. Although he cannonades and burns 500 buildings (including a Company factory with £300,000 worth of goods inside) the British for the moment are fighting a losing battle. Charnock by

now, in 1686, has been made Governor of the Bay of Bengal,
answerable to a Council of Directors based in Madras. He is in
Hooghly again but he and his men are forced to retreat downstream to Sutanuti, which is one of three villages almost on top
of each other on the east bank; the other two are Govindpur and
Kalikata. A large army is chasing them so they fall back again
to the island of Hijili, in the mouth of the Ganga, which is
diseased and without water, and where half these Europeans are
dead within three months. There are peace talks and Charnock
returns to Sutanuti, but by the beginning of 1687 there is hostility again and this time Charnock sails out of Bengal and
down to Madras in the frigate *Defence*.

The Emperor Aurangzeb had long since deposed his father,
Shah Jehan, and shifted his Imperial capital from Agra to Delhi;
most of Charnock's troubles, indeed, resulted from the change
in ruler. Aurangzeb, however, was a calculating man and Charles
Stewart probably accounts as well as anyone for what happened
next. He writes that the Emperor, 'being highly incensed against
the English, had commanded them to be expelled from every
part of his dominion; but as Aurangzeb ever made his passions
subservient to his policy and was sensible that he derived a
considerable aid to his revenue by the commerce carried on by
the English; also, that their ships of war could much annoy his
subjects ... putting a stop to the pilgrims visiting Mecca ...
authorized his ministers to form a treaty with Messrs Weldon
and Navarro, two English commissioners who had been sent
from Bombay by Sir John Child, the Director General of the
Company's settlements, to solicit peace.' So a treaty was formed
and Charnock sailed for Bengal again, but not before he had
insisted on obtaining the Emperor's firman, or personal licence,
to trade on the most advantageous terms. Charnock was a calcu-
lator, too.

Thus we come – at 22° 33′ North 88° 23′ East, in the middle
of the monsoon – to the foundation of Calcutta. In view of what
was to follow from this landfall, the moment should have been
recorded in something more memorable than Charnock's blank
prose. But he, after all, only knew that he was returning to his old
anchorage at Sutanuti and probably didn't expect his settlement

to last indefinitely anyway. He was rowed ashore, with an escort of 30 soldiers, to a village whose thatched huts had been pillaged and burned in the Nawab's pursuit of three and a half years before and he logs this in characteristically deadpan style. 'August 24, 1690. This day at Sankraal, I ordered Captain Brooke to come up with a vessel to Chuttanuty, where we arrived about noon, but found the place in a deplorable condition, nothing being left for our present accommodation, the rains falling day and night.' And then he pitched his tents, and brought provisions from the boat, and it was left to Rudyard Kipling two centuries later to provide the serenade in some of his most thumping and ungainly verse:

> Thus the midday halt of Charnock – more's the pity! –
> Grew a City
> As the fungus sprouts chaotic from its bed
> So it Spread
> Chance-directed, chance-erected, laid and built
> On the silt
> Palace, byre, hovel – poverty and pride –
> Side by side;
> And, above the packed and pestilential town,
> Death looked down.

At least Kipling could see which way Calcutta was heading by then. Charnock, with less than a couple of years to go before he died at the age of sixty-two, certainly couldn't. He and his people were struggling for survival and a report from May 1691 suggests how difficult it was for them. 'They lived in a wild and unsettled condition at Chuttanuty, neither fortified houses, nor godowns,* only tents, huts and boats.' The nicest thing left to him was probably the marriage of his daughter Mary to Charles Eyre, a future knight and Governor of the Bay, in Calcutta's first English wedding.

The most vivid reporter of the early years was Captain Alexander Hamilton, whose ship was constantly sailing in and out of the Hooghly round the turn of the century. We get a picture of Charnock sitting under a large tree, smoking a hookah and

* Storage sheds.

sipping arrak punch, clad in loose shirt and pyjamas; which, much floppier than Western fashion dictates nowadays, is still one of the most comfortable garments for Calcutta and, in white cotton, one of the most frequently worn. There he would receive his English and Indian merchants and talk with them till the light began to fade, when they would be dismissed so that they should get safely home before robbers and wild beasts appeared. Hamilton had no love for Charnock, who 'reigned more absolute than a Raja' and who had natives whipped near his dining room, so that he could hear their cries as he ate. It is not certain that the two ever met, for Hamilton's *New Account of the East Indies* was not published until the first decade of the eighteenth century. So his stories must be taken with reservation; but at least they put some flesh on the bare bones of Company memoranda.

Hamilton was an early objector to the site. Mr Job Charnock, he writes, had chosen it 'for the sake of a large shady tree ... though he could not have chosen a more unhealthful place in all the River; for three miles to the North-eastward is a Saltwater lake that overflows in September and October and then prodigious numbers of Fish resort thither, but in November and December, when the Floods are dissipated, those fishes are left dry and with them putrefaction affects the air with thick stinking vapours which the North-east winds bring with them to Fort William, that they cause a yearly Mortality. One year I was there and there were reckoned in August to be about 1,200 English, some military, some servants to the Company, some private merchants residing in the town and some seamen belonging to the Shipping at the town, and before the beginning of January there were 460 burials registered with the Clerk's Book of Mortality.' Such unpleasantness was of no great concern to the Company Directors, however, far away in Leadenhall Street; they were much more exercised over the chartering of a rival combination, though the two were happily united within a decade. And in spite of demonstrations on their doorstep by Spitalfields silkweavers, angry at the importation of cheap Indian textiles, they were in expansive mood in Bengal. Fort William was started in

1696 out of brick dust, lime, molasses and cut hemp ('as hard and tougher than firm stone or brick' all the same, and known as pucca construction) and named after King William of Orange three years later. At the same time the Nawab was persuaded to sell the three villages 'with rents, uncultivated lands, ponds, groves, rights over fishing and woodlands and dues from resident artisans, together with the lands appertaining thereto, bounded by the accustomed notorious and usual boundaries in exchange for the sum of Rs 1300 current coin of this time'.

Watching all this, Captain Hamilton is seeing a pattern emerge that is to repeat itself on an increasing scale in Calcutta for a long time to come. He remarks of Mr Weldon, who comes to the town as a Commissioner in 1709, that 'His term of governing was very short and he took as short a way to be enriched by it by harassing the people to fill his coffers.' A seaman's wife, 'a little inclined to lewdness in her husband's absence', entertains a couple of Armenians, and they quarrel over her; Weldon reprimands both but gives one man sole rights to the woman for Rs 500 cash. Life sounds even lustier just up the road. 'Barnagul is the next village on the River's side above Calcutta, where the Dutch have a house and garden; and the Town is famously infamous for a seminary of female Lewdness where Numbers of Girls are trained up for the Destruction of unwary Youths, who study more how to gratify their brutal passions than how to shun the evil consequences that attend their folly, not withstanding the daily Instances of Rottenness and Mortality that happen to those who most frequent those schools of Debauchery.' The air of disapproval is so strong and the haphazard use of capital letters so pointed, that it is sometimes rather difficult to remember that this is a seadog writing. Possibly Captain Hamilton was a secret maritime evangelist, for he takes pains to note that 'In Calcutta all Religions are tolerated but the Presbyterian, and that they browbeat.' He also tells us that the Company has a good hospital here 'where many go in to undergo the Penance of Physic, but few come out to give account of its operation'. And he observes that on the other side of the river from rising Calcutta, where the twin city of Howrah now is, there are docks for repairing and fitting ships' bottoms, and a pretty good garden belonging to the Armenians. Note the precision – 'ships' bottoms', not just 'ships'; this is a seadog after all.

The Armenians are a puzzle in the origins of Calcutta. The Dutch we know about; they had settled twenty-five miles upstream at Chinsurah in 1653 and they were to stay in their Fort Gustavus until they were ceded to William IV together with £100,000 in exchange for Sumatra. We had, of course, fought them in between. There was a bonny scrap in 1759 when a Dutch fleet of seven ships came up the Hooghly without pilots – either a marvellous or a lucky piece of navigation in that treacherous river – and attacked a handful of East Indiamen anchored below Melancholy Point. They were beaten off after they had shot the *Duke of Dorset* through and through, leaving ninety cannonballs in her hull, without even managing to kill one of her crew, because the Englishmen had lined their quarters with bags of saltpetre, a crazy fire risk to take. This was the occasion when Colonel Forde, observing Dutch soldiers put ashore, and knowing the two countries were nominally at peace, wrote to Robert Clive – no longer a depressed Company bookkeeper but a brilliant soldier and Governor – for an Order-in-Council to fight. And Clive, who was playing cards when the message came, wrote back in pencil; 'Dear Forde – Fight them immediately and I will send you an Order-in-Council tomorrow.'

We know about the French, too. They had founded a colony at Chandernagore in 1673, a little way down the river from the Dutch, and not until Napoleon was out of the way did the British feel at ease in this proximity. Strong and flourishing under Dupleix, bombarded a little later by Admiral Watson, the story of the French on the river is one of recurring dispossession and retrieval. The longest period the tricolour was missing from the flagstaff of the Administrateur's house was from 1794 to 1815. Indeed, it outlasted the Union Jack in Calcutta, in Bengal, in all India. The little colony remained in French hands until it was gracefully handed over after a referendum of its people in 1951. Nearly twenty years later, its singularity was almost entirely dissolved in the absorbing atmospheres of Bengal, leaving only traces of the past among a few rotting tombstones, a sign outside a shop exclaiming 'Wine!' and *'Liberté, Fraternité, Egalité!'* still faintly inscribed upon a decaying gatepost. And a Bengali poetry magazine circulating in Calcutta under the title *La Poésie*, because its editor was educated in French Chandernagore.

We also know about the Danes, though they were not to found their mission station at Serampore for half a century yet. But the Armenians remain a problem to the student of Calcutta. They had probably been in India at least as long as the Portuguese and possibly before. The standard history of their association with the country asserts, a little vaguely, that they had come overland, by way of Persia, Afghanistan and Tibet, as commercial birds of passage before 'any other Europeans'. They settled at the invitation of the Emperor Akbar, who made a Queen of the Armenian Mariam Zamani, and who allowed her kinsfolk to build a church at Agra in 1562. By 1690, so we read, 'The Armenians were the most favoured subjects of the Delhi Government ... and had been held in high esteem by the Mogul Emperors from the days of Akbar downwards for their loyalty and integrity.' They did very well for themselves in Bengal, whenever it was they arrived, and they showed pleasure in their new masters when they got the chance. When George III had recovered from his madness in 1789, and the news reached Calcutta, 'a general expression of joy was made by all the inhabitants'. But the most conspicuous and brilliant illuminations were displayed by an Armenian merchant by the name of Catchick Arrakiel. His loyalty did not escape the notice of Lord Cornwallis, who on interrogating him what particular interest he felt in the life of His Britannic Majesty, received this reply: 'I have, my lord, lived under his Government for near thirty years, it has never injured me, but on the contrary has always afforded its protection and this, with industry, has enabled me to accumulate a very plentiful fortune.' His son was so grateful for this protection that he raised and kept at his own expense a company of 100 Armenian volunteers to defend the industry of Britons and others when the regular Army was in the Deccan. And a British voice approvingly remarks at the start of the nineteenth

century that the Armenians are the most respectable and perhaps
the most numerous body of foreign merchants in the capital.
They trade with China to the East, Persia to the West, and most
places in between. Their information from all sides is deemed
the most accurate and minute of anyone's in their profession.
They are attentive, regular and diligent in business, and never
do they think of departing from their lives and indulging in
dissipation even after a competency has been acquired.

The question is, when did these worthy merchants arrive in
the Hooghly? What were they doing between the building of a
church at Agra in 1562 and the founding of a capital city at
Sutanuti in 1690? Mesroub Jacob Seth, the author of the Armenian history, claims that the merchant Khojah Israel Sarhad, a
favourite of the Bengal Nawab, came down from Delhi to negotiate on the Company's behalf the sale of the three villages a few
years after the foundation and Charnock's death. This, together
with Hamilton's references, appears to be the earliest report of
Armenians in the district.

The problem arises because of a gravestone in the Armenian
Churchyard in Calcutta. The building is eighteenth century, a
cool oasis in the middle of a crammed bazaar. But half way
across the yard, which is completely paved with graves, there is a
black granite slab marking the tomb of 'Rezabeebeh, wife of the
late charitable Sookias.' And the date on it is 21 July 1630. Does
it mean that there were Armenians already trading from Sutanuti
or Kalikata when Charnock finally dropped anchor and that his
log forgot to mention them? Or is it just the slip of a mason's
chisel? A small point, maybe. But in the Calcutta Club of an
evening they can engross themselves for hours in lighter topics
than that. And the whisky, for an hour or two, might not taste
quite as Scotch if it were suddenly established beyond doubt that
the capital of the Raj had been started not by a gentleman adventurer from England, grown honourable in the Company's service, but by a tradesman from Isfahan with no pedigree at all.

The start of the eighteenth century sees the middle of the three
river villages giving its name, already Anglicized, to the whole
spreading settlement; presumably because the first substantial

buildings (judiciously for storage, not comfort) have been erected at Kalikata, away from the still makeshift living quarters of Sutanuti. It sees Bengal declared a Presidency, junior by several years to Madras and Bombay, but soon to overtake both in power and prestige. It sees Job Charnock's son-in-law, now Sir Charles Eyre, President of Bengal and Commander-in-Chief of the United East India Company's Fort William. It sees the beginnings of a remarkable expansion throughout India which, as Philip Woodruff has remarked, is within little more than half a century to present the Company Directors in England 'with an empire at which they looked with the incredulous elation, shot with sharp twinges of doubt, of a village grocer who has inherited a chain of department stores and is not quite sure whether they will pay him a profit beyond his dreams or drag him down to ruin'.

By now, young men are heading for the Hooghly in boatloads from the Thames. As Company servants they are required to salute the captain of the Indiaman on his quarterdeck whenever they see him during the voyage, they appear at meals to a roll of drums and they must have their cabin lights out at ten p.m. sharp. They are mere Writers on the Company payroll and the Company pay is not excessive. The young man has had to find for his passage and his keep on board ship. And although he is fed and accommodated free in a Writers' building on arrival, he must furnish his rooms and obtain servants, washing, candles and many other necessities at his own expense. Young Robert Clive, making a similar journey (to Madras) within a few years, complains to his father that on the Company's stipend of £3 10s. a month it is as much as he and his colleagues can do to live at all, what with the dearness and scarcity of everything. The immediate prospect, on top of all this, is three or four years of drudgery with account books. No wonder Clive twice tried to blow his brains out and pined, of all places, for Manchester.

It was a system based upon a grasping premise in England and it made for grasping behaviour in India. It spawned men with an eye to the main chance above all things, who were shortly to discover that although they might have come to Calcutta penny-pinching, they could rapidly acquire a fortune if they set about it in the right way. Their sense of direction would soon be established for them if they took a look at their immediate lords and masters. The settlement was governed by a Council of nine members. The President, who was also First Member, received an emolument of £100 a year; his eight assistants by now received £40 a year. In addition to these salaries the Members in Council were given free board and lodging and a palanquin allowance of Rs 30 a month. On the face of it they were not doing much better than their Writers. But every one of them was also allowed to trade freely and privately – as other Company servants were not – and the profits on free trade in Bengal could easily amount to several hundred times a Member's salary. And before very long, regulations notwithstanding, the Writers and other underlings were inspired by this example to follow it as best they could. The result was that even Clive, a fairly ruthless rogue from childhood, seems to have been shocked by his first acquaintance with Calcutta, and that was after an experience of Madras. It was not only the most wicked place in the Universe in vague terms. Precisely, it was that 'Corruption, Licentiousness and a want of Principles seem to have possessed the Minds of all the Civil Servants, by frequent bad examples they have grown callous, Rapacious and Luxurious beyond Conception . . .'

At about this time a Nawab of Bengal, Mir Kasim, was writing to the Governor to describe what it meant for an Indian to be on the receiving end of this philosophy. 'And this is the way your Gentlemen behave; they make a disturbance all over my country, plunder the people, injure and disgrace my servants . . . Setting up the colours and showing the passes of the Company, they use their utmost endeavours to oppress the peasants, merchants and other people of the country . . . In every village and every factory they buy and sell salt, betel-nut, rice, straw, bamboos, fish, gunnies, ginger, sugar, tobacco, opium and many other things . . . They forcibly take away the goods of the peasants, merchants etc. for a fourth part of their value, and by ways of violence and oppressions they oblige the peasants to give five rupees for goods which are worth but one rupee, and for the sale of five rupees they bind and disgrace a man who pays a hundred rupees in land-tax; and they allow not any authority to my servants ...' There were good men in the Company service prepared to back all that to the hilt.

Calcutta was beginning to thrive on this creed and its expatriates were beginning to make themselves at home. They had built St Anne's Church in 1709, they had completed the Fort in 1712, they had made George Pomfret the District Grand Master of the Freemasons in 1728 and their 'Star of the East' was to be the oldest Lodge outside England. They were to open their first theatre, in Lalbazar, in 1745. They had sent a deputation to Delhi, led by the merchant John Surman, to buy up another thirty-eight villages, including Howrah across the river; and, remembering two excellent precedents, they had not forgotten to include Dr Hamilton in the party. They were in luck once more, for the Emperor was thinking of marriage but had a troublesome swelling in the groin. Surgeon Hamilton worked wonders, like Dr Boughton before him, and in due course, when both treatment and marriage had been proven, the villages were made available for Calcutta's first suburban development.

If there was already looting and corruption by the British on a growing scale, there was even more deeply established rapacity and greed by a line of Mogul Emperors in the capital and their placemen in the country. The Emperor and his senior ministers could be wonderfully accommodating if the foreigners presented them with chiming clocks, China screens, pieces of ambergris, Persian horses or plain rupees; but if a Bengali peasant fell behind with his rent, his zamindari landlord was quite liable to stitch him up in a pair of baggy pantaloons with two or three half-wild cats for company. And after Aurangzeb died in 1707, the Empire was in such a chaos of mismanagement that the English and the French were presented with perfect conditions for their fight to take the upper hand in India. Lord Macaulay, who was to know Calcutta well in the nineteenth century, is not always to be trusted for anything except a faultless ear for colourful English prose, but his summary of the four decades after Aurangzeb also rings true. 'A succession of nominal sovereigns, sunk in indolence and debauchery, sauntered away life in secluded palaces, chewing bang, fondling concubines, and

listening to buffoons. A succession of ferocious invaders
descended through the western passes to prey on the defenceless
wealth of Hindostan ... and every corner of the wide Empire
learned to tremble at the mighty name of the Marathas ...
Wherever their kettle-drums were heard, the peasant threw his bag
of rice on his shoulder, hid his small savings in his girdle, and
fled with his wife and children to the mountains or the jungles,
to the milder neighbourhood of the hyena and the tiger.'

It was the threat of assault by these invaders that had an
alarmed Company finding Rs 25,000 for the excavation of the
Mahratta Ditch in Calcutta in 1742. The English town was now
a mile long and a quarter of a mile wide, with a Black Town of
natives, four miles in circumference beyond it. There were
400,000 people of both races living here and in outlying villages,
and with nearly fifty vessels a year coming into the Hooghly,
trade in Calcutta would soon be worth £1 million per annum.
It was well worth Rs 25,000 spent on extra defences. So the
Ditch was started in a great arc round the Company property,
but after three miles had been dug the threat of the Mahrattas
receded and it was never finished. Calcutta could sit back again
and, always keeping a weather eye cocked for the gentlemen just
upstream at Chandernagore, wait for the next blood-stirring
thing to happen.

It started to happen almost at once with the French and English going to war, but that was at home, and ships moved slowly,
and the news didn't reach India for ages. When the despatches
arrived, the Governor of the French East India Company, Dupleix, made his first move for the mastery of Southern India, a
thousand miles away. There followed a long, untidy, intermittent
campaign, with the French manipulating one puppet prince,
Chanda Sahib, and the English another, Mohammed Ali. And
Robert Clive, his book-keeping abandoned, his commission as a
Company soldier taken up, his age not yet being twenty-six, discovered and established his military genius, marched on the
village of Arcot in terrible conditions, held it under siege for
fifty-three days in worse, effectively ended Dupleix's career, and
went home to England to enjoy the applause. And that, for
the time being, was that.

Calcutta had watched this at a distance, sharpening meanwhile its own primary instincts for trade, not war, welcoming the attention of the native princelings, who were increasingly minded to use its security as a bank. The latest batch of Company recruits from England had included a Junior Writer called Warren Hastings, who was beginning to struggle along in the Writers' Building on £5 a year. Roger Drake had been made Governor at thirty and was otherwise engaged in the affairs of the Masonic Lodge. One of his Members in Council was John Zephaniah Holwell, magistrate and another Mason. Some distance from the city, the Company outpost at Kasimbazar was under the management of Mr W. Watts, but he was best known for his recent marriage to a very remarkable lady.

She had already been widowed twice, by Mr Templer and Mr Altham, and after Mr Watts had served his time she was to enjoy a fourth union with the Reverend William Johnson (known locally as the Reverend Tally-Ho), the Presidency chaplain. He eventually retired to England with a fortune but 'Begum' Johnson was really wedded to Calcutta and stayed behind, holding celebrated whist parties in Clive Street, the ever engaging topic of conversation in the city. She died in 1812, when she was eighty-seven, much loved, much spoken of and always absorbing; having grandmothered an English Prime Minister (the second Lord Liverpool) and having chosen her burial place at the invitation of an Indian Governor-General; it was almost alongside Job Charnock's in St John's churchyard and richly deserved by then.

A little farther up-country, in his palace at Murshidabad, the Nawab of Bengal was dying. Mahabat Jang's name meant terror of war, but he had been chiefly noted for a rule of some dignity and wisdom and for a singular aversion to the harem, having taken but one wife at a period when the Nawab of Oudh was said to accommodate 800 women in his quarters. He had no son, and when the throne became vacant in April 1756 it was occupied by his grandson Siraj-ud-Daula. He had certainly been spoilt as a child groomed for succession, and what followed after his enthronement at the age of twenty-five was doubtless an impulsive attempt to enrich himself quickly. He picked a quarrel

with the Company and, with the first signs of monsoon in the
sky, he marched on Calcutta with 30,000 foot, 20,000 horse, 400
trained elephants and 80 pieces of cannon. He also held Mr and
Mrs Watts captive, for Kasimbazar had been taken *en route*
without a fight, Ensign Elliott, in command, having shot himself in despair. This was the first British indignity in an episode
which, wretched and heroic in turn, has been codified for ever as
the Black Hole incident. It is a disputed story, but let us have it
now in the standard version received from the man who comes
best out of it, John Zephaniah Holwell.

Calcutta, in 1756, was a decently held place but it was not
heavily fortified. Fort William protected a number of warehouses on the river bank, it included a large tank of rainwater,
it could be used as a refuge by the Europeans of the city, who
were only a fraction of the 400,000 population. It had four bastions, with between eight and ten guns apiece, and curtain walls
that were eighteen feet high but not four feet thick, and the
whole enclosure was 210 yards by 120. Apart from this, Calcutta's only defence was the unfinished Mahratta Ditch and for
at least a couple of years there had been an anxious correspondence with London on this inadequate state of affairs. 'When the
Nawab's intention of marching on Calcutta was known,' writes
Captain Grant, who was the Fort's Adjutant-General, 'it was
felt time to inquire into the state of defence of a garrison neglected for so many years, and the managers of it lulled in so
infatuate a security that every rupee expended in military service
was esteemed so much loss to the Company.' The defences, such
as they were, had about 250 men manning them, of whom only
sixty were Europeans; the rest, mainly Indo-Portuguese, were
commonly referred to as 'black Christians'. And only one
officer, Captain Buchanan, had ever seen active service. To this
uncertain collection of soldiers was now added a swiftly drum-
med up militia of perhaps 260, again mostly Armenians, Portuguese and 'Slaves'.

Grant says that the military wanted the European houses close
to the Fort demolished, to allow a better field of fire, but their
owners refused to hear of it, 'not knowing whether the Company would reimburse them the money they cost'. Siraj-ud-

Daula was now, on 16 June, approaching Dum Dum and the British set fire to the native bazaars in his path; when they found their own Indians plundering the ruins they beheaded them on the spot. And then, perhaps 2,500 strong, they took refuge in the Fort and locked the gates. They had been panic-stricken from the moment a threat had been rumoured but now they seem to have largely dissolved with fright. There was some stout fighting by the eastern battery and women busied themselves making cartridges, but by 19 June courage had oozed so fast that there was a rush to the boats anchored in the river. One of the ¯rst to take himself off was the Governor, Roger Drake, who was shamefacedly to explain later on that he had fallen asleep with exhaustion; on waking, and seeing boats preparing to sail in confusion, he had assumed all to be lost and so prudently but reluctantly joined the retreat.

All was very nearly lost, in fact, but Holwell was still standing by his militia and other Europeans had not yet quit; and the first thing they did after the indecent rush to safety was to secure the river gate to stop more desertion. This could be nothing more than a gesture, for the houses by the ramparts were now all on fire. There had been twenty-one vessels in the river when the siege began and several of them were still in sight, drifting while they watched the end of Calcutta. Holwell made signals for them to return and pick up those who remained, but not one vessel stirred in their direction. The humiliated bitterness of the British in India at this cowardice was to last a long time, and it is clearly reflected by the Calcutta raconteur Busteed, writing more than a century later. 'Drake had the hardihood to plead, that by bribes and threats he had tried to induce some boats which he passed on his way down to go back, but the native crews were afraid. As a survivor bitterly retorted, if he as President had hoisted his flag upon his vessel and led the way back, all would have followed him. But he showed no stomach for this, especially when the commander of his vessel did the reverse of advocating it by using, in Captain Grant's hearing, the matchless argument that the attempt would indeed be attended with danger!!' Two exclamation marks in 1882, and no wonder.

And another exclamation mark at least implicit in what im-

mediately followed. For the Nawab's men now came swarming
into the Fort by ladders over its walls and though they promptly
relieved the survivors of their watches, their silver buckles and
other valuables, they didn't kill them. 'It is right,' says a slightly
surprised Busteed, 'to remember this unexpected forbearance.' Instead, they lodged their captives in the Fort's punishment cell on
the Eastern wall, at ground level, with an open verandah between
it and the parade ground. It had a small barred window and it
had always been known as the Black Hole by soldiers. Holwell
reckoned it was an 18 ft cube; at any rate, it was an impossible
place to put 146 people on 20 June. The monsoon, late that year,
didn't start to fall until 21 June; the historic captivity was thus
spent on what would be the hottest and sultriest night of 1756.
There is no reason to suppose that what happened was due to
anything more than thoughtless stupidity by Siraj-ud-Daula; it
was, after all, a brutal age all round; the same week had seen these
captives decapitating their own servants.

What happened was ghastly and noble, according to Holwell.
With bodies pressed unbearably close, people soon began to die,
and two of the first to go were the Reverend Mr Bellamy and his
son, the Lieutenant, hand in hand in a corner. With the floor
soon strewn with corpses 'my poor friend Mr Edward Eyre
(Member of the Council) came staggering over the dead to me
and, with his usual coolness and good nature, asked me how I
did; but fell and expired before I had time to make him a reply'.
Holwell did enough to live by sticking near the window whenever
he was able and by sucking his shirt sleeve to relieve his thirst.
When six o'clock in the morning came and the door of the Black
Hole was opened, twenty-three people were still alive and one of
them was Mrs Carey. Most of them were told to be out of town
by sunset on pain of having noses and ears cut off if they stayed;
and drums beat a message to all who could hear, that Calcutta
should henceforth be known as Allinagore. Holwell and three
others were held for over a fortnight in case they could lead the
way to treasure. The survivors took off to the ships and were
received with much care and attention by the Dutch settlers up
at Chinsurah. And Holwell lived to be eighty-seven in England,
where they called him Governor by courtesy (though he had

briefly been a deputy Governor), having first put up in Calcutta a monument, at his own expense, to those who were in the Black Hole with him.

This story is still circulated with his details in English history books, though there is reason to believe that some of it is fabrication; that, at the most, sixty-four people went into the Black Hole with no Mrs Carey among them, and that twenty-one survived. Not that the legend is likely to be disturbed in Europe by reduced figures. Holwell's monument having collapsed with neglect, Lord Curzon had another one built when he was Viceroy in the twentieth century. But today there is merely a tablet in an arch next to the General Post Office, which the visitor has difficulty in locating; it is surrounded by crowds of pavement tradesmen in lottery tickets, suspenders, sunglasses and ballpoint pens; and they grin and chant 'Black Hole of Calcutta' in the most mocking fashion.

Six months later Robert Clive, now returned from the acclamations of England, led a punitive expedition from Madras. He recaptured Calcutta without difficulty in one sortie at night and then went on, for he was conscious of a larger strategy, to take Chandernagore from the French. Siraj-ud-Daula now found himself enmeshed in intrigue, the British openly wringing concessions and compensations from him while covertly negotiating to replace him with his uncle, Mir Jafar. The cards were at least cleanly laid down on 23 June, 1757 at Plassey, twenty miles from Murshidabad. The monsoon damped down the Nawab's ammunition, Clive's soldiers did the rest, and Siraj-ud-Daula was led off to the provincial capital and assassination; after a seemly interval Clive followed and made a state entry into Murshidabad.

He now began to exact much more than retribution for the sack of Calcutta the year before. Within a month, a hundred boats were sent downstream to the British city, laden with 7,500,000 silver rupees; six weeks later another four million rupees went coasting into the Calcutta treasury, to be received with flags flying and bands blaring. This was the compensation money. Clive was no longer content with that. On behalf of the Company he annexed nearly nine hundred square miles of land south of Calcutta, known as the 24 Parganas; the Company now

became the zamindars, the landlords, of this area but Clive had
been kingpin in the operation and he proceeded to take the king's
share of the rents. It was to yield him £30,000 a year till the day
he died and a grudging Company had no option but to wait bale-
fully for his funeral and a reversion of the annual windfall to
Leadenhall Street. On top of this, Clive extracted a spot payment
of £234,000 compensation for all the trouble he'd been put to in
Bengal. Then he wrote to his old father in Shropshire, telling him
to repair the family home and make ready a seat in Parliament.

At Plassey, some historians suggest, Clive had laid the foundation stone of the British Empire in India. It is an arguable point.
What he certainly did was to start something inseparable from
Empire and more sinister in itself. As Percival Spear says, 'the
financial bleeding of Bengal had begun'. The British had so far
secured their position with varieties of trade, quiet and violent,
fair and extortionate. Now they began to rob the bank. When
Mir Kasim superseded Mir Jafar as Nawab in 1760, he was
obliged to hand over £200,000 to the Council in Calcutta. When
Mir Kasim was replaced three years later and a more obedient
Mir Jafar was reincarnated, 'presents' were made in the following
order; £530,000 to the Council, £300,000 to the Company and
£250,000 to the military. And beneath these swelling patrons of
Bengal, the smaller leeches began to hang on. The incoming
independent merchants of Calcutta were now allowed to conduct
their private trade duty-free and so undercut their Bengali competitors. With the military holding the whole countryside in
submission and the Nawab merely an administrative puppet by
kind permission of Clive's troops, they could employ armed
gangs to browbeat villagers and Nawabi officials alike into almost
any terms they chose.

It was the freest trade imaginable if you happened to be born
on the right side of the counter and it both ruined Bengal and
took the Company to the brink of bankruptcy. It became scanda-
lous enough for a Burke to denounce it far away in a House of
Commons. Here were not tradesmen, here were *conquistadores*;
'animated with all the avarice of age and all the impetuosity of
youth, they roll in one after another; wave after wave; and there
is nothing before the eye of the native but an endless hopeless

prospect of new flights of birds of prey and passage, with appe-
tites continually renewing for a food that is continually wasting'.
It became alarming enough, in certain quarters and in certain respects, for the Company to send Clive back to Calcutta as
Governor in 1765, after five years at home spent acquiring the
Barony of Plassey among other things. On the Company's behalf
this time, Clive accepted from the Emperor in Delhi the appointment of revenue minister for Bengal, Bihar and Orissa; an arrangement of mutual interest, for it ensured regular payments to
both Delhi and Leadenhall Street which had been vanishing of
late. Clive also began to impose strict instructions on Company
servants. The size of 'presents' was now to be severely limited and
private trade on the side was now out of the question. People
henceforth must toe the Company line or be shipped back home.
For a moment or two, Clive established order if not justice. Then
he sailed for England for the last time, after a couple of years'
hectic work. He left behind him what had been an almost totally
repugnant age, for which he was partly responsible. It is with
relief that one can now see Warren Hastings resolutely moving
into the wreckage of it.

Descendant of a Norman invader, son of a Balliol vicar,
nephew of a Customs man who got him into Westminster School,
and ward of a Company Director who put him up for India,
Hastings had been hunched over his Writer's ledgers in Calcutta
till 1752. He had then been posted as Mr Watts' assistant in the
factory at Kasimbazar. Siraj-ud-Daula's men had caught him on
the march to the Black Hole, and Hastings had been imprisoned
in Murshidabad until a local Dutchman bailed him out. Hastings
was back in Kasimbazar when Holwell and his three companions
arrived in chains from Calcutta and he fled to the Dutch at Chinsurah. Here he found a wife who already had two daughters, for
her husband had just been trampled to death in the Black Hole.
This second marriage of hers was also to be sliced by tragedy and
in it we begin to detect the streak of melancholy that is never far
away from Warren Hastings afterwards. They have a son in 1757
and a daughter the next year, but she dies. Mrs Hastings herself
dies in 1759 and within five years diphtheria has taken the son as
well. Somehow Hastings survives it all. He marches as a

volunteer in the army to recapture Calcutta. He returns to Kasimbazar and is happily in charge, making money on the side like
everyone else, selling imported coffee on commission and dealing
in salt. In 1761 he is brought to Calcutta as the Governor's assistant, with a seat in Council, and George Vansittart is helping him
to a government contract for the supply of transport bullocks.
When he leaves for England in 1764, he has £30,000 invested in
India. When, four years later, he sails for Madras to be second to
the Governor there, he leaves a standing order with Messrs Warren of Cecil Street to be sent three chests of claret and one of hock
each year.

And now, in 1772, at the age of thirty-nine, he returns to
Bengal as Governor. He has not been entirely free from the spirit
of the times so far and he will not be able to change that spirit
very much during the thirteen years of his rule in Calcutta. He
can be seen, indeed, as a man who continues to make privately
the most of his public opportunities. In his first year as Governor
he ships fifty chests of opium on his own account. He has Spanish
dollars invested in the China market. In 1776 he clears £25,000
in England from the sale of diamonds. He can be caught accept-
ing a suspicious £15,000 from one of Mir Jafar's wives, the
Munny Begum, who was an ex-dancing girl from Agra sophisticated enough to smoke the hookah and to talk non-stop to visiting Englishmen from behind her scarlet purdah.

Nevertheless, a new morality begins to creep into Bengal with
the accession of Warren Hastings. It is not merely that he is
generous as well as acquisitive, though he paid a pension to Mrs
Hastings' Goanese maid until she died long after leaving the
family service, and he slipped the Reverend Tally-Ho Johnson
£100 when marriage to the redoubtable 'Begum' loomed, and
when he heard that his uncle's illegitimate daughter was to marry
he sent £600 and enough to set her up with a nursery school in
Chelsea; such liberality was not uncommon among gentlemen of
means. The morality of Hastings is more subtle and complex
than that. He says, 'as to my friends, I shall be glad to serve
them, but as to my friends' friends I neither can nor will serve
them'. And he seems to prove it. He only once wilfully abused his
power, and even at this lowest point, when he brought the forger

Nuncomar to trial and death, the most obvious thing about him was that he had been goaded beyond reason.

Hastings returned to Bengal two years after a famine there had wiped out maybe a third of the inhabitants. Calcutta had only just been described as a straggling village of mud-houses, with the whole ground south of Chandpal Ghat thickly covered with jungle. The ramparts of the old Fort William were crumbling, with huge gaps in them like the one left when Siraj-ud-Daula blew up St Anne's. But there was still some life in the old fort, such as the circulating library and a so-called chapel next to the ruined Black Hole, available for worship on Sundays, used for the sorting of piece-goods on weekdays. Christians otherwise took themselves to premises next door to Selby's gambling club, where the red mission church of the Danish preacher Kiernander stood; having lately lost his wife, he now drove around Calcutta in a four-in-hand and gave banquets and ogled two distinctly fat and reputedly rich ladies in his congregation.

His was not by any means the highest living in the place. It would scarcely match the scale of the local Commander-in-Chief, Sir Robert Baker, who ran a private trade in saltpetre and opium. Or of Richard Barwell, that stereotype of a rising breed of men, the British Nabobs. The son of an ex-Governor who was now a Director of the Company in London, his reputation in Calcutta ran in several directions at once. He was the outstanding flicker of bread pellets across the dinner tables of the community, able to snuff out a candle at four yards, when pellet-flicking was an esteemed amusement; it went on for years until someone flicked someone else once too often, was flattened with a side of mutton, challenged to a duel and all but killed. Barwell was also known as a man who would gamble on anything and though he seems more often than not to have lost heavily, he eventually went home with enough money to buy an estate at Stanstead in Sussex and a Parliamentary seat at St Ives. His ambition in chief had been to get rich quickly and he could hardly go wrong, gambling debts notwithstanding, with a father in Leadenhall Street and a sister Mary also in London to watch stock prices and elections and to inform him where to lay his commercial and social bets in Calcutta. He had a liking for Locke and Dryden. But mostly he enjoyed the company of others, whether this meant flicking bread pellets with them, playing cards with them or dancing with them.

Calcutta, when it had a mind to, could mount an exquisite ball. It could revolve for a night round the delightful Miss Sanderson, who so captivated young men that sixteen once turned up simultaneously wearing a livery modelled on her pea-green French frock with pink silk trimmings. At some cost in that dreadful climate, no doubt, as a reporter of the period tries to convey. 'Imagine to yourself the lovely object of your affections ready to expire with heat, every limb trembling and every feature distorted with fatigue, with a muslin handkerchief in each hand, employed in the delightful office of wiping down her face while the big drops stand impearled upon her forehead.' In the end, Miss Sanderson married Richard Barwell.

This does not sound like life in a straggling village of mud-houses and it was that no longer, for Calcutta was expanding again. In place of the old Fort William, Clive's new one was finished; and, bearing in mind the old garrison's handicap with almost no field of fire, a vast area alongside had been ordered empty of everything but trees and a parade ground, or maidan. Business in real estate and mortgages was brisk and mansions were going up. Hastings built one himself in the rising suburb of Alipore, obtaining tons of marble from Benares for the staircase. He began to see Calcutta as the first city of Asia and not merely in size or wealth. He was more ambitious than that.

Unlike many of the British settlers in Bengal, he had on his first visit struggled with the language. By now he could speak Bengali and Urdu well and he had a grasp of Persian, which was the tongue of the Muslim court. He decided to create an *élite* of British officials, speaking the local languages and mindful of the local traditions, who would work more effectively within a hierarchy that was still curiously balanced between the Emperor's court in Delhi and the Company's offices in London. The object for Hastings, was not British Empire but a pervading British influence in India, and it was not to be a mindless one. So he drafted the plan to establish a Persian chair at Oxford and he drew up a scale of financial inducements to the study of Bengali in Calcutta. Under his influence a new manner of men began to appear.

One of them was Charles Wilkins, who within a year or two had completed a set of Bengali type-faces and started the first vernacular printing press in India. Another was Nathaniel Halhed, who composed a Bengali grammar. Jonathan Duncan became a Persian scholar and Henry Colebrooke became an expert in Sanskrit. William Jones, presiding over the Asiatic Society which Hastings founded in 1784, was to leave the most startling mark of all by arguing a common source for Indo-European languages. These men were the Orientalists, the first serious British students of Indian culture, whose conclusions were to be most strenuously disputed half a century later by Lord Macaulay. They evoked a golden age in India's cultural past and they shared their discoveries with the native intelligentsia of Bengal. Racial privilege was anathema to them. They were rationalists, classicists and cosmopolitans for the most part and, put simply, they believed that both races in India had much to give to each other. They were, patently, an *élite* and in the Calcutta society of their day they must have seemed a very rarified group indeed.

Parliament, meanwhile, had stepped into the East India Company's affairs. The 1770 famine had not only killed off people; it had demolished much of the revenue, which was how they tended to see Indian famines in Leadenhall Street. By 1772 the Company was in such straits that it went to the Bank of England for a loan, which was turned down. So it asked the Government for £1 million, and the money was advanced at the cost of a Regulating Act the following year. From now on, the Company's dividend was limited to six per cent until the loan was repaid, and surplus receipts went to the Exchequer, with all accounts and correspondence submitted to Parliament. A Supreme Court was created for Bengal. Above all, a royal Governor-General was to sit in Calcutta from now on, with obscure but tacit authority over Madras and Bombay, and the first one was to be Warren Hastings at a salary of £25,000 a year. If Robert Clive had indeed laid the foundation stone of British India at Plassey, Lord North had just raised the scaffolding in London.

Hastings was to rule with a Council of four Members (at £10,000 apiece), each with a vote equal to his own, and this was to bedevil all he tried to do until a Member died and tipped the balance. One of the new Members was already in Calcutta, locally born and bred, and he was Richard Barwell. Two others, General Clavering and Colonel Monson, were powerfully connected at home; Clavering, indeed, was not only to be second to the Governor-General and Commander-in-Chief, but he was George III's private choice to succeed Hastings as soon as possible; and Monson's wife, the Lady Anne, was the great-granddaughter of Charles II. Then there was Philip Francis. He was the son of a chaplain to the Fox family and he had been a War Office clerk. He was also almost certainly (though it was never proved) the Junius whose scurrilous attacks on public figures made vivid reading in the *Publick Advertiser* at the time. He was engaging, he had soft hands, women liked him, and he was to leave his wife and children behind in England because he thought, among other things, that Betsy was not intellectually up to the company he was now about to keep. When the Indian appointment came up he had been unemployed for a year, some piece of patronage having broken down, so he set off for Shropshire and within a couple of months had the Clive family utterly charmed. And his future was secured. Doubtless he had told them, as he was to tell others later, that he thought the Government of Bengal 'the first situation in the world attainable by a subject'.

In April 1774 this bundle of rulers sailed in the East Indiaman *Ashburnham*, in consort with another vessel, the *Anson*. That contained the new judges, led by Chief Justice-elect Sir Elijah Impey. He had been at Westminster with Hastings, in company with William Cowper, Edward Gibbon and a brace of future Prime Ministers (Shelburne and Portland). He was to stay healthy in the taxing climate of Bengal by making sure that his court always rose for the day at one o'clock and by taking regular holidays by the sea, either at Chittagong or at nearby Beercool, where the beach was 'totally free from sharks and other noxious animals except crabs'. He was also to complain bitterly before long that he had not been able to lay up more than £3,000 a year since coming to Calcutta.

On 19 October the new men disembarked at Chandpal Ghat at noon exactly, which Francis thought 'a comfortable season for establishing the etiquette of precedency'. This was scarcely done to the satisfaction of General Clavering, for one. A royal salute of twenty-one guns from Fort William had confidently been expected but a mere seventeen salvoes were ordered instead. Worse, there were no guards, no person to receive the gentlemen or to show the way, no state. Just awful heat and confusion, not an attempt at regularity, and a Governor-General who only put down his work when his colleagues and judges were on the doorstep of his house. 'But surely,' remarked a member of the entourage, 'Mr Hastings might have put on a ruffled shirt.' It was a bad start to a relationship already undermined by six months of plotting on the voyage from England. It was never to improve. Francis was soon to be dispatching his slanders to Lord North or Baron Clive in England. One letter concedes that Mr Hastings has some little talents of the third or fourth order, the next claims that Mr Hastings has wholly and solely sold and ruined Bengal. He kept this up right to the end, which was not until 1818 in England, where both Hastings and Francis died within a few weeks of each other. It was Francis who lobbied Burke for the impeachment at Westminster. It was now Francis who stimulated his colleagues in Calcutta to be rid of the Governor-General. They were willing accomplices, for the most part; Monson until he died within two years of arrival, Clavering until he followed soon after, having left strict instructions that Mr Hastings was not to be informed till he was buried. Only Barwell seems to have been rather more concerned with his pellet-flicking and his gambling; he had a duel with Clavering one day at Budge Budge, in which both missed with pistols and civilly apologized.

The Three, then, attacked Hastings over his organization of the revenue and they attacked him over his conduct of a war against the Rohillas beyond Oudh. They snubbed him at his tenderest point, and she was Mrs Imhoff. The two had met on an

East Indiaman bound for Madras, Hastings with his Member's commission to Fort St George, Marian with her child and her husband the Baron, an impoverished miniaturist seeking a cadetship in the Madras army. Eventually the Baron returned to England, the child sometime after, and much later there was a divorce. The Reverend Tally-Ho Johnson then married Hastings and Marian in St John's, Elijah Impey giving her away, and it was a love match that lasted deeply and passionately until Hastings died. But for the moment it was another small and mean weapon in the hands of Francis, Clavering and Monson. They finally nailed their quarry at his weakest point, though the wound did not bleed him till the impeachment at Westminster. This was the trial and execution of Nuncomar.

Nuncomar, seventy years old at his trial, had held many posts under a succession of native governments in Bengal; when Siraj-ud-Daula was Nawab he was Governor of Hooghly. He had become a wealthy Rajah and he was an unprincipled old rogue whose path had crossed that of Hastings during the latter's first period in Bengal. Hastings disliked him intensely with that coldest arrogance which he seemed to reserve for Indians he judged shifty and underhand, though no Englishman had yet shown greater warmth to Indians in general or to individuals who passed muster with him. The dislike was mutual. No sooner had Nuncomar scented where the wind lay with the new Council of Bengal than he was cultivating its acquaintance in the most pointed fashion. Finally, he gave Francis a document purporting to prove that Hastings had been taking bribes and worse. It was like manna from above to the Three and they canvassed their new ally in return, attending his levees, receiving hospitality at his house. Only the door of the Hastings residence remained firmly shut on all these comers. And then, quite suddenly, the city was agape with the drama of events. The news spread that Nuncomar had been thrown into gaol, charged with forging a bond six years before. And forgery, as the British of Calcutta patronizingly knew, could be regarded as little more than a peccadillo among Indians.

The trial was conducted with speed, in eight days flat, and in spite of Sir Elijah's preference for short sittings the judges heard argument from eight in the morning till late each night, retiring twice a day to change their linen. Nuncomar fared well in his prison, eating sweetmeats for the most part, and receiving messages of condolence from Lady Anne Monson and from the gentlewomen of General Clavering's house; Clavering's aide-de-camp also paid him a call. In court the sittings were not only extended beyond the norm, but ran through a Sunday as well and at the end Sir Elijah made a summing up that was to cost him impeachment, too, thirteen years later. The entirely European jury found Nuncomar guilty, he was refused leave to appeal, and he was sentenced to death as a felon. A number of petitions on his behalf were either ignored or were stillborn, including one that Francis proposed from the Three but which Clavering and Monson declined to sign. Nuncomar hanged within seven weeks and he died with much dignity. And for every man in Calcutta who thought that he had got what he deserved, there were two convinced that he was the victim of judicial murder. After the two impeachments, posterity became as much inclined to take the first view as the second. At this distance the biggest pity of it seems to be that Hastings, of all people, should be tainted by it.

But tainted he was, and goaded he still was, and he was to remain so long after he and Francis had fought their duel. By the time enmity had reached that stage both Monson and Clavering were in their graves but Francis was still single-minded in his pursuit of prey and prize. The calumnies continued on their way to London; the Governor-General was now glorying in General Burgoyne's surrender in America, he was preparing a retreat in Switzerland, he was totally incompetent in directing a war against the Mahrattas near the Malabar coast. In the end Hastings turned on his tormentor, determined to destroy him morally by exposing his dishonour if possible, willing to obliterate him physically if that failed. Characteristically, he laid his plans with care. He sat down and wrote a minute he proposed to put before a Council which was now less weighted against him, though with Barwell soon to leave India anything might shortly happen; indeed, at any time a ship might sail in from London bearing both the warrant that was to depose him and the new favourite who was to succeed. It was a long and provocative document but the essence of it went as follows: 'My authority for the opinions I have declared concerning Mr Francis depends on facts which have passed within my own knowledge. I judge of his public conduct by my experience of his private, which I have found to be void of truth and honour. This is a severe charge, but temperately and deliberately made, from the firm persuasion that I owe this justice to the public and myself as the only redress to both, for artifices of which I have been a victim, and which threaten to involve their interests with disgrace and ruin. The only redress for a fraud for which the law has made no provision is the exposure of it.' Then he packed Marian Hastings out of town, to stay with the Dutch Governor at Chinsurah. And he waited six weeks until Philip Francis had got over a bad bout of fever. On 14 August 1780, he had a copy of the minute sent round to Francis's house, with a note to say that the original would be on the Council's table the next day.

They met at six in the morning on the road to Alipore, by a double row of trees that had once been a walk of Belvedere Garden. Colonel Watson, the Chief Engineer at Fort William, was already there with Francis when Hastings arrived with Colonel Pearse, the Commandant of Artillery (the one with a Begum wife and a half-caste son at Harrow). Colonel Pearse thought the place very improper for the business, so near to the road and the hour close to riding time when horsemen and women might soon be passing by. So they walked some distance towards Mr Barwell's house, and found a retired and dry spot. Colonel Pearse discovered that both gentlemen seemed unacquainted with the procedure on these occasions (as they were; Francis had never fired a pistol in his life and Hastings only once or twice) and took the liberty to tell them that if they would decide on their distance, he and Colonel Watson would measure it out. Watson suggested fourteen paces, which Hastings thought rather a lot, but didn't object, so it was done. The gentlemen next had to be told where to stand and when to fire. Then Francis had some trouble with his priming, coming thrice to the present and down again, until it was discovered that his powder was damp. Neither he nor Hastings had brought enough for more than one shot, but provident Colonel Pearse had a spare cartridge and supplied his man's adversary with dry powder from that. And at last they were, after a fashion, ready to kill each other.

They presented together and Francis fired first but missed. Colonel Pearse said afterwards that it would have been possible to count three before Hastings pulled his trigger. He fired, Francis sat down with a bump and a cry that he was a dead man. Hastings shouted 'Good God, I hope not' and ran up to him. Francis, in fact, had the ball in his side and was bleeding heavily. Pearse and Hastings wrapped a sheet round the wound while Watson dashed for a palanquin from Belvedere, to carry him into town. That evening Hastings sent a message to Francis, asking him if he might call on the convalescent. Two days later, Francis declined 'as civilly as possible' through Colonel Watson, while Hastings was writing to a friend that he hoped 'Mr Francis does not think of assuming any merit from this silly affair'. Both had behaved like English gentlemen of the period for half an hour or so, while conducting a deadly business which deceptively reads like a piece of comic opera. But within a month Francis was back in Council and the deep hostility between the two continued.

Even if Job Charnock had duelled with Captain Hamilton, it is doubtful whether we should have known so completely what went on. But from the time of Warren Hastings onwards we begin to form detailed pictures of Calcutta. The age of Charnock and his immediate successors is a period of small and indistinct cameos because men were then too busy hacking at the jungle for existence and profit to sit down and describe for posterity the minutiae of their lives, which in any case were probably emptier than we care to think. So we get the bare bones of history and little else. Even at the time of the Black Hole there is not much reporting of social trivia from Bengal; the chronicles, such as they are, are all of trade and campaigns and crucial events. But from the last quarter of the eighteenth century we find ourselves deeper and deeper in a mass of social literature which becomes more and more comprehensive as the eighteenth century slides into the nineteenth.

It is partly because newspapers begin to appear with the first number of the *Bengal Gazette* in 1780. It is partly because ladies have started to arrive with much time on their hands and large diaries to fill; parting gifts from England, no doubt. First it is Mrs Kindersley, then it is Mrs Fay, later it will be Emma Roberts and later still the Hon. Emily Eden. But it is also because there are now men in Calcutta who can apply a pen to words as well as to columns of figures, who can absorb what is happening around them while waiting for the fortune to grow; who can occasionally perform both feats as well as some professional task and remain remarkably indifferent to the possibility of a fortune. It is the age of, among others less vivid, William Hickey – attorney, dapper man about town, occasional painter and diarist extraordinary – who can both introduce the New Cutch Club to a new drink (burnt champagne) and maliciously but indelibly say all that needs to be said about an Army chaplain, Mr Blunt, in one sentence. 'This incomprehensible young man got abominably drunk, and in that disgraceful condition exposed himself to both soldiers and sailors, running out stark naked into the midst of them, talking all sorts of bawdy and ribaldry, and singing scraps of the most blackguard and indecent songs, so as to render himself a common laughing stock.' Perhaps poor incomprehensible Mr Blunt had just been celebrating the recent rise in the salary of Bengal clergy, from Rs 800 to Rs 1200 (when 10 rupees were worth one sovereign). Or maybe he had landed some other windfall, for parsons dabbled in trade like everyone else. Officially they had leave to send up to £1,000 a year to England through the Company's bills, but some did very much better than that. Mr Parry had a two thirds share in a salt, betel and tobacco cartel which yielded him a profit of £2,800 in the first year of trading and over £2,200 in the next.

We must beware of an error that too frequently overtakes us when we consider Victorian England, of assuming that everyone is living at the same presentably high standard as the popular stereotype; there would be comparatively poor Europeans here, too, sweating it out in barracks and ship as well as in the Writers Building. We hear nothing of them. We hear only of households like that of Mrs Fay, barrister's wife and dress-maker, who first came to Calcutta in 1780 and returned three times to die there in 1815. One of her early letters home describes their eating habits. 'We dine at 2 o'clock in the very heat of the day. I will give you our bill of fare and the general price of things. A soup, a roast fowl, curry and rice, a mutton pie, a forequarter of lamb, a rice pudding, tarts, very good cheese, fresh churned butter, excellent Madeira (that is very expensive but eatables are very cheap). A whole sheep cost but Rs 2, a lamb R 1, six good fowls or ducks ditto, 12 pounds of bread ditto, 2 pounds butter ditto, good cheese two months old sold at the enormous price of Rs 2 or 3 per pound, but now you may buy it for R 1½. English claret sells at this time for Rs 60 a dozen.' She might have added that you could also obtain best Durham mustard (Rs 2 per lb), pickled oysters (Rs 8 a bottle) or marmalade (Rs 12 per jar) through H. Davies of Tank Square. And by the time Mrs Fay died, soda water was coming in from Messrs Schweppes.

These were trenchermen, and every June the newspapers had to warn them against overeating in the desperate weather ahead, if they didn't want to follow the surgeon of an Indiaman who had dropped dead after consuming a hearty meal of beef with the thermometer at 98 degrees. They were also powerful drinkers. A man would easily tipple three bottles of loll shrub (claret) or two of white wine at dinner and even ladies put back a bottle a day ('fashionably or medicinally' as Mrs Fay delicately has it). They did their best to keep the climate at bay. Every family had its ab-dar, the servant whose duty was to stay up all night, constantly moving an earthenware jar of water in a larger receptacle containing saltpetre and water, which produced something nearly as cold as ice by morning; the real thing did not arrive until the enterprising Frederic Tudor cut enormous blocks off frozen Wenham Lake in Massachusetts and in 1933 sailed them to Calcutta for storage in the domed Ice House on Bankshall Street. They also had the punkah, usually at mealtimes only, which had probably been introduced by the Portuguese. But the climate generally won in the end, one way or another, if people stayed too long. It often enough took them in a roundabout way when they had barely settled down, as it did Rose Aylmer, who died at the age of twenty after 'a most severe bowel complaint brought on entirely by indulging too much with that mischievous and dangerous fruit, the pineapple'. A memorable death, nonetheless, for it inspired one of Charles Lamb's favourite poems, written by Walter Savage Landor, who had fallen in love with young Rose during an intoxicating hour in the Swansea Circulating Library before her parents took her East.

The climate made them go carefully with their office hours; from nine to noon in the hot season and again from seven to nine, from ten till two and from seven to nine in the rest of the year. They would have gone riding or walking before they started work, of course, and until 1818 all the horse races in Calcutta were run before sunrise. When evening came they could pretty well take their pick of amusement. A drive usually came first, in a variety of carriages, along the Course, which ran south from the Esplanade by the Maidan. Once a week there would be a public evening mounted by three or four of the most prominent ladies of the city, a conversation party which started at ten o'clock or even later and offered a couple of hours' babble with cold supper before going home. There would be subscription assembly balls at the London Tavern in Vansittart Row, and it was said that many Englishwomen died of consumption brought on by the excessive strain of dancing through the night. There were endless card tables, offering ombre or quadrille but mostly whist; Lady Anne Monson was a very superior whist player. There was magnificent and desperate gambling, with Philip Francis calculating that on one blessed day in the year of our Lord he had cleaned up £20,000 at whist. There was boating on the Hooghly in the cool evening breeze, when parties would take to a budgerow or a mourpunkhy, a snake boat which was eight feet wide and sometimes one hundred feet long, paddled by thirty or forty men; but the most dazzling craft of all was William Hickey's 48-footer, manned by a crew of fourteen rigged in white linen jackets and trousers with red and green turbans and cummerbunds.

The cultivated, who were trying to keep up with their Sterne and their Richardson, could also enjoy their theatre. The city's first one had been demolished when Calcutta was sacked by Siraj-ud-Daula, but a replacement had been built in 1772 and the New Playhouse followed three years later. David Garrick had a hand in promoting the first and supervised the despatch of scenery for the second, and the grateful local patrons sent him two pipes of Madeira for his kind interest. Then they watched *The Critic* or *Venice Preserved* or Shakespeare from a seat in the pit at Rs 12 or a bench in the gallery at Rs 6; or they went along to see what Mrs Bristow, that enthusiastic amateur, was offering in the private theatre at her house on Chowringhee; and Mr Playdell's fine voice was much in demand for his tonic rendering of *Let me approach my sleeping love*. Calcutta left it to the Russian adventurer Herassim Lebedeff, though, to produce the first Bengali plays at Lebedeff's Theatre in 1795.

This was, overwhelmingly, a masculine society. There were more women in Calcutta than in any other British settlement, to be sure, and many a girl came in high hope of a husband; if she got someone in the growing civil service, after all, it meant an assured income of £300 and a pension when he died; and she wouldn't need to wet nurse any babies, for the climate was an excellent excuse to farm an infant to an ayah. So the young spinsters arrived and Sunday morning on the church steps became a great time and place for casting an eye over the latest boatload of beauties. And before long they were making their first tentative acquaintance with the hookah, inviting a gentleman of their choice to share the mouthpiece for a refreshing puff, whereupon the man knew that he was at least in with a chance. Or they might dabble with a pinch of his prime Macouba, for Calcutta was a great place for taking snuff. They would patronize the two Frenchmen who settled into the community as fashionable hairdressers, M. Malvaist charging two gold mohurs a month for attending to ladies, M. Siret charging Rs 8 for cutting ladies' hair and Rs 4 for dressing it, with half prices for gents. For the gents of Calcutta were increasingly mindful of a certain pace that was set in London society. Mr Hastings might have preferred a plain brown coat but the general taste in such matters ran to waistcoats of gold brocade or blue satin, sprigged and flowered at Rs 200–300 each. Calcutta, in fact, began to outstrip London in its fancies after a while; by the time William Hickey got home he was given to understand that the wardrobe he had built up in India was, by the most tailored canons of St James's, just a little too loud.

It was a society which thrived on scandals and gossip of scandals. Much of the gossip was circulated, for the two indiscreet years of its life, in the *Bengal Gazette*. Everyone knew that the latest fragment purveyed about Marian Alipore referred to the Governor-General's lady, and that greedy old Poolbundy was none other than the Chief Justice, so-called because Sir Elijah had helped his cousin to a contract (or pulbundi) for the upkeep of bridges and embankments at Burdwan. Eventually the *Gazette*'s freebooting proprietor, Augustus Hicky, went too far and Hastings had him up for libel. There had been plenty of scandals for Hicky to choose from. Hastings and Mrs Imhoff was juicy enough, but nothing was better than Philip Francis and Madame Grand.

She was Mlle Catherine Verlée, to start with, daughter of a French official at Chandernagore. When she was not yet fifteen she married George Grand, a member of the Company's civil service who had sailed to India in the same ship as William Makepeace Thackeray's grandfather. Twelve months later, Grand being out at dinner with Richard Barwell, ('the happiest, as I thought myself, of men') Philip Francis scaled the walls and took himself to the young Madame behind a locked bedroom door. A dutiful ayah raised the household. By the time Grand got home Francis had disappeared, but a jemadar was holding Mr Shee (he was later knighted) flat on the floor; Mr Shee had merely rushed in to help after hearing an alarmed whistle from Francis. There were recriminations, there were tears, and Madame Grand was parcelled off to her parents at Chandernagore, till Francis pursued her and installed her in his house at Hooghly. There was talk of a duel, with Francis being supported by his redoubtable cousin Major Phil (Fighting) Baggs, but it evaporated into a Supreme Court action in which Grand sought £160,000 damages. He received £5,000 and soon after left Calcutta for some other station. Only months later, Madame Grand herself sailed for Europe alone. There she eventually became the Princess Talleyrand, hostess to statesmen at the Congress of Vienna, wryly remembered by Napoleon on St Helena, last heard of in extreme old age surrounded by parrots and snuff in a house on the Rue de Lille in Paris. And when she died, randy old Talleyrand merely said that her death simplified his position.

It was, above many things, a heavily introverted society. It could hardly be otherwise, given the difficulties of travel outside Calcutta. You could go by boat up the Ganga to Benares, but that took 75 days. Dacca was 37½ days away and it took the best part of a month to be transported as far as Murshidabad. Apart from the boat, the palanquin was the only method of travel abroad. The passenger reclined on cushions in this glorified sedan chair, sipping loll shrub or some other refreshment, while four bearers staggered and stumbled along the jungle trails; and, weeks later, he would reach Benares for Rs 500 or Patna for Rs 400. Much better stay at home, even though the streets were so dimly lit that William Hickey once scraped his face rather badly on a wall *en route* to a party, even though there were certain conveniences like window glass absent from practically every house but the Governor-General's, even though there were plenty of local hazards like tigers stalking any kind of meat just behind Chowringhee and footpads of both races who made the Maidan a deadly place at night; and there was that awful spot in Bowbazar which was becoming known as Gulla-kutta Gully, or throat-cutters' lane.

But at least, you could comfort yourself, villains were properly dealt with if caught. Thieves were generally branded on the hand and pilloried for hours, though Ramjoy Ghosh in 1795 stole tenpence and was first gaoled for a few days before being carried to Burrabazar and whipped for four hours up and down the street until he was discharged half dead at Chitpore Bridge; he might, alternatively, have been flogged all the way from Loll Diggy, the great tank of water where old Fort William was, along Lalbazar as far as the house of Mr Willoughby Leigh in Bowbazar. Dacoits, who killed as well as robbed, were savaged to death; fourteen caught in 1789 were pinioned to the ground, one by one in sight of the others, where their right hands and left feet were hacked off at the joints; the stumps were then dipped in hot ghee and the mutilated bodies were left to perish slowly in the sun. Only Mogul jurisdiction contrived more hideous executions than that.

The chronicles of these times do not mention Bengalis much, except in subservient capacities. There was, in fact, by now a rising mercantile class among them, distantly accepted by the British, having its share in the plunder of Bengal, soon to become much closer to the new masters of the country. The way was almost open for a bright young lad of the district to become as rich on his wits as any red-faced sprig from Kensington. Russomar Dutt worked as a clerk for Hawke Davis and Co. at the turn of the century for Rs 16 a month until the accounts got inextricably confused; the firm offered Dutt Rs 10,000 to straighten out the mess, which he did, and was rich thereafter. There were natives making plenty of money before that. A member of the Tagore family was letting his house on the Esplanade to Company servants for Rs 800 a month, and if an Indian had property he invariably rented it to an Englishman at a very high price. It had long been commonplace for a man to take a local mistress on arrival in Calcutta, as William Hickey took his lovely Jemdanee; and sometimes these liaisons became so deeply affectionate that the *Calcutta Gazette* in 1809 could advertise for sale 'a garden house and grounds situated at Toltalah Bazar, which to any gentleman about to leave India, who may be solicitous to provide for an Hindostanee Female Friend, will be found a most desirable purchase'.

But mostly the British regarded the natives as servants of one kind or another. They were part of that mob of bheesties who crowded all day round Loll Diggy to fill skin bags with water, eight gallons at a time, for their masters. They were durwans (doorkeepers), peons (footmen), hurcarrahs (messengers), houccaburdars (stewards), mussalchees (dishwashers), dhobies (laundrymen), or sirdars (chief bearers). They were that army of menials attached to your household; one family of four had 110 servants, the bachelor William Hickey had sixty-three, and thirty or forty was common. They were the sharks who extracted extravagant wages from you (head cook Rs 15–30 a month, bearer Rs 4, syce Rs 6–8, wet nurse Rs 12–16) and so in 1785 you and the other Company employees asked the Directors in London to do something about it, perhaps by fixing a pay scale; then you drifted along to the London Tavern or the Harmonic House in Lalbazar, to sup a dish of coffee and to riffle through the newspapers for R 1 inclusive. And eventually you sailed for home, taking your fortune with you. Samuel Tolfrey, under-sheriff, returned with Rs 600,000, which is six lakhs, which was then £30,000. Thomas Farrer, who defended Nuncomar, walked off with £60,000 and became Member of Parliament for Wareham. And the tales these people told when they reached home were so enticing that, within a few years, the Prince Regent himself was lobbying the Governor-General for a post in this fabulous land. He was turned down.

This was the society Warren Hastings bestrode like a colossus for thirteen years. The clearest symptom of his management was Pitt's India Act in the last year of his power, which subordinated the Company even more to the authority of Parliament. The best of his achievement was a shift in the governing cast of mind, though this did not show itself at once. Immediately after Hastings there was Sir John Macpherson, a Skyeman best remembered for singing ballads with equal verve in Gaelic, Spanish and Hindustani and for helping himself on his way to the top by interesting the Nawab of the Carnatic in electricity and the magic lantern. His successor Cornwallis, lately surrendered at Yorktown, thought that Sir John's twenty months in office had bequeathed him a 'system of the dirtiest jobbery' and proceeded to clean it up. He called the Calcutta warehouses 'a sink of corruption and iniquity' and did what he could there, too. And then he went on to make the Permanent Settlement. Only a few years before, Frenchmen had been storming the Bastille and what Cornwallis now did was almost as revolutionary in the context of Bengal.

Traditionally, the revenue had been collected by the hereditary zamindar, a word which literally means landholder, but which

covered anyone from an owner to a tax-collector. The zamindars paid dues to the Mogul's government, later to the Company's government under the revenue licence that Clive had
secured in 1765. In turn they collected what they could extort
from the peasantry in their areas; and the difference between
the two sums, a jealously-held secret, represented their income.
It was a system complicated, as far as the British were concerned,
by the vagueness of Hindu and Muslim land-law which recognized force as the only title to land possession. This was anathema to the rising rulers of India, who were Whigs with a
belief in justice founded on private property and commercial
transaction. It was substantially this philosophy that they now
imposed in Bengal; the peasant was to be secure as long as he
paid fixed dues to the zamindar, who was to hold his position
while he could produce a fixed revenue to the government. It
was well-intentioned, it was civilized, it was very English. It
meant that the zamindar was a recognizable proprietor who
could be sold up like any other squire who failed. What it did in
the end was to break up a potentially brutal but always close
relationship between peasant and zamindar and lay Bengal wide
open to a new breed of speculators from Calcutta and even
farther afield; it made the peasant even more uncertain of his
future than before. And it was the beginning of the end of
Muslim supremacy in India.

It was part of Cornwallis's permanent aversion to corruption
and in this it was enormously misplaced. He had little time for
most of the British he found in Calcutta but his distaste for the
Indians was even greater. He verily believed that every native
of the country was corrupt, and said so; just as the Marquis of
Hastings (who gave us the word Eurasian) was to say within a
generation that 'The Hindu appears a being nearly limited to
mere animal functions and even in them indifferent'. The same
language was to be repeated until the British left Calcutta, but
from now on new voices could be heard from time to time and
the first of them was Sir John Shore's, who governed near the
turn of the century. 'When I consider myself the Ruler of
twenty-five millions of people,' he declared, 'I tremble at the
greatness of the charge ... I consider every native of India,

whatever his situation may be, as having a claim upon me; and that I have not a right to dedicate an hour to amusement further than as it is conducive to health and so far to the despatch of business.' That was the genuine tone of the Raj as the Raj was to imagine it for a century and more to come. It was the voice of the Clapham Sect, for Sir John, like a good many of his successors and their administrators, believed in a profound alliance with the Testaments – with, if anything, a slight preference for the Old over the New. It was also an echo of Warren Hastings.

Lord Wellesley arrived. Where Cornwallis had been preoccupied with corruption and Shore had been preoccupied with making land reforms work under the Ten Commandments, Wellesley was preoccupied with living like a prince and with dislodging the French once and for all from India, together with any damn-fool revolutionary notions that might now be infiltrating with them. His younger brother Arthur came, too, and promptly marched on the Mahrattas in the West; he was soon to win more applause with battles at Talavera, Salamanca, Vittoria and Waterloo. Yet nothing that either Wellesley did in India was to have greater effect than Lord Richard's idea of a college at Fort William. It sprang, indeed, from that anxiety of his about revolutionary influences. He wished to transform the young men of the Company, prone to instability under the social pressures of Calcutta and a prey to the money-lenders now thriving in the city, into reliable functionaries of government. 'To fix and establish sound and correct principles of religion and government in their minds at an early period of life,' he was to write later, 'was the best security which could be provided for the stability of the British power in India.' To this end he would create something comparable to the institutions of Oxford and Cambridge in Calcutta. Knowing well enough that the Company Directors would not tolerate anything that cut into their profits, he financed it from a levy he imposed on all civil servants in India. And he found an unlikely ally in the person of William Carey.

Carey was a farm labourer's son with a remarkable talent for languages; he is said to have been proficient in Latin, Greek, Hebrew and Dutch before he was fifteen. He had renounced the

Church of England and become a Baptist minister and he had arrived at the Danish missionary settlement of Serampore in 1800 with four sons and a psychotic wife. Two of the six missionaries there, Fountain and Ward, had police records in England for openly supporting the French Revolution. In 1799 Wellesley had tried to seize a clutch of Baptists on suspicion of spying, being prevented only by the refusal of an American ship's captain to hand them over and by the asylum offered at Danish Serampore. The talents of this community were such that by 1805 the Mission Press – run for a start by the printer Ward on a contraption Carey bought in Calcutta for £40 – could print any work in Bengali, Urdu, Orya, Tamil, Telegu, Kanarese or Marathi.

Carey's flair for language was now harnessed to Wellesley's brainchild, though the Governor-General remained cynical enough of Baptists to hire him at a lower salary and status than Henry Colebrooke or any other teacher. Fort William College now became the focal point of intellectual activity among the British, though the campus was not in the fort itself but in the Writers' Building. Its young men found themselves writing essays on distinctly non-commercial topics; whether the Asiaticks [sic] are as capable of as high a degree of civilization as the Europeans; whether the natives of India under British Government enjoy a greater degree of tranquillity, security and happiness than under any former government. There were disputations in Indian languages, held in Wellesley's gorgeous new Government House, though this description comes from 1818, when the Marquis of Hastings was in command: 'In a state chair covered with crimson velvet and richly gilt, with a group of aides-de-camp and secretaries standing behind him, sat the Governor-General. Two servants with state punkahs of crimson silk were fanning him and behind them again were several Native servants bearing silver staffs. Next to him, on either side, were seated the examiners, and below them again, the most distinguished ladies of the Presidency. Next in an open space were two small rostrums for the disputants, and chairs for the professors; the room behind these, and fronting the Marquis, was quite filled with company, and in the rear of all, the bodyguard was drawn up in full uniforms of scarlet with naked sabres.'

This, then, became much more than a forcing house for loyal civil servants. True, Fort William supplied gold medals for proficiency; and William Taylor, winning his in the 1830s, smartly melted it into earrings for his girl friend. But this was also the starting point of literary patronage and a depot of linguistic research. In the first five years of its existence, Fort William published more than a hundred original works in oriental languages. The time was not far distant when Mr Lockett, the chief librarian, could boast that he supervised the largest collection of orientalia in the world; the Escorial had 1,851 volumes, Oxford 1,561, the Seraglio in Constantinople 7,294; but Calcutta, in 1818, had a grand total of 11,335 printed and manuscript sources. Orientalism became its obsession from 1807 onwards, when the Company Directors decided that the European part of the curriculum should be taught at Haileybury in Hertfordshire, where the young men would be indoctrinated with the best British values before exposure to the cultural and other hazards of Calcutta.

Education was generally in the air. Another Serampore missionary, Joshua Marshman, published his *Hints Relative to Native Schools*. It contained a programme for national compulsory education, no less, in which peasant children would learn to read and write with a vocabulary of four thousand words. They would also have simple arithmetic and later become conversant with astronomy, geography, natural philosophy, mineralogy and chemistry; all this would 'rectify and enlarge their ideas of the various aspects of nature around them'. This was in a city with a population of well over half a million, containing educational places for only 4,180 Indian children; nevertheless, the Calcutta School Society within a few years was able to report that 'printed instead of manuscript school books are now in common use. The branches formerly taught are now taught more thoroughly, and instruction is extended to subjects formerly neglected, viz. the orthography of the Bengalee language, geography and moral truths and obligations ...' David Hare, a retired watchmaker, assisted in the establishment of the Hindu College, which was mostly the creation of Bengali *nou-*

veaux riches such as the Tagores, the Mullicks, the Debs and the Ghoshals, and its pupils were soon offering inflated prices for copies of *The Age of Reason*. Horace Wilson, who had come to India as a Company surgeon, who had worked on the Calcutta Mint and then managed the Hindoostanee Press, now started his Sanskrit College, which was not only Orientalist but scientific as well; and though none of the Indian graduates in the College hospital had by 1831 been allowed to perform any major operations, they were regularly allowed to conduct minor ones like 'opening little abscesses and dressing sores and cuts'.

A result of all this intellectual activity in Calcutta was the birth of the Young Bengal movement and the start of a period which has been glorified as the Bengal Renaissance. The hero of the first was Henry Louis Vivian DeRozio, the Eurasian son of an officer with an English firm. He was educated in one of the private English schools of Calcutta and he was captivated by Robert Burns, the French Revolution and English radicalism. He wrote verse, and one of his poems hailed the liberation of the Greeks at Navarino. He edited Bengali newspapers and he was teaching senior classes at the Hindu College when he was in his teens. His followers were, unlike himself, almost entirely the sons of high-caste Hindus who were rapidly becoming Anglicized. He turned them into atheists. It was rumoured that some of the Hindu College boys at prayer would recite passages from the *Iliad* instead of sacred mantras, and one lad, asked to bow before the image of Kali, said 'Good morning, madam' as well. And this within a year or two of the treaty of Amiens, when the British community had officially marched down to Kalighat, accompanied by military bands, to present a substantial sum of money to the goddess in her temple as a thanksgiving for an end to a period of war with France. The Young Bengalis also drank, 'cutting their way through ham and beef and wading to liberalism through tumblers of beer', as a shocked contemporary noted. The French tricolour that the students hauled to the top of the Ochterlony Monument one day might have been disregarded or even been quietly pleasing to their elders, but not this; not this and atheism as well. A scandalized parent complained that his boy now had his hair cut, wore European shoes, ate food without bathing, didn't know how to write bazaar bills, uttered unintelligible Bengali and could tell of any mountain or river in Russia but could give no account of his own country. So DeRozio was sacked from the staff of the Hindu College by Hindus, died of cholera soon after, and left a rudderless Young Bengal which did not long survive him.

The Bengal Renaissance was much more substantial; indeed, it became the history of the Bengalis from the moment Rammohan Roy hoisted himself from poverty at the start of the nineteenth century. His father had been an old-fashioned zamindar, who lost his property as a result of the changes made by the Permanent Settlement, who was imprisoned and who died a ruined man. The son emerged from this wreckage by, curiously enough, starting to lend money to Englishmen. He was also employed by one of the earliest students at Fort William College, John Digby, and he was soon in contact with some of the Orientalists. It is a matter for scholastic argument how many of Roy's subsequent ideas were drawn from them, how many were original to him. But before long he was writing his famous tract denouncing suttee. This was at a time when in three consecutive years – 1815 to 1817 – 253, 289 and 441 women were known to have been burned alive with their husbands' corpses in Calcutta. He started an Anglo-Indian school, he compiled a Bengali grammar, and twentieth-century Bengali scholars tend to regard him not only as the Father of Modern India but as the founder of Bengali literary prose.

He was one of those men whose reputation is apt to be enlarged almost annually with the passage of time, so that now it is a little difficult to see him as he probably was. But he clearly restored a racial pride to the Bengalis when they badly needed such a tonic. He was a man of moderation who could launch a new Hindu sect which eventually evolved into the Brahmo Samaj and which has remained the spiritual refuge of the intellectual, the Anglicized, the man who is sceptical of extreme dogma; its propositions were so sympathetic to some Christian feelings that the Unitarians, at least, were happy to reprint pamphlets by Rammohan Roy. Hard-line Hindus, of course, reacted against it and adherents of the Samaj were to know persecution from people who shared the same essential faith; they were sometimes smeared with treacle and then covered in wasps, by incensed gurus and their mobs. Roy had fed on Bentham, Montesquieu and Blackstone and two things that he said suggest the splendid balance of his intellectual diet.

When Wellesley began to censor the press in fear of revolutionary ideas, Roy lobbied for freedom on the grounds that the Company Directors might judge for themselves 'whether the systems introduced in their possessions proved so beneficial to the natives of the country as their authors might fondly suppose or would have others believe, and whether the Rules and Regulations which might appear excellent in their eyes are put strictly into practice'. And when Young Bengal was applauding that tricolour atop the Monument, Roy said, 'To assert that if the Natives had enjoyed the blessings of the French Revolution they would by this time have been treated like men, and assumed a proper position among the nations of the earth, is to write absolute nonsense. Let him read Thiers and Allison before he again ventures to long for a revolution which would have turned the Hooghly into a revolutionary torrent and established a permanent guillotine in Tank Square.' Revolution, in fact, was to come to Bengal and it was to be made by the spiritual descendants of Rammohan Roy together with those who merely used his name as a watchword. It was to be aggravated by the reversal of a climate that had been fostered unwittingly by Wellesley and Hastings with their support for the influence of Fort William and its Orientalist teachers. And, ironically, the wind began to change just as Roy and his followers were looking West for a temperate salvation, with the arrival in Calcutta of a new British overlord, whose background was radical and whose inclinations were for reform.

This was Lord William Bentinck, a disciple of the Utilitarian philosopher James Mill who had lately written a history of India without ever having been there or knowing any of its languages, who regarded the Indian past as an age of total darkness. Lord William was a vigorous man and, just as Wellesley had forbidden the sacrifice of children to sharks at the mouth of the Hooghly, he now proscribed suttee and began to stamp out Thuggery. He swiftly changed a deficit of £1 million a year in the Indian economy into a surplus of £1½ millions and he did it partly by cutting military allowances. He also dismantled Fort William College, whose students had largely become idle fellows with mounting debts.

He had received the services in Calcutta of Thomas Babington Macaulay, as Law Member of his Council. Before leaving England, Macaulay was deep in the controversy between the Orientalists and the Anglicists, between those who would synthesize two cultures and those who would Westernize everything possible. Now, in 1835, he delivered the famous minute on education, which was to establish entirely English standards in India. Lord Macaulay had not found one Orientalist, it said, 'who could deny that a single shelf of a good European library was worth the whole native literature of India and Arabia'. Lord Macaulay believed he was not exaggerating when he said that 'all the historical information which has been collected from all the books written in the Sanskrit language is less valuable than what may be found in the most paltry abridgements used at preparatory schools in England'. His conclusions added up to what he expressed more concisely elsewhere, that 'to trade with civilized men is infinitely more profitable than to govern savages'.

That might almost have served as a civic motto for Calcutta. Instead, it marked the end of a period where there seemed to be growth and the promise of greater fruitfulness in every direction. Physically the city was, indeed, becoming the first in Asia. When Lord Valentia arrived in 1803 in the course of a world tour he remarked how 'Chowringhee, an entire village of palaces ... altogether forms the finest view I ever beheld in my life'. The patronage of Lord Wellesley was such that in England he was being hailed as another Medici, and the seat of his government as a second Florence. There was soon to be a Lottery Committee to finance construction work, and both Town Hall and Strand Road were to be created from the proceeds. By the time Bishop Heber came, much pleased to discover that his hymn 'From Greenland's icy mountains, From India's coral strand ...' had already been translated into Bengali, he was able to write this: 'Of European towns I am most reminded of Moscow. The size of the houses, which are frequently occupied by more than a single family, their Grecian architecture, their number of servants, the Eastern dresses and the hospitality of the place which, though much diminished, is still profuse and incessant, continually remind me of what I saw in a different climate; and if you will recollect the Russian prints which I had in Hodnet, you will have no bad idea of our China bazaar and our Cossitollah.'

That was in 1823. By then, in spite of the periodic crises of the Company, trade and Calcutta were both flourishing. Where there had been six insurance companies in 1804, there were to be fifteen in 1832. Where the Kidderpore Docks had built 35 vessels between 1780 and 1800, they had launched another 75 between 1800 and 1805. And where, in 1790, there had been 15 managing agency houses in Calcutta, by 1813 there were 14 Scots, 10 English, 12 Armenian and 2 Portuguese merchants in the city. These private managing agencies were a particularly significant factor in commercial growth here. As the historian of the Bengal Chamber of Commerce has suggested, they were the bone upon which the flesh and sinew of Indian commerce were to grow. They originated in private London anxieties to intrude upon the monopoly of the East India Company, and their function was to run a profitable trade in Calcutta on behalf of absentee gentlemen in the City. The system was open to the most notorious abuses. The agent, with his connections and his instincts for profit both sharpened on the spot, could make deals that were not in the interests of his unwitting employers in London and it was not infrequently the case that an agency would flourish while the various companies it managed were drained of all profit – or, at least, kept at the subsistence level necessary to maintain the contracts. Siblings would be installed in sinecures to the accompaniment, no doubt, of some growls in the boardroom at home but with the final and unassailable assumption that the local manager must know what he was doing. Thus the agencies grew with Empire and even survived its passing, with fewer Englishmen sitting behind the executive desks after India's Independence, but still enough to maintain the thin black line of tradition on the right side of the ledgers. When the agencies were abolished in 1969, one of the oldest and most honoured names in the commerce of Calcutta, Andrew Yule and Co., was still managing nine companies, its origins still unmistakably preserved in the name of a jute factory up the water; Cheviot Mills, no less, on the steaming banks of the tropical Hooghly River.

There is an air of bounce and vitality by the Hooghly in these early years of the nineteenth century, and it is perhaps conveyed obliquely by the tone and style of an advertisement that appears in the *Calcutta Gazette* in October 1814, on the eve of the great Hindu festival and holiday, the Durga Puja: 'The principal days of entertainment are the 20th, 21st, 22nd, on which Nikhee, the Billington of the East, will warble her lovely ditties at the hospitable mansion of Raja Kishan Chaud Roy and his brothers ... Nor will the hall of Neel Money Mullick resound less delightfully with the affecting strains of Ushoorun who, for compass of voice and variety of note, excels all damsels of Hindustan. Misree, whose graceful gestures would not hurt the practised eye of Parisot, will lead the fairy dance on the boards of Joy Kishun Roy's happy dwelling. At Raja Raj Khrishna's may be viewed with amazement and pleasure, the wonderful artifices and tricks of legerdemain by an accomplished set of jugglers, just arrived from Lucknow. Baboo Gopee Mohan Deb, urged by his usual anxiety to contribute to the amusement of the public, has besides a selection of the most accomplished nautch girls, engaged a singularly good buffoon, whose performances and those of a boy, who has the uncommon faculty of being able to dance with impunity on the naked edge of two sharp swords, may claim the title of unique. Besides these, the respective residences of Baboo Gopee Mohun Thakoor and Gooro Pershad Bhose, have each its individual cause of attraction, and promise to repay by a full measure of delight those who are content to forsake the calm repose of peaceful slumbers for the hum of men and squeeze of crowded assemblies.' The native of Bengal has now been elevated to the rank of entertainer in the public prints as well as servant in the private places. A handful have become founding members of the Calcutta Chamber of Commerce in 1834. There are men like Sheikh Gullam Hussein, Ram Dollal Dey and Dorabjee Byramjee running their own ships out of the Hooghly in profitable trade. And even Lord Macaulay's minute is constrained to admit that 'I have heard the very question on which I am now writing discussed by native gentlemen with a liberality and an intelligence which would do credit to any member of the Committee of Public Instruction'.

The growth does not now cease, but the atmosphere begins to sour. It will soon be so embittered that the Bengali journalist Girish Chandra Ghosh will be writing that men like Jones, Colebrooke and Wilson 'respected our fathers and looked upon us hopefully at least with melancholy interest, as you would look on the heir of a ruined noble. But to the great unwashed abroad today, we are simply niggers – without a past; perhaps, without a future. They do not choose to know us.' For 1857 will have come and gone, bringing to Calcutta the lustre of the first Indian University and the disgrace of the Mutiny. The second of these was entirely British.

There had been mutinies of sepoy soldiers in Bengal before. In 1764 Hector Monro had suppressed one by lashing a score of insubordinates to the muzzles of field guns and blowing them to bits. In 1824 the 47th Native Infantry at Barrackpore had refused to march on Burma, whereupon their Commander-in-Chief had shattered them with grape shot at close range. But in the great Indian Mutiny, where there was savagery on both sides from one end of Northern India to the other, nothing but British panic happened in Calcutta. The rising began at Meerut in May and by the first week in June it had spread steadily eastwards. The city then quartered three and a half sepoy regiments at Barrackpore, and they were certainly seething with discontent; so was another sepoy regiment at Fort William. If the worst came to the worst the British could only muster a weak wing of the 53rd Foot and artillerymen in Calcutta, though there was a complete regiment of the 78th Highlanders up at Chinsurah. As rumour circulated, the civilian population settled into various postures of defence. Volunteer Guards were formed, with four guns, five troops of cavalry and seven companies of infantry. A tradesman in Dalhousie Square barricaded himself in and waited at the top of the stairs with a loaded gun, molten lead and boiling water.

On Sunday 14 June, the British were emerging from Matins in their churches when the news went round that the sepoys had mutinied at Barrackpore and were marching into the city centre. It was untrue; the sepoys had been disarmed by the Highlanders. But it started a headlong panic. Colonel Malleson, who was· there, described it like this: 'Those highest in office were the first to give the alarm. There were secretaries to Government running over to Members in Council, loading their pistols, barricading their doors; Members of Council abandoning their houses with their families and taking refuge on board ships in the river. Crowds of lesser celebrities, impelled by these examples, having hastily collected their valuables, were rushing to the Fort, only too happy to be permitted to sleep under the Fort guns. Horses, carriages, palanquins, vehicles of every sort and kind, were put into requisition to carry panic-stricken fugitives out of the reach of imaginary cut-throats. In the suburbs almost every house belonging to the Christian population was deserted. Half a dozen of determined fanatics could have burned down three parts of the town. A score of London thieves could have made their fortunes by plundering the houses in the neighbourhood of Chowringhee which had been abandoned by their inmates.' Dr Mouat compared the scramble of people across the Maidan, babbling for the safety of the Fort, to 'what might have been if a modern Herculaneum had been evacuated in broad daylight on the approach of a visible eruption from a neighbouring volcano'. Sardonically, Girish Chandra Ghosh observed that 'The state of feeling now exhibited by the notabilities of Chowringhee and their humbler satellites in Cossitollah is very much akin to that which drew the laughter of the world on the aldermen of London and their militia when Boney was a stalking horse in the imagination of the British people.'

The Great Eastern Hotel became another rallying point for the British and from there they sent out their patrols of Volunteers (armed by Messers Manton and Rodda) to scout the city till midnight, while in the poorer Eurasian quarters people loosened their fear by firing fusillades of blank cartridges for hours on end. Nothing happened. On Monday morning everyone went sheepishly home and started to relieve bruised feelings with a

campaign for retribution upon those who had threatened but
not harmed them. The Governor-General, Lord Canning, was
abused because he would not dismiss loyal sepoys from guard
duty at Government House. The hysterical temper of the British
civilians was poured into the columns of the local press, including the Poet's Corner of *The Englishman* :

> Barring humanity pretenders
> To hell of none are we the willing senders
> But, if to Sepoys entrance must be given,
> Locate them, Lord, in the back-slums of Heaven

It even found its way into art criticism. 'Portrait of Captain
Hazelwood, which may be seen in Thacker and Spink's Gallery.
The friends of the gallant officer will at once recognize the
likeness and feel confident that no undue lenity on his part will
be shown to the murderers of women and children, for he has a
stern expression of countenance, as if he had just given the order
to hang them and their favourers.' Had this been Meerut, Delhi
or Cawnpore, where Europeans had been butchered by mutineers,
this would have been a valid Old Testamental reaction. But no
one had laid a finger on Calcutta. It was plain terror mixed
with shame and it became racialism of a kind the city had not
known before.

The East India Company was now liquidated and its 16,000
soldiers were quick-marched into the British Indian Army.
Victoria was proclaimed Queen Empress and the Governor-
General was translated into her Viceroy. Within four years,
Indians were serving alongside Englishmen on the Imperial
Legislative Council and on the presidential assemblies of Bombay, Madras and Bengal. The high noon of the Raj was upon
the land and its heat was unevenly deployed, in Calcutta most
distinctly of all. From here, the Imperial capital, the Government
and its supporting Indian Civil Service ruled with something
between benevolent despotism and hurt reproach; and sometimes, intermittently and by the light of its day, it performed
even more creditably than that. Standing apart from Government, at an increasing distance, was the other British commu-

nity of merchants and tradesmen and their various hangers-on. Of them, Sir Bartle Frere was now writing that 'the English here are almost generally openly discontented, disinclined to remain here or to care for India, and disposed to look at things in anything but an Indian light ...' They did stay, of course, for there was still much money to be made from Bengal.

The fifties had seen the first Indian railway-train, hauled by the 'Fairy Queen', pull out of Howrah for Hooghly and it had seen another line opened from Calcutta to Raniganj, 120 miles away; coal, not as good as the best Welsh or Pennsylvanian but profitable nonetheless, had been discovered up there and fifty pits were working it by 1860. Dundee had started to supply power-driven looms to turn jute into gunny sacks and other heavy packaging; by 1885 there were to be twenty-four of these power-driven factories in Calcutta, with 52,000 operatives, and expatriate Scottish managers in the city were rubbing their hands and regarding that scrofulous plant as 'gold on silt'. In 1861 regular auctions of tea from the gardens up-country around Darjeeling began in Calcutta and, from then on, more and more of the crop was sold direct to overseas buyers in Mission Row and less and less was shipped to London for resale by the moguls of Mincing Lane. Trade was coming along so comfortably that the Bengal Chamber of Commerce could toss £54,000 in the direction of Lancashire, which was in some difficulty because of the American Civil War; in 1869 it was handing Rs 8,250 to a Mr Cooper for trying, but failing, to open up an overland trade route to China.

This was to be a half century of headlong commercial rush, accompanied by the first bridge, a pontoon affair, across the Hooghly to Howrah in 1874, the appearance of horse-drawn trams in 1880 and the installation of a telephone system in 1882. It was to be checked only by the opening of the Suez Canal, which soon persuaded the directors of the Peninsula and Oriental Steamship Company to shift their Indian headquarters from Garden Reach to Bombay; a rare example of Calcutta suffering from the primary instincts of commerce which had served it so well so far. Not that the business community needed to worry overmuch about a small loss of prestige. In 1853 the total value of import and export trade for the whole of Bengal had been just less than £29 millions. By 1901 in Calcutta alone it was worth nearly £111 millions. Buried somewhere in the middle of that goldrush is the strangely foreign figure of Surgeon-Major Ronald Ross, sending his servant Mahomed Bux from the laboratory of the Presidency General Hospital in search of mosquitoes, getting them to bite the poor fellow on his return, but finally discovering that this was how malaria happened. That was in 1898 when, at the other end of the city, Captain Bertie Clay was inventing a bullet with a soft lead nose in the small arms factory of Dum Dum; it was designed to punch a hole the size of a fist in Afridi tribesmen who were undeterred by conventional ammunition, and the 2nd Battalion, The Yorkshire Regiment, who tried it out in the field, reported a shot at one thousand yards which went right through a man after first penetrating the mess tin and thirteen folds of rolled greatcoat belonging to someone in front of him; 'the bullet', they said, 'was in good shape and not distorted in any way'.

The Bengalis, meanwhile, were becoming more difficult to contain in peace. Their educated *élite*, the bhadralok (literally the respectable people, the gentlemen), had long been aware how heavily the economic condition of the land had been weighted against its natives. They could quote (in English) things that conscience-stricken Englishmen had said on the subject; what the economist Montgomery Martin had said in 1840 about previous decades, for example, that 'We have during this period compelled the Indian territories to receive our manufactures, our woollens duty free, our cottons at 2½ per cent, while we have continued during that period to levy prohibitive duties from 10 to 1000 per cent upon articles they produce from our territories ... a free trade from this country, not a free trade between India and this country.' The uneducated ones merely experienced the effect of such things as facts of life, together with the evident contempt and worse of the average Englishman they met. In 1861 a Society for the Promotion of National Feeling among the Educated Natives of Bengal was launched, inviting everyone to speak and write Bengali, not English, to wear dhoti and chadar instead of hats and coats, to abandon British foods and hotels, to adopt indigenous games and physical exercises and to take up Hindu medicine again. New names, belonging to the cultural descendants of Rammohan Roy, began to travel through the bazaars and their owners began to demand greater participation, more freedom and less subservience in the running of their land; we shall hear more of them later.

And for a little while they found some Englishmen in and around Government willing to listen with sympathy. There was Allan Octavian Hume, for example, Customs commissioner and ornithologist, son of a great English radical who, instead of retiring to London, set himself up in Simla and helped to found the Indian National Congress to promote liberal and secular ideals. There was even a Viceroy, Lord Ripon, a Gladstone man, who in 1882 wrote a memorandum aiming to help 'the small beginnings of independent political life'. It was Ripon who brought in the Ilbert Bill, which would have allowed Indian judges sitting alone to try Europeans in the courts. Nothing demonstrated more clearly the distance between the best men of Government and the general men in the streets of British Calcutta. These openly abused the Viceroy as his carriage passed by, gangs of indigo planters came in from the country to do the same, and there was a threat to kidnap him. *The Englishman* declared that 'We are on the eve of a crisis ...' and ranted in the same tones it had once used before, when a planter called Rudd had actually been sentenced to death for killing one of his native workmen without provocation. On that occasion the Government had stood fast and Rudd was hanged; this time it watered down the Ilbert Bill so that a European would be tried at least by a jury, half of whom must be European too. A typical British attitude of these years was represented by a correspondent to *The Englishman*, writing about Calcutta Corporation, which had lately been created with an elected majority of councillors, which meant a majority of natives. 'Sir,' wrote this gentleman, 'With reference to the question of the Municipal Government of Calcutta, I beg to submit that the present system is perfectly preposterous. Calcutta is a purely English city. The city belongs and has always belonged to the English, and the native community in it is simply a foreign and parasitical com-

munity which would cease to exist if the English were to abandon it. Its site was selected and the land taken up for it was taken
up by the English. They founded it, built it, occupied it, maintained it, defended it, regulated it, and it is still from their commerce and enterprise that its revenues are now developed. The
English race, in its capacity for self-government, is admitted by
all nations to have never been surpassed by any race that has ever
been recorded in history. The Government of India in the pleni-
tude of its wisdom has, however, taken out of the hands of the
English race the management of their own city, which they built
for themselves, and which they support by their own exertions,
and in which they live, and has handed it over to their native
followers, who live by them and who are notoriously unfit for
the discharge of such functions – as is only too manifest at the
present time ... The end, however, is not far off. The nations of
the world will refuse before long to be done to death by cholera
and other loathsome diseases which are diffused from Calcutta
over the surface of the globe, in order that Bengali babus may
hold places of importance for which they are unfit and in which
all they can do is to exercise their talents for chatter, and enable
Government to say "See how liberal our administration is in
India to the natives." '

Sympathy in Government did not last long. There had been
too many insurrections in Bengal since the Mutiny, mostly of
peasants rising against indigo planters, who notoriously ran their
properties on medieval principles. Acting Chief Justice Norman
had been assassinated while entering the Town Hall in 1871 and
that still cut deeply even after Lord Ripon had come and gone
again. There was a strong element in the ICS who believed
Ripon and his ideals were the feeblest possible responses to a
situation requiring the most decisive and muscular central administration; talk of delegating some authority to Indians was
to them the fatuity of the milksop. They got what they wanted.
They celebrated Her Majesty's Diamond Jubilee first with an
earthquake. And within twelve months, in 1899, Lord Curzon
arrived in Calcutta and began to be a real Viceroy.

He began by demanding a more efficient administrative machine. A bill to reconstitute Calcutta Corporation at once offended

him, so he scrapped it and produced a new measure himself, which reduced the elected representation and ensured that the Corporation would remain firmly under British control. He decided that the administration of Calcutta University had 'fallen into the hands of a coterie of obscure native lawyers who regard educational questions from a political point of view' so he appointed a commission of reform without a single Indian member. It was possibly the largest single insult that could have been offered to the highly self-conscious and educated bhadralok. And then Lord Curzon turned his attention to the vast and increasingly troublesome province in which his Viceregal throne was set.

At the turn of the century Bengal was administratively a collection of provinces, each with distinctive historical, sub-racial and cultural differences; besides Bengal proper it included Bihar, Chota Nagpur and Orissa. It contained 78 million people. For years the Government had toyed with the idea of dismantling this cumbersome unit, to make it more manageable for hard-pressed civil servants. One reason for Curzon's next move was certainly administrative convenience. A larger reason was totally political. In October 1905 a partition line drawn down the middle of Bengal proper created two provinces. To a new East Bengal was added Assam; to the western half of Bengal the people of Bihar, Chota Nagpur and Orissa remained attached. From now on East Bengal was overwhelmingly Muslim in character. And in Bengal to the west, the preponderantly Hindu Bengalis of Calcutta and its hinterland found themselves numerically dominated by Oriyas, Biharis and others with whom almost the only thing they shared was a religion. This meant that the bhadralok, entirely upper-caste Hindu in character, were isolated from most fellow Bengalis and surrounded by people of alien traditions. It was the bhadralok of Calcutta who for the past half century and more had been more vociferously and intelligently critical of British rule than anyone else in India. They were now to be cornered in the hope that their influence could be reduced; or at least, in the expectation that it could be prevented from spreading.

It was an obtuse miscalculation by Curzon. What his partition did was to trigger a form of revolution in Bengal that con-

tinued almost until the British finally left India in 1947, that
incited other people in the sub-continent to imitate the Bengalis.
It was to cripple the politically moderate unity of the Indian
Congress. It was also to play its part in stirring the rivalries between Muslims and Hindus, which were to come home to Calcutta at their most ghastly extreme in 1946. Immediately, it set
the land aflame with opposition. Curzon had already experienced something of Bengali intransigence. When he was
meddling with Calcutta Corporation, Surendranath Banerjea
had led twenty-eight Indian councillors out of the Town Hall
with a vow never to return till official impositions were removed,
and there had been press campaigns, protest meetings and angry
deputations ever since. Something much tougher now began to
happen, though Curzon did not stay to watch it. He resigned
his Viceroyalty two months before his master plan was put into
effect, and left Lord Minto to deal with the repercussions.

On the eve of partition a public meeting in the Town Hall
announced that all true Bengalis would boycott all British goods
from now on. They would vow themselves to the purchase and
use only of swadeshi (literally, of one's own country) things.
And as the swadeshi movement began to swell, people began to
open new schools dedicated to nationalism through education;
Sarala Debi started a gymnasium in her father's house at Old
Ballygunge for the physical regeneration of Bengali youth. The
Bengali newspapers, their columns hot with passionate denunciations of the Raj, found their circulations soaring; *Amrita
Bazaar Patrika* went from 2,000 copies a day in 1904 to 7,500
in 1905, *The Bengalee* rose from 3,000 to 11,000, *Sandhya* from
500 to 7,000.

Then terrorism began. Bengalis were reminded that Kali the
Terrible had been created by the gods to destroy demons who
would take their kingdom from them, and the parallel was
obvious. Someone was sent off to Paris to learn about revolutionary explosives and before long there were backyard bomb
factories from one end of Calcutta to the other. Young men
organized into small and highly disciplined groups began to use
them, not always finding their mark, aiming occasionally for a
District Judge up-country but killing a couple of English gentle-

women instead. Foreign newspapers such as *L'Humanité* applauded their bearing when they were caught and stood their trial with composure. For the British turned fiercely on these assassins and the population that urged them on. Newspapers were suppressed, editors and printers were imprisoned, hundreds of Bengalis at a time were rounded up and grilled. Security officers descended almost daily on Calcutta University and its surrounding student bastions; and at the very least they would bear away any copy they could find of *War and Peace* or Jethro Brown's *Underlying Principles of Modern Legislation* with that sinister first chapter entitled 'The Challenge of Anarchy'; but they were almost as likely to haul somebody off for deportation on information laid by a secret agent previously insinuated into the campus.

This was to be one pattern of relationship between the British and the Bengalis until deep into the 1930s. It was not to be changed by Lord Minto, even though he had merely inherited another man's blunder and wished to make real concessions to Bengali feelings. Together with John Morley, a new Liberal Secretary of State for India, he constructed an Indian Councils Act which would allow Indian majorities on legislative councils in every province. He got rid of the Lieutenant-Governor of East Bengal and Assam, the monocled Bampfylde Fuller, who ruled his province with a zeal that his patron Lord Curzon had approved and intended. But neither of these strategies cooled the Bengali hotheads. They continued to sling their bombs and they still preached anarchy, when Lord Minto returned to England and when Lord Hardinge took his place. They were not even restrained much when Lord Hardinge engineered part of what they asked for and when, on top of it, he infuriated the British in Calcutta as carefully as Curzon had antagonized the Bengalis with partition. Lord Hardinge, at least, knew exactly what he was doing.

When Hardinge came to Calcutta in November 1910 the population of the city was well over one million. There were perhaps 14,000 British among them, insulated from the native mob by 16,000 half-caste Anglo-Indians whose loyalty to the Raj established them in positions of minor responsibility on the railways, in the post offices and along other vital lines of communication. The British themselves had a power quite separate from that of Government and they used it without scruple for the interests of anyone else; they applied pressure on Government through the Chamber of Commerce and through the columns of their four newspapers, *The Englishman*, *The Statesman*, *Capital* and *Commerce*; and when these devices sometimes failed to produce desired results, they wrote letters home to influential friends lurking in and around Westminster. They were obstinate and they were arrogant (they inhabited the second city of the whole British Empire, after all) and Hardinge was to snub them utterly and unforgivably. So was someone else, and he was George V.

The King had visited India as Prince of Wales in 1905–6 and he had thought then that the partition of Bengal was a mistake. On his own throne he now told his Viceroy that he still thought so. After getting his bearings, Hardinge agreed. The King was anxious to return to India as Emperor, to attract in person the loyalty of his increasingly restless subjects there, and he believed that nothing but goodwill would follow if he told them face to face that Bengal was to be reunited. At this point the Viceroy's Home Member in the Imperial Council, John Jenkins, suggested that Indians might be even more mollified if the Imperial throne were removed from Calcutta to Delhi. Delhi, after all, had a magnetism for both Hindus and Muslims that Calcutta could never match; it was where the Pandava Princes had engaged in epic struggles with the Kurawas in far distant times; it was where the Moguls had proudly ruled in the name of the Prophet. There was the additional thought that Imperial Government might function more coolly and more comfortably if it were shifted from the violent atmosphere of Bengal. So a decision was taken, and a magnificent Durbar was planned, and memoranda shuttled back and forth for six months between Lord Hardinge and Lord Crewe in the India Office at home. There was enormous and quite remarkable secrecy. Only a dozen people in each country were aware of what was to happen. Even Queen Mary hadn't heard a thing until she arrived in India and Lord Hardinge brought the matter up in his first audience with the royal couple.

The King proclaimed his news on a Durbar field of brilliance in Delhi. His Queen wore a crown with 4,149 cut diamonds, 2,000 rose diamonds, 22 emeralds, four rubies and four sapphires. He had 20,000 of his British and Indian troops drawn up in full-dress parade before him. There were trappings of Maharajahs, Rajas and princelings galore to make that December day in 1911 a gorgeous memory for everyone present and there were 50,000 of them at least. And when King George said 'We are pleased to announce to Our people that ... We have decided upon the transfer of the seat of the Government of India from Calcutta to the ancient capital of India ...' there was first of all a stunned silence in his audience. Then there was wild and incredulous cheering all round.

In Calcutta that week, life had proceeded at its normally assured pace, with its customary sounds of turbulence from certain sections of the native community. The London Repertory Company was playing *The Rivals* at the Grand Opera House and *The Passing of the Third Floor Back* was on at the Empire. There was some tut-tutting in the Bengal Club at the news of a hurricane on the South coast, which naturally meant somewhere between the Goodwin Sands and Portland Bill. The King Emperor would be visiting his capital city soon, when he had finished showing the flag in Delhi; full-scale Durbar quite proper, of course; the Mutiny had been at its worst up there, so it was a good idea to impress those people with maximum pomp and circumstance from time to time.

On Durbar day, five thousand troops paraded on the Maidan. As noon approached, when the King would speak in Delhi, a bugle call was followed by a royal salute of a hundred guns, then a feu de joie, after which the whole parade advanced on the flag while the band played 'The British Grenadiers'. Captain Brancker, Quartermaster-General at Fort William, read the proclamation in a loud and clear voice which could be distinctly heard by troops and spectators. Half a mile away the Deputy Sheriff, Mr E. W. Foley, did the same from the steps of the Town Hall. The list of Durbar honours was read out, with a Kaiser-I-Hind Gold Medal for Mr Lindsay, joint secretary of the Calcutta Club, and a knighthood for Mr Justice Ashutosh

Mukherji. A Royal Clemency was announced for 651 prisoners in the Calcutta gaols. They included ten Europeans and a couple of political detainees, and many of them went straight down to Kalighat, to bathe in the river and to make sacrifice to Kali. They are said to have cheered when His Majesty's name was mentioned and Bengalis generally were mightily pleased at the King Emperor's news. At a meeting in College Square sometime later, Surendranath Banerjea said that future generations would point to December 12 as the start of a new epoch in Bengali history; he also said that reunification represented 'the triumph of British justice and the vindication of constitutional methods in our political controversies'. Even the bully boys with bombs, who had long since decided against constitutional methods, briefly held their fire with gratification.

The British seem at first to have been totally crushed by the news. Their papers next day merely recorded events in Delhi, the bare facts of proclamation in Calcutta, and added that 'Durbar day passed off quietly' there. After that they let their feelings go, and these were infinitely more bitter and angry than the 'chagrin and disappointment' Lord Crewe had foreseen among members of the commercial community in one of his memoranda to Hardinge.

One by one, in the next few days, the newspaper reporters picked up the grudges and the smarting calculations of the British man in the street. 'It is the European community that will suffer and every member of that community will have to bear the burden,' said one gentleman under interview. 'It is quite likely that, Delhi being a great distributing place, goods that now come to Calcutta will go to Bombay and Karachi.' Another entrepreneur, who had invested a lot of money in developing estates and building houses and blocks of flats, was very despondent. 'Calcutta is done,' he said, 'and men like myself, who have tried to cope with the demand for places of residence, have lost our money.' The head of one of the biggest firms in the city, deciding that he spoke for tradespeople generally, said that 'we have spent a very great deal of money in recent years in order to cope with the business which the influx of the Government officials and cold-weather visitors has brought us. Now it seems to

me that there will be no cold-weather season in Calcutta and we
need not have extended at all, for our premises for the most
part were quite big enough for the ordinary population of Calcutta. We are the people who will suffer ...' A man wise in the
ways of influence remarked that 'As everyone who has had dealings with the Government knows, little satisfaction is to be
obtained by writing and it is only by personal contact and personal explanation that we can make Government officials realize
our needs.'

For weeks now, the correspondence columns of the local press
were to be filled with letters which the sub-editors thoughtfully
presented under the generic headline 'The degradation of Calcutta'. The correspondents never put their names and addresses
to these communications; they signed them Civis, A Liberal
Disgusted, Ichabod, Patria Cara, An old Anglo-Indian and
Cricket. Their general flavour was perfectly reproduced in one
of the leading articles *The Statesman* was publishing at the time:
'It is upon the Government of India and in particular upon
Lord Hardinge that the responsibility rests for what can only be
described as an insult to the people of Bengal and to the people
of India, rulers and ruled alike ... The Viceroy and his Council
decided the matter without consulting a single prominent man
in the Province, whether official or unofficial, and then they turn
round and plead for a generous view from the people they have
insulted. Our answer is that before Bengal can look at the question on its merits, the men chiefly responsible for this utter
disregard for the principles of constitutional government must
go. Lord Hardinge has made use of his high office to mislead
the King ...'

Within a few months Lord Crewe, briefing the first Governor
of the reformed Bengal, was to characterize these people thus:
'The Calcutta English ... community includes, I am sure, a
number of honest, capable and likeable people; but I am not less
sure that they are spoilt children in many respects, full of their
historical and social importance, anti-Indian *au fond*, and keen
to scent out 'disloyalty' in any independent expression of
opinion, hidebound too in class prejudices.' And, indeed, only
The Statesman's turf correspondent appears to have viewed the

disaster philosophically. 'Would a change of capital from London to the ancient capital, Winchester,' he asked his readers one morning, 'have any effect upon racing at Epsom, Newmarket, Ascot or Doncaster?'

Calcutta was not, of course, *done*, as the property developer had feared. There were still two or three decades left in which an Englishman could turn his fortune out of it. The essentials of its life continued, bereft only of the opportunity for some to have a pointed word in the most useful ears, stripped merely of the most glittering social functions that were patronized with a sigh periodically by the latest Viceregal tenant of Government House. Nothing but these most superior benefits of Empire was to be missing from the lives of the British citizens for more than a generation to come. Yet a line *had* now been broken, which stretched back vividly and firmly at least to Warren Hastings and, in a way, even beyond to Job Charnock himself. For this was the first time the Raj had retreated before its subject people. This was symbolically the beginning of an end, not only for the British of Calcutta but for the alien rulers of India as a whole. There were even a few men, mostly in London, who could see it as such. And maybe they allowed themselves a wry grin when they realized that the moment in 1912 when it was appointed that Calcutta should cease to be capital of India, was none other than April Fool's Day.

3

POVERTY

WHEN the international and jet-propelled traveller disembarks
at Dum Dum he finds, if he has come by the right airline, that a
highly polished limousine awaits his pleasure. It will be 6.30 or
thereabouts in the morning, and the atmosphere will already be
faintly sticky with heat and so unmistakably sweetened with a
compound of mainly vegetable odours that the visitor can almost taste it. He need fear no discomfort at this stage, however,
for he is to be transported into the city in air-conditioned splendour behind delicately tinted windows. From this smooth and
relaxing position he can begin to observe how the other half of
humanity lives. From the outset he notices some things which
are reassuringly familiar. Along the first mile of this wide and
tarmacadamed airport road are spaced the very same collection
of gaudy hoardings that signal the way in and out of Heathrow
or J. F. Kennedy or Fiumicino; 'Try a Little VC-10derness',
says one – and some untidy idiot seems to have thrown up a collection of chicken coops in the shade of BOAC. Beside these
homely reference points, however, the peculiarities of India are
to be seen. The road is bordered by ditches and ponds, all
brimming with water, in which women even at this hour are
flogging garments clean, in which men are taking the first bath
of the day. Beyond the spindle-elegant sodium lights, with buz-
zards and vultures perched on top, stand thickets of bamboo-
and-thatch huts among avenues of palm. Along a canal, a large
black barge top-heavy with hay is being poled inches at a time
through a mass of pretty but choking mauve water hyacinth.
And in the distance, lurking on the horizon, a range of tall
factory chimneys is beginning to smoke.

Calcutta is announced with a pothole or two. Then a bus is
overtaken, such a vehicle as the traveller has never seen before;
its bodywork is battered with a thousand dents, as though an

army of commuters had once tried to kick it to bits, and it is not
only crammed with people, it has a score or so hanging off the
platform and around the back like a cluster of grapes. It is
lumbering and steaming into a suburban wasteland, stippled with
blocks of dilapidated flats; and maybe Bishop Heber's imagery
was not so far-fetched after all, for these are not at all unlike
some of the homes for the workers you can see in Moscow today,
though there they are not coloured pink and they certainly
haven't been decorated with the hammer and sickle in crude
whitewash on the walls. Swiftly, the outer Calcutta of these
revolutionary symbols now coagulates into the inner Calcutta
which is unlike anywhere else on earth. The limousine now
lurches and rolls, for there are too many potholes to avoid. It
rocks down cobblestoned roads lined with high factory walls
which have an air of South Lancashire about them. It begins to
thread its way through traffic along thoroughfares that have
something of Bishopsgate or Holborn in their buildings.

It is the traffic that makes it all unique. A traffic in trams
grinding round corners, a traffic in approximately London buses
whose radiators seem ready to burst, in gypsy-green lorries with
'Ta-ta and By-by' and other slogans painted on the back, in
taxis swerving all over the road with much blowing of horns, in
rickshaws springing unexpectedly out of sidestreets, in bullock
carts swaying ponderously along to the impediment of everyone,
in sacred Brahmani cows and bulls nonchalantly strolling down
the middle of the tram-tracks munching breakfast as they go.
A traffic, too, in people who are hanging on to all forms of public transport, who are squatting cross-legged upon the counters
of their shops, who are darting in and out of the roadways between the vehicles, who are staggering under enormous loads,
who are walking briskly with briefcases, who are lying like dead
things on the pavements, who are drenching themselves with
muddy water in the gutters, who are arguing, laughing, gesticulating, defecating, and who are sometimes just standing still as
though wondering what to do. There never were so many people
in a city at seven o'clock in the morning. Patiently the driver
of the limousine steers his passage between and around them,
while they pause in mid-stride to let him through, or leap to get

out of his way, or stare at him blankly, or curse him roundly, or occasionally spit in the path of his highly polished Cadillac. Presently, and quite remarkably, he comes to the end of the journey without collision and deposits the traveller and his luggage upon the pavement in front of an hotel. And here, the traveller has his first encounter with a beggar. He had better make the best of it, for beggary is to be with him until the end of his days in Calcutta.

No one knows how many beggars there are in the city; the only clue is the estimate that there are 400,000 men in town without a job. There is beggary all over India, but nowhere is there beggary on the scale of Calcutta's. There are not many places where a European can move a hundred yards in the certainty that his charity will not be invoked. An old man with one leg, using a quarter staff in place of the other like a figure from Bruegel, stumps up and mutters subservience with downcast eyes and outstretched tin bowl. A woman rushes to your side and almost thrusts her sleeping child into your face, supplicating mournfully. These are commonplace figures of the landscape. So are the children who come at you with terrible histrionics in which tears begin to stream and sobs become uncontrolled and hands are held upstretched below chins to the cry of 'No Mamma, no Papa, paise, paise'; and round the corner there is a dwarf woman with the same cry on her lips, though her bandy little legs must have been carrying her around for the best part of fifty years. There are beggars who are horribly mutilated; a small boy without feet or hands, who clumps along an arcade upon wooden blocks which have been strapped to his knees and elbows, while he holds a bowl between his teeth; a man who lies on his back outside the Grand Hotel, his limbs at grotesque angles, squirming violently while he bangs his tin on the ground for attention; and twenty-five yards away, another fellow who uses one arm as a crutch to lever the rest of an apparently lifeless and rigid body along, while tendons stand out on his neck like ropework and his mouth bares its teeth in a werewolf grin. It is said that many of these beggars have been deliberately maimed at birth, to be run in stables for more profitable business. And there is surely a degree of tactical organization to the beggary of Calcutta that is sometimes admirable. Where flashy Park Street turns off Chowringhee there are traffic lights and by these a score or more of beggars customarily stand, waiting for the cars and taxis to pull up at red; whereupon they flush from the pavement like sparrows from a hedge and pester the passengers who have not wound up their windows quickly enough; and for two years, to my certain knowledge, a woman with a baby and a face made hideously piebald by leucoderma was regularly among them.

The average European was not conditioned to live with beggary of this nature in the middle of the twentieth century and after a while he finds himself being unpleasantly exposed by it. At first his conscience troubles him so much that he dispenses charity to all who approach him. But then, one day, a woman to whom he has given all his loose change counts it carefully and pursues him angrily for more; he finds himself looking carefully over his shoulder, before tossing coin in yet another bowl, to see how many of the beggar's fellows are within pouncing distance; and before long he is giving very selectively indeed. As long as he remains in Calcutta he is emotionally split in two by the children who come at him and will not let him go, as though he were a second Pied Piper. Sometimes he has observed them being ordered onto him by a pavement tradesman, sometimes they are pestering at his left hand while a parent is beseeching at his right, sometimes they have been playing alone in the gutter until his shadow falls across their game. However they come at him, they eventually corner him, by their dogged persistence, by their interminable numbers, in a frightful dilemma of his own; for he finds that while half of him wants to pick them up and hug them, the other half would willingly kick them hard across the street if he dared. But the most terrible beggars of all are the men, women and children who shuffle into his path with a whisper and only half a gesture of entreaty and who, when the rich man in a moment of excessive guilt or charity thrusts one whole rupee in their direction, do not take the note but stand looking at it blankly; for they cannot comprehend the wealth represented by 6p or 12 cents – current coin of this time.

The sleepers on the streets present no such problem, being

inert, so that they can be avoided at will. A census was made of them one night in 1961 and the tally was then thirty thousand; eight years later a local newspaper referred to seventy thousand; and neither figure can be taken as a precise reckoning of Calcutta's utmost destitution, which could be either more or less than any systematic calculation. On the one hand, the city is too complex and sprawling for everyone living in the open to be accounted for; on the other, it is an observed fact that many people prefer to sleep on a blanket in the comparatively open air of the streets rather than stifle in the foetid atmosphere of a Calcutta slum. Nevertheless, there are vast numbers who clearly have nowhere else to go. They are to be found late at night and every morning throughout the centre of the city, lying under the arcades of Chowringhee and beside the standpipes of Bentinck Street. There are squadrons of them around the approaches to Howrah Station across the river, in addition to the platoons who sleep inside the station itself. You can find them at intervals along the great curving length of Lower Circular Road and you have to step over their bodies as you move out of the dancing lights of the Ballygunge crossroads. The nights of Calcutta, indeed, flicker with the small fires made by street campers and you are never far from the smell of their acrid fumes; they flare and smoke in the angles of walls, along gutters, even beside tram tracks in the middle of roads. And wherever a fire is, bodies are huddled beside it. Sometimes they still lie there during the day and they are so reduced that they do not even sweat any more; they lie in some shade from the blistering sun, almost and sometimes totally naked, their hair matted, their sinews clearly visible, their skins bone dry and very dusty, the texture of an abandoned inner tube. They die like that, eventually, and the kites which forever swing lazily in the skies of Calcutta congregate in a swirling circle high above the corpse, waiting for it to be alone.

Sometimes these inhabitants of the streets construct lean-tos, if they are in families, of any material they can find. There is a peculiarly awful series of them against a high brick wall at the bottom of Bepin Behary Ganguly Street, where it approaches the hubbub of Sealdah Station, in a junction which marks the spot where Job Charnock's famous tree once stood. For five hundred yards or so there is a confusion of packing cases, corrugated iron, cardboard, straw matting, odd bricks and wads of newspaper arranged into a double-decker sequence of boxes. Each box is approximately the size of a small pigeon loft, with room in it to squat and only just to kneel. No English miner would dream of keeping his pigeons in anything so ramshackle and primitive; he might, indeed, fear the attentions of the RSPCA if he did. In Calcutta each box, one on top of the other, is the sleeping and loving quarters of a family. The rest of their life is conducted on the pavement where they cook and play and quarrel together; and in the gutter, where they wash themselves and their rags in the gush of fractured standpipes.

Sometimes these people are taken from the streets on the threshold of death. If this happens then almost certainly it will be because a truck has cruised that way, driven by one of Mother Teresa's Missionaries of Charity; there is scarcely anyone else in Calcutta who will even notice their dying. But the nuns have a refuge specifically for dying destitutes. It is right alongside Kali's temple and it is called Nirmal Hriday. It is a highly scrubbed and totally antiseptic shed, with little in the way of pious decoration. It is crammed with stretcher beds, row after row of them, and their moribund occupants. There are people in here in their twenties but hardly anyone looks less than sixty years old. They lie very still, blinking and clawing at food, but otherwise not moving at all. They have been brought here because of a curious and alien philosophy that has gradually been evolved in and out of Calcutta by these women in the white muslin saris that are bordered in blue; it is simply a conviction, unfathomable to the deepest dogmas of Hinduism, that there is some point in bringing a human being who has been totally neglected since birth to a place where he can at least die in a scrap of dignity and with somebody aware of his end. So the nuns move perpetually down the rows of stretchers, dishing out food to those who can eat, cropping the heads of those who are lousy, dressing the sores of those who are rancid, mopping up the ones who are squittering incontinently. There are moments in Nirmal Hriday when a visitor can believe he has reached the backside of hell. A young Englishman wrote this in his journal for 1969: 'A man of forty, he looked seventy – with a gangrenous leg – with a rag wrapped round it; we had to take him outside because of the stench to hose his leg down. The water started the blood flowing over the green flesh; bone and muscle dropped off. The foot was just a skeleton and you could see right through his leg up to the knee. A crow came down and picked up a bone that had fallen from his foot (they're hungry, too). My stomach didn't think much of this and added to the mess flowing down the drain.' When these people die they are not given a Christian burial; the nuns would think that profanity; they are given the cremation and the consignment to the water that they and their ancestors have always craved. Occasionally they do not die, they are restored to a kind of health, and they are gently asked to leave, to make room for more of the really dying. There are always plenty of those.

Mother Teresa's nuns are also almost the only people who care for Calcutta's lepers, and there are reckoned to be something between 35,000 and 40,000 of those. With one exception, the hospitals cannot or will not take them and when the police find a leper wandering at night in the rich suburb of Alipore, it is the missionary convent they ring for a truck to convey the wretch out of the way. Most of the lepers have to fend for themselves, but the nuns look after eight colonies containing ten thousand around the city. One lies beyond the slaughterhouse at Entally, where Calcutta begins to ooze out into the eastern swamplands. It is a smoky, grimy, industrialized area with cobbled streets that are permanently choked with cows of skin and bone and not much else, which are mysteriously no longer sacred and which are being driven in lurching procession to the butcher; or which, having sometimes dropped dead *en route*, are carried the rest of the way lashed to carts pushed by men, their carcases flopping ghoulishly, their eyeballs glaring at the gritty sky. A few hundred yards further, on the other side of a railway bridge, not far from a vast garbage dump, upon the muddy banks of a creek, is the leper colony of Dhapa.

There are people here in various stages of disease. Some lie on beds inside mud huts with their limbs bandaged. A boy sits against an outside wall, his arms and legs smeared with a blue ointment; next to him is another child with finger stumps which are raw and quietly bleeding. There are lepers in the early stages of mutilation helping lepers who have already been crippled for life. A woman uses the grey stump of her hand like a wooden spoon to stir a pot of steaming liquid, for it has no feeling left, and the ghastly image that comes to a Western mind is of some particularly hellish production of the witches' scene in *Macbeth*. Next to her a gaudy pop-art representation of Kali has been propped against the wall alongside an iron trident garlanded with marigolds. The nuns come once a week with medicines and call in regularly to treat the worst cases; they also bring cats to keep down the rats from the garbage dump and the slaughter-house, which would otherwise begin to chew a leprous limb without its owner even noticing. But the lepers are mainly on their own, looking after each other, making shoes to raise some kind of income, having children and now usually managing to rear them free of leprosy, with the nuns to keep an eye on things and administer drugs; for it is possible to halt the disease in its tracks provided you act early enough, when the first scaliness appears on the skin. A patient tries to convey what it is like, when you find you must make your life at Dhapa: 'Mother, I am an educated man. I was a clerk in a very good position. I earned 650 rupees per month. One day the neighbours got up a petition and said his face not properly well, children in the compound, and the police came. The police came and said within two days I must go. I said what must I do. They say you are an educated man, make your own arrangement. Then I know only Mother Teresa will help me. I am an educated man and my motto is leprosy is not a disgrace, it is an illness.'

The destitutes and the lepers represent the extremities of Calcutta's poverty. The norm is in a sense even more appalling. For that is what this society appears to have settled for on behalf of huge proportions of its people. In the city of Calcutta proper, the heart of this sprawling metropolis bordering the Hooghly, there are something over three million people. More than a third of them live in slums, of which the most notorious kind is the registered slum, or bustee. The figure generally quoted for the number of bustee dwellers is 700,000, but as that was an estimate made in 1961 the true figure will now be considerably greater. The bustee is legally defined by municipal act as an area of land occupied by a collection of huts not less than ten cottahs (which is one sixth of an acre) in extent. It is, moreover, a definition of ownership and tenant relationships, not a description of building characteristics. It involves three parties: one is the owner of the land, who pays Corporation taxes and leases parts of the holding to others; another is the thika tenant or hut owner, who builds dwellings on the land, pays the landlord for the privilege and rents out the rooms he has constructed; at the bottom of the pile comes the bustee dweller, paying his rent to the thika tenant, ultimately obliged to the landlord. In 1967 it was estimated that there were 20,000 thika tenants in the city proper, owning 30,000 huts between them, each producing an average of Rs 80 a month in rent. But the bustee is an awful fact of life throughout the metropolitan area of Calcutta. People lie in bustees from Budge Budge in the South to Kanchrapara in the North, which is even higher up the Hooghly than that old Dutch settlement of Chinsurah. Some of the nastiest are to be found directly across the river, in the twin city of Howrah, which is to Calcutta what Southwark is to London, what Birkenhead is to Liverpool, what The Bronx is to Manhattan.

There is a typical bustee out near Calcutta's second university at Jadavpore. It starts on the edge of upstanding middle-class houses and it trails off into the railway lines; so many bustees do. The huts are made of wattle, they have tiled roofs, they have mud floors. They are so congested that there is nowhere more than an arm's span in the dirt-track lanes that separate one row from another. And open drains run down the middle of each lane, so that you tend to walk them at the straddle. People sit in these lanes chopping wood, cooking at open fires, even buying and selling at tiny stalls. As many as seven or eight sleep in one room of a shanty, for which they pay Rs 10 to 15 a month to their thika tenant. There is no electricity, which means that there are no fans; and the fan in Calcutta is a minimal necessity of life for any European, no luxury for any Indian. There is a standpipe providing water for 125 people. There is also the khatal.

The khatal is the rich man's method of stabling his cattle upon the premises of the poor. Every bustee contains them; it is one way of acquiring a minute income from the rich man, and there is also the consideration of dung which can be collected, shaped into small pats, placed upon the baked earth for drying in the sun, and then used as fuel for the fires. The people have to put up with the filth of these dozen beasts, sitting there tethered under a shady roof in the middle of their homes, and they also have to find vegetation for the wretched animals to eat. In exchange they are allowed to milk them, as long as the cows are not dry. The rich man expects to be paid for the milk, of course; he comes down to the bustee once a month to settle his financial transactions with the people.

There are other forms of slum in Calcutta. Up at Baranagar, which is almost within sight of the Howrah Bridge, there is a jute mill which was built and profitably maintained for nearly a century by Scotsmen. Eventually it passed into the hands of Indians, who run it now, almost a model of its kind. It is circumscribed by a high brick wall and in spite of the purely Indian setting – the long row of cooped-up stalls across the street, their owners cross-legged on the counter, the bicycle rickshaws being pedalled laboriously, with much ringing of bells, over the cobbles – in spite of all this, the essence of the mill and its vicinity is still ridiculously British. That raw red brick with its patina of dirt, that gateway with a wrought-iron arch curving above it, those factory attendants in khaki dungarees checking people in and out, those workmen wheeling their bicycles away after a shift, are all part of an industrial landscape which originated half way across the earth and which can still be seen in a thousand examples from Dundee to Bolton and back again. The street curves downhill slightly, alongside the high wall, towards the river, where the mill has its private pier for barges come to collect its gunny sacks and its other makings of jute. And at the bottom, on the bank of the river, those Scotsmen built some homes for their workers; for their Indian foremen, to be precise.

They stand in terrace rows and they are made of the same glazed brick as the factory, a couple of storeys high. They contain a total of 630 rooms and 1,500 people inhabit them. One room on the ground floor is 10 ft by 6ft and three men share it; there is space inside for nothing but them, a string from one wall to the other with clothes hanging from it, half a dozen metal cooking vessels and a few religious pictures tacked into the brickwork. But they have themselves added a short bamboo porch to give them a little extra space for a kitchen of sorts, a small angular horseshoe shape two bricks high; an open drain runs within two feet of it. The men live here by themselves because, like so many men in Calcutta, they find that ends can be made to meet more often if the wife and children stay behind in the village, which may be somewhere in the back of Bengal or even farther afield. Once a year these three men return to their families for two months allotted leave, a fortnight of it paid. Each collects Rs 200 a month for a forty-eight hour week and absolutely no chance of overtime. He has six per cent of his wages deducted for an unemployment benefit scheme. He spends Rs 70 a month on keeping himself alive. The rest he sends home to his family. These three men have lived like this since they came to Calcutta in 1956. By the norms of the city, they are not too badly off, even though the pumps of unfiltered water supplied by the company work out at one for every hundred people, even though the solitary latrine for the whole colony of 1,500 is so foul that most people instead take to the Hooghly.

There is also a little electricity here, not in the rooms of course, which don't even have ventilation, but enough to provide two or three lamp standards along the end of the terrace rows. And at night, in the pools of light these create, this colony of company slums can be seen as a haunting throwback to a distant age in a distant place. People sit upon their haunches in the lamplight and gamble with cards; they lean and gossip beside small stalls which are set up even in here, with shelves bearing spices in jars, tobacco in boxes and garish glassy beads threaded into necklaces and bangles on string. On the outer rim of the light, where the thick shadows fade and the deep blackness begins, grey figures steal back and forth, quarrel by one of the pumps, sit very still with their backs to a wall and squat upon their heels to piss in a gutter. There are flickering lights from oil lamps inside some of the buildings. There is iron-blue smoke from fires drifting in small clouds just above head height. There are mangy dogs, their coats almost bald with disease and undernourishment, scavenging listlessly in corners. It will have been something like this in the stews of Whitechapel early in the nineteenth century.

The sewerage of Calcutta is from the same era, as the city approaches the last quarter of the twentieth century. Along the whole thirty-mile length of Greater Calcutta there is not much of even remotely modern sewerage, and modern in this context means anything up to a hundred years old. Instead there is what they call the service privy. This is a small brick shed with a platform above a large earthenware bowl to receive the shit; it is usually fully exposed and unprotected from flies. It is supposed to be emptied daily by Calcutta Corporation, but things do not happen that way in Calcutta. It is sometimes weeks before the Corporation sweepers arrive. Even with the service at its best, the bowl has usually long since overflowed across the surrounding ground. Howrah, with a population of half a million, contains nothing but service privies. Apart from Howrah and the city proper, there are 126,000 of them in Greater Calcutta. The city itself has another 42,000. Its bustees alone contain 17,000. Unutterably nasty as the service privy is for those who must use it, its implications are much more awful than mere squalor. It represents the beginnings of cholera, of every other gastro-intestinal disease in creation, with smallpox and tuberculosis thrown in as well. For the stinking mess around the bustee's privy is washed straight into the ponds and tanks of water in which the people clean themselves and their clothes and their cooking utensils. Every year, when the monsoon falls, the incidence of cholera in Calcutta rises from its service privies. It is endemic and sometimes it is epidemic; in 1958 there were 4,900 cases and 1,765 deaths in Calcutta City alone. And this place is not much equipped for the medical care and attention of its poor people. In the whole of West Bengal there is not even one hospital bed for every thousand people. It occasionally happens that an ambulance takes a sick man to hospital, where the doctors refuse to treat him, whereupon he is returned by ambulance whence he came; which, as often as not, is to the pavement.

It is just possible for the Western mind, contemplating Cal-

cutta from a safe distance, to grasp some of the incidence of its
poverty. It is almost impossible, except from personal experience,
to understand how congested the poverty is. But some comparative figures can give an inkling. Calcutta is obviously one of the
most overcrowded places on earth. In fact, the last time anyone
made a count (between 1961 and 1963), it was found that the
city contained 102,010 people per square mile. Even by Indian
standards this was an enormous density. Calcutta's nearest rival
at the time was Ahmedabad, with 56,540 people per square mile;
in Delhi the figure was 41,280, in Bangalore it was 49,220. In
1963, the city the Western world laments as the most shockingly
overcrowded it knows, New York, contained 27,900 people per
square mile. The average figure for twenty-two cities in the
Central United States was 13,500; Los Angeles rated an agora-
phobic 7,870. Figures do not diminish in Calcutta; the density
will be appreciably greater by now. In 1961 the average dwelling
along the Hooghly consisted of 1.55 rooms, with three people
living in each room. But in 1957 it was calculated that seventy-
seven per cent of all the families in Calcutta had less than forty
square feet of living space per person.

Life is squalid, it is claustrophobic and it somehow continues
on a pittance. A man earning Rs 200 a month by tending a loom
in a jute mill at Baranagar is a princeling among such people. He
is, for a start, at least semi-skilled, which means that he will
have had some education in a city where sixty-four per cent of
the adults are illiterate. And he is comparatively secure in his
employment. So, in a smaller way, is a man like Bheddari Poshman, who at the age of sixty-five pulls a rickshaw through the
pouring traffic of Calcutta. It is not his own rickshaw, of course;
the middleman flourishes in India as he flourishes nowhere else;
the rickshaw man rents his vehicle for one rupee a day from a
fellow who owns forty of them. He then runs and trots and jogs
anything between ten and twenty miles a day to make a living.
He charges his customers anything between an equivalent of ½p
and 1p a mile, which means that he earns Rs 3 to Rs 7 a day,
with takings on the higher side on Saturday and Sundays; for he
keeps going seven days in the week. Poshman manages to do this,
in spite of his sixty-five years, on a diet which one would have

thought insufficient even to keep him standing on his legs without support. At the start of the day there is eight ounces of rice or a similar amount of the cereal called chhatu, mixed with some chili and onion for flavour; there is some tea around noon, and chappatis in the evening. Nothing else. Nevertheless, this is still living on a slightly higher income than the infinite number who are employed as servants in Calcutta.

In 1965 the American Woman's Club of the city compiled an instructive booklet for the guidance of new members recently arrived from the States. It included prevailing wage rates for servants, and it should be borne in mind that in many cases the terms of engagement probably meant that the employee ate at his employer's expense on top of his wage, and his lodging in a shed at the back of the house; though whether this also allowed him to carry food away to his immediate relations would depend upon individual American or European generosity. The instructions to the new hirer of servants went as follows:

Bearer – Rs 90 to Rs 120 or more a month. The higher paid bearers act as butler-bearers, combining the duties of serving man with those of major domo. *Cook* – Rs 90 to Rs 110 a month. Does marketing and cooking. *Cook-bearer* – Rs 100 to Rs 125 a month. Acts as cook and bearer usually for a single person or for a couple. Occasionally may be employed by a larger family *Sweeper* – Rs 60 to Rs 75 a month. Does cleaning and heavy work. *Ayah or nanny* – Rs 60 to Rs 75 a month. Takes care of children. The ayah usually doesn't live in. The nanny is usually a more experienced person, lives in and receives higher pay. *Personal ayah* – Rs 35 to Rs 75 a month, depending upon whether the service is full or part-time. Acts as lady's maid, washes, irons and mends women's clothing, etc. Single women with jobs find a part-time ayah a great help. In homes with pre-teen or teenage girls it is suggested that an ayah be hired as a personal maidservant for the women of the family. *Driver* – Rs 130 to Rs 165 a month. Drives and takes care of the car. *Mali* (gardener) – Rs 60 to Rs 75 a month. Takes care of the garden. *Durwan* (guard) – Rs 60 to Rs 80 a month. Acts as watchman and gate-keeper. *Dhobi* (laundryman) – Rs 45 to Rs 50 a month. For a part-time employee who washes, irons all linens and clothing, including the servants' uniforms two or three times a week. Rs 70 to Rs 80 or more for a full-time employee for large families who require daily service. He may live in. Rs 30 or more for ironing only, for families who have their own washing machines.

Living in, it should be explained, means the shed at the back of the premises. It does not mean having a room in a household of Westerners. The servants, as likely as not, dwell in the nearest bustee.

The strains of life at this level are sometimes quite alien to the experience of the Western world, and at the most there will be merely suggestions of them in the slums of Southern Europe and the poor men's ghettoes of North America. They could only be guessed at in Calcutta until a year or two ago. But towards the end of 1968 the Anthropological Survey of India, whose head-quarters stand just off Chowringhee, began eight months' study of life in one bustee which has been sunk just beyond the glow of neon lights near Rashbehari Avenue, in the South of the city. There are sixty-one hutments here, almost all of one storey on a couple of acres, with mud or brick walls, with tin or tiled roofs. Each of them contains anything from eight to forty families. There are 2,451 people altogether, mostly Bengalis, seasoned with immigrants from Bihar, Uttar Pradesh, Orissa and Nepal. They represent something like forty different castes between them. The vast majority of them have come to Calcutta from the villages of Eastern India but the next largest group are some of the refugees who have been flowing into the city from East Pakistan ever since Partition in 1947; after them come a handful whose life began in some other Calcutta slum, and there is a sprinkling of people who once knew something a bit better than this in some other Indian city. They are labourers and ayahs, masons and lathe-operatives, tram conductors and office peons, and they pay monthly rents between Rs 9 and Rs 35 for each room. For this there is a service privy and an open bathing space to each hut. There are seven tubewells and two taps of water for the entire bustee. Right alongside this is the kothabari, the middle-class land of bricks and mortar rising to a couple of storeys (homes are mostly no higher than that in Calcutta), of commercial hoardings and street lights of neon which glare so fiercely at night that the bustee seems to be a place of total blackness with half a dozen guttering candles to mark that it is there at all. It requires some courage for an outsider to step alone into such a place after dusk.

There are 441 families in the bustee and for most of them income can be almost anything up to Rs 150 a month. In many, the wife is out earning money in the morning and evening and it is the man who is cooking, cleaning and caring for the children. A newly-married couple may go to the cinema two or three times in the first few months, but after that recreation together generally stops. When the wife is at home the man takes himself to a tea shop or plays cards near a street lamp with his friends. The women do not often have friends, only acquaintances. The wives living in the same hut often cooperate in family matters, but it is usually for what each can get out of the other later on; they quarrel and fight a great deal. So do the husbands and wives. The women, with the self-esteem of earning power, sometimes call their husbands 'Dokno' or she-man and say 'I am not afraid of him; I do not depend on him.' And sometimes men say 'I have not allowed my wife to work in spite of the hardship I have to endure, because then she will no longer obey me.'

Where the man is the only bread-winner, the wife is subservient and gets no help at all in domestic affairs. The children of both sexes are taught to cook and do other chores from an early age; the local primary schoolteacher is frequently asked by a parent to let a small boy go home early so that he can prepare rice for the family. From the age of eight the boys begin to stay away from home. By the time they are twelve they have usually started a job and they spend most of the money on themselves; the girls usually get jobs as servants a little later. The parents complain that their children are not respectful once they have ceased to be infants, but what they really mean is that they are disobedient. Children frequently abuse their parents in sexual terms; they are not very old when they start to beat their parents, and this frequently continues for the rest of their lives together. Abuse and beating is common among brothers and sisters as well, and the relationships between them soon become as impersonal as those between people without blood ties. A young man is known to borrow money from his elder brother at five per cent interest.

A striking thing about the people of the bustee, in a land where kinship is highly esteemed, is how little contact they have with relations outside the immediate family. It is usually only the husbands who maintain any contact at all with adult brothers and sisters, aunts and uncles and cousins. Some people have difficulty in recalling the name of their grandparents. And when there is a marriage in the bustee, only the very closest relatives attend. Yet somehow, marriages seem to stand the strain of this life surprisingly well. The rate of husbands deserting their wives is under five per cent, though there are fifty unmarried couples who, on one side or the other, abandoned earlier unions. There is a certain unspecified amount of illicit sex by both men and women who are married.

There are obvious reasons why relatives should lose contact with each other. One is the expense of travel and another is the difficulty as well as the expense of accommodating someone who might have come to Calcutta from a home village in Bihar to see a son or a niece. But the moral obligations of family hospitality also break down because one side has become wealthier than the other. A man living in the bustee will not visit his aunt and her husband who reside in the adjacent kothabari because he feels they are above his station, and the residents of the kothabari will certainly never descend to the bustee. A small trader who lived in the bustee for three years eventually moved out to Jadavpore, because he thought it would improve his wider family relationships. Moreover, a middle-class Indian can be shocked (you can smell it coming off the pages of the anthropologist's report) by some of the relationships that do occur in the bustee. 'I had,' he writes, 'opportunity to observe the behavioural pattern between "vasur" (husband's elder brother) and younger brother's wife, between daughter-in-law and mother-in-law, son-in-law and mother and father-in-law, between maternal nephew and uncle, etc. In all cases the element of respect seems to be lacking and the social distance has been shortened considerably. Smoking biri or cutting joke with elderly persons has become common. Normally a brother's wife when talking with "vasur" must veil herself and use a gentle tone and should show no petulance. The "vasur" on the other hand, should be reserved in his behaviour. Though this is the ideal norm, none of these conventions are observed in the bustee. I have at least one case to show that sexual relations exist between "vasur" and his younger brother's wife.' And sadly, he notes two cases of incest five years previously, the families having since left the bustee.

Fifty yards away is the towering kothabari, but it is a world apart from the bustee, inhabited by the babus of the bhadralok class who are separated from these slum dwellers by education, wealth and general demeanour. Not by caste; twenty-eight of the bustee families were born at the Brahmin level of Hinduism, which is as high as a mortal can be in this order of things. Practically every other caste is represented there in descending steps of precedence. And none of them deal with the lowest babu except in the relationship of master and servant, tradesman and customer. Yet the bustee dwellers have no strong feeling of community among themselves, in spite of their shared squalor and poverty. A man who has lived there as long as anyone knows everybody inhabiting the same hut and almost everybody living along the same lane; but what he knows is simply their name, which hut they live in and what job they do. A common saying there is 'People will be good to you as long as you please them', and mutual help doesn't often get beyond one family siding with another for a specific purpose. Even when there is a marriage or a death here, where people are living tightly on top of each other, the majority are merely sympathetic watchers. A few years ago the Calcutta Rotary Club decided to try and improve conditions in the bustee, with the help of the inhabitants. The plan collapsed because the inhabitants wouldn't stir themselves, they wouldn't even find a few paise each month to keep the paths and drains clean. When they had grievances or wanted anything done, they preferred to argue it out with their thika tenants rather than turn to any well-meaning group of outsiders.

The poverty-stricken of Calcutta are not always as apathetic as that suggests. You can find colonies of refugees who have hauled themselves a little way out of the gutter, which is where most of them begin life in the city. They will have arrived, as their kinsmen are still arriving from East Pakistan, with nothing but their rags, a bundle of cooking things and other small possessions. They will have found a length of pavement which has not yet been tenanted, they will immediately have gone a-scavenging round the backsides of warehouses and shops, for packing cases, decrepit dustbins, tattered tarpaulin and pieces of rope; and, soon, yet another shanty of refuse will be obstructing the pedestrians in the shadow of Howrah Bridge or the evening strollers along the willowy fringes of the Dhakuria Lake. But then the men of the colony will discover a piece of ground with greater possibilities and the entire shanty collection will be moved onto it with speed, lest other incomers stake their claim first. They will stick together, these people, bound by ties of distant blood and communal flight and equal dispossession, and some of them will get jobs in this overpoweringly awful but still bountiful city, and money will be saved and used with the finest calculation.

One day, the visitor will encounter Mr Chatterjee, lately of Dacca, now of Gariahat, who will invite him to come and inspect the marvel that has been wrought in twenty laborious years. The marvel will be four hundred families inhabiting pucca dwellings, brick or cemented sheds but very pucca nonetheless, built by the refugees themselves. There will be tolerable space between these dwellings, maybe two arm spans or a little more. There will be fans and electric lights inside each home. There will be three long sheds and these, Mr Chatterjee will proudly explain, are schoolrooms which they have constructed themselves and which they have staffed out of their own resources. And then he will ask you kindly to notice the lamp posts dotted here and there throughout the colony. They represent the largest triumph of all; for in the face of all this self-help over two decades, the Corporation's heart has lately been melted and only last week the visitor would have been able to watch municipal employees erecting the last concrete post and installing the final sodium light fitting.

There is a much harsher self-help than that, and it is represented at its nimblest by the kangali. The kangalis have an equivalent in almost every great city of the world, and the scugnizzi of Naples are probably the closest to them in the West. For the kangali, too, is the child of the streets. If he ever knew his parentage, he probably left it behind in a bustee. He is more likely to have been born on a pavement and to have been abandoned there; in which case he will have been lucky, some say, not to have been picked up by the lackey of some frightful creature who might have bound up his soft limbs, or even worse, so that he would grow misshapen and maimed, the more effectively and profitably to function thereafter as the most pitiable of beggars. A kangali will say, with more unblinking nonchalance than anyone ought to have between the ages of six and twelve, that he is an orphan, or that his father is a drunk, or a gaolbird who has been wrongfully imprisoned, or even – in a flight of not improbable fancy – a murderer. But now he, the kangali, has freed himself from the dragging burden of this domestic presence, or the lack of it. He has become one of a small band of little brothers and they have a total freedom of the streets.

The kangali is not a begger. He offers service for money. You meet him when you have parked your car on your way to the cinemas of Chowringhee, or when you are bent on one of the brassy night clubs of Park Street. He is going through the motions of windscreen-cleaning before you have even turned off the engine and, sahib, he will guard your property while you are gone in exchange for a rupee. He guards it well, in company with his brothers. And if you think that, in the prevailing economy of Calcutta, his rates are rather on the high side, you will do well to remember that if you turn him down, the evening will be much more expensive in the long run, when you have returned to a vehicle which has lost three door-handles, two windscreen wipers and one petrol cap at least. So keen is the kangali to be of assistance to allcomers that when a friend drops you from his car in Strand Road, so that you can dawdle over a Hooghly sunset, a kangali will be asking you, burra sahib, whether you now require a taxi before your foot has even touched the pavement.

Thus he acquires his small competence in life. He does not acquire enough capital to set himself up as a shoeshine boy very often, and even where he did and began to collect his parapher-

nalia of polishes and brushes and shoe-box, he would face the
vicious jungle law of Calcutta commerce and be trounced from
his stand by many larger shoeshine boys than he, with wives and
children to support out of their small foothold among the smart
set. Something more than a beggar, then, something less than a
tradesman, the kangali spends his rupees on the cinema. Or he
purchases cigarettes; not those raw tobacco leaves tied with cotton, an inch and a half of perfumery which will only burn as
long as you suck, which are sold in Kensington Market in
London as 'real Indian cigars' but which in Calcutta are called
beedies and known as the poor man's gasper; not beedies, but
genuine babu cigarettes, like Gold Flake and Capstan and other
products of the Imperial Tobacco Company.

He does not spend his money on quarters or food. He sleeps
with his fellows on the pavement or in a park. He eats what the
restaurants or others have thrown away. At night you can see
these small boys rummaging among the great stinking middens
that are dumped on Bentinck Street or at the start of Lower
Chitpore Road. They are collecting bones with fragments of
meat still sticking to them, scraps of green vegetable that have
been discarded as refuse, spoonsful of rice that have been
scraped from the half-finished plates of wealthy diners. And
twice a day they repair to their particular piece of pavement, or
their corner in the park, to cook up this pottage and consume it
with relish; for they are growing boys, and they are always
hungry.

They are also firm in their adherence to a gang. They stick
together in half dozens under a leader who is slightly older and
tougher than the rest, who maintains a form of discipline among
them, who determines what their next communal strategy shall
be. This is very rarely a form of crime; these are not chhentai,
which is the Bengali label attached to a pickpocket or a thief who
snatches and runs. They will affront the law half a dozen times a
day and it is useless to tell them that something is illegal or
frowned upon even by this all-embracing society, for they will
just giggle in your face. It is pointless to throw religious precepts
at them, for they are irreligious and a Hindu temple is merely
another place where they can scrounge food or money. But be-

fore the kangali bands turn to theft, they will assiduously scavenge for rags, for paper, for empty bottles, for anything at all that can be sold in a city where absolutely everything has a place and a price on the market. They will take care of each other, going without food to provide more for one who is sick. They will sometimes play like children, though their games will probably be with incomplete packs of cards discovered in some dustbin and their stakes will be cigarette butts and occasionally cash. The one thing they will not do, as long as they remain kangalis, is surrender their urchin freedom to any more beholden way of life. Only as a kangali reaches his teens does he begin to find substitute allegiances and excitements for those provided by his gang. He is finally seduced by sex, like many a boyo before him, and presently discovers that the need to mind the burra sahib's car, to nail the flimsiest sort of income, is even more imperative than it was when he was simply an orphan of the streets.

A few of his fellows will doubtless mature into goondas. The goonda, when fully fledged and at the height of his powers, is almost the nastiest customer in Calcutta. A straightforward definition in the dictionary will call him a ruffian, but in Bengal he is a ruffian who is prepared to kill and rob as well as to brawl in back alleys. The police detectives, who study goondas as closely as anyone, are apt to place their origins far away in the time of the East India Company and toss up a quotation from Macaulay to emphasize their point. And, indeed, his Lordship did once write that 'The servants of the Company obtained, not for their employers but for themselves, a monopoly of almost the whole internal trade. They forced the natives to buy dear and sell cheap ... Every servant of a British factor was armed with all the power of his master, and his master was armed with all the power of the Company. Enormous fortunes were thus rapidly accumulated at Calcutta, while thirty million of human beings were reduced to the last extremity of wretchedness. They had been accustomed to live under tyranny, but never tyranny like this.' Having fed you Macaulay, the detectives will remind you that these wealthy British Moguls employed armed servants, called paiks or lathials, to attend to their defensive and offensive interests. When the Indian Mutiny was over and the Company was disbanded, the Queen Empress ordered the dissolution of these small private commandos and the dismissed paiks and lathials promptly began to use on their own account their highly cultivated skills of bullying, blackmail and robbery.

These, say the detectives with assurance, were the spiritual ancestors of the goondas; and though that isn't faultless history – for the dacoit was somewhat in the same line of business even before Job Charnock came to Bengal – it isn't entirely beside the point. The Goonda Act of 1923 was directed against political hotheads as much as barefaced brigands and the true goonda's most immediate model was the mobster who appeared in numbers during the Second World War, when Calcutta was a strategic centre of South-east Asia Command and there was a vast and illicit traffic in military equipment, military rations and military luxuries; when some highly respectable members of local society needed good men and true to help them seize this main chance and no questions asked. And shortly after, there were two years of almost continuous communal riots, in which the strong-arm men were able to consolidate a distinctive position in the city and an unhealthy respect.

The goonda will generally have taken to his trade in the middle of his teens and he will be at the peak of his unpleasant performance between the ages of twenty-one and twenty-five. More likely than not he will live in a bustee or, if not there, in a building of some sort; he is very rarely homeless. He probably lives in Central Calcutta, though he is almost as likely to come from somewhere north of Chowringhee and is scarcely ever based in Alipore or any of the richer southern suburbs. If he has a comparatively regular income it will not often amount to Rs 250 a month, and more frequently it will be less than Rs 100. And while the city's prisons at any time will accommodate goondas who have come from all India, even from China and from Burma, the vast majority are born and bred in Calcutta; but very few refugees find their way there, and those that do tend to be novices. Very rarely do goondas have much in the way of education, though when the police made a close investigation of those in their custody some years ago they discovered that two

were good painters, twelve were decent singers, three could play
the tabla (the drum that accompanies the sitar) and one wrote
tolerable poetry. There was also an international footballer
among them.

The goonda is not always a splendid physical specimen. He
tends to be more efficient with a medium build and he is very
often handicapped in some way, minus an eye or a hand, or
totally deaf. But always he has an excellent pair of legs. His
choice of weapon depends upon his state of health. A dagger or a
knife is commonplace, a pistol belongs to the most successful
and to those with the greatest reputation in the hierarchy of
goondas. Then there is the bomb, which is frequently just a
bottle of soda water used as a formidable missile; you shake it
vigorously until the gas is almost on the point of bursting the
glass, whereupon you hurl it and generally achieve a most spectacular effect. Policemen in Calcutta long ago discovered that a
well-trained goonda with only one hand was capable of throwing
ten soda-water bottles a minute, which is quite enough to keep a
crowd at bay twenty-five yards away. And this is what a comparatively weak goonda uses for his getaways, though the majority will mix their bombing of strong opposition with their
knifing of feeble adversaries. This desperate talent is sometimes
employed in the course of direct robbery and looting, and it
is frequently placed at the disposal of the shiftier gentlemen of
Calcutta's commerce, who deem it prudent to equip themselves
with protectors against rivals in trade and amorality, and sometimes against the police; they, at any rate, are in a direct line
of descent from those old Nabobs and their henchmen. But for
twenty-five years, at least, the goondas have made profitable
alliances with the party politicians of Bengal, who have found
them extraordinarily effective in resolving any uncertainties that
might linger in the mind of a peasant voter as polling day approaches. No one party has had a monopoly of their services on
these occasions, or even for sustained campaigning in between.
The goondas have found themselves in the role of highly-
esteemed party workers on behalf of at least ten different varieties
of Communism, within the merely tepid ranks of Indian socialism and, as much as anywhere, among the political descendants

of Mr Gandhi, who now manipulate Congress in all its internecine manifestations.

The goonda's prey can thus be almost anyone at all, and it is
possible that those who suffer most from his terrorism are the
very poorest people in Calcutta, who must be bludgeoned or
bribed into a political allegiance they will not otherwise follow,
or those hundreds of thousands in the city who live in genteel
poverty and who offer some source of plunder without the means
to defend it. Many of these last are refugee families from East
Bengal. Their ancestors will have been zamindars and not so
very long ago they themselves will have had great land holdings
on the other side of the delta, with mansions of substance much
patrolled by servants. But because they are Hindu and not
Muslim they will have found, one agonizing day after the 1947
Partition, that the balance of local power was no longer to be
endured and they will have assembled what possessions they
could move and what money they could promptly convert to
cash and carry on their persons, and they will have bumped
and lurched across the border in a bullock cart or a rattletrap
car or a collapsing lorry, leaving the bulk of their wealth behind
them. And so you discover them one day in Calcutta.

They are dwelling now – Papa, Mamma, three children and
perhaps a grandparent as well – in three rooms high above a
street, though they also make use of the roof to hang out their
washing and to get out of each other's way from time to time.
Papa will have secured a job as an insurance clerk and Mamma,
being literate too, will have contemplated looking for work but
after a dozen years will still be undecided, for such a thing is not
quite seemly for a lady of gentle birth. A mutual friend will take
you to them. You will remove your shoes on their threshold
after climbing two flights up a dingy and communal staircase
(for there are other families in this building, so many that your
hosts have quite lost count) which is exposed to the street
through high and barred openings on each landing. You will be
received in a room decorated with calendars, with an antique
radio, with a shelf full of books, with a plant in a pot; for these
have been cultivated people. Mamma and Papa will insist that
you be seated in the one easy chair, while they sit cross-legged

upon the large bed which fills a third of the room and which is where four people sleep every night, Mamma and Papa at one end, their two daughters at the other. They will offer you refreshment from a silver cakestand, savoury biscuits sprinkled with salt and poppy seed, and sweetmeats of almond paste, and small dishes of those tiny silver balls which are too sweet for words and which the children of the West love to have scattered across their birthday cakes. There will be a cup of tea with curdles of milk floating on the top, but before everything there will be a glass of water which it would be discourteous to refuse but which, as the mutual friend is making clear with sidelong gestures and frowns, is at the very most to be acknowledged with a token sip, for almost certainly it has been drawn from an unfiltered tap and will be teeming with every sickening bacteria in Calcutta.

Your hosts will pretend, with exquisite manners, not to notice your aversion to a cold drink on this parching afternoon, and they will talk with composure, without any emotion at all, of the opulent life they once led. They will discuss the dreadful state of Calcutta today and then, for old habits die hard even in so destructive a place as this, they will invite you to come and look at their landscape. They will take you to their roof, where two saris and a sheet are hanging limply in the fug, and there you can inspect the street below. It will reek with a refuse of rotting green coconut shells and other garbage, with crows hopping on top and pariah dogs poking below. Rickshaws will be swaying past that sacred cow which is sitting with confidence in the middle of the road. A beggar woman will be creeping up the pavement, bent more than double with infirmity or deception. She will be totally ignored by everyone passing her, except a couple of Sikhs almost as ragged as she, who surreptitiously slip a something into the tin which is held towards passers-by in a tentative gesture containing only half a hope of any return. Your hosts will contemplate this without a trace of sadness, without a suggestion that it marks a painful fall in their fortunes. Their bearing implies that it is as completely within the order of things as that sun which is sliding like a scarlet gong below the level of the roofline and beyond the waters of the

Hooghly at the end of the disreputable street. They see you to
the top of the slatternly staircase, which is the threshold of their
home, and bid you to return at any time and be welcome. And
when you come back the following year you discover that the
miniature car which your mutual friend presented to their son
has been carefully preserved, its paintwork still immaculate, in a
glass-fronted cabinet alongside six china cups and saucers and the
silver cakestand; not a toy from Woolworth's any more, to be
gradually broken by a small boy, but a treasure from England to
be marvelled at by all.

Not all the genteel poor are refugees. Most of them have been
born here, have been given a fingerhold upon a Bengali's greatest
prize, which has always been education. They have been taken
into the university and they have been spewed out again at the
other end of it upon a labour market which has not for fifty years
been capable of absorbing all their qualifications. Even Lord
Curzon used to nag about that. At Dum Dum there is a beaming
little man, maybe thirty years old, whose job it is to lead certain
visitors from overseas out of the Customs hall and across the
passenger concourse to where their airline bus awaits them outside, making quite sure that their baggage follows them intact.
He is employed to do this and nothing else by the State Tourist
Bureau. And if he discovers immediately that the traveller he has
just picked up in Customs is disposed to be friendly, he will offer
to be of service at any time he can possibly be helpful in Calcutta. He will casually hint that he has many times thought how
splendid it would be if he could make his way to England and
perform some more useful task there. And then, amid mutual
smiles, best wishes and shaking of the hand, he will remember
on the steps of the airline bus to present his card to the visitor.
It identifies him as Gour Kanjilal, Master of Arts (Hons), tourist
officer; and very thankful indeed to have a regular and secure
job in the service of the nation and the foreigners.

Had he been luckier in his vocational search he might have
become a teacher; in which case, being a graduate, he would have
welcomed a report by a pay commission in 1970, suggesting
that his salary for primary school work might be raised to Rs
300 a month, or in a higher secondary school to Rs 350; with

Rs 350 at that time being the equivalent of £19.50, or rather less than 50 American dollars. And though it is true that in Calcutta you could then buy onions for 50 paise a kilogram, a dozen eggs for Rs 4, a very small chicken for Rs 2·25 and baby hilsa caught in the estuarine waters of the Ganga for Rs 5·50 a kilogram, it was also true that an everyday sari for your wife would cost the best part of Rs 30 and an attaché case of papier mâché, whose handle came away the moment it was picked up full of clothes, anything up to Rs 75. Nor was any teacher or well-educated airport courier absolved from the need to queue at the ration shop for the weekly allowance of rice and grain and sugar; only people much more prosperous than they could afford the prices fixed and schemed upon the city's ever ready and highly stocked black market.

The supply of any food in Calcutta is liable to run short at almost any time and even the rich are apt to bump into restrictions when they eat away from their carefully-planned and well-provided domestic pantries. A man taking his lunch at a middle-class restaurant like the Kwality in Park Street, and ordering mutton korma, is likely to be reminded that this is Tuesday and therefore a meatless day; on seeking prawn curry forty-eight hours later he will possibly be told that fish is off, it being Thursday, of course. There are maybe a thousand ration shops for rice and grain in the city because these are the basic foodstuffs for almost all its people and because if there were not a little to give to everyone each day there would be starvation for most and more corpses than usual upon the streets within a week. And lodged in everybody's consciousness, located somewhere in many people's memories, is the frightful time when this has happened and when famine has been declared.

A man is less likely to starve under famine conditions in Bengal than in some parts of India. If the devil wished to lay the largest odds on a human being rotting to death with no food in his belly he would set him down in the middle of the North of the sub-continent, where quite regularly the two vital monsoons from South-west and South-east fail to meet and spray all the land with water. But Bengal is bad enough. There have been periodic years of starvation stretching back into its ancient history. Of the twenty-two famines that occurred in various parts of India during the age of British trade and rule, Bengal experienced seven, either alone or in company with some other area. Probably the worst it has ever known was the famine of 1770, which is supposed to have annihilated a third of its population, so many millions of people that the figure means nothing at all to an occidental except another unbelievable eastern statistic. There were other famines in 1783, in 1866, at the turn of 1873 and 1874, in 1892 and in 1897. Then came 1943, which Bengal had to itself, and even now no one is quite sure how many people lost their lives in that disaster. Communist party literature puts the deathroll at twelve million, which will be a gross exaggeration. A year after the event, statisticians at Calcutta University were committing themselves to three and a half millions; certainly no one in Bengal believes the official inquiry commission's final estimate of one and a half million to be anything like realistic enough. Whatever the truth of the catastrophe, it scarred the soul of Calcutta in a way that partly explains some of its history since.

There was a war on, and for most Indians, Bengalis as much as any, it was a war being waged by and on behalf of the British, not them. The Bengali hero Subhas Chandra Bose, indeed, had been in Berlin and was on his way to Tokyo to organize an Indian National Army, and before the year was out he had declared war on the Allies himself in the name of a Provisional Indian Government. The majority of Indians were ranged against Bose largely because there was a King Emperor in London with his cousin Mountbatten commanding an enormous military machine from Delhi and his general Slim manoeuvring a Fourteenth Army nearby in Burma. In the circumstances, it was a little difficult for Indians not to acquiesce in the martial directives of their masters. By the middle of 1942 almost the whole of Burma had been in Japanese hands and the British had neither the energy nor the inclination to spare for anything other than fighting the Japanese back.

Several things made the famine happen. There had been a long run of indifferent rice harvests and, except for 1937, Bengal had needed to import rice every year between 1934 and 1941. One source of outside supply, Burma, was now cut off. There were sixty million Bengalis and nearly forty-six million of them were peasants depending upon a pitiful agriculture for their livelihood. A government which could wage war carefully and sometimes effectively was much less capable in accounting for the needs of the people in the territory it was defending. The official records of recent rice crop yields were hopelessly unrealistic, giving no clear sense of how much might be expected from a subsequent harvest or any idea of what the requirements from outside might be if there should be a total failure. Official policy did little more than to stockpile huge quantities of food in the factories of Calcutta for the use of munition and other war workers. There had been a flood and a cyclone in 1942 which had quite destroyed the aman crop – the winter paddy harvested between the end of November and early January – around Midnapore and throughout the 24 Parganas; and all over Bengal the aman crop was desperately poor. So the peasant farmers began to stockpile, too, keeping from the market a third more than they usually did. And when famine had actually begun, it was made worse than ever by Government policy. In April 1943 a Boat Ordinance required every craft in Bengal to be registered under military supervision, to prevent an important means of local transport from falling into enemy hands: the result was that twenty-five thousand boats at once went out of commission, preventing the cultivation of delta lands and fishing in the estuary of the Hooghly. And in the first seven months of 1943, some eighty thousand tons of food grains were exported from the province. Something like that had happened in the famine of 1873, when one million tons of rice and ninety thousand tons of wheat were exported on the orders of the Viceroy and the Secretary of State in London, in spite of pleas by the Lieutenant-Governor of Bengal, Sir George Campbell, that the food should remain in India.

In human terms the blame for 1943 was not entirely British, though it has been seen as such in Calcutta since. The British did nothing at all to relieve the disaster until Lord Wavell became Viceroy in October, when he immediately visited the city and at once ordered the army to intervene. But from start to finish there had been a Provincial Government sitting in Calcutta, Indian almost from top to bottom, and it had performed no better. At a food conference in Delhi in December 1942, when the local aman crop was clearly heading for trouble, the Prime Minister of Bengal, Mr Fazlul Huq, had said 'We do not require for the next few months any rice, even though we are in deficit.' For months to come his ministers were making similarly reassuring noises; on 9 May 1943, the Food Minister of Bengal, Mr H. S. Suhrawardy, declared that although the province was undergoing certain difficulties due to hoarding and profiteering, there was sufficiency of foodgrain for the people of Bengal. A few days later he told an audience in one of the richer suburbs of South Calcutta to go forth and preach the various evils of over-eating. Profiteering there had certainly been for nearly half a year by then; prices had been soaring since the start of January and by the time the Food Minister spoke they had risen 600 per cent. And in April a post mortem on a man found dead in the street had discovered that his stomach contained nothing but undigested grass. Quite suddenly, it was noticed that there were possibly more destitutes than usual in the city though, Calcutta being what it was, some people could forgive themselves for not having observed this sooner.

They were, in fact, by then entering the city in staggering mobs. A lot of them began to crowd together for shelter under railway sheds at suburban stations. A lot more began to line the pavements in exhausted family groups. A reporter described how one family had settled on Lower Circular Road, the husband lying inert while the three children watched their mother cooking some vegetable peelings. 'The wife looked slightly better than the husband but . . . I could count her ribs from a distance of ten feet. The intestines seemed to have disappeared altogether from the abdomen. She was not more than twenty-five years old yet there was no womanly breast. Only two nipples dangling from two parched sheets of skin, from which everything else seemed to be dried up . . . One of the children, a girl, had swollen limbs. In some parts of the legs the skin had cracked and a liquid discharge was slowly trickling out. Her face was writhing

in pain but she had not even the strength to cry.' Among those
who came to Calcutta was Jagaddhari Haldar, a man of sixty
from Basar Gopinathpur in the 24 Parganas. The cyclone and
flood of the previous October had destroyed everything he possessed; it had swept away his house, his foodgrains, his animals
and his utensils; it had drowned his wife, his mother, his younger
brother, his sister-in-law, his three nephews and his two nieces.
He had survived by climbing a tamarind tree, and since then he
had been roaming the land looking for food. A few yards from
him on the pavement was Sarathi Bagdi, a young mother from
Sarkerchak, also in the 24 Parganas. Her husband had died of
dysentery, so she had come to the city with her son, aged seven,
and her daughter, aged one. She had left them on the street while
she went round a corner to urinate and when she returned they
had disappeared. When the reporter found her, ten days later, 'we
offered her food but she merely went on weeping'.

Where people like these had not lost everything in the cyclone
and the flood, they had sold all they possessed before coming to
Calcutta. They had first sold their ornaments for less than the
lowest market price. Then they had sold all the parts of their
homes that anyone would buy; the doors, the window sills, the
corrugated iron sheets of the roof. This had brought them a
little food and time. But then they had started to eat wild roots
and leaves. In Howrah, by now, heaps of snail shells were to be
found in front of almost every house. There was much worse
than that to come. In the villages of Bengal, widows who had
lived for years with brothers and their families were being asked
to leave and fend for themselves. Husbands were forsaking wives
and wives were abandoning sick husbands. Parents were stealthily
leaving immature children to their fate and drifting off to look
for food. Mothers were leaving babies at the gates of wealthy
men.

In Calcutta, children were wandering from door to door crying 'Mago! Ekthu phan deo' (Mother! Give a little gruel).
Charitable institutions began to set up street kitchens and they
would give the hungry a ration of gruel on leaves; when the
gruel slopped off onto the ground the people would throw themselves after it and lick it up. The Government set up a kitchen,

too, but it offered only bajra, a coarse grain that was too heavy for starved stomachs and produced bowel complaints. People began to eat dogs and they began to scramble among the refuse heaps for scraps, even when these were mixed up with discarded surgical dressings thrown out by the hospitals. Their hunger had become so terrible that religious taboos were forgotten or ignored; orthodox Hindus, who will never normally accept anything to eat or drink from anyone of another faith, were taking food from the hands of Muslims; and Muslims were receiving succour from Hindus.

In July a member of the provincial assembly asked that Bengal should be declared a famine area, to obtain outside relief, and Mr Suhrawardy said that this was not necessary. He could, after all, see plenty of food in the shops of Calcutta and it is very strange that the starving people seem to have made no attempt to raid these places. There were soon to be a hundred thousand of them in the city. In August came the first reports of people selling their children in the villages. At Khulua a woman disposed of her daughter for Rs 15 after the father had gone looking for food and never returned. At Burdwan a three-month-old girl was traded for Rs 5 at the same time. In Malda, Bhogurdi Mandal was charged with murdering his only son Mozzaffar, aged three, because he could not feed him or anyone in his family; none of them had touched food for most of the week before he killed the boy. In Calcutta someone spotted the body of a child, partly eaten by dogs, on the pavement in Cornwallis Street. Only two or three weeks before, in Delhi, the Home Secretary to the Government of India, Mr Conran Smith, had told the Council of State; 'I may say that the Government of India view with misgivings the tendency in some quarters to overdramatize the situation, possibly with the best intentions, and they have no hesitation in condemning the tendency in other quarters to exploit the situation for party political and sectional ends.' At the beginning of July the Secretary of State for India, Mr L. S. Amery, had been telling the House of Commons in London that 'There is no overall shortage of food grains, India has harvested a bumper crop of wheat this spring. There is, however, grave maldistribution.'

In Calcutta by then the newspapers had been reporting what they could discover of the horror for nearly two months. They were beginning to turn up some appalling figures. In the village of Contai, 500 people died on the streets between July and September; in Burdwan, 97 died in August; between July and November, 2,000 were to perish in Satkhira. On 9 September, the Government of Bengal stopped supplying the papers with relevant figures but the public clamour was such that the service was resumed two days later; but from now on the journalists were forbidden to use the word 'starvation'; instead, people dying of hunger had to be called 'sick destitutes'. On 28 September, 325 sick destitutes were admitted to hospitals in the city, where they died of their sickness. On 27 October, an unofficial relief organization disposed of 170 corpses that had just been sick and destitute. The next day a Bengal Destitute Persons (Repatriation and Relief) Ordinance was passed, and between 30 October and the following January the police cleared 43,500 starving people from the streets of the city, and sent them back into the country. Only just in time to strike a note of sympathy, Mr Suhrawardy had on 10 October finally announced that 'Bengal is in the grip of an unprecedented famine'.

The nightmare was not nearly over. In October the burning ghats by the Hooghly were stacked for days on end with bodies for cremation. And from Dacca a news agency reported that 'Recently, a famished fisherman who was reduced to bone and skin, came from the interior and took gruel in the free kitchen of the union. He lay down nearby. In the morning the people were shocked to see that a portion of his body had been devoured by jackals. His life was still not extinct. It is believed that when the jackals attacked him at night he was too weak to resist or call for help. He died later.' In London Mr Amery was now telling the House of Commons that he understood the death rate in Bengal to be a thousand a week, though 'it might be a bit higher'. It was, in fact, something like eleven thousand a week at that time and, in Calcutta, *The Statesman* said almost as much in a leading article: 'All the publicly available data indicates that it is very much higher and his [Mr Amery's] great office ought to afford him ample means of discovery. The con-

tinuous appearance of effort on the part of persons somewhere
within India's Governmental machine, perhaps out here, perhaps in Whitehall, to play down, suppress, distort or muffle the
truth about Bengal, is dragging the fair name of the British Raj
needlessly low.' It would have cost something for a newspaper
with *The Statesman*'s background to publish that, for the British
in Calcutta were still a proud and arrogant people. There is no
sign at all that they took any comfort from the knowledge that
at this moment some Indians were behaving even more miserably than the worst of their own countrymen; for there were
food profiteers who were mixing ground stone and dust with
rice, who were putting plaster of Paris in wheat flour to give
it whiteness and weight.

Cholera now came in the wake of famine and in one week, in
the district of Naogaon alone, one thousand people died of it;
yet in the same few days, on 21 October, Mr Amery was telling
Parliament that there was no shortage of medical supplies and
no widespread outbreak of disease. Within three weeks it was
announced in Delhi that 2,233,000 people queued each day at
feeding centres throughout Bengal; in Calcutta, hundreds fought
each other beside a row of dustbins which contained nothing
but particles of refuse and putrid food. On 4 December, Major-
General D. Stuart made a radio broadcast in which he admitted
that 'The reports you have seen in the newspapers of the numbers requiring medical treatment and clothing are not exaggerated ... In the first place malnutrition coupled with the
advent of the cold weather and shortage of personal clothing
and blankets, has made a large percentage of the poorer people
easy victims to malaria, cholera and pneumonia, which are rampant throughout a large number of civil districts.' It was impossible, by now, for anyone in India to ignore or dilute the truth,
and nobody was trying to any more, though the figures which
demonstrated the full extent of the disaster did not begin to
appear for some months yet. It was the end of March 1944 before the news agencies reported that in Dacca, 22,866 people had
died in January, compared with 7,194 in January 1943.

Even at that date, horror stories were still being printed almost every day. On 26 March, the *Hindustan Standard* reported

from Mymensingh: 'The dead body of a destitute woman was found yesterday morning in a vacant house by the District Board road off Sarish station. The body was seen lying all day long without any arrangements for removal. At night, jackals dragged the body out and mostly devoured it up. The remaining part of the body is being devoured by dogs and crows in front of the eyes of hundreds of passers-by this morning.' By this time Bengal was merely suffering from the awful after-effects of famine. Nearly a century before, Sir Bartle Frere had described in the context of another catastrophe what was happening now: 'Men are death-stricken by famine long before they die. The effects of insufficient food long continued may shorten life after a period of some years, or it may be of some months. But invariably there is a point, which is often reached long before death actually ensues, when not even the tenderest care and most scientific nursing can restore a sufficiency of vital energy to enable the sufferer to regain even apparent temporary health and strength.'

Early in 1944 there was plenty in the land again. By the middle of the preceding November a man from *The Times of India* had been able to write that 'a grim but not uncommon spectacle in East Bengal today is to find a whitened skeleton in the corner of a field bearing the richest rice crop in half a century'. By the spring a new Governor of Bengal, the Australian Mr R. G. Casey, was guilty of nothing more than an insensitive analogy when he said 'I am convinced that there is plenty of rice in Bengal for all the people of Bengal. The difficulty is that it is unevenly spread ... Our task is to spread the butter evenly on the bread.' He might have chosen his words more carefully, but there were Englishmen open to charges much graver than that and a member of the Bengal provincial assembly had already made one of them. 'I would like the fact to be more widely known in India,' said Dr M. R. Jayakar one day in the chamber, 'for few newspapers have reported it, that at the last debate in the House of Commons on the Indian food question, the attendance of Members varied from 35 to 53 out of a total of 600 and odd ... This knocks the bottom out of the old superstition that these 600 and odd men can govern India from 7,000 miles away. Is it not time that this Punch and Judy show was ended?' He was speaking in November 1943, when the effects of the Bengal famine were to be seen at their worst. And Punch, without letting on to Judy, was already losing interest in the show.

Calcutta has known nothing of famine since 1943, yet starvation has become a permanent factor in its life, such a commonplace that it is scarcely remarked on any more. It is very difficult for Westerners, certainly for the British, to understand quite what starvation means in terms of the person to whom it is happening. This is partly because the English language in the West has become debased at this point; the vocabulary of extreme hunger unto death has been used so flippantly so often that it has almost ceased to convey its true meaning. An Englishman will frequently say that he is starving when he means that he is ready for his second large meal of the day, and he has never in his life known the day which has not contained two large meals and several snacks. He will use the word famished as an alternative to starving in exactly the same way. There are places in the North of England where a man will say that he is starving when he is merely chilly enough to move closer to the fireplace. Famine, on the other hand, has almost sunk without trace in our understanding because it has for too long carried entirely biblical overtones or because it has become tediously associated for a generation with a number of charitable organizations which are forever making demands upon our purses and our consciences. Starvation has nothing at all to do with its contemporary English usage, and famine is quite obscured by the Christian mythology and by the publicity apparatus of charity. Starvation and famine really mean a man who dies with a stomach containing undigested grass; a child whose body has started to split open with lack of food, so that its liquids begin to trickle out; a fisherman who is so weak that a dog begins to eat him before he is dead; a crowd which goes scavenging among poultices full of blood and pus and scabs in the hope of finding something putrid but edible there, too.

It is also very hard to understand what the starvation and the other parts of Calcutta's poverty are like, at a distance, because of the effect they have on the man who is reporting them at first hand. You find, when you have returned from the leper colony at Dhapa, or from the death shed of Nirmal Hriday, that you have the very sketchiest recollection of whåt these people actually look like in their extremity. There is something quite intolerable about peering too closely at those sores and those mutilations and most of all at the eyes (which I cannot describe) that go with them. No derelict human being should be examined as a specimen by another human being, unless it is by someone who can give him something to mend his condition; whatever that may be. For the same reason you return from Calcutta, unless you are very tough or a professional, with a camera which may be full of exposed film but which contains hardly any record of people. Quite apart from the risk of violence when the camera is raised, which is considerable, you are also deterred by the indecency of the act.

Maybe these are among the reasons why comparatively few Western hippies are to be seen in the city. They are to be found in hundreds at places like Benares, where they live in boats moored in the Ganga for months on next to nothing, where they idle along the interminable ghats in their blue jeans and with their embroidered satchels, and where occasionally a Western face may be observed gliding by in a rickshaw, a vision of flowing muslin and long hair who has lately been dignified there as the Italian swami. But in Calcutta hippies are few and far between and they do not stay long even when they come, though Allen Ginsberg spent months here a few years ago, becoming curiously obsessed with the spectacle of incinerated corpses at the Nimtallah burning ghat. The reputation of the city has stopped most hippies in their tracks elsewhere in India; and on first acquaintance it is enough to destroy any romantic illusions about gentleness and brotherly love and a dominating concentration upon the beatific vision. It is a place where disagreeable statistics are translated into men and women and children without number. The Reserve Bank of India published a report in 1970, pointing out that if the baseline of poverty be taken as a calorific rather than a financial measurement (this being agreed upon in India's case by experts), then seventy per cent of the nation's people live in absolute poverty, an increase of eighteen per cent in seven years. In Calcutta you can see this for what it is in almost any hundred yards you care to choose from; you can see it, you can feel it as it brushes past you, you can smell it, you can almost taste it. Most of the time you struggle with yourself and with the poverty-stricken to avoid bumping into it or treading on it.

Calcutta is a place where people devise the most ingenious methods of adding to a pittance if they have one, or of acquiring one if they have not; at the Zoo in Alipore, across the road from Warren Hastings' old house, a keeper has trained his elephants to take coins, not biscuits or sweets, in the tip of their trunks from the visitors. And a Zoo keeper is not nearly at the bottom of the human pile in Calcutta. At the bottom of the pile are those who squat upon its pavements, scarcely noticed in life by the people walking by, claiming attention in death only because the kites have started to circle overhead or because the crows have begun to prod at their bodies. In the end they have not even had the energy or the willpower to destroy themselves, as some do. If it were not lost in the far bigger problems of Calcutta, there would be the problem of those who jump off the Howrah Bridge in despair. A man leaps in front of a train pulling into Sealdah Station and, misjudging the angle, merely loses both legs at the thigh; whereupon he is taken to Nirmal Hriday and there, eventually, he dies. In 1967, 4,682 people were known to have committed suicide in West Bengal; in 1968 there were 5,800; in the first six months of 1969 there were 2,873.

All these things are terrible in themselves. They are made much more terrible in Calcutta because they are to be seen alongside all the signs of opulence. One day you pass an emaciated man standing outside the window of a fashionable shoe shop on Chowringhee. He is without shoes himself, but that is as unremarkable as the grimy rags that hang upon his body. It is his stance that catches your attention. His knees are faintly bent, his shoulders are curved forward, his head hangs almost upon his chest while his eyes gaze unblinking at the lowest row of shoes. His hands dangle by his sides but he is utterly motionless. He suggests not envy, not anger, not desire, but absolute incomprehension and total defeat. He is still there, not having shifted an inch, when you return half an hour later. It is at about this time that you are struck anew by the memory of something seen on your journey into the city from the airport. It dawns on you that the messy collection of packing cases and tin sheets standing in the shade of the BOAC hoarding was not a couple of chicken coops at all, but the best that a handful of people could manage in the way of a house. The ironies of such wealthy advertisement next to the deepest deprivation in Calcutta are so huge and so frequent that you might almost suspect some-one of gigantic and tasteless caricature very deliberately carried out. Down in Ballygunge there is a long and gleaming metal hoarding, from the same stud as 'Try a Little VC-10derness', and it invites all-comers to 'Dial Panam and Ask for the World'. Smoke drifts across its surface in the evening, for within fifty yards there are half a dozen families cooking by the gutter. Somewhere else the bedtime people are catching the eye with 'Ever Thought of Dunlopillo as a Gift?'; and five yards below the lights which keep the thought uppermost through the night, a man is sleeping on the pavement without even a blanket to his name.

And then there is the advertisement with a specially-constructed concrete foundation, half-way up Park Street, where it begins to curve from middle-classiness to the downright pro-letarian tramtracks of Lower Circular Road. The foundation consists of a concrete roof supported by four concrete posts on the very edge of the pavement and at first sight it looks as if it might be a bus shelter. It has been erected solely to bear the weight of the sign perched on top – 'Fedders Lloyd, the world's largest-selling air-conditioner!'; and a picture to go with it. Al-most every day there is someone lying prone and exhausted under that concrete roof, which provides a splendid shade from the searing sun. Once, a family moved into it. There is a broken standpipe a few yards away in the gutter and there the woman would dhobi clothes and draw water, khaki though it is, for cooking. Her two small children would splash and play in the water. Her husband could occasionally be seen taking a bath in that gutter, which also accommodated two or three discarded green coconut shells. Sometimes the children would rush up to a rich pedestrian and beg something from him, and because they were generally full of smiles and giggles and did not pursue their quarry more than ten yards down Park Street, they more often than not collected a few paise. But mostly the family kept to themselves.

They had been there only a day when it was noticeable that they had made an alteration to the Fedders Lloyd shelter. On the three sides that did not border the gutter they had raised a minute wall of mud, no more than three or four inches high, which linked one post to another. It was the boundary of their home, and inside it their three tin bowls, their iron pot and their two old blankets were laid out, the only things they possessed apart from the winding sheets the parents wore and the beads that dangled at each child's crutch. They lived there for more than a week, and when the parents were not cooking or washing they were usually, one at a time, just lying very still. Then one morning they were gone, and only their little mud wall was left behind. Possibly they had infringed the Bengal Destitute Persons (Repatriation and Relief) Ordinance of 1943, or some subsequent equivalent, by having sheltered without permission or payment beneath an advertisement they would not even be able to read. Nor would they be able to read another notice facing them on a wall just across Park Street, not so well turned-out as the one promoting Fedders Lloyd but demanding attention nonetheless. There are now many more of these in Calcutta than there are those of commercial origin and they usually come in a kind of durable whitewash or a shade of dolly-blue. This one said: 'No hope left. Only anger.'

4

WEALTH

FOR this is a very wealthy city as well as a squalidly poor one and the two elements live so close together, they present such grotesque contrasts, the one has so frequently begotten the other, that anger is the most natural and the healthiest response in the world. In a sense, Calcutta is a definition of obscenity.

It has little in the way of exotic wealth. There are parts of India where a town or a village is still dominated by the presence of a local prince, whose patronage extends through hovel, market place and temple. He may be physically withdrawn, and he will certainly be taxed to the marrow by the State, but he is still there and his influence and his employment still count. A few miles upstream of the ghats at Benares there is a great white palace on the South bank of the Ganga. Part of it has become a museum and the visitor may inspect a romantic collection of objects; a shed full of palanquins and broughams, and coaches to be drawn by four horses; another packed with howdahs chased in silver, tasselled with silk and emblazoned with heraldry, in which majesty would sit and sway on top of elephants; a long gallery full of muskets and pikes and wicked swords like the one whose curved blade has ball-bearings racing up and down a channel in the middle, the more easily to decapitate a victim. But much of the palace is still a very private place, where a Maharajah and his family sit and control the considerable remnant of a king's ransom, and from which they still carry weight in the affairs of Benares. Calcutta is not like that. It is not by any means devoid of nobility. It accommodates the Maharajah of Cooch Behar, the Maharajah of Cossimbazar, the Maharajah of Mayurbhanj, the Maharajah Ruler of Sonepur State, the Maharajah of Nattore and the lady Maharani Bahadura of Nadia. It is home for the even more exalted Maharajadhiraja Bahadur of Burdwan, Sir Uday Chand Mahtab. Yet while these people still dwell in palaces of a kind, they are distinctly suburban palaces. While Burdwan still takes the platform of the British Indian Association chiefly to lament the fact that zamindars have fallen upon evil days and to suggest that the land-holding community has been denied justice, Cossimbazar avoids publicity and keeps his feet sticking firmly to the ground in a collection of china clay mines.

And there or thereabouts lies the wealth of Calcutta. This is the wealth of the warehouse and the foundry, of the dockside and the bank, of the metropolis and the *entrepôt*, of the stocklist and the showroom and the ringing tradesman's till. It depends hugely upon a peasantry toiling over the earth under the eyes of a landlord and his men, but these are hidden from its sight behind the smoke of its factories, beyond the rumble of its overpowering traffic. Calcutta is by far the richest city in India, even though its various problems have started to turn this richness into a collapsing wealth. It is possibly the richest city anywhere between Rome and Tokyo in terms of the money that is accumulated and represented here.

To get rid of a few measurements, this is where, between 1956–7 and 1966–7, 46·9 per cent of India's exports left the country and where 30·4 per cent of the imports arrived. It is where, in 1964, 15 per cent of India's manufacturing industry was based, where 30 per cent of the nation's bank transactions occurred, where 30 per cent of the national tax revenue was produced. And just behind Calcutta is a hinterland that has always swollen its wealth, that in the first place provided the excuse for Calcutta being here at all. The Mogul rulers of India knew Bengal as their Paradise on earth, and this certainly wasn't because it was comfortable to live in. The British soon came to the same conclusion and Charles Stewart had decided by 1813 that 'The province of Bengal is one of the most valuable acquisitions that was ever made by any nation.' It has always been the source of profit. In 1963, West Bengal was producing 95 per cent of India's jute, 92 per cent of its razor blades, 87 per cent of its electric fans, 80 per cent of its sewing machines, 78 per cent of its railway wagons, 74 per cent of its rubber shoes, 70 per cent of its enamelware, 56 per cent of its electric lamps, over

50 per cent of its crockery, 49 per cent of its paint and varnish, 31 per cent of its radio sets and its soap, 30 per cent of its finished steel, 29 per cent of its coal, 25 per cent of its tea and 21·5 per cent of its paper and paper boards.

Add to West Bengal a strip of southern Bihar, a slice of northern Orissa, a fragment of western Assam, and you have what has justifiably been called the Ruhr of modern India. Within less than 300 miles of Calcutta, which is not very far in Asia, almost the whole of the republic's iron and steel industry is concentrated today in townships cleared out of jungle to make room for blast furnaces, coke ovens and rolling mills. Durgapur, Jamshedpur and Asansol may suggest elephants, bullock carts and the most exotic Orientalism to the Western mind, but they are chiefly the tropical cousins of Middlesbrough, Pittsburgh and Essen. There is a network of similar towns in this hinterland, each with its special development of industry. There are more iron and steel works at Rourkela and Kulti, engineering at Midnapore and Ranchi, textiles at Cuttack, locomotive works at Chittaranjan, an oil refinery at Barauni, a great mixture of factories at Patna and Siliguri. The industry is based upon an endless supply of manpower and a vast accumulation of natural resources. For this hinterland conceals beneath its jungle, in the firmer ground outside the delta, not only iron and steel and petroleum, but limestone and copper, manganese and dolomite, china clay and asbestos, bauxite and graphite, titanium and mica, fire clay and kaolin, chromium, kyanite, talc and potash. There is also much timber and there is tea in the hill country even farther to the North. And all of it gradually being plundered from the earth and sent up and down in some shape or form, by railway, by truck, by lighter and sometimes still by bullock cart, to Calcutta.

It would not have been so if there had not been a mighty river here, wide and deep enough to let the biggest sailing ships that man could make come tacking into the middle of this Paradise; they once used to voyage from Europe as far as Patna, which took them well over a month beyond Kalikata. The river's origins are far away across a sub-continent of sweltering earth. It has started in the foothills of the Himalyas to the West

and it has come tumbling in a cascade of sky-blue water past
Rishikesh, where the Maharishi Mahesh Yogi once received the
Beatles in an air-conditioned bungalow built on the proceeds of
Western adulation, and where there is a township totally given
to spirituality and alms, vividly decorated with green and red
cast-ironwork, dominated by a Victorian clock-tower, looking
and feeling like a cross between Blackpool and Lourdes. Much
later the river has rolled powerfully past Benares, a deep sea-
green now, past the four miles of ghats and the buildings bearing signs advocating birth control and the piles of timber with
people waiting their turn to incinerate their dead; and in the
dawn, ghostly figures have started to creep down the ghats in
dozens, in scores, in hundreds and then in thousands to bathe
in its sacred waters, while birds have meditated on this humanity
and perhaps taken thought for their own souls, perched upon
rails which have been staked out in mid-stream especially for
this purpose. All this time the river has been called the Ganga,
though people have called it by other names as well at different
places along its course. They have known it as Daughter of the
Lord of Himalaya, Born from the Lotuslike foot of Vishnu,
Dwelling in the Matted Locks of Siva, Taking Pride in the
Broken Egg of Brahma, Triple-braided Stimulator and Cow
That Gives Much Milk. But always, and above all else, they
have known it as the blessed Ganga, Mother of the World.

Eventually the river has reached Bengal, and there it has been
unable to contain itself in a single headlong rush for the sea. It
has become divided into so many channels that it is doubtful
whether anyone has ever counted them all. Until the middle
of the nineteenth century the mainstream swept confidently past
Calcutta in the guise of the Hooghly, but then it began to edge
its current towards the Padma and each year since then, more
and more of the true Ganga has taken this way to the South,
through the East Bengal of what is now Pakistan, with no great
Indian city to use it on the rest of its way to the sea. There are
gloomy men who call the Hooghly a dying river, though it certainly doesn't look it yet. It pours in a khaki torrent, a third of a
mile across, between the twin cities of Calcutta and Howrah so
fiercely that there is always a foaming bone in the teeth of the

merchantmen pulling anxiously at their anchor cables and their buoys. It is still so full of life that even its pilots have to take a daily briefing on its latest wayward movements, for it is one of the most treacherous rivers in the world. There are 125 miles of it between Calcutta and the Bay of Bengal and they are punctuated by sixteen sandbanks which are never quite the same shape and depth from one sailing to the next. The most dangerous one of all, the James and Mary, a shoal three miles long and 600 yards wide in the middle of the estuary, was troubling Streynsham Master and Thomas Bowrey in the seventeenth century just as it has troubled mariners ever since. So were the Hooghly's tidal bores, which now come rushing up to Calcutta on 144 days in every year and even at that distance from their start they are usually six feet or more in height. The newspapers give warning that they are due so that merchantmen can warp themselves into the safety of the Kidderpore Docks, while the country boats can prepare to ride them hazardously in midstream, and people – if they can read – can crowd for their lives on the very topmost steps of the ghats. There are sudden squalls to beware of, that can turn a laden barge over in an instant, or an overladen motor launch on its way up from Diamond Harbour to Kalighat full of pilgrims who will drown in the twinkling of an eye. And there is always the lurking possibility of a cyclone which can devastate the city, wreck thirty-six large vessels and throw steamships high, dry and smashed to bits upon the land, as one did in 1864.

The Hooghly exposes Calcutta in cross-section like the rings of a sawn-off log. Scarcely a mile above the city centre it proceeds past palm trees which only half conceal temples and the steadily decaying palaces of old zamindars and Nabobs, together with the worst slums in creation. There are crocodiles here, just as there are leopards around Dum Dum and the other boundaries of the city, and while both sometimes snatch a human being, the crocodiles at least are occasionally caught and put on stuffed display in some ambitious motor-showroom along Chowringhee. Then, quite suddenly, there is all the activity of a great cosmopolitan port. On the right is Howrah, which in 1848 was called the Wapping of Calcutta and which does big business in the way of

docking and shipbuilding, where oxy-acetylene flashes burst out
of deep and cavernous shadows. On the left is Calcutta proper,
and close to the river are high buildings in which most of this
tremendous commerce is manipulated. They appear much smaller than they really are, though, for the sky here is full of the
Howrah Bridge; and there never was a bridge which dominated
a landscape as much and in so ungainly a fashion as this one.
From any distance it looks as though it was trying to crush the
life out of everything beneath, for it is a graceless thing, a great
fretworked grid of steel built only to bear footpaths and roads
and tramtracks and certainly not to beautify a skyline. There are
many bridges in the world constructed upon similar principles
and they usually seem to leap across an intervening space with a
spring of their own; even Sydney's metal coathanger manages a
pleasing arch across the harbour. But here, it is as if the Howrah
Bridge had merely been clamped down over the city, or dropped
across the river, and it looks every ounce of its 27,000 tons.

Far from being crushed, life is teeming in its shadows. Early
in the morning there is a market down here, where scores of
people sell thousands of flowers in garlands of orange, in
swathes of blue, in bunches of crimson and in posies of white,
and the servants of the rich come in hordes to buy the freshest
tiny blooms to decorate their masters' dinner tables, while others
scramble and barter for something beautiful and precious to
give to Kali and the other gods. Lithe young men stand in rows
or in intermittent ones and twos, their naked torsos gleaming
with sweat while they press up and touch toes and swing long
dumb-bells in dangerous-looking arcs, in something that is a
combination of physical jerks, religious exercise and sheer racial
pride. Nearby, corpulent old men lie like sows bereft of their
litters, while some wiry helot pummels each back and massages
each gut and rubs each scalp and strokes in oil from top to
bottom. And always there are people washing here, slapping
clothes up and down against the stone steps of the ghats, jump-
ing into the water and splashing just for fun, or quietly ladling
the sacred liquids of the Hooghly from tin bowls upon their
almost private parts. They pay no attention at all to the occasional rime of ashes and sodden fronds of marigold that come

drifting down from one of the burning ghats above the bridge. For there is much death here as well as life; and daily, bodies are cremated on steps like these on a bonfire of logs, with a blowing of flutes, before being scattered in the river. But sometimes in Calcutta a man will die and his people will not even have the money for his burning; so they quietly slip him into the Hooghly and the next day, on mudflats a mile or two downstream, dogs are seen chewing over a floppy, seemingly rubberized thing, which by some mysterious chemistry has been bleached almost totally white from head to toe.

Below the bridge lies the shipping and all the river traffic of the East. Every craft here was built for merchandize. There are no posh liners in the Hooghly, come to see how the other half lives. It has not been possible to cruise up here in all the old Imperial splendour of the P and O, with lascars on the decks and foxtrots in the lounge, since 1931, though Bombay was still enjoying an occasional whiff of that past until the spring of 1970. The shipping at Calcutta comes from the strictly tradesmen's lines of Ellerman, Elder Dempster, Bank, Clan, American Export and half a dozen others. It has tramped in the hard way from the River Plate, from St John and Halifax, from Odessa and Varna, from Singapore and Port Swettenham, from Liverpool and Hamburg, from Melbourne and Yokohama. It has rust dripping down its sides and underpants drying on its stanchions and only small bikinis of awning to protect its crews from the sun. It waits very patiently, sometimes for weeks on end, while lighters clutter its sides and the Hooghly is much more busy with the comings and goings of smaller fry.

There are flat boats moving round here with cargoes of hay so huge and overwhelming that the boat itself is invisible and all you can see is a floating haystack on the water; they are often moored in their dozens just above Howrah Bridge, like an aquatic farmyard, and their crews have created a tunnel inside each stack, which makes a sort of home. There are tipsy little boats, long, slim, with low pointed prows, canting over at speed as the wind leans into their lateens. Outriggers flick by, bearing fishermen off to look for bhekti and hilsa. Sharp-stemmed and narrow lighters, with a canvas shelter stretched tight in a hump over the sterns, are parked in rows where they toss and bump each other like a flotsam. And down the middle of the Hooghly there is always a procession of vessels moving rather grandly under square sails cocked at a jaunty angle, known as junks to the European and noayka to the Bengali. They are to be seen at their best when the wind has dropped, however, or when they are trying to make way against it. For on the high curved poop, the serang leans against his tiller above the great triangular sweep of a rudder plunged vertically into the water, while in front of him four or six men stand up and work oars the size of saplings in one of the most graceful movements imaginable. In perfect time together they take three measured and swinging paces along the deck, dip in the blades and then lean back from the shafts while the boat slides forward under their pull. Rhythmically, almost studiously, they and their craft get the better of this turbulent river, which flows so fast that any boat trying to move straight across it rocks and rolls like a mad thing.

The Hooghly bears all this traffic along, past the ghats and beyond the strollers along Strand Road, which Lord Hastings created as a promenade for ladies and gentlemen. It carries it past the point where the master mariners could satisfy themselves that Calcutta knew how to deal with pirates, whose bodies were hung from gibbets there until 1820; for the next thirty years they were drowned instead off Prinsep Ghat. Opposite is Shalimar, with its ropeworks and a big red neon sign advertising Shalimar Paints, though once it was a country retreat with a miniature garden modelled on the original Shalimar in Lahore, which had been laid out by Shah Jehan's chief engineer and where pale hands were loved by heartsick young Englishmen. On the Calcutta side is the opening of Tolly's Nullah, the creek that wriggles away up to the temple at Kalighat and then on to Warren Hastings' old house and wealthy Alipore; Major Tolly dredged it afresh in 1775 so that pilgrims should still be able to bathe in Ganga water when making sacrifice to Kali; water buffalo now hide in it from the heat, with only nostrils, eyes and horns poised above the surface, and children play skidding games on its steep banks of greasy black mud. The Hooghly is broadening now, turning into its dogleg, and at an

angle the Kidderpore Docks have started to succeed the rich
southern suburbs, infinitely more complex than Colonel Watson
could have imagined when he started to engineer the first berth
within a few days of acting as second to Philip Francis in the
duel with Hastings; for now the docks sweep away in range
after range of warehouses and gantries and superstructures
which are all locked in against the disturbance of the tides.

Calcutta is not quite finished yet, but the worst is over by the
time the Botanical Gardens come up to starboard, which Bishop
Heber thought just like Milton's idea of Paradise and which Sir
Joseph Hooker used as a base while he was collecting and com-
piling his famous flora of British India before returning to his
Directorship at Kew; and in the gardens is the largest banyan
tree in the world, which is supposed to have started life two
centuries ago on top of a wild date-palm, under which a fakir
would sit and beg, but which is now an astonishing growth like
a self-made jungle, with over six hundred trunks of its own,
covering so much ground that you can never quite get it all into
one photograph however far back you stand. There are occasional brickworks to follow beside the river after this, and a vast
Bata shoe factory to port, with two or three townships posted
along the banks, but now the Hooghly is making speed, full of
intimidating little eddies and swirls, through proper Lord Jim
jungle to the Bay of Bengal. In spite of all the horrors that it
passes and occasionally inflicts, it is a captivating river, and its
romance is precisely the romance of Conrad, who saw it briefly
once, when he sailed as mate in the *Tilkhurst*, bound from
Singapore to Dundee in 1885, just before he wrote his first short
story.

It is famous for its sunsets, whose exhausted transformations
are best witnessed from somewhere near the Gwalior Monument
on Strand Road, where Sepoy Ganga Din and Sepoy Juggernauth Misser and Naick Runmust Singh and a variety of Bom-
bardiers, Roughriders and Farriers, led by a Major-General C. H.
Churchill, are commemorated for a battle they fatally won in
1843. Almost always the sun has become a disc the colour of
blood orange by the time it is apparently motionless just above
the factories across the Hooghly. The cloudless sky is pure

orange by now, the river is nearly golden not khaki, the Howrah Bridge has lost its hazy, noon-time pallor and turned to hard grey steel instead. Suddenly, the sun begins to move, not changing colour by even the slightest fading of its heat, but the sky begins to shift from orange to pure white and the river begins to dazzle with more light, as though it were going to recover from a false alarm of dusk. Immediately, the junks and the other boats still plodding up and down acquire a new and sharp outline, which makes them individual and distinguishes them from the blur of the opposite bank. You can now see the sun sliding perceptibly down near the sign of Shalimar Paints, its circle unbroken in one instant, its bottom edge flattened in the next. Everything changes rapidly now. The sky moves again from white to something less vivid than orange, more nearly the colour of burnished gold. Behind you, bats begin to skim and skirmish around the squat grey bastions of Fort William, lying low within its earthworks. On the river, guttering lights are lit inside those tight-humped shelters on the barges, the neon sign at Shalimar begins to jerk and splutter into advertisement, the Howrah Bridge begins to dissolve upstream. As the last kite flogs itself hastily home past the fort and over the tree tops of the Maidan, the sun has become a crescent, thin as a wafer and pure blood now, and the sky has almost completed its spectrum to deep mauve. The bridge has almost vanished, the opposite bank is a lurking shadow, the boats between are the vaguest shapes. Suddenly, like the throwing of a switch, darkness. And a thousand small lights, flickering over and beside water, with a mustard glow in the sky behind as Calcutta makes ready to pass the night.

Flowing into Calcutta like the Hooghly is a rich commodity of human beings. It has been thus ever since the foundation and it has never for a moment diminished. Over the past half century this flow has become a torrent, too. These people have been an indirect source of Calcutta's wealth since the day they were born and they have come to the city to share it at last, for there has been scarcely anywhere else for them to go if they were to have a chance of living above that dreadful line marking absolute

poverty. At the start of the sixties the hinterland from which Calcutta has drawn its wealth contained 145 million people – and
it now has well over 150 millions – living in one of the least
urbanized areas in the whole of India. According to the 1961
census the proportion of urban to total population throughout
the nation was 19 per cent. At that time only West Bengal, with
24·5 per cent, exceeded the national average among the states of
Eastern India and this was entirely due to the vast compression
of people into the 200 square miles of Greater Calcutta; outside
the metropolitan district only two and a half million Bengalis
out of 28·4 millions lived in towns, a proportion of only 9·2 per
cent. Even today, in the four hinterland states of West Bengal,
Bihar, Orissa and Assam, there are only sixteen cities with
populations exceeding 100,000; and on the Indian scale of being,
100,000 is very nearly an insignificant number of anything;
there are almost that many people on the pavements each night
in Calcutta. In such a situation Calcutta represents, for all its
well-known poverty, the possibility of personal wealth not to be
obtained elsewhere. At the beginning of the sixties the average annual income per head of population was Rs 194 in Bihar, Rs 259
in Orissa, Rs 319 in Assam and Rs 327 in West Bengal. In the
whole of India it was no more than Rs 334. But in Calcutta it
was Rs 811. Only Delhi and Bombay could better that, and they
are much too far away for any Bihari peasant to contemplate
migration in their direction; he can walk to Calcutta if need be
in a matter of weeks, but he would be dead before he was even
half way to the capital of India. And even if, when he reaches
the city, he cannot find work he can find many rich people
from whom he can beg enough to stay alive until something
better turns up. There is no one to support the destitute in a
Bihari village, for everyone there is almost destitute himself.

The plight of such people was displayed with much subdued
militancy and a great deal of warm camaraderie at a congress of
peasants in the village of Barasat, not far beyond Dum Dum, at
the beginning of 1970. It was held under the auspices of the
Communist Party of India which, within India's great and per-
plexing variety of communism, is the party which holds most
strongly to the undefiled truths revealed by Moscow alone. Bara-

sat is where Bengali serfs rose up against the infamous planters
in one of the local revolutions which followed the Mutiny, and
in the literature of the congress there were even references to
'the notorious despot Warren Hastings'. There were many displays of propaganda, of course; stands bearing drawings to illus-
trate the domination of India by the British, others showing the
life and times of Lenin, photographs demonstrating the people's
struggle in Vietnam. Very small and articulate boys led illiterate
old men round these displays, gravely pointing to the pictures
with their canes while they described the meaning and significance of each one. Older girls dispensed tea and chappatis to
hungry comrades while their brothers, wearing red berets and
carrying bamboo quarter staves, marshalled crowds who were
not in the least disposed to be unruly. It must have been a bit
like this in Russia when the Narodniks were planning revolution
before Lenin turned up, or in the backblocks of Kweiyang before Chiang Kai-shek was sent packing into Formosa. There
were many, many speeches for days on end, for this is what the
congress had been called for, and there were delegates to hear
them from every part of India.

One of them was a man called Sibsankar Jha, who had fratern-
ally come from his party cell somewhere in Bihar. He was small,
he was dark, he had a shy, attractive smile and he wore his party
badge dangling lopsided on the breast of his dhoti. He was forty-
six years old, he was the father of seven children and he and his
family inhabited one room made of brick and five others constructed of thatch in a little compound of their own. He was a
peasant farmer owning five acres of land, which meant that he
was far better off than the average peasant farmer of Bihar.
Most of it was rice paddy but the crop had failed for three successive years and so the family income had depended almost
entirely upon what they could grow of sugar cane instead. The
rice would bring them in Rs 3,500 in a decent year but the sugar
cane had a smaller market and made only Rs 2,000.

Sibsankar Jha and his family had last eaten meat so long ago
that he could not remember when. They enjoyed milk every
other year, when their buffalo cow had calved, and once a day
they ate rice as a luxury. Otherwise their diet consisted of grain

and pulses, which is a crop of low nutritional value that can eventually cause beri beri if taken for too long in too much quantity. Two children were at school, while the eldest, a young man of twenty-two, had acquired his BA at Bihar University. But he was unemployed; he was, in fact, learning to type to give himself a saleable skill, riding a bicycle eight miles each way every day to his lessons, which cost Rs 5 a month. The family were permanently in debt and this was quite the most terrible thing in their lives. The beginning of Sibsankar Jha's loan is a bank which lends money to a credit society at six per cent interest. The credit society then advances money to a money-lender at an interest of ten per cent. The moneylender then gives Sibsankar Jha the cash he wants on condition that he pays interest of twenty-five per cent. Some people say that these figures are, if anything, on the low side of such transactions in this part of the world. And Indian economists will tell you that no local substitute for this system of usury has yet been devised. In Sibsankar Jha's case, it meant that he could see the time rapidly approaching when he would have to sell his land in order to pacify a moneylender who would no longer be prepared to grant him a loan. And if that happened, Sibsankar Jha would probably have to do what many Biharis have always had to do, at last go down to Calcutta to look for work.

If that happened he would probably hold onto his little compound so that his family could stay behind and at least have shelter, while he prospected the city for a new home. If he was lucky he would find work. He might get a job as a labourer in one of the jute mills of Calcutta and if this were so he would be a fortunate man. There are many worse things that can happen to a Bihari peasant in the city. The wages are comparatively high and though the work is hard and rough, it is not by any means as bad as some employment there. If you go into the shed of a jute mill and you have had any experience of a Lancashire cotton mill, you find that the differences between them are fewer than you might have anticipated. The noise is about the same, though the humidity here is appreciably higher and there is generally much less natural light. The jute operative is considerably worse off than the cotton worker in the conditions of his labour insofar as his is a much dirtier job. The atmosphere is dusty as well as humid and for the men slashing the filthy bundles of raw jute into hanks that can be managed by the washing machines and then the looms, a management careful of its workers would provide protective masks; which certainly doesn't happen in Calcutta. But elsewhere there are no thick clouds of dust; you can see fairly clearly to the opposite end of the shed, two or three hundred yards away, across row after row of clattering machines.

A great number of the men working these looms, slashing the dusty bundles, pushing the finished gunny sacks and the hessian mats into the warehouses on trollies, are immigrants to Calcutta. One day they left their villages in search of work, in the hope that eventually their families would be able to follow them. But the weeks tended to stretch into months and then into years because the workman, though obtaining employment, has never had quite enough money to keep his wife and children on the higher cost of living in the city; and, above all, because he has not been able to find anywhere they could all live together tolerably by even the impoverished standards they have been accustomed to. And so he has shared his tiny room with two or three other immigrant husbands and fathers, each week he has gone to the General Post Office in Dalhousie Square or to one of its branches, and there he has queued for a small but vital postal order and sent it back home to his wife. Every year, Calcutta despatches the equivalent of £14 million in this way and for this purpose, for there are very many men sharing in its wealth, which at any level is much greater than that of any village. So it has remained what it has always tended to be, a city dominated by men, to a greater extent maybe, than any other in the world. It was so in the East India Company's heyday and it was unchanged when the twentieth century began. In 1901 there were no more than 515 women to every thousand men. In 1961 there were still only 612.

In such circumstances is jute manufactured, still accounting for almost a quarter of the country's export trade in spite of heavy competition from East Pakistan, which acquired most of the jute-growing lands at Partition. Calcutta and West Bengal almost monopolize what was left, between them. There are nearly two million families dependent upon growing jute in Calcutta's hinterland, and in the city there are 200,000 people working it in the mills; of the 109 jute mills in India, 98 are to be found in West Bengal. It is a vastly profitable trade for those who control it, in spite of its great dependence upon fluctuating world markets. The British ran it almost from top to bottom of management until they left, though the fantastically golden years had become just a little dulled by then. The time for a well-respected man with his origins in the Scottish Lowlands to be running jute mills in Calcutta was during and just after the First World War, shortly after he and his compatriots had been howling with rage and bitter prophecy at the transfer of the capital to Delhi. Apart from any normal manufacturing during the war years, the millowners were then selling eight million sandbags a month to the War Office to protect the brave lads in Flanders and elsewhere. One of them boasted to the Governor of Bengal that they could rise to ten millions if asked. They and their friends in the city made so much money out of their war production that in the first few months of peace they surreptitiously began to coin a local epithet for Armistice Day. They called it Black Friday, because it was going to make such a severe cut into their profits. Then they consoled themselves at the Saturday Club, where they could hear forty Goanese musicians dressed like Central European ringmasters, playing 'In a Monastery Garden'; or took their wives to dinner at Firpo's new restaurant, whose management had imported a jazz band and furnished the premises in the best P and O Louis Quinze style. For five or six years after the war the bonanza went on, with the average dividend from the jute mills exceeding 100 per cent and frequently reaching 150 per cent. Mr Nehru was one of the Indians who bitterly noticed in those years 'within an hour's drive of the palaces of Calcutta, semi-naked women, wild and unkempt, working away for the barest pittance, so that a broad river of wealth should flow ceaselessly to Glasgow and Dundee as well as to some pockets in India'. And though the enormous fortunes that expatriates had always made out of Calcutta had dwindled by the 1930s, though their controlling interest in its treasure had to be abandoned on Independence Day 1947, the

British continued and still continue to play a very decent hand in the wealth of the city.

There are many British firms in the Bengal Chamber of Commerce which have been connected with the city for several generations, such as the descendants of Sir Thomas Lipton, who entered the local tea trade in 1890, or Brooke Bond, who followed in 1902. The chamber's membership is littered with dozens of other old, familiar trading titles – Associated British Machine Toolmakers, Associated Electrical Industries, Atlas Assurance, The Avery Company, British Insulated Callender's Cables, Eagle Star Insurance, English Electric, National and Grindlays Bank, Imperial Chemical Industries, Norwich Union Life Insurance, Wiggins Teape and many more. Occasionally a British firm modifies its title in the interests of tact, as the Imperial Tobacco Company of India did when it became the India Tobacco Company at the end of the sixties, though this doesn't necessarily save it from local suspicions of lingering Imperialism. A purely Indian tobacco company not long ago bought two full pages in *The Statesman* in order to mount what it called an exposé of the foreign monopoly in India's cigarette industry. This pointed out that while 60,000 million cigarettes were smoked in the country each year, only 12,000 millions were produced by totally indigenous companies. It claimed that in recent years not only had many Indian companies found themselves working below their full capacity, but that some of them had been obliged to shut down a total of ninety-six factories, including eleven in Calcutta. It suggested that the market was dominated by two foreign giants, the American Tobacco Company of the United States, and the Imperial Tobacco Company of Great Britain, working in consort as the British American Tobacco Company Ltd. It claimed that in the case of ITC, the foreign shareholding amounted to ninety-four per cent of the company's total. And it is perfectly true that the British companies remaining in Calcutta still try to pay a good dividend to investors at home, while attempting to keep the city afloat with their investment on the spot. They do not always succeed in both objects and at least one of them, the Calcutta Tramways Company Ltd, is virtually a British charity to the city, for although it still has shareholders in the United Kingdom it is run by the West Bengal Government, which expropriated the concern some years ago.

It is instructive to read the files of these British firms in the Board of Trade's company registry in London. One of the thickest, running to two or three volumes, is that of the Calcutta Electric Supply Corporation, which began to generate power for the city as the Indian Electric Company in 1897. This has managed to do rather better for itself than the tramways company. There was not a year between 1965 and 1968 when something called the Adjusted Profits of Calcutta Electric (gross profits before deducting depreciation and after deducting debenture interest) were less than £3,487,000 and in 1965 they were £5,132,000. Even in 1969 they were £2,810,000 and, as the chairman pointed out in his annual report for the year, this meant that when loans, interests and several other encumbrances had been dealt with, no less than £1,177,971 clear profit could be declared, paying a dividend for the year of 9 per cent. He was not entirely happy about this figure which was, he said, £20,405 less than the Reasonable Return agreed upon by the Electricity (Supply) Act of 1948. 'As I have said before', he remarked on that occasion, 'the lot of industrial management in Calcutta today is not a bed of roses – this is especially so in the case of a public utility like ours.' Now, Calcutta Electric provides more than 10,000 very badly needed jobs in the city, quite apart from producing electricity, and although these employees are doubtless as dutiful as any workmen there (at least they always get a vote of thanks for their services in the annual report) the fact is that the chairman was on that occasion speaking during a high wave of industrial and political unrest in Calcutta. This, and several other trying local factors, was reflected in the Corporation's next annual report, which could only present a clear profit for 1970 of £787,301 – and this time, the Reasonable Return was missed by the margin of £449,000. Nevertheless, it was possible to make an *ex gratia* payment of £6,000 to a retiring director and donations to charitable organizations in India amounted to £743 that year, as against £521 in 1969.

One of the difficulties for a British company like Calcutta Electric, doing business in the city but registered in London with

its head office in Bloomsbury, has been its subjection to Indian
Corporation Tax amounting to 70 per cent. It was chiefly in
order to reduce this to the rate of 50·6 per cent imposed on
domestic companies in India that in January 1970, the firm
shifted its headquarters to Chowringhee Square and controlled
itself from Calcutta. Where, until 1970, it had two Indian directors in Calcutta and five Englishmen living either in Suffolk,
Sussex or London, it now has four directors resident in India
and three in Britain. The list of shareholders remains unchanged
by a strategy which, after all, has been adopted chiefly for their
benefit. Half the shareholders have for many years been Indians,
a majority of them inhabiting the more salubrious parts of south
Calcutta. The other half are sprawled on fixed and fluctuating
incomes throughout the length and breadth of the British Isles
and elsewhere. There is a Burnside in Derby and a Bushell in
Richmond, a Callow in Maidenhead and a Ballantyne in Glasgow, a Hook in Exeter and a Wylie in Belfast, a Thompson in
Tunbridge Wells and a Ward in Brighton. There is a clergyman
in Bury St Edmunds and a lady living on the Costa del Sol.
There are companies and groups of shareholders, like the Scottish Union and National Insurance Company of Edinburgh,
which holds 10,000 shares, and Twenty Nine Gracechurch
Street Nominees Ltd, which holds 3,725. The list of British
shareholders in Calcutta Electric is a long and lingering one, in
fact, a very paradigm of the British connection with the city
itself.

Calcutta's commerce is manipulated most carefully and trans-
acted most powerfully in the streets around Dalhousie Square.
This was once Tank Square, when the burra sahibs sent their
bheesties to draw water by the bagful from old Loll Diggy, and
the tank is usually brimming today, though it is now circum-
navigated by tramcars and a high fence is intended, and utterly
fails, to discourage people from so much as washing their clothes
in the water and putting them to dry on the sloping concrete
banks of the tank. On one side is the Writers' Building where the
Government of West Bengal, when there is one, functions loudly
behind Early English openings and classically pedimented entrances which have been uniformly colour-washed in burnt

sienna. Opposite is the pale ochre skyscraper of the Telephone
Bhavan and, between the two, the square is dominated by a
green copper dome above a Doric colonnade, which belongs to
the General Post Office, and very nearly to the army of pavement tradesmen who also skirmish up its steps and over the
inlaid brass line which marks a boundary of the first Fort
William.

In the streets to the North and West, along Lyons Range, up
Clive Row, down Fairlie Place and beside the full length of
Netaji Subhas Road, are stacked the offices and company headquarters of Bengal's new Nabobs and their British progenitors.
Trim-suited and Westernized very often, but sometimes in
chadar and little astrakhan cap, the babus come each day past the
armed guards on the door (for there is much money here and
there are many impatient poor) and up to the boardroom in
quietly-humming lifts. And down below, in the deep shades cast
by the Royal Exchange and the buildings round about, the streets
seethe with the passage of clerks in pastel shirt and slacks which
deteriorate to highly-pointed shoes over fluorescent socks, or in
brilliant white dhotis with bare legs ending in sloppy rounded
shoes and no socks, all of them bearing leather briefcases and
canvas pouches and documents zipped into plastic folders. The
traffic in people is so great here that the pavements are inadequate to contain them and they overflow onto the roads and
become as confused and shapeless as a football crowd coming
out of the stadium after the final whistle, swirling and darting
in every direction between the cars, the handcarts, the taxis and
the lorries, leaving small and intermittent spaces where workmen in shabby khaki shorts, their chests glistening through the
holes in their singlets and their heads swathed in grubby makeshift turbans, are flinging sand upon tarmac which is gently
bubbling in the heat.

Not all the private wealth of Calcutta is schemed and pro-
grammed in these few streets; there is many a thriving little
empire conducted from one of the rising tower blocks beyond the
Maidan. But this is Calcutta's Wall Street, its City, its Bourse.
It is rife with company directors whose pay cheque may only
amount to Rs 5,000 a month but who can safely slip almost all

of that in the bank, for everything they possess – house, cars, servants, refrigerators, pots and pans – is thoughtfully taken care of by a board which is very wise in the ways of self-defence against India's high taxation rates. It is full of men like the late Shri Y. L. Agarwal, whose colleagues once took a very large advertisement in *The Statesman* in his revered memory; there was an uplifting text beneath the photograph of a gentleman who gazed at the readers benignly from behind his horn-rimmed spectacles and who passed away on 26 December 1967. 'Shri Agarwal,' so it said, 'dedicated his whole life to the betterment of the scrap industry and set us the guide-line we religiously follow. Our Humble tribute to him lies in our achieving the Certificate of Merit recently awarded to us by the Government of India for the highest export of scraps.'

This is where the biggest giants of Indian business abide. The mammoth Tata Iron and Steel Corporation is anchored here, which may be compared to the Bethlehem combine in the United States. And here, in an almost too tasteful suite of offices at the top of the Royal Exchange, are to be found the Birla Brothers, who can only be compared to the Fords or the Rockefellers or the Krupps as a wealthy dynasty, but who are otherwise totally unique. If it is possible to conceive of a London family which owned Imperial Chemical Industries, Shell, Unilever, British Leyland and half a dozen lesser concerns the size of Sainsbury's, it is just possible to grasp the position of the Birlas in the Indian order of things and their ridiculous hold on the national economy. In assets it may be that Tata of Bombay – who founded Jamshedpur fifty years ago and started the airline which was eventually nationalized into Air India – are still slightly ahead of Birlas; but the Birla Brothers are growing at a rate which far exceeds anyone else's. They have a total monopoly of motor car production in India with Hindustan Motors and they own one of its biggest newspapers, the *Hindustan Times*; they control the Indian Shipping Co. Ltd, the Hindusthan Investment Corporation Ltd, Hind Gas and Industries Ltd, Jayashree Textiles Ltd, Minerals and Minerals Ltd, Textile Machinery Corporation Ltd, Universal Electric Co. Ltd, Universal Cables Ltd, and the Usha Development Co. Ltd – all of which merely gives an idea of their range, for these are simply a few of several dozen Birla enterprises.

They came from the deserts of Rajasthan in Western India, like every other Marwari family. There was once a Birla Prime Minister of Jaipur State and, half a century ago, his son set out by camel from the ancestral home at Pillani to seek his fortune in Bombay. He made it as a bullion broker there and from it founded the commercial House of Birla, which had almost achieved its present consuming size by the time he retired to Benares where his sons, the Birla Brothers, would come from time to time to seek his sage council. They have congregated elsewhere outside Calcutta when necessary and, not infrequently, careful newspaper readers of India's equivalent of the European court circulars have been able to note items issuing from the Rashtrapati Bhavan in Delhi like this one: 'Nov. 5 (1956) – The following came to lunch: Shri Ghansyamdas Birla, Shri Brijmohan Birla, Shri Lakshmi Narayan Birla, Shri Basant Kumar Birla, Shri Gangaprosad Birla, Shri Madho Prosad and Shri Prabhu Dayal Himatsingka.' This has meant that all the important members of the Birla family, together with their solicitor, have been breaking rice with the President of India. They have always been deeply involved in the politics of the nation, and the Congress Party for several decades would have been quite lost financially without them. Gandhi himself looked to them for support and stayed with them often. He was assassinated on the prayer ground of their Delhi mansion and another great Congress and national leader, Sardar Patel, was nursed through his last illness by Birlas in the same place.

They have a colossal and well-publicized reputation for charity. Among many other things, they have founded a university in their native village of Pillani, they have built the splendid Lakshmi Narain Hindu temple in Delhi, they have set up the Birla Education Trust. Calcutta has benefited from a Medical and Relief Society, the Birla Industrial and Technological Museum, and, at the top end of Chowringhee, the only planetarium in the country, whose dome houses a collection of projectors and optical equipment expensively imported from East Germany. Oddly, not a single Birla rupee has yet gone in the direction of Mother Teresa and her sisters, who exist on charity which they then pass on to those even poorer than themselves. And the Birlas have many, many rupees. Twenty years ago, when India was just emerging from war and dominion, their total output was worth £45 million, and they have been expanding ever since.

They have also, once or twice, been investigated for the possibility of evading their taxes on a monumental scale. In 1948 an Income Tax Investigation Commission under Mr Justice Varadachariar was set up and two years later reported that the following Birla concerns were culpable of evasion: Cotton Agents Ltd Rs 1 crore 10 lakhs, Birla Brothers Ltd Rs 90 lakhs, Model Knitting Ltd Rs 15 lakhs, R. K. Kejrinal Groups Rs 24 lakhs, Loyalka Groups Rs 40 lakhs, Birla Cotton Mills Ltd Rs 2 crores, Orient Paper Mills Ltd Rs 2 crores.* No sooner had it dropped this bombshell than a Birla nephew, Sarojmall Mohta, filed a suit with the Supreme Court, challenging the basis of the Commission's constitution; and the Court found that the Act under which the commission had operated offended Article 14 of the Indian Constitution, that the commission was therefore void. So the investigated cases were handed over to Government officers for further action, and nothing more was heard of the tax evasion cases officially. But an advocate of the Calcutta High Court, who also held his Master's degrees in economics and commerce, eventually published two books, which amounted to a one-man investigation of the Birla companies, immensely detailed in its evidence, garnished with photostats of relevant documents. And though the first book, in two volumes, is now twenty years old and the second has been on sale since 1957, the Government has done nothing very much apart from setting up a judicial commission of inquiry into Birla affairs, at the end of 1969, in response to the lobbying of left-wing MPs who drew its attention to the findings of the Dutta Industrial Licensing Committee some months previously. But Mrs Gandhi's decision in 1969 to abolish managing agencies would not have been welcome in the House of Birla which, among other roles, is the managing agency in excelsis with assets in 1967 of more than £265 millions.

* A lakh is 100,000; a crore is ten million.

The Birlas have that mansion in Delhi, they have ample re-
treats at Mussoorie and at Nainital in the hills, but home as well
as headquarters has long been in Calcutta. At the headquarters
in the Royal Exchange the initials of the leading Birlas – L.N.,
K.K., B.K., G.P., S.K., M.P., B.M., and G – are engraved beside little sliding panels to indicate whether each is in or out. On
the top storey of the building, above the accounting machines
and the electric typewriters, the Birlas lunch and negotiate their
business in air-conditioned opulence, seated upon red leather and
under soft diffused lighting, while the food is served through a
wrought-iron grille; it is vegetarian and no drink is taken with
it, nor do the Birlas smoke, for they are exceedingly rigorous
in their religious observances. They are also exceedingly careful of their privacy and their security. Across the city in deepest
Alipore, far from the contamination of the bustees, lies Birla
Park, surrounded by a high wall invigilated by guards who
scrutinize each visitor very carefully at the gate and then announce his coming by telephone to whichever of the Birla families is prepared to receive him. For inside the wall are several
separate Birla dwellings, one for each active brother, as well as
various communal features of a considerable and highly cultivated landscape. Here is a breakfast garden shaded by bamboo,
there is a Japanese garden modelled exactly on the traditions of
Honshu, and much of the space in between is occupied by lily
ponds and crazy paving and shrubbery and coadstone urns, not
nearly as worn-out as those of the Mullicks at the Marble Palace.
But the climactic moment for a visitor to Birla Park is the discovery of a possession that marks this astonishing tribe for who
and what and how they are in the context of Calcutta, above all
the other things that they own and control and manipulate from
one end of India to the other. It somehow signifies their real
wealth much more than any calculation of rupees that might be
made even by an accountant not employed by the Birlas. It is an
ice-skating rink, insulated frigidly from a normal temperature of
100 degrees in the shade. Such is the environment of an interview which one of the ladies of the compound, Mrs Sarala Birla,
gave one day to a man representing the magazine which Pan
American Airways give away to their passengers. When he asked

her what she would do if she found herself Prime Minister of India, she began her reply with the words 'Make people work ...'

There are aerial photographs of Calcutta to be seen in this or that guide book which might make any stranger wonder what on earth was all the fuss about poverty in this city. They have usually been taken from the top of some high buildings a few blocks East of Chowringhee. From such a vantage point, what is visible through a carefully-positioned lens consists of wide streets much shaded by trees, stretching unbroken by anything more ominous than a glaring modern tower block to what is clearly an enormous park, with an intriguing prospect of a few ships' funnels and the Howrah Bridge indistinctly on a heat-hazed horizon beyond. The streets will probably be Rawdon or Hungerford or Wood or Camac, or what used to be Theatre Road but is now Shakespeare Sarani, or what was once Harrington now translated as Ho Chi Minh. The park is indeed enormous for it is the Maidan, and that stretches for two miles in one direction and one mile in the other. You could take a similar photograph from somewhere along the very top end of Broadway, looking towards the Cloisters, and it would be just as unrepresentative of New York as a whole; or from high above Cromwell Road where it is crossed by Queen's Gate, with the camera aimed past the Albert Memorial, and it would give you the same highly selective view of London.

This is not yet Alipore, where the unbelievably rich of Calcutta live; Alipore is the next stop South, beyond the Maidan and the Racecourse, proclaimed on one side of the road by the Zoo and on the other by the old Hastings house at Belvedere, with its Bengal tiger still flexed above the entrance to what is now the National Library. Nor is it Old Ballygunge, where there is another well-landed enclave. Here, just before Alipore, here is the residential district of those who by the most comfortable Western standards are pretty well to do, who by the norms of the city are rich beyond comprehension. It is also the territory of the imperial and ex-imperial brainwashers – the Soviet and United States Information Services, the British Council. It would not be safe to say that there is no bustee within a mile, for Calcutta has

a horrible habit of surprising you with just where she can park a
couple of thousand poor, at the end of a side alley leading off a
fairly respectable-looking road. But pavement sleepers are comparatively thin upon the ground here and you could easily walk
a quarter of a mile at midnight round these streets without
stumbling over a bundle of rags that stirs and proves that it is
still alive. For the most part, when the gutters run with water
here it is because someone is handling a pump deliberately fixed
at a street corner to provide for small tradesmen, taxi drivers and
anyone else far from or without a domestic tap, and not because
a standpipe has been smashed into a permanent gusher. The
movement of people here is much like that along the spacious
roads of New Delhi above Connaught Place; scarcely more
crowded than in a British suburb, with a group of idlers gossiping by a corner, a handful of cyclists wheeling along, a coolie
striding beautifully with a great basket of vegetables on his head,
taxis rolling past the potholes and honking baritonally at every
intersection, rickshaws with their sleighbell ring, and maybe a
man with a pair of half-dressed monkeys on a lead, who stand up
and prance the moment he shakes his little cord-lashed drum
in the hope of attracting your patronage. The houses here stand
back from the street behind walls that are not repellently high
and there are sometimes lawns, with the mali rearranging a
water sprinkler, sometimes gardens that are vivid and intoxicating with bougainvillæa and jasmine, sometimes courtyards
with a range of sheds just inside the wall that could contain
ponies but which harbour the servants instead. All this is the
province of the superior tradesmen, the managers and the rising
young executives of Calcutta.

The province is terminated to the North by the busy brash
line of Park Street, which links Chowringhee and the Maidan
with the tough underside of Calcutta represented by the Lower
Circular Road. In a sense, Park Street is its focal point also, for
this is where many rich drift when work is done, where they take
much of their amusement, where many of their values are
paraded in public, where they can be seen making fastidious contact with the poor; or very carefully and blankly avoiding it.
Park Street was not always a combination of honky-tonk and

urbane shopping centre, as it mostly is today. Its name came out of the deer park which Sir Elijah Impey had here. The exclusively erudite Asiatic Society built headquarters at the Chowringhee end, where the spiritual descendants of Jones and Colebrooke still come to pore over the twenty thousand increasingly dusty volumes of orientalia. And towards the Lower Circular Road, where the bright lights have faded, where garish neon has given way to butter-coloured and standard electric, is the cemetery where the old British masters of India buried their dead and raised astonishing monuments to their memory. But the pyramids of Park Street Cemetery are now almost (though not quite) a world and a century or two away from the general flavour of the thoroughfare at its upper and fashionable end. Right alongside the Asiatic Society's drab and unobtrusive frontage is a high and faceless hotel whose cultural origins lie somewhere in the post-war concrete jungles of the midtown United States; and, indeed, this is where the Pan American limousine finishes its journeys from Dum Dum, depositing its last passengers at Reception before being parked itself in the mezzanine garage. And this is the aspiring tone of the next five hundred yards of Park Street.

The Park Hotel contains a night club called the In and Out, where there is 'Cabaret by Heather. Also Mina in exotic Oriental and Continental dances. Music by Paul Correia with Hazel at the mike. Panday with his telepathic wonder show. Reva, the lady with the radar mind, answering all the innermost questions.' There are many other niteries along the road, like the Moulin Rouge, the Blue Fox, the Mocambo and Trincas ('Enchanting Eve, popular Toto, Shilling's Fentones, irresistible Iqbal Singh. Morning discotheques from ten a.m. to noon') and once you are over the threshold it is scarcely possible to distinguish one from the other. The lighting is concealed and barely adequate even for flirtation, the menus are almost the size of the tables-for-two and the liquor comes at a price to make an Englishman gulp in this wettest of all Indian cities, where only Thursday is theoretically non-intoxicating. When an irresistible Iqbal Singh or an exotic Mina is not performing, the ledge at the top of the room is invariably occupied by a three- or four-piece band whose players may have been born and bred in Bombay or points East but whose music, deafening even when it is meant to be soothing, was beginning to die down in London or Manchester ten or fifteen years ago. There are usually special lighting effects playing upon the band, a succession of greens and oranges and blues slowly flooding glass panels behind and around the instrumentalists, which are identical to those which used to suffuse the most popular British cinema organists in the thirties and the forties. It is generally a nostalgic indulgence to be there and a relief to get outside again, even though this means forsaking the crisp pleasure of air-conditioning for the sopping humidity of the night.

The shopping style of Park Street is Westernized, too. There are occasional cubby-hole tradesmen, usually dispensing tobacco or pan or bootlaces, but most business is conducted behind plate-glass windows with a till instead of an old tin to contain the currency. There are emporiums here which sell anything from plastic toys and lavatory paper to patent medicines, bottles of lime-juice, and biscuits which have been packaged by the factory in several layers of waxed or tin-foiled paper to prevent them going rotten in the climate. There are shops which do a roaring trade in nothing but saris and silks. There are businesses which specialize in pop-up toasters or thermostatic irons but which, in all their electrical commodities, never offer a vacuum cleaner for sale, because in Calcutta a human carpet sweeper is infinitely less expensive and much more durable as well. Park Street also includes two or three of the best bookshops in town, where you can purchase your Basildon Bond notepaper as well as Mr Manchester's account of a President's death, but very little that is not written in English. It contains a rambling auction sale room, where bargains can be obtained in garden statuary, middle-aged upholstery, mounted buffalo heads and bundles of electro-plated cutlery which have been abandoned by the latest British family to leave the land. At several points there are news stands – a sheet or two of cardboard on the ground, bearing five or ten yards of Indian newspapers and Western magazines running a gamut from *Time* to *True Confessions,* from *New Statesman* to *Health and Efficiency.*

It has restaurants as well as eating places which are chiefly night clubs, and here there is a very fine demarcation line between those which cater for the shopkeeping or the rickshaw-owning rich and those which pander to the executive rich. The first of these people are rather more likely to eat in family outings at the Chinese house next to the auction rooms, alongside Westerners who feel like a break from curry. The decor is universal chinoiserie and *My Fair Lady* is coming moderately loud and clear through amplifiers, but when the dhobi arrives with his enormous load of newly-laundered tablecloths he counts it piece by piece with the management upon the floor beside the diners. Somewhat more polished than this is the Kwality just over the road, where the clientele is in rather better business or still clinging, like the handful of Anglo-Indian ladies who pop in at teatime for a gaudy icecream confection with nuts on top, to the fading remnant of an ascendancy which the British and mixed blood once gave their sires and their grandams.

At the Kwality the tinned music is so perfectly muted when it is there at all that you cannot identify the tunes, the management would not dream of exposing their laundry before the customers, and their own professional aspirations were perhaps accomplished by the beginning of 1970 when they finally achieved wall to wall carpeting throughout their establishment. Before that, the long aisle between the tables was bare, and all day a humble man in khaki would move up and down crabwise on his haunches, swabbing the floor with a damp cloth around each chair leg and between each dining foot, without ever raising his eyes from his task. Nobody seemed to notice his presence; in fact, nobody was obliged to, for the slightest movement in his direction from customers, waiters or anyone else, was enough to make him deftly swivel his body out of the way, to avoid all possibility of contact.

India sometimes seems to be the intruder here; it becomes the great amorphous power which the British used to feel claustrophobically surrounding them and threatening them. It is still there, waiting to be harnessed and bidden and used for the pleasure and necessity of alien values. There is no getting away from it. At almost every intersection along Park Street there are rickshaws waiting for passengers. There are small boys waiting to clean shoes. There are men of no apparent vocation gossiping around the tobacco stalls, smoking beedies which they have lit from a smouldering length of rope that someone has thoughtfully tied to a lamp-post. There are people coming and going perpetually, bearing burdens of indiscriminate size and composition, heaving and sweating until late at night behind bullock carts that are not rumbling and lurching fast enough, their storm lanterns swinging and jerking at the back. They are all in some way at the disposal of the other people moving in and out of the shops, the restaurants and the clubs, whose colour may be identical, whose dress (particularly in the case of women) may often derive from the same tradition, but whose mannerisms suggest both ownership and alienation.

In the Kwality at lunchtime some ascending young entrepreneur, who has had his two girl friends round-eyed and giggling at his story of a dashing drive up the Grand Trunk Road to Durgapur, will suddenly shoot his elegant cuffs and bellow 'Bearah' across the room; what he really wants is the waiter with the bill, but the jargon of command was settled long ago in this city by men infinitely paler than he, and he can even imitate to perfection their intonation as well as their vocabulary. At night he and his blood brothers will emerge from a similar restaurant or club, together with their women, and they may pause for a moment before collecting their cars or hailing a taxi to purchase a balloon from a man who is almost hidden beneath a bobbing mass of them; or to buy a garland of those small, white, bell-shaped and stickily sweet-smelling flowers whose name is mogra. Then they will stroll, more easily, more indolently, much more slowly than any Westerner would dare to, past every beggar on Park Street without even a glance in their direction. And if a beggar should persist in his entreaties while these rich people are chattering and laughing at the kerb before getting into a car, he will be dismissed without anyone actually looking at him, with a gesture which is at once one of the most delicate and one of the most appalling that a human being ever contrived. It is a movement of the hand and wrist at the end of an arm which is not quite outstretched. Ladies of the British royal family are inclined to render their own stunted version of one element in it, to signify gracious condescension as they pass their subjects by in a car. But here the hand is upturned, the wrist rotates freely and the fingers flow one after the other away from the body. The gesture is delivered with the suspicion of a shrug in the shoulder and it means, at one and the same time, 'I don't even recognize your existence' and 'Don't you dare to pollute me with your presence' and quite simply 'Fuck off'. In it you detect a dismal truth about the gap which separates the people who frequent Park Street. For it is not India which threatens and encompasses on the outside, but the poor. And it is not the merely Westernized who are surrounded and besieged but the rich, who were in this land when all its people were Hindu, whose original alienation is vanished in antiquity, being simply fortified by the Moguls and buttressed by the British, being grafted into both these strains, the mannerisms being those of the last who happened to lead along this way.

And because the British were the last rulers, because the ambitions of the nation are rising towards an economy and a form of civilization that has been instrumentalized in the West, the executive rich of Calcutta are to be found casting themselves as carefully as they can in the same mould. The home revolves around the drawing room and if there is a concession to Mother India it is not very often taken farther than the food or the row of dolls or masks or brightly-painted clay animals or other native craft symbols ranged along the mantelpiece or upon the shelf over the pelmet. There will be a radiogram, possibly a tape recorder, and even here there will be a refrigerator, for that is a symbol as well as an important piece of equipment. There will be a bottle or two of whisky, for that lubricates business friendships as splendidly in Calcutta as it does in Cape Cod. The adolescent and mature women of the household will wear the sari or other forms of Indian dress, for nothing the West has yet devised is more graceful or engaging than such local garments; but the men, the boys and the little girls will have imported clothes in their wardrobes and little else. The children will be encouraged to call their parents Daddy and Mummy with, as nearly as they can manage it, both the accents and the sentiments of Surbiton. Daddy will play golf if he can pass muster with the very particular member-ship committee of exclusive Tollygunge, and both he and Mummy will go to regular parties at which the pattern is in-variably one of ball-room dancing with dinner following around midnight, because the Indian habit is to go home after you have dined with your host; which may or may not be one reason why the executives of Calcutta, faithfully following the precedents of the West, are notoriously subject to chronic gastric troubles. The dancing will be strictly 'ball-room', with nothing nearly as vulgar as the Twist or its subsequent variations. The music will come off the radiogram and its general tempo is suggested by the list of best-selling long-playing records issued by the Gramo-phone Company of India Ltd (part of the EMI empire) for 1969; which included, among the top eight discs, Nat King Cole, Danny Kaye, Mantovani, Joe Loss, Enoch Light, The Ventures, The Seekers and 'All Star Discotheque Dance Album'.

This is a confused culture, then. It can have an executive arriving in the office at the start of Durga Puja, which is Bengal's major Hindu festival, and greeting his staff with 'Happy Puja' – which precisely identifies the man for the hybrid he is. For al-though he himself will be nominally Hindu, he will have been curiously claimed by his position, his wealth and his ambitions, for a variety of Christian British rituals. There will be no great family reunions at Christmas or New Year because, more likely than not, sisters and brothers will still be firmly settled in Hindu traditions, but there will be heavy drinking and there will be all-night parties; it is even known for a family like this to consume hot-cross buns for breakfast on Good Friday. An advertisement recently offering refrigerators for sale, did so with the picture of a lady in a sari regarding the latest model, under the inviting heading 'Wilt thou take this Leonard . . .' And just as the relation-ships between parents and children, generally prized in India as in few Western societies, can be seen crumbling under the pres-sures of extreme poverty in the bustees, so they can be noticed splintering under the blandishments of wealth and alien custom in the executive suburbs. The children tend to be left with grandparents when there is a foreign business trip to be awarded

and increasingly when there are annual holidays to be taken up
in Kashmir or down at Gopalpur-on-sea.

At the apex of this society are the clubs of Calcutta. There are
two kinds of commercial traveller regularly making their way
into the city from some other part of India, or even farther
afield. One is the man in small business who is hoping to improve an uncertainly secure position by some careful barter
around the side streets of Dalhousie Square or along the calculating length of Brabourne Road. He will probably spend his
few days in town lodged in some entirely Indian hotel like the
Minerva, where foreigners are looked upon as curiosities, where
the rooms glare with neon strip-lights and the shutters are always firmly shut, where the bathrooms *en suite* are walled in
undecorated concrete, where food is taken in a slightly jazzy
restaurant next door, where the servants sleep on the staircase at
night because the hotel is home as well as work to them, and
where the lad who carried your bags briskly demands a second
rupee on top of the tip you have already given him. The traveller
lodging in such a place will probably be entertained one evening
by his most benevolent or most anxious contact to the high life
of the Blue Fox or some other resort in Park Street. He will
proceed no higher than this up the social scale of Calcutta.

But let some captain or rising subaltern of industry fly into
Dum Dum, and one of the first things he will pass after his
transit through the arrival lounge is a notice board with gilt
lettering upon a gravy-coloured varnish. This is a roll of the
eighteen clubs in Calcutta available to anyone who might be
welcome and at ease in White's or Boodle's or the Athenaeum or
some other equivalent in St James's, London. Here is the Auto-
mobile Association of Eastern India Club, the Ordnance Club,
the Calcutta South Club and others of a second rank. Above
them rise the Royal Calcutta Turf Club, the Bengal Club, the
Tollygunge Club and the Calcutta Club itself. The man who has
an entrée here would never dream of staying at a purely Indian
hotel, but will instead book himself into the Great Eastern Hotel
or the very Grand Hotel, whose clientele is cosmopolitan, whose
lobbies have their own shops, whose bedrooms are as ample and
highly equipped as almost anything that Europe and the

Americas have to offer, and whose commissionaires, rigged in turbans and cummerbunds like princes on one of the old durbar days, are employed to spend a proportion of their time shooing the beggars away from the immediate vicinity of the entrance; and, when they are not doing that, to open and shut the door before any guest can even contemplate the risk of fatiguing himself, while they offer him a smart salute and a great clumping together of heavily-booted heels in the process.

At the Tollygunge, which is said to be the most select of these establishments nowadays, they have acres of parkland, quite apart from other possessions up to and including stables, a golf course and a swimming pool, and here people can sit and toy with their drinks upon easy cane chairs beneath trees, while they perhaps imagine themselves on an uncommonly stifling day at home in or on a visit to the suburban woodlands of England; and half of them are probably quite unaware that in the lee of the wall that encircles this oasis, lies yet another of Calcutta's bustees. At the Royal Calcutta, apart from the usual club amenities, there is of course the racing, which can be observed from the grand enclosure for Rs 15 (please note that no cheques or IOUs can be accepted at the ticket boxes). At the Bengal Club, which was once the supreme unofficial headquarters of the Raj and which would never permit an Indian to pollute its membership, they sadly have had to auction their impressive Chowringhee frontage and retreat into reduced circumstances at the back. At the Calcutta Club they were always more civil to the natives of the country, and the main staircase is hung with the photographs of club presidents whose faces have from the start very carefully been alternately white and brown; and in this amiable atmosphere, two thousand gentlemen who have each subscribed Rs 1,500 to belong, can further enjoy the sensation that goes with the knowledge of four thousand other gentlemen anxiously waiting to get in.

There is a common form to all the clubs, whatever their distinctive caste marks might be. These are places where you can sit out on a lawn as trim and almost as close shaven as a bowling green while the rest of Calcutta, at the very worst, merely roars at you from somewhere beyond the high and mighty wall. You

can probably take your good lady along for a drink before dinner
and if the servants, who are uniformed in the same style ordained
for those commissionaires at the Grand and the Great Eastern,
do not attend to your needs smartly enough, you can punch the
highly-polished brass bell provided on each open-air table to
bring two or three of them scurrying at once. But in spite of
the heterosexual· lawns and lounges and dining rooms, the focal
point of all this clubmanship remains the purely masculine
smoking room and bar.

Here you may encounter the Maharajadhiraja of Burdwan,
spruced up in his brocade smoking jacket, or the vigorous Commissioner of Police, Mr Ranjit Gupta, who when not engaged in
his constabulary duties can be discovered playing polo or re-
viewing books for *The Statesman* or delivering witty lectures on
the Battle of the Jhelum, in which Alexander the Great is supposed to have crushed the Indian Prince Porus in 326 BC. Here
are doctors who, like the majority of men in their profession,
have at the earliest opportunity rushed out of the State medical
service, where the emoluments are so low that a teaching professor will collect no more than Rs 2,500 a month; they are said to
make quite Rs 20,000 a month in Calcutta out of private prac-
tices which exact Rs 128 (or about £7) for a house visit. Here
are barristers who, in this litiginous place, are reputed to amass
Rs 50,000 a month, which puts them more or less on the same
financial footing that Sir Elijah Impey and Thomas Farrer
enjoyed when they were here. Here are men who help to keep the
immaculately white premises of Hamilton's, the jewellers, in very
fine fettle in Old Court House Street, and whose weekly shopping generally includes its ration of St Emilion at the equivalent
of £10 a bottle and Dry Monopol at £14. There are gentlemen
around these mahogany tables who still seal their correspondence with red wax and who complain about their laundry bills,
which must indeed be taxing when a chap who wishes to clothe
himself in white drills and ducks all the time – as many in Calcutta do – reckons that he needs fourteen pairs of trousers and
shirts to keep himself going, with another ten of each in reserve,
just to be on the safe and presentable side. Then they poke each
other in the ribs, and take a rise out of old Shanti there, who is

keeping himself very much to himself because he either won or lost Rs 600 at gin rummy here last night.

There is another manner of clubman in Calcutta and he is the most judiciously rich fellow in the whole city. He has positively insisted on entertaining you in his house, which lies in one of the thoroughfares beyond Park Street. It has not been an excessively opulent home, judging by appearances, but it has been distinctly well-appointed, with a skinned tiger lounging over the back of the sofa, and a terrace beyond the dining room on which the family are wont to sit with their guests in the evening, while the fans whirl and click overhead and the crickets jingle in dozens among the bushes beneath, and the occasional cries of people in poverty are heard from the alleys beyond the trees. There have been subsequent visits, for it has been difficult to refuse such great warmth and hospitality pressing you almost daily to return. There has even been an excursion with your host's wife (tactfully chaperoned by your host's daughter) who has very badly wanted to show you the latest exhibition of the arts centre that she patronizes; and joy has completely though a little nervously been unconfined when on the threshold of the club premises Lady Mookerjee, the grand patroness of Calcutta's arts and crafts, has descended from her chauffeur-driven car and graciously exchanged pleasantries.

Your host, in these few days, has meanwhile been dragging the conversation over his whisky away from arts and crafts and people and his business and yours, and towards the verge of politics. On discovering that you are a moderately radical soul yourself he has confessed that, by Jove, he is of much the same mind. He has then told a quite remarkable story, in the circumstances of these surroundings. He has mentioned once before that he owns an hereditary piece of land and bungalow near a village several miles south of the city, which he and his family use for weekends and holidays. The story is that one weekend he went down and found that someone had daubed his gateposts with the hammer and sickle. Your host summoned the village headman and asked him, with great sternness, who had done this thing. On tracking the fellows down he put on a great display of anger until he had them trembling before him. And then (he begins to chuckle at this point) he pointed out to them that he was very angry indeed; but not because his gateposts had been daubed. His anger proceeded from the dishonour thus done to the hammer and sickle. He made them an offer on the spot and it was that if ever again they felt like proclaiming their politics on his premises, they should bring a proper flag, that he would then provide the rope and the flagpost to fly it from.

Your host has been watching you very carefully while he has been telling this tale and when you have smiled rather feebly he has let it be known that he has some contact with the Communist world in Calcutta. And indeed he has. Before you know where you are, he has taken you to meet the ancient Muzaffar Ahmad, one of the founding fathers of Indian Communism, by whom he has been received (somewhat distantly) as a kind of disciple. A few nights later he has taken you to a great rally on the Maidan, conducted by the Communist Party of India (Marxist), where all the party bosses have been speaking, led by the former Deputy Prime Minister of West Bengal and the most powerful Communist in India, Jyoti Basu. The highly disciplined young party militiamen on the makeshift gate have refused you both entrance, whereupon your host has written a note to Mr Basu and within minutes the pair of you have been escorted to a couple of the best seats beneath the platform. Your host has very kindly translated the speeches, when he has not been applauding them, for they have almost all been in Bengali. When the rally has finished, he has suggested a nightcap in his club, and just before he has driven you both into the car park he has asked that you will ... er ... of course ... er ... not mention where we have been in front of his other friends and colleagues upstairs. In that smokeroom, a little later, your host has been sitting in a circle of cronies, jesting about the richness of life in Calcutta, poking hearty fun at the card losers, complaining with the best of them about the local breakdown in law and order since these damned Communists were first allowed to get away with it. And no casual observer could possibly tell that he was not as distant from Jyoti Basu as the Maharajadhiraja of Burdwan himself.

That clubman is not by any means unique, and it would be

unreasonable to be too scornful of his running with both hare and hounds. A man born into the landed customs of Calcutta has been born into a tradition of cynical opportunism which has been more obvious here from the first foundation than in most places on earth. He is living in a city where the instincts for self-preservation have always been primitively uppermost in a majority of its people out of awful necessity; and where things have reached the stage that even the rich can no longer think themselves confidently insulated by their wealth from the possibility of catastrophe. They are beginning to betray themselves, as they have never been obliged to before in many generations, as creatures not substantially different, when it comes to the pinch, from impoverished peasants who abandon or sell their children in time of famine. A rich man called Roger Drake once established some such precedent in this city, even if it was not already to be found somewhere in the area before him. And a compatriot of his, much later, ran off another of his gaudy little verses, not entirely inconsequential, to fix Calcutta as he knew it eighty-odd years ago:

> Me the Sea-captains loved, the River built,
> Wealth sought and Kings adventured life to hold.
> Hail, England! I am Asia – Power on silt,
> Death in my hands, but Gold!

If Kipling had been composing today, he might just have sacrificed his scansion to turn his last line the other way round. For there is many a man in the city today, with gold in his hands and the worry of imminent doom twitching his nostrils.

5

MIGRANTS

THE best place to start sampling the cosmopolitan mixture of Calcutta without undue menace or harrassment, without too much risk of injury from traffic or population, is at a junction a few yards beyond the square containing the offices of *The Statesman* newspaper and the Calcutta Electric Supply Corporation. This is where Chowringhee begins straight ahead, where the Maidan starts to roll away to the right, where grey and vastly overloaded trams go lurching and clanging across your path from their Esplanade terminus at the top of the Maidan and down Dharamtala Street to the left. High up on the buildings nearby and just round the corner are the neon signs proclaiming Chanda Paints, Britannia Biscuits, Bush Transistors and Philips; and there is a cinema a few yards away called Paradise. Separating the square from this crossing is a comparatively low building, with many domes, all blindingly whitewashed. It is the Tipu Sultan Mosque in which, at any time of the day, you may see men sitting in meditation or bending themselves double upon mats in profound acknowledgment of Allah. Rickshaws and taxis are parked among rotting vegetation outside one of its entrances and its surrounding pavements are full of people hawking anything from haberdashery to tobacco. Its railings by your left shoulder have been decorated for twenty yards or more by a man who is selling calendars and posters. He has garish reproductions in colour of the current Indian film stars and he has calendars topped off by pop-art beauties of indeterminate status who are fluttering their eyelids and their elegant fingers at the passers-by. And, dangling from the railings of these Muslim premises, he has any number of intimidating representations of the Hindu's most powerful goddess, Kali.

When the policeman, standing on his little platform under his black umbrella in the middle of the crossroads, switches the

traffic in your favour and lets you plunge over to the arcades of
Chowringhee, you may easily lose your bearings for a moment.
For the next half mile or so you will be safe from the terrible
sun but you will have to brush and sidestep your way, it seems,
past half the people in India as well as a sprinkling from beyond. On the corner, a couple of Bengalis will be purchasing
from the cubby-hole tobacconist something wrapped up in a
green leaf which looks distinctly unsmokeable and is; for it is
pan, the all-India digestive, aperitif and snack, a pinch of
crushed araca nut and other spice to be chewed with betel for its
stinging bitterness and then spat out, leaving the lips, the gums
and the pavement an arterial bloody red. Two or three Chinese
will be jostling them as they stand; for the corner is congested
and the pavement just there is not wide, and there will be babus
moving in every direction with briefcases clasped beside their
large and swaggering bellies. You will fall into step behind a pair
of Sikhs who are holding hands or who, if they are not doing
that, are each for some unfathomably Sikh reason cradling their
testicles in one careful palm as though they were afraid these
might suddenly drop off and go rolling down Chowringhee.
There will be beggars, of course, for very soon the Grand Hotel
will appear and already a number of lobster-coloured Westerners
like yourself will be nervously making their way up from its
direction. Small boys will be trailing them like puppies, pros-
trate men will be imploring them from an emaciated inertia, and
a woman with a sleeping baby over her shoulder will be gliding
into their paths, one at a time, with her hand outstretched; she
has a ring through her nose, her ankle is tattooed, she is very dark
indeed and she may be a Birhor, one of the nomadic tribespeople of Bihar who live in huts made of leaves, who hunt
hares, monkeys and porcupines with bows and arrows, but who
occasionally find it necessary to exist in another kind of jungle
in Calcutta.

There will be many turbans along this arcaded pavement,
which is wide, because it was constructed chiefly for the passage and shelter of British masters in this country. There will be
turbans, there will be dhotis, there will be quite a lot of half
nakedness, there will be many men striding along in great white

flapping pyjamas. There will also be as many men neat and
dapper in Western shirt and slacks and they will line the pavement edge until the arcade runs out, with benches or just sacking
stacked with all manner of things they wish to sell. You can
buy a gaudy tie in this next few hundred yards without stepping
inside one of its many shops, or a ball-point pen complete with
refill, or a set of compasses and dividers and rulers for a school
desk, or a bucket and a basin for the kitchen; you can pick up
a universal spanner cheap, or a hammer and chisel, you can try
on a hat for size, or take a cotton frock home to your woman,
or collect a plastic aeroplane for a small boy who has toys. The
men offering you goods from their stalls will not lobby you as
persistently as the beggars, for beggars are mobile as a man with
possessions is not, but they will press themselves upon you as
you pass them by with cries that cajole, promise, harangue and
occasionally threaten implicit and awful deprivation if you do
not buy. Presently you will observe, in a little space between
these tradesmen, a man sitting at a desk with a typewriter on
top. It means that you are approaching the street leading
down to the Corporation offices, and you will see such men in
Calcutta in the vicinity of any place where typewritten applications, petitions or other documents may be required of people
who either don't have their own machines or perhaps can't even
write. They frequently sit in rows, they sometimes do not have
a desk, and there are usually two or three of them squatting and
bent more than double on the pavement outside Park Street Post
Office. Here, on Chowringhee, because prospective customers
will almost certainly be bound for the municipal offices, the
typist will knock off letters in Bengali script, but next to the
High Court you will find typewriters with Hindi characters, and
there is said to be a man in Burra Bazar whose machine will
type Urdu. And alongside the freelance typists there are generally freelance handwriters, carefully plying their pens while
ancient illiterates whisper messages in each scribe's ear.

The Grand is engorging a coachload of tourists, who are looking slightly flustered as they cross five yards of shaded but
nonetheless steamy arcade from one lot of air-conditioning to
another, while the durwans at the hotel door bristle and defy

the beggars to shuffle a barefoot step nearer. Across the road, under a tree on the edge of the Maidan, stands a holy sadhu in a dirty sheet, with mud smeared on his arms and the white mark of Vishnu painted on his forehead, leaning on his quarter staff with his begging bowl in one hand; he is staring at the new arrivals to the Grand, almost without blinking, and he is always in the same spot whenever you pass, never known to move from that place from one day and night to the next. And though you may become accustomed to his watchful presence after a while, you can never pass the front of the hotel without feeling that you are crossing some electronic beam which may suddenly open the ground beneath your feet and send you packing where the sadhu may think you properly belong. But always you proceed past Firpo's, where the very richest people eat, with another great husky fellow on the door, while the pavement tradesmen begin to thin out and the odd Brahmani bull occupies half the arcade so that it can munch and ruminate in the shade. It has probably salvaged a newly discarded coconut husk, green and still juicy, from the gutter where there is a long train of rotting brown ones. Adding to them at every street corner are men with piles of fresh coconuts, whose top they neatly open up with one chop of a machete so that some weary pedestrian can slake his thirst on the tepid and slightly sour water inside. Or the bull may have snatched a piece of sugar cane (and had his rump angrily belted for doing so) from the bundle beside a juice machine. There will be a couple of men doing business with this, one of them sitting on the ground stripping the canes while the other turns the handle of a great cast-iron wheel, like an old-fashioned mangle, which drives a collection of cumbersome cogs and crushers over each cane until the juice drips out into a tumbler, or into one of those tiny baked-clay cups which are to be used only once by devout Hindus and then cast away for the sake of cleanliness, to make even more refuse on the streets.

Just here, past the Westernized elegance of the Grand and Firpo's, you can see how fastidiously clean the people of Calcutta are, for hereabouts the broken standpipes reappear after an absence of several hundred yards since the crossroads on the threshold of Chowringhee. Round every one of them, from all ends of the city to the others, there are always people washing. There are women doing modest wonders to themselves beneath their solitary winding sheets, and there are men and boys clad only in skirts who are pouring and sloshing brown liquid over each other from brass bowls or simply cupped hands. They go on like this, from dawn to dusk, or they submerge themselves in the great tanks of water that are posted here and there around the city, or they rush down to the Hooghly if it is near at hand and splash about on the ghats. They are conceivably the cleanest people on earth in themselves and in their homes even if they may be the filthiest creatures in the world when it comes to public hygiene. And such is the incredible and endless public filth of Calcutta that even here, along elegant Chowringhee, the complex smells of the city, which are always based on some form of decay, steam into your nostrils until you can almost taste them; a compound of incense, and cooking spice, and industrial grime, and rotting vegetation, and gallons upon gallons of staling urine from both animal and human being. So accustomed to this impregnation do you become that after a while you even stop trying to distinguish one of the more agreeably tantalizing odours from its fellows, you forget to wonder whether the whiff that came at you from that alley belonged to turmeric or cumin, to marigolds or mogra. And you only wrinkle your nose from then on when you pass a particularly large and long dump of garbage on which, bereft as they almost entirely are of public lavatories, half a dozen men are at that very moment emptying their bowels or their bladders.

With the complex of smells you are also assailed by Calcutta's complex of noises. There are few places here where silence is kept even in the middle of the night for there is always, at the very least, someone crying for something. In the daytime the minimum you can expect to hear is a muted rumble if you stand in the middle of the Maidan, where there is nothing but two or three hundred people between you and the nearest road half a mile away. Stroll over here, to Chowringhee, and you can break the rumble down into its clamouring elements. Much of it is traffic-based, and if one sound rises above the threshing noise of engines it is the sound of Calcutta's taxi horns, which are very old-fashioned and mounted outside the driver's window as often as not, with a large black rubber bulb which he squeezes to produce a deep and bronchitic honk that would sound well from the belly of a sick cow. On the pavements there are other sounds. There are boys who want to polish your shoes and who, when they are not doing this, are banging their brushes on their boxes in order to attract a customer. There are disabled beggars who are banging their tins on the ground. Itinerant key-makers are scurrying along (curiously, they always seem to be in a hurry) with uncut keys, metal discs and various tools slung together on metal hoops which they shake at everyone as they go in a frenzied clash. Every ten yards or so, someone will be clearing his nose and throat and then spitting, in a cleansing operation which tears at the ears and nerves of more delicate acquaintances, which the refined may like to call hawking but which people from Lancashire have always identified more accurately, even in its gentler local form, as grolching. Usually within earshot there is the sound of some procession, religious or political. If it is the second, then cries of 'Zindabad' will be hurled into the air, which is the local vivat. If it is the first, then almost certainly it will be accompanied by a band and there will be drums plopping, pipes doodling and the clang of bells exactly like those that used to hang above the cow catchers of railway engines crossing the American prairies. But the most haunting sound in Calcutta, if it isn't that of the taxi horns, is the one that the rickshaw men make. Every one of them has a small brass bell, shaped like an infant's pram harness bell, which he fastens to his wrist or fingers with a length of cord. When he runs with a passenger swaying behind, it jingles like a sleigh bell. He also uses it when he is parked by a kerb and waiting for customers. He taps it on the metal of his shafts then, or against the nearest lamp post, to attract your attention, when it has a dull and hollow but almost anvil ring. And there is nothing more eerie or ominous than to go late at night down a street in Calcutta, where very poor people are settling to sleep almost under your feet and the scarcely less poor are standing in shadows, to walk from one inadequate pool of lamplight through a patch of darkness to the next pool of light, and to be pursued all the way by the wordless sound of one rickshaw bell after another being tapped out to mark your passage.

Above all, along Chowringhee during the day, if you have the ears to hear it, there is the sound of people speaking in polyglot tongues. At one end are those Bengalis taking pan and gossiping in their own language. At the other, where the arcade has finished and the Museum railings have begun, there is a very smart young Sikh who accosts you in English on behalf of some unmentioned cause or charity of his own, who pins to your chest a paper symbol with his very first movement in your direction, and who accuses you hotly of insulting the Indian flag if you try to step out of his way (which is almost impossible). In between these two extremes you hear people gossiping in Hindi, in Urdu, in Oriya, in Tamil, in Telegu or in half a dozen of the other languages that network the sub-continent. There may not be a man in the world who could understand what all of them are saying and to an average untutored Westerner it is merely a confusion of voices producing sentences which are quite indistinguishable, with the occasional English word or phrase popping out at right angles from a flow of completely foreign usage; for 'social security' and 'gramophone' and 'piano practice' and the like do not yet appear to have achieved translations. And somewhere along the arcade, between one group of gesticulating tradesmen and another, a fellow is briskly handing out leaflets which bear the indistinct photograph of a man wearing a stethoscope and which carry a message in three languages. 'Salutation,' says the English version, sandwiched between the Bengali and the Hindi scripts. 'Death is in weakness, life is strength Patients suffering from impotence in every state of weakness that is before urine or after, morbid discharge of semen nocturnal emission any kind of illness concerning urine and burning are treated medically with guarantee. Before marriage or after. Dr Dogra has passed from England, USA, UK England health home with good-reputation X Meet Dr Dogra once. Address: – Kalighat near Basusree cinema 121B Monohar Pukur Rd Cal–26 Beside Raj Hotel Consult, 8 a.m. to 1 p.m. evening – 4 p.m. to 9 p.m.' (*sic*)

There may not be another city containing such a hotchpotch

of people as this one, with so many crucial differences of sub-culture, of race, of religion, of caste and of language riddling them and holding them apart even when they are thrown most crushingly together. Ten years ago, Calcutta had reached the point at which, in the city proper, Bengali was the native tongue of only two thirds of its inhabitants; and in the metropolitan district of Greater Calcutta five years ago, something over half the work force was provided by people who had originated out-side either India's or Pakistan's slice of Bengal. The baffling com-plexities of these people is illustrated as well as may be by the fact that, twenty-odd years after a Partition which was supposed to divide the sub-continent into two distinctive states on a basis of mutually hostile religions, Calcutta was to be found with thirteen per cent of its population (close on a million people) still practising Muslims who mostly spoke neither Bengali nor Urdu but Hindi as a first choice. At the other end of the racial-religious scale, Calcutta contains enough Jews to support three synagogues and a variety of Christians ranging from its 700 or so Armenians to its handful of Catholics bearing names like DeSouza, Gonsalves and D'Rozario, who doubtless find them-selves dreaming from time to time of the days when, under King William's charter to the East India Company, English Protes-tant clergymen were required to learn Portuguese within twelve months of their arrival in the city.

You find people living in communal pockets in Calcutta, just as you find its varieties of trade concentrated in what must be uncomfortably competitive huddles. You find, for example, that almost all its native Christians (excluding the British, that is, who are still mere birds of passage) are congregated along a broad corridor of streets extending eastwards from the Maidan; and you find, if you turn left into Lower Circular Road at the bottom of Park Street, that the next three-quarters of a mile are occupied by men selling bits and pieces of motor-bikes, internal combustion engines, mudguards, axle grease, bicycle lamps and almost everything concerned with getting you or maintaining you awheel, with scarcely anything poked in between one of these stalls and the next, or overlooking the similar trade taking place on the pavement, except the occasional fly-blown butcher's shop. But to enjoy Calcutta's various propinquities at their most marvellously excessive, it is best to head half a mile North of the Maidan and the top of Chowringhee, and to start making your way up Lower Chitpore Road, which may not be immediately obvious to you, for it is known almost as frequently by the name Rabindra Sarani.

Calcutta's wide open spaces, actual and comparative, are now behind you and its centres of high finance, government and law are to be found somewhere to the left, one after the other, between Dalhousie Square and the river. Just here, where Bentinck Street becomes Lower Chitpore Road, is where Calcutta becomes desperately congested. Instantly, as the tramtracks curve from one into the other, you feel as if you have entered some deep canyon. This is an illusion, for the buildings on either side are no more than a couple of storeys high but they and their contents have simply spilled out onto the pavements beneath canvas and rattan awnings. And while each building and its frontage is a shop without windows it is also, as often as not, a fragment of cottage industry besides. A third of the city's work force is employed in this way. The building will contain two or three men somewhere in the back who are making the things displayed on the floors and the shelves of the front room and on the trestles thrusting out almost to the kerb; and one or maybe two brothers in commerce will sit cross-legged in the middle of the finished goods, hailing pedestrians to come and buy. There are sequences of these shops, sometimes lasting for a hundred yards or more before giving way to a fresh range of another commodity. You can thus work your way for a start through a stratification of footwear, picking and choosing velvet slippers with curling points and gold embroidery, or winkle-pickers in patent leather, or tanned hide sandals which look most becoming but which tend to have tacks that rise in the first half mile and blister you cruelly, or the local equivalent in plastic of Woolworth's flip-flops. Finish with the shoe shops and you can move to the shops which specialize in ribbons and buttons and the ones which sell nothing but handbags and gloves. Ahead is still the stretch which competes to offer you brassware and the length of road where the shops sell chunks of marble, with the patterns of

Carrara, Genoa and Purbeck on them, which mean that yet another old Nabob's palace has been demolished and scavenged for what its ruins are worth. And even after that there is the crossing with Mahatma Gandhi Road, where you can buy the best quality bhang and ganja in Calcutta; the first being the shredded and dried leaves of cannabis, the second being its flowering tops; ganja being for chewing when it isn't smoked in hookahs, bhang being for rubbing into fragments to spice drinks and confections on festival days when it isn't mixed with tobacco cigarettes for smoking on any day at all.

There is so much trade along this road that there is scarcely room for anything else, although, this being Calcutta, much else manages to squeeze in somewhere. Because the pavements are almost totally occupied by shopkeepers and their possessions, everyone has to walk on the roadway. Here, for a start, he is competing with trams going in two directions, with maybe three feet between them and the kerbs. There will be taxis crawling between the trams, driven almost invariably by Sikhs, who mysteriously gravitate towards the transport industry wherever they migrate; in Calcutta they usually have a friend sitting for company in the front seat, they generally know far less than any passenger which direction to take, and they proceed with much blowing of horns, with a mixture of alarming dash which quite naturally takes them onto the wrong side of the road to avoid a tram or a pothole, and great caution, which causes them to switch off the ignition when they are brought to the briefest halt, so as to save on petrol and to delay the moment when the engine will explode with too much heat. Barging between the trams and the taxis and cars are the bullock carts and the high-sided lorries, with 'Public Carrier' above the cab, usually manned by dark fellows from Bihar or Uttar Pradesh, who have slogged into the city centre each day from their colonies down near the docks in Kidderpore or among those high and bleak buildings with Communist devices daubed on their sides which you have noticed at Maniktala on your way in from the airport. Most of the coolies in towns are Biharis, too, though not many of them come along this stretch of Lower Chitpore Road, for they need a little space and free passage to do themselves and their loads justice, and

neither is available here. But watch a coolie striding along the
Red Road across the Maidan and the poetry of movement is at
once transformed to something more exciting than a cliché; for
his hips rotate and his muscles swivel in perfect co-ordination
down the length of a furrowed back and there is a great give in
his step and his shoulders every few paces, while his head levelly
bears a basket containing maybe half a hundredweight of vegetables; or he and three fellows move smoothly, without that
giving spring in their steps, balancing the corner of a plate-glass
sheet or a bedstead or a wardrobe, or almost anything at all.
Coolies may be scarce just here, then, but there is always a bhari
or two from Orissa to increase the traffic with their cans of water
slung from the ends of a pole across their shoulders which they
are selling to the shopkeepers and householders who are devoid of
taps; or if not bharis with their tin cans, then genuine old-
fashioned bheesties bearing goatskins, though in this case they
will be on their way to some thirsty Muslim, for no good Hindu
will drink anything that has been tainted by leather.

The start of Lower Chitpore Road conceals what is left of
Calcutta's old Chinatown. A generation or so ago the whole of
Bowbazar between here and Chittaranjan Avenue is said to have
echoed to the clop of wooden sandals and the ivory click of
mahjong pieces, to have been largely peopled by men and
women in blue boiler suits (which must have been uncommonly
stuffy) and to have boasted at least one opium den. Then the
Corporation in one of its rare spasms of development moved in
and began to pull much of the area down to make room for high
blocks of something or other. Not many high blocks have yet
gone up, but most of the Chinese have been dispersed around the
city, leaving a small colony who do not wear boiler suits very
often, who patronize their Nanking Restaurant for its Peking
duck and other homely dishes, and who worship at the Sea Ip
Temple in Chhatawallah Gully, with its collection of antique
Chinese weapons, its cooking, its chapel and its curved roofline
with two large porcelain fish standing on their tails on top. You
would never see this unless you knew where to look for it with
a steadfast sense of direction, so confusing and haphazard are
the side streets and offshoots everywhere in North Calcutta.

The Nakhoda Mosque is a different matter, for it dominates the main road the moment you walk into it, like a brick-red cliff pierced by Mogul galleries and topped by a thicket of minarets and a couple of copper-green domes. It is big enough to accommodate ten thousand at their prayers, and there are many times in the year when its courtyards, its marble hall and its balconies are full and overflowing. It is the centre of a Muslim community which contains its own infinite varieties and complicated patterns within the larger confusions of the city as a whole. Not all the Muslims live nearby. A number came as servants and hangers-on to the Nawab of Oudh when he took refuge here two centuries ago and they have remained stranded in their own enclave down South at Garden Reach. But just round the corner there are Muslim Gujeratis who do well for themselves in the textile trade and there are Muslim Tamils who make a living on the boats on the Hooghly; there are Muslim Kashmiris and Punjabis and Afghans as well. There are Muslims here from Indian places in between. They are sprawled across every possible area of Calcutta's working life. They are kharadi, or woodworkers, churihar, who make glass bangles, mirshikar, who trap and deal in birds, ghosis, who own those awful khatals in the bustees and make a decent packet out of the milk that flows from them. There are many hajjam among them, and every few yards you will see one squatting on the pavement while he delicately shaves his cross-legged customer's face. While the majority of all these people belong to the Sunni sect of Islam, there are others like the Shias, who look sidelong at the Sunnis because it was men of their blood who murdered the Prophet's Shia grandson in the seventh century AD, and others still, like the Lal Begi, who make particular devotion to a Turkish saint of enormous piety and long-blessed memory. It is, of course, exceedingly difficult to pick them out from any other group of non-Western people in the city; impossible, unless someone has told you what subtle sign-manuals to look for, like the red or black shirts worn by one or another sub-group of Muslims from Rajasthan.

The only time you can be quite sure you are watching Muslims and not Hindus or Christians (Sikhs being obvious, with their turbans, their beards and their bangles showing) is during one of their festivals. The most spectacular of these, in a part of the world where religious festivals are very spectacular indeed, is Muharram. Up in Murshidabad they go in for extravagant exhibitions of fire-walking and flagellation then. Credible friends who have seen this tell you that members of one Muslim sect will walk straight across pits of fiery coals so hot that onlookers find it difficult to sit within ten yards; that they will emerge not only with feet unblistered but with not so much as the hairs singed from their ankles. Later in the day, men will scourge themselves with small hooked knives on chairs till their backs are deeply scored with bloody wounds; but next morning no sign of this remains except a faint hairline scab such as a thorn scratch might have left after two or three days of healing. Yet if someone from another sect attempts either the firewalking or the flagellation, he is in just as much trouble as an Englishman might be, strengthened with nothing more faithful than his weakly bob in the direction of the Thirty-Nine Articles. In Calcutta there is no public firewalking or flagellation (though goodness knows what happens privately in obscure corners of this city) but there is much parading about the streets near the Nakhoda Mosque. The traffic comes to a halt on the climactic day of Muharram, locked solid for hours, while banners pass the end of the road with bands playing, and men dressed in all the panoply of Islam dance like dervishes with bloodthirsty cries as they sweep and swish the air around them with great curved and gleaming swords. Even if it means being jammed uncomfortably in a car till long past dinner time, by traffic so close and rigid that you can't open the doors to get out, it is worth sweating it out just for a craning peep at the Muharram parade; until a more than uncomfortable thought occurs and you wonder just what would happen if one of those whirling swords swept wider than usual and accidentally removed some bystanding Hindu ear.

All this is the packed and providential essence of Lower Chitpore Road. And the totally peculiar thing about Calcutta is that if you moved two hundred yards in almost any direction you could be at the edge of some social or religious or cultural condition which was basically alien in some important respect to

what is to be found here. Almost across the road from the Nakhoda Mosque, for example, is Armenian Street, which eventually
leads, after some long-distance contortions, to the Armenian
Church. One of the biggest middens in Calcutta is usually
dumped in the gutter beside its little lychgate, but if you pass
through that you are in one of the clearest and neatest open
spaces for the best part of a mile. The yard is paved with grave-
slabs and here, as well as the puzzle commemorating the Mrs
Sookias who was evidently dead and buried on this spot before
Calcutta was officially born, there is a tablet to poor Esahac
Abrahamian who died a hundred and seventy odd years ago
from wounds received after he had fought (and killed) a lion in
one of the gladiatorial contests that were sometimes surreptitiously laid on in the ruins of old Fort William. On a Sunday
morning you could mistake the congregation here for Anglo-
Indians, so sallow are their complexions, so very familiar are
those best Sunday suits and uncomfortably starched shirts the
men are wearing.

The church itself, with its thick and almost Norman piers
supporting faintly Mogul arcadings, and with its spotlessly
white walls, could quite easily have been transported from somewhere much farther West than its real point of origin in Persia,
though the solid cane-bottomed chairs rather give the game
away from the start. There is a black-bearded priest, much coped
and crowned, much attended by acolytes, much given to dis-
appearing in small procession behind the altar with gongs beating, incense drifting and candles guttering. There is a small
choir of boys in dapper grey suits and girls dressed like Bohe-
mian peasants in billowy white muslin frocks with red bodices
and red kerchiefs over their hair. They sing to the accompaniment of a lady in a smart pink two-piece suit, seated at a har-
monium in the corner, and their chants are skirling and
Slavonic. The people in the congregation cross themselves repeatedly and attend to their prayer-books, which are printed in
yet another of Calcutta's bewildering scripts. And when they
leave, scarcely one goes home to Armenian Street, for that is in
decaying North Calcutta. These are far from decaying people,
for they have come in cars and taxis and in these they disperse

across the middle and southern parts of the city. One of them gets into her waiting taxi and is carried with many a lurch and plenty of honks to the vicinity of Park Street, to the private hotel which her late husband bequeathed her, still named Killarney Lodge as he named it, still with a photograph of Balmoral Castle hanging outside one of its bedroom doors, precisely as he left it.

There is another people who once thrived round here and then moved off to better things, and they are the Marwaris. Their ancestral homeland lies at the other side of India, in the largely desert region of Rajasthan, which is so very arid that it is common to see nomadic shepherds mounted in long camel trains, driving huge mobs of sheep and goats in search of pastures as far away as the outskirts of Agra and even Delhi. Rajasthan before Independence was divided into several princely states based upon towns like Jodhpur, Jaipur, Bikaner and Udaipur, and the Marwaris were traditionally the moneylenders attendant upon these courts and their surrounding society; they were also very often Jains, a sect which began as a monastic organization that parted company from Hindu Brahminism at about the same time as Buddhism, to become another religious development. They are pious people, who support fourteen schools in Calcutta alone, simply to train a priestly caste of men to serve as domestic chaplains in the Marwari households of the city. A handful of Marwaris settled in Calcutta a century ago; between 1890 and 1920 they increased their numbers here by 400 per cent, and since then they have never ceased to flow eastwards into the city, to fasten on to its commerce and to manipulate and multiply its wealth. For a start, they colonized this part of the city as moneylenders and traders, but then they began to move into the property market and after that into the highest levels of industrial management and ownership. They were shrewd enough and had capital enough to buy up land adjacent to the new roads that were being cut by the Calcutta Improvement Trust after the First World War and they were sometimes caught out in something more than shrewdness.

Marwaris were discovered at the profitable end of the great ghee scandal in 1917. Ghee is clarified butter, a basis of cooking

in every solvent Hindu household and, being a by-product of the
sacred cow, a highly important element in religious practice and
diet. In 1917 rumours began to circulate that Calcutta had suddenly become a great market for adulterated ghee, which in this
land means something between a criminal act and a cultural
disaster. Marwaris by then had almost a monopoly of the ghee
trade and when samples were taken it was discovered that only
seven out of sixty-seven test cases contained pure ghee; one
sample consisted of only five per cent ghee, the rest of it being
some unmentionable and untouchable fat; another sample didn't
have a drop of ghee in it. In the scandalized uproar which followed, the local Brahmins summoned learned priests from
Benares to advise them what to do. After deliberating for a
couple of days, these sages reported that anyone in the city who
could possibly have been defiled by the adulterated ghee would
have to purify himself by the Hooghly in a ceremony lasting
four or five days, accompanied by scrupulous fasting. 'The result of this edict,' the observing Governor of Bengal, Lord
Ronaldshay, says, 'was electrifying. Three thousand Brahmins
gathered on the banks of the Hooghly forthwith ... by the
morning of 19 August there was a vast concourse of between
four and five thousand undergoing purification.' And the Marwari Association fined its shifty traders up to Rs 100,000 apiece.

That will be one reason why the Marwaris are at least suspected and more frequently detested by almost everyone else in
Calcutta, particularly by Bengalis. There are others. Suspicion
and distrust have only been increased by the perpetual refusal of
Marwaris to lend themselves to any cause other than those of
purely private and sectarian interest. They ostentatiously held
themselves aloof from the swadeshi movement at the time of
Curzon's partition, boycotted the local boycott, and continued
to trade in any commodity that might be profitable to them.
They offended Muslims by their deeply Jain distaste for the
slaughter of cows (curious in a people who were capable of
adulterating ghee) and were so surrounded by hostility in the
Burra Bazar part of the city, which they largely shared with the
Muslim community at the time, that by 1918 they were import-
ing armed guards from Rajasthan to defend their homes and their

warehouses; which only increased their offence. Yet their isolation was to become, ironically, even more profitable to them. For the British, struggling to contain local nationalism, were very ready to replace a stroppy Bengali who might be in some position of influence or substance with someone politically more reliable, whenever possible; and the most reliably apolitical Indians around Calcutta during the first three decades of the twentieth century were the Marwaris, even though they were carefully cultivating Mahatma Gandhi on the side from the moment it seeemed he might become a power in the land. So they prospered exceedingly in the last few years of the Raj.

When Independence came, and a lot of British investment was withdrawn, Marwari capital was swiftly popped into its place. When British managers decided, as they increasingly have decided over the past twenty years, that their current contract to work in Calcutta should be their last, Marwari managers have generally been found the most competent and the most accessible to take their jobs. And when British directors have bowed to the inevitable and relinquished their seats in the process of Indianization, almost always it has been a Marwari who has slipped into the boardroom behind them. An Indian has characterized them to an Englishman thus: 'They do not, as you do, think of an ever-expanding market: they mark off an area, turn their attention on it in detail, set out to pick the bones absolutely clean'; which is a habit psychologically formed perhaps by an ancestry in the desert, where vultures are known to do the same thing. In Calcutta today, you will not find many Marwaris living in the confounding congestion of Burra Bazar or the Lower Chitpore Road. They are domiciled much more comfortably, more frequently, in Old Ballygunge, beyond Park Street, and down in deepest Alipore; which are places where the masters of this city have always lodged for preference. Their most conspicuous success story is that of the Birlas. Their most glittering monument is the Jain Temple, a shrine of filigree delicacy and sherbet sweetness built by a jeweller, with mirror-glass mosaic smothering its interior, with precious metals and stones inlaid upon its principal deity, and with very fat goldfish waiting to be fed in its adjacent pond.

BENGALIS

ENCIRCLED by this maze of migrants are the Bengalis, the only natives of this strangely beloved Kalkatar. These are the Basus, the Boses, the Mitras, the Sens, the Duttas, the Chowdhurys, the Chakrabartys, the Roys, the Majumders, the Banerjees, the Chatterjees and the Mukherjees of the city; or variations of these names, for there are thirty-one ways of rendering Chakrabarty, ranging from Chackerbutty to Chuckervertty, and there are fourteen forms of Mukherjee, eleven of Banerjee, eight of Chatterjee. The Bengalis have distinctive personal habits, like a Bengali way of sitting, which consists of resting on your left hip and left hand with one leg drawn up, unlike a Bihari, who simply crosses his legs and sits on his heels. They have their own New Year's Day, which is 15 April, when their astrologers take counsel and advise that in 1377 (which is also 1970) life in Calcutta will be eventful and unpleasant because Saturn is in an unfavourable position. They have a Bengali way of declaiming, either in the theatre or in politics, a rhetorical style of pumping out words and phrases on a rising intonation to a final explosion, which mesmerizes in the theatre but which can make a Communist party meeting sound alarmingly like a Nuremburg rally. A more commonplace adaptation of the same trick has been beautifully described by a European who knows Bengalis better than most: 'Whenever we ran into an acquaintance – that's to say, every two hundreds yards or so – we would stop and my guide would launch into a long introduction: "This is Dr John Rosselli, he's half-Italian, he has a wife and two sons in England, he's from the University of Sussex, he teaches history, he's studying Bengali, he learnt it in London at the School of Oriental and African Studies, he eats sitting on the floor in the Bengali posture" (beaming smiles all round) "he eats with his right hand, and oh yes, he's eaten khichuri, and ilish mach – but of

course he has a bit of trouble with the bones – and he's had
paish" (a special sweet). "Ah, paish! Paish!" everyone would say.
It was like going about with one's own herald extraordinary.'

There are probably more generalizations made about the
Bengalis than about any other people in India. Some of them are
demonstrable, but some are so far-fetched that you wonder how
they could have originated. Considering the history of Bengal
over the past hundred years, it is impossible to believe the legend
of the Bengali as a gutless and pacific individual, an excellent
fellow for talking but no good at all for action. Yet in the nineteenth century a British ruler, Mountstuart Elphinstone, was
noting that while every Mahratta above the rank of messenger
invariably sat in his presence, in Bengal there was scarcely a
native allowed (or, by implication, daring) to; and in the twentieth century another representative of the Raj, Mr R. G. Casey,
was remarking that 'he is probably the cleverest and quickest of
Indians but ... practically no Bengalis serve in the fighting services'. At the beginning of the nineteenth century Charles
Stewart even ventured to suggest that 'should the English ever
be driven from all the other parts of India, they may find in
Bengal an asylum where no enemy will venture to follow them.
They are secure from a foreign invader, they are equally safe
from any insurrection of the natives, whose mildness of dis-
position and aversion to war are such that nothing short of the
most atrocious cruelty or of religious persecution could induce
them to draw swords against their present masters.' Which is
almost a comical misjudgement in view of all that was to follow.
It is said that the Bengalis of Calcutta are particularly soft-
spoken and courteous, though East Bengalis believe them to have
honey on their lips and poison in their hearts; and this may be
so, for we have the word of Bengal's most distinguished living
writer in English, Nirad C. Chaudhuri, for it. The most celebrated Bengali social scientist, N. K. Bose, has written that 'The
Bengalis seem to have a strong sense of local patriotism. The
range of their social combinations also appears to be small. Small
combinations take place easily among them for building up a
library, a club for physical culture, a sports or a social service
organization and the like ... A Bengali seems to feel happier in

the company of those with whom he closely agrees, rather than in the company of others with whom he may have points of difference. Unities are not stressed; differences are not easily tolerated.'

There is a rampant fiction that the Bengalis have never soiled their hands with trade and commerce, preferring to dwell loftily upon a plane which is intellectually and spiritually higher than anyone else's; it is usually repeated in Calcutta by someone who has just remarked caustically that Kalwars have cornered the local scrap-iron market. Yet when the Bengal Chamber of Commerce was founded in 1853, the good Bengali names of Gurucharam Sen, Harischandra Bose, Ramgopal Ghose, Rajendra Dutta, Kalidas Dutta and Shyamcharan Mitra were among those of the first members; the flourishing coal, shipping and banking combination of Carr, Tagore and Co. had belonged to the Calcutta Chamber which preceded it; and when India's first jute mill was started at Rishra in 1855, it was a joint effort by George Auckland and Shyamsundar Sen. In the days when East India Company writers depended upon Indian banians to find them house, horse and enough money to get along with, there were quite as many Bengalis as anyone else waiting by the wharves along the Hooghly when the latest boat came in, to secure their share of young Englishmen and offer them the benefits of their agency. It was in this fashion that the Tagore clan began their rise to remarkable power and prestige in the city and abroad. In the second half of the eighteenth century there were millionaire Bengali banians like Hidaram Banerjee and Monhur Mukherjee, while the Bengali merchant and shipowner, Ramdulal Dey, was eventually so rich that American traders used to borrow from him.

Where the Bengalis did not dirty their hands was when they were upper-caste landowners, refusing to till the soil in person. Unlike most men of their status and position throughout India, they maintained that manual labour was degrading. They had usually obtained their land after long service and good conduct as some kind of officer (a khan, maybe, or a chowdhury or a sarker or a mazumdar) working for the Mogul Emperor. One of the biggest such landowning families were the Subarna Roy Chowdhurys, the leaseholders who sold the first three villages of Calcutta to the Company for Rs 1,300 current coin of that time; it was they who in 1809 replaced the original temple at Kalighat with a new one and it was Subarna Roy Chowdhurys again who gave old Loll Diggy its name in Tank Square by pouring red dye into the water (and thus making it Lal Dighi) as an act of gracious patronage during the colourful Holi festivities. People such as this were the original bhadralok of Bengal, who became so respectably refined in the changing times of India, carefully avoiding the dialect and coarse speech of the lower castes while embracing eagerly the best of Western culture as it was made available to them, that they became even more alienated from their own people. They would boast, eventually, that their activities in the nineteenth century were as much as anything destroying the class structure of traditional Hindu society and they would then await the applause they felt this claim deserved. In fact, apart from making things hot for the British, they had merely achieved some demolition of the barriers separating the upper three castes of Bengal. By the time the British removed their capital from Calcutta to Delhi, it was not not only men of the ICS who regarded this Bengali *élite* as headmen in 'a despotism of caste, tempered by matriculation'. It was a Bengali periodical which wrote one day 'These irreligious, luxury-loving beggars are the creation of English education. The country and society have nothing to do with them. The mass do not know them, neither do they care for the mass. By virtue of their begging through the Congress they secure high posts, start subsidized papers and try to win fame and respect in the country.'

Education (and its by-products) has been prized in Bengal more obviously than in other parts of India. Calcutta University has recently been described as the world's largest degree-granting factory, which it probably is; at the same time it is almost certainly headquarters for the most aggressive student population on earth, and the principals of Berkeley, the Sorbonne or the London School of Economics, who doubtless feel they have a hard time from undergraduates these days, can count themselves lucky not to sit where a succession of Bengali Vice-Chancellors have been for the past few years. Yet the university symbolizes something more (and conceivably even more extensive) than revolutionary anger and mass-produced qualifications. If you go up College Street you find yourself in what might well be the biggest second-hand book market in the world. It is not just College Street itself which contains one shop after another full of literature, for perhaps half a mile, together with stalls full of books and pamphlets on the pavements over the same distance; the same goes for ten or a dozen streets round about. Much of it is printed in Bengali or other Indian scripts but, at the very least, half of this treasure comes in Western typefaces. Nor is it all by any means examination fodder. You can poke around many of these shops and find one genuine and purely pleasurable old edition after another; and the bookseller will be well content with your company and your chatter about books long after he has realized that this time he is not going to make a sale. He and his fellows are perhaps the only tradesmen in town who will leave you alone if that's how you prefer to be. They are part of a climate that is as inseparable from Calcutta as the monsoon.

There are far more poets in this city than there are novelists in Dublin, and a much bigger difference is that in Calcutta the writers have usually at least put pen to paper. You can see a lot of them every weekend on the Maidan, generally in groups of twenty or thirty, holding a Mukta Mela, which is a kind of cultural jamboree in which poets recite their verses to each other, composers sing the ballad they have just finished, artists discuss their most recent brushwork and lots of people simply roll up to listen, for the whole thing is entirely informal. On any night of the week there will be much music in the city; an East German ensemble sweating their way through Schubert in the Max Muller Bhavan for the wealthy, perhaps, but in many places there will be recitals on sitar and tabla, at which office clerks will sit rapt and intoxicated with understanding while someone thrillingly executes the major raga Jayjayanti (and if his thumri has some nice alamkarik combinations, so much the better). There will be extravagantly-staged Bengali theatre, depending upon symbolic gesture almost as much as Peking opera. There will be much cinema. This is the city of Satyajit Ray, after all, though it probably values him less than do Western connoisseurs and has lately taken to heaving bricks at his cameras whenever he tries to film on location in Calcutta; for there is much professional jealousy in the film world and here politics enter everything and Ray, like the Frenchman Louis Malle, has been unacceptably realistic in his artistic responses to Calcutta. Nevertheless, it esteems the cinema and produces much film, even though more often than not this provokes the local critics to begin their newspaper columns; 'So it goes on: one incompetent Bengali film after another that is neither minimal art nor more than minimal box office.' But creation is everything here.

This urge has produced more publishers in Calcutta, it is said, than in all the rest of India. They sometimes operate from small back rooms which probably accommodate half a dozen members of the family at a time, as well as the man of literature. And so great is the clamour of other men of literature to get their thoughts and observations into print, that such a publisher sometimes makes quite a modest living from launching books of 28 pages and 1,500 words (complete with source notes) on serious topics at two or three rupees per copy. No author of a thumping bestseller in the West ever put more of himself into these small classics. One of them begins with the dedication 'To the Memory of my Beloved Cousin Chirantan Bhattacharya, a Sergeant of Calcutta Police Knocked Down Dead by a Fleeing Lorry on 28 October 1965', and there is a verse to go with it. Then there is a foreword. Then comes a preface; 'In 1958, on request of my friend Sitangsu Chatterjee, I contributed a series of articles on DeRozio to the *Radical Humanist*. Since then many a friend of mine has been urging upon me to bring them out in the form of a booklet. I have been in search of a publisher for all these years and at last find him here . . . My publisher looked through the manuscript by chance and practically snatched it away from me for publication. Words can hardly express my gratitude to him.' Then comes the book proper.

This great local pressure to execute and create for yourself, in whatever way you can, perhaps accounts for the fact that even the very best artists in Calcutta, like Jamini Roy with his delicate linear paintings, and Meera Mukherjee with her metal sculpture rooted in ancient traditions which she is gradually restoring to her people, find it difficult to sell their works in a place which is not always stuck – even inside the plaintive Bengali community – for the odd rupee; that and the fact that most of the rich in Calcutta do not often wish to know about Bengali culture. Yet the Bengalis are so proud of this side of themselves that they will quite solemnly assure you, and believe it to be true, that one of their scholars had translated Moliere into their tongue before ever the English heard him in theirs. Nor do they fail to point out that the three Nobel prizes so far associated with India were each awarded for work done in Calcutta. The most cherished, naturally, is the one Rabindranath Tagore won for his verse epic *Gitanjali* in 1913, for that was Bengali through and through. But the city's first honour from the Nobel committee came with Sir Ronald Ross's medical prize in 1902 for making that break-through in malaria, up at the Presidency Hospital with his servant Mahomed Bux. And though C. V. Raman was a Madrassi, he collected the physics prize in 1930 for discovering some important thing about the diffusion of light while he was occupying a professorial chair at the university here. These are scarcely coincidences. Calcutta has always been better provided with intellectual facilities than anywhere else in the country. Above all, it has evolved an atmosphere for perpetual cerebration, even if much of its thinking has often been wildly and extravagantly impractical.

It has been persuasively argued that the Mutiny failed in Bengal as it did nowhere else in Northern India because not only had local nationalism (which has frequently taken precedence here over Indian nationalism) not at that stage focussed on a political objective, but because the natural leadership in Bengal was obsessed with acquiring whatever advantages the British could give them; that whereas in Delhi people thought of expelling the foreigner and establishing Indian government, in Calcutta the educated were content with assuming equality and sharing in administration. One Bengali poet, Iswarchandra Gupta, even went so far as to celebrate in verse the victory and the retribution of the British when they recaptured Cawnpore from the mutineers. The tide turned against the British in Bengal very largely because of the appalling behaviour of these badly-frightened foreigners in Calcutta and elsewhere after 1857;

and because the education which the Bengali *élite* acquired and sought from their Western teachers was bound to promote a fervent desire for freedom, being based as it was precisely on those values. The first effective thing the educational apparatus of nineteenth century Calcutta did for the Hindu Bengalis (from whom the bhadralok exclusively came) was to draw them far ahead of the Bengali Muslims in power and influence. The Muslims, having been dethroned in India by Westerners, were not inclined to embrace Western values until their pride had started to heal again by the beginning of the twentieth century. Significantly, of 2,738 college students in Bengal in 1881–2, only 106 were Muslims; only 8·7 per cent of the 44,000 high school students were Muslims in that year; while in 1871, the Bengal Government service was officered by 60 per cent Europeans, 30 per cent Hindus and only 4·5 per cent Muslims.

The Bengali's pantheon, therefore, is stocked with Hindu figures who were invariably Westernized to some degree, who were usually wealthy or landed or both (these being caste marks of the bhadralok), who spoke passionately of freedom from the beginning, who did not at first speak against the British with great hostility, but who progressively can be seen in more rebellious attitudes until they are out for downright revolution against the Raj. Education was not totally monopolized by the bhadralok; there was, for example, the low-caste blacksmith Panchanan who was employed by the printer Ward at Serampore, where he became skilled in making typefaces, though not as skilled as his son-in-law, who eventually cut type for fifteen oriental languages, including a Chinese fount with 43,000 characters in it; and there was Ram Camul Sen, a village boy who became a clerk's assistant in the Magistrate's Court and then rose on his native brightness and his friendship with Horace Wilson to a managing post in the Hindoostanee Press and a fortune of Rs 1 million. But the prototype godling of Bengalis remains Rammohan Roy, who came from a bankrupt zamindari past, who made his own fortune, who unfashionably denounced suttee, who was so enamoured of freedom-fighters that he broke his leg while rushing up on deck to catch his first sight of a French tricolour in Capetown Harbour when he was sailing to England in 1830, and who

– Hindu that he was of sorts – was eventually buried amidst Graeco-Doric monuments at the Arnos Vale cemetery in Bristol.

Not many of these men were as besottedly Anglicized as the poet and playwright Michael Madhusudan Datta, a quaint and overwrought figure who crammed most of his output into a couple of years towards the end of the Young Bengal period and the start of the real renaissance. He based most of his work on Hindu mythology, though he became a Christian at one stage and he composed both in Bengali and in English. But while he used his native traditions he gloried in something more distant. He would claim that two thirds of his work derived from Greek artistic inspirations; he hailed Milton as divine and he once wrote to a friend; 'Here you are, old boy, a Tragedy, a volume of Odes, and one half of a real Epic poem! ... If I deserve credit for nothing else, you must allow that I am, at least, an industrious dog ...' Today, in Calcutta, where men of letters and culture talk, they still refer to him as 'Michael'; or, rather more often, as 'poor Michael'. But they give Keshub Chandra Sen his full name, for he still demands a very full respect. He went to England, like many other Bengalis of that age, and there he told them that 'You cannot hold India for the interest of Manchester, nor for the welfare of any other community here ... If England seeks to crush down two hundred millions of people in this glorious country, to destroy their nationality, to extinguish the fire of noble antiquity and the thrill of ancient patriotism and if England's object of governing the people of India is simply to make money, then I say, perish British Rule this moment.' That was in 1870, and the English were so impressed by his style and competence if not by his sentiments, that they devised a small test for Keshub Chandra Sen one day, requiring him without any warning to lecture to them upon the subject of 'O'; which he promptly did for the following hour.

They were much more frosty when they received Surendranath Banerjea, though he had not by then had his series of clashes with Lord Curzon over the administration of Calcutta Corporation. Banerjea was the son of a doctor, a westernized Calcutta Brahmin, and he obtained most of his education at Doveton College among boys who were mostly British or Anglo-Indian.

1 Calcutta 1971 – A crossing along Chowringhee, always congested and always with an armed guard for the policeman on point duty; for this is a perpetually violent city.

2 (above) Two of the most impressive monuments to British rule. Lord Curzon was responsible for building the domed Victoria Memorial. An officer of the Bengal Engineers copied the Bell Harry Tower of Canterbury Cathedral when he designed St Paul's Cathedral (in the foreground).

Two men who have
helped to make
Calcutta what it is.

3 (left) Rabindranath
Tagore, Nobel
Prizewinner and most
glittering member of a
highly talented and
influential Bengali
family.

4 (below left) Jyoti
Basu, leader of the
CPI(M), and the most
powerful communist
in India.

7 (above) Visiting wealth is likely to spend the night in the Great Eastern Hotel. On the pavement outside, a handful of the thousands who have to make do with something less comfortable.

5 (top left) The lawn – and patient service – at the Tollygunge Club. A focal point of the enormous wealth that has been accumulated in Calcutta.

6 (below left) Ochterlony Monument on the edge of the Maidan; focal point of political rallies.

8 (above) A slum of makeshift shanties by a suburban railway line. A commonplace of Calcutta today. Some of the one million refugees who have come to the city from East Pakistan since 1947 have been living in conditions like these ever since.

9 (top right) Poverty does not necessarily mean filth. Wherever you go in the city you see people washing all day long – as often as not at broken stand pipes in the gutters.

10 (below right) Park Street Cemetery, the ultimate mausoleum to the Raj. Thackeray's father is buried here, along with Walter Bagehot's father-in-law, Fanny Burney's half-brother, a son of Charles Dickens, and scores of other Empire builders.

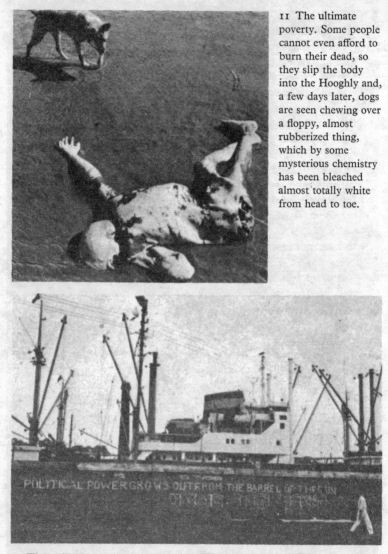

11 The ultimate poverty. Some people cannot even afford to burn their dead, so they slip the body into the Hooghly and, a few days later, dogs are seen chewing over a floppy, almost rubberized thing, which by some mysterious chemistry has been bleached almost totally white from head to toe.

POLITICAL POWER GROWS OUT FROM THE BARREL OF THE GUN

12 The voice – and the mood – of Calcutta in 1971. From one end of the city to the other walls are now covered with slogans like these.

He took a degree and then he went to London to sit for the racially exclusive ICS examination, which only one Indian before him had managed to pass; he was successful, together with two other Bengalis and a lad from Bombay, but at once Banerjea and another candidate were disqualified for having (inadvertently, it seems) falsified their ages by nine months. He challenged the decision at the Queen's Bench and was successful. Three years later, the ICS sacked him for an error which would have earned an Englishman nothing more than a reprimand. Banerjea returned to England to get this decision reversed, was unsuccessful this time, and was turned down when he tried to make a fresh career at the Bar, because he was a dismissed Government employee. 'I felt,' he wrote later, 'that I had suffered because I was an Indian, a member of a community that lay disorganized, had no public opinion, and no voice in the counsels of their Government. The personal wrong done to me was an illustration of the helpless impotency of our people.' He was given a chair in English literature at a Calcutta college run by Indians and from it he began to run his campaign of Indian nationalism. He founded the bhadralok Indian Association (which counterweighted the landholders' British Indian Association) and he made much of his propaganda through the columns of the *Bengalee*, of which he was editor. He was bitter in his hostility to Curzon, both over the Viceroy's gerrymandering of the Corporation and his crass stupidity and Imperialism over Partition. But he was never an extremist, though extremists were on the way in Bengal, and he was partly responsible for loosing them. He is to be remembered typically, perhaps, for his warm response at that meeting in College Square after George V had revoked Partition. And for something Lord Minto wrote a little later: 'It was simply marvellous,' to Curzon's successor, 'with the troubles and anxieties of a few months ago still fresh in one's memory, to see the "King of Bengal" sitting on my sofa with his Mohammedan opponents, asking for my assistance to moderate the evil passions of the Bengali . . .' Another British ruler was to say of Banerjea even later; 'I have a soft corner in my heart for Surendranath; we have done him a grievous wrong but he bears no malice.'

No Englishman could possibly have made such an assessment of Subhas Chandra Bose, who became Netaji, revered leader, to many Indians and a rival in their affections to Gandhi himself. Bose was born into a Bengali family living in Orissa in 1897, his father a lawyer and a member of the Bengal Legislative Council. He had been educated by Baptists before he started to read philosophy at the Presidency College in Calcutta, which expelled him for leading a communal assault on an English teacher in 1913. He was readmitted and he went on to Cambridge, where he was to write a letter home to say that 'what gives me the greatest joy is to watch the whiteskins serving me and cleaning my shoes'. He got into the ICS without difficulty but resigned within a year to join Gandhi's movement, now beginning to stir across India. To his disgust the Mahatma was talking some nonsense about non-violence and Bose began to drift off in the direction of Chitta Ranjan Das, who was a considerable Bengali poet, Calcutta's leading barrister, and a highly successful defender of nationalists in court. Das by this time had already worked his way through the foothills of Congress in company with such people as Banerjea and the English Indophile Annie Besant; he had claimed the leadership of the extremist faction which was opposing Banerjea and the moderates and he was about to leave Congress to start the new Swaraj Party which would head the fight against the British. He picked young Bose as chief of the pickets which were enforcing the boycott of British goods in Calcutta's shops; and when, in 1924, the Swarajists won control of Calcutta Corporation, Das became Mayor and Bose his first executive at a salary of £3,000 a year. Bose was still only twenty-seven and his personal mythology had scarcely begun to take shape.

He was arrested for suspected terrorism and, without being charged, he was sent down to the great concentration camp of a prison in Mandalay. Das died while Bose was there; his own health began to break, but when the British offered to release him if he would take refuge in Switzerland he replied that he was not a shopkeeper and he did not bargain. He watched Nehru become general secretary of Congress, which was yet another movement in the wrong direction, according to Bose. He is said, at this point, to have foresworn women and alcohol until India should be free, and it was a reputation that he was to maintain carefully but hypocritically until his death. The early thirties were now upon him, the years of civil disobedience on a massive scale in India, and Bose was in and out of prison several times. When not there he was either enjoying election as Mayor of Calcutta, making an uneasy peace with Gandhi, or travelling in Europe; and there he was always warmly welcomed by a motley collection of politicians, from Ribbentrop to Stafford Cripps, from Hitler to Clement Attlee, from Eamon de Valera to Eduard Benes. At home he was crowned with the Presidency of Congress in 1938, arrived at its annual assembly on a carriage drawn by fifty-one bullocks through fifty-one gates of honour, and almost at once began to find himself outmanoeuvred for the ultimate hallmark of Indian approval by the shrewd Gandhi, who preferred the more biddable Nehru as his first lieutenant.

When war broke out and India was bundled into it whether she liked it or not, Bose began to stump the land with speeches demanding the immediate transfer of government from the British. Not surprisingly, on 2 July 1940, he was arrested; the excuse being seditious talk at a demonstration he had organized in Calcutta for the removal of the memorial Lord Curzon had erected to the victims of the Black Hole. He was sent home after going on hunger strike for six days. Nine days before his trial was due to start, he fled from the city by car, disguised as a Muslim teacher. He wore other disguises before he reached the Italian Legation in Kabul; in Peshawar he posed as a Pathan, later he pretended to be a deaf mute; and he tried to find the Russian Embassy in the Afghan capital, for he was not particularly happy about the Nazis and their ally, only settling for the Italians after getting lost several times. The Italians, however, were most obliging and Bose, identified in his new Roman passport as Orlando Marrotta, got to the Russian frontier, took train to Moscow, and flew into Berlin on 28 March 1941.

For the next two years his life among the Germans was uneasy and uncertain. He immediately asked if he might broadcast anti-British propaganda, but Count Ciano, Mussolini's son-in-law and Italy's Foreign Minister, vetoed the idea; he already had

the Grand Mufti of Jerusalem and ex-King Amanullah of
Afghanistan making similar applications and could visualize a
number of wires getting badly crossed. Bose then asked that all
Indian troops taken prisoner by the Germans and Italians in
North Africa should be sent to him for brainwashing and even-
tual parachuting home along the North-West Frontier, to spread
disaffection among the population of British India. He was
allowed to brainwash them but Hitler forbade the parachuting
because he was by no means ready for an Indian revolt. So Bose
amused himself further by devising a flag for a potential Indian
Legion, a green, white and saffron tricolour, with a Bengal tiger
springing across it. He had a daughter by Emilie Schenkel, whom
he had first known in 1934, when she was his secretary at the Free
India Centre in Berlin, and to whom he was now married in
secret; for he had the appearances of a vow to keep up among the
other Indians in the city. And he constructed his post-war, post-
revolution aims for India. For a few years after the British had
been removed, there would have to be a dictatorship, for no
other form of government would be ruthlessly effective enough
in tackling India's chronic internal dissensions and factions. She
needed a Kemal Ataturk, and he would be Subhas Chandra Bose.

In February 1943, just as Bengal was beginning to starve
to death, Bose sailed out of Kiel in a U-boat and eventually
flew from Sumatra to Tokyo. The Japanese received him with
acclaim, particularly on their new territory of Singapore,
where Bose in July attended a series of public functions and
private consultations with the military; and such was the mark
he made there on his first visit that for several years after
the war the anniversary was commemorated as Netaji Week. He
accepted the Presidency of the Indian Independence League,
which had been founded in Japan between the wars, and with it
the allegiance of an Indian National Army which the Japanese
were forming from sympathetic Indian prisoners. In August,
Bose was in a position to offer 100,000 tons of rice to starving
Bengal, as a gift from his league. The British turned the offer
down. On 23 October 1943, his Provisional Indian Government
declared war on the Allies and within five months troops bearing
the banner of the springing tiger had crossed the Indian frontier

after battling their way through Burma. Neither Bose nor the 25,000 soldiers of the Indian National Army were to advance again. They were beaten back out of their homeland by Slim's Fourteenth Army. After the British victory and the Japanese defeat at Imphal, Indian troops serving the British discovered Indian troops serving Bose dead of starvation in the ruins of the garrison, though Bose by then was in Rangoon. Under the pressures of headlong retreat and one lost battle after another, troops of the INA and their Japanese brothers in arms began to quarrel. There were more and more desertions to the ranks of British India. The dream of a second Kemal Ataturk was destroyed and Subhas Chandra Bose was thinking of making his way to Russia when he took his last flight from Singapore to Tokyo. On 18 August 1945, his plane rolled down the runway on Formosa after refuelling there, was airborne for a few moments, then crashed into a hillside. A few hours later Netaji died very calmly, though he had been terribly burned.

There are many people in Calcutta today, many more right across India, who refuse to believe that Bose is dead; they say quite fiercely sometimes that the British imprisoned him, or that the Americans enslaved him, or else they suggest that he is safe in some good Communist land, waiting for the right moment to come and redeem them from a bondage that has puzzlingly continued even though Indians now govern themselves. In 1970, indeed, the Speaker of the Indian Parliament's Lower House presided over a meeting which demanded a judicial inquiry into the circumstances leading to the 'disappearance of Netaji'. In Calcutta they have renamed their most important commercial thoroughfare after him as well as erecting two statues to him. One is at the edge of the Maidan, near the Governor's Raj Bhavan, where Subhas Chandra Bose stands with his right arm raised in what could be a benediction upon the high-noon sun. And there, on his birthday, crowds come to place portraits of this hero against the high plinth, to garland him with flowers, to watch the guard of honour's horses nervously pawing the ground when the sirens begin to wail and the firecrackers start to burst at 12.15 p.m. precisely, the instant Netaji was born; and then the military band plays the old marching tunes of the Indian

National Army, and everyone goes home in quite high spirits.

There is only one name rivalling that of Netaji to produce a warm response from a Bengali, and that is Tagore. This is not a name so much as a dynasty and every element in the rise, the predominance, the lustre, the aspirations and the sad decline of both Calcutta and West Bengal is embodied in the fortunes of this astonishing family. It was a Tagore who moved over from Kalikata to Sutanuti to make way (with suitable compensation) for Clive's new Fort William after Plassey; it was a Tagore who contracted the first business partnership with a European, Mr Carr; it was a Tagore who became the first Indian to pass the ICS examination; it was a Tagore who composed the Indian national anthem as well as bringing the first Nobel prize to India as a native of the country. From the very start of Calcutta, a Tagore has been standing at least upstage but more frequently dead centre at every scene change of the whole, rambling epic performance. The most remarkable thing about the Tagores, considering their history, is that Bankim Chandra Chatterjee, and not one of them, composed 'Bande Mataram' (Hail to the Mother), which is Bengal's own particular and fervent regional anthem.

This has always been a family of colossal and shrewdly accumulated wealth. They were banians when the British arrived but they were soon very much more under the leadership of Dwarkanath Tagore, who was Rabindranath's grandfather. Dwarkanath acquired the makings of his fortune as zamindar and head dewan (chief native officer) of the East India Company's salt and opium department, but soon he was investing in industry with the advice of Lord William Bentinck himself. He became director of the Calcutta Steam Tug Association, which was so profitable that envious people labelled it The Thug. He bought up the *Bengal Herald*, the *India Gazette* and the defunct *John Bull*, which later became *The Englishman* and the voice of the Raj. He was Director of the Union Bank, he owned indigo factories, and when the Chowringhee Theatre was burned down, he snapped up the land for Rs 15,000 and began to make a profit on it. He launched the Landowners' Association in 1838, the year after he had neatly established his own position in life when he pressed the Government for the appointment of a Deputy Magistrate who 'should be taken from the respected class of people and not selected merely to increase the salary of those who are at present employed ...' His eldest son Debendranath was just as successful in keeping the family fortune well topped up, and so was every other commercial leader of the clan in generations to follow; the start of the twentieth century saw Surendranath Tagore helping to float the Cooperative Navigation Company with a capital of Rs 2·5 millions at the same time as he was secretary of Hindusthan Cooperative Insurance with a capital of Rs 10 millions.

The Tagores were vigorous Hindus with a reforming streak in everything they touched. Dwarkanath worked with Rammohan Roy for free trade and a free press, went to England, and returned with the Member of Parliament George Thompson to campaign for the spread of education in Bengal and more opportunities for Indians in Government service. Debendranath was almost a founding member of the reformist Hindu Brahmo Samaj and once despatched four Brahmins to Benares to inquire whether the Vedas were infallible. At the same time he spent a great deal of energy in fighting the missionary instincts of Christianity, starting the Hindu Charitable Institution, a free school for middle-class Hindu boys who would there be shielded from the influence of Serampore and its brothers in Christ. The Tagores wanted to see a reformed Hinduism, not one vitiated by outsiders or by apostates; Prassanakumar Tagore, lawyer and founding Fellow of Calcutta University, was one of the Hindu College directors who sacked young DeRozio from its teaching staff for his blasphemous ways; and Debendranath was so strict in his observances that he once forbade his cousin Jnanendramohan to address the Brahmo Samaj in English, just as he once refused to accept a letter from a son-in-law because it had been written in the same language. The movement of the Bengali bhadralok from ingratiation and willing acceptance of the British to suspicion and then hostility is clearly outlined in the history of the Tagores who, indeed, were generally to be found setting the bhadralok pace. In 1830 Prassanakumar was publicly forecasting a day fairly soon when distinctions between conquerors and conquered would disappear and Indians would be accepted as fellow subjects of the Crown. By 1867 Debendranath had started the Hindu Mela to encourage Bengali pride, fellow to the recently formed Society for the Promotion of National Feeling Among the Educated Natives of Bengal, both of which were anticipating the boycottery of the swadeshi movement by two or three decades.

With their wealth, their reforming zeal and their nationalism, the Tagores were also preposterously. accomplished as well as interested. Dwarkanath and Prassanakumar were among the first Indians to be admitted to the erudite Asiatic Society in 1829, nearly half a century after it was opened. Debendranath composed a Sanskrit grammar. His eldest son Dwijendranath was a mathematician, a philosopher, a writer in prose and poetry and a very decent flautist; he also invented Bengali shorthand. Dwijendranath's nephew Balendranath was the first recognized critic of Bengali art, but died young before he could fulfil even greater promise. This century has seen a Tagore painter, a Tagore Professor of Fine Arts at the university and a Tagore musicologist. All this, and Rabindranath Tagore as well.

When this greatest of the Tagores was born in 1861, Debendranath had already produced seven sons and the polymathic Dwijendranath was twenty-one years old. Within a dozen years the new boy was getting into the family stride for by then, it is said, he had translated the first scene from *Macbeth* for a teacher at the missionary St Xavier's college he was attending. Given Debrendranath's suspicion of proselytisers it is surprising that Tagore was ever allowed near these Jesuits, but he was soon withdrawn and placed in the hands of his brothers in that rigorous Bengali household up the Chitpore Road, where Western manners and speech were totally taboo. From them he learned most things, from music to wrestling, and started composing early in his teens; and he curiously imitated Chatterton by publishing a series of poems not under his own name, but as the Padavali of Bhanu Singha – a deception that was never recognized until Tagore himself acknowledged it much later in life. When he was seventeen he sailed for England with his second brother Satyendranath (the Tagore who broke the ICS examination barrier) and for the next eighteen months he attended lectures in English literature at London University, wrote a sentimental verse drama called 'The Broken Heart', and made friends with many English. When he got home he plunged into his literary profession by demolishing poor Michael Madhusudan Datta's major work in a critical essay; and then went on to write a series of considerable poems himself that marked him, among cultured Bengalis, as someone to watch.

He was in his early thirties when his father switched him onto another tack of the Tagores, by sending him to look after their estates at Silaida, many miles from Calcutta, near the River Padma; and there, when he wasn't settling tenant disputes and boating round the property, Tagore was editing a literary journal in an old indigo planter's hut. By the turn of the century, having added novels and plays to his music and his verse, being already loaded with honour and reputation in Bengal (though India as a whole waited for the world's acclaim before adding its own), he retreated to another family home in the country, which his father had built for religious meditation as much as anything.

Rabindranath was always torn between town and country; when he had established his own home, much less restrictive than his father's, he once wrote 'When in the village I become an Indian. The moment I go to Calcutta I become a European. Who knows which is my truer self?' At Santiniketan he now built a school which was to evolve into a university, as a protest against an education system which he feared and despised as yet another industrial manufacture alien to the Indian tradition and destructive of the human spirit; his students here were taught the brotherhood of man in the open air. And in the next few years he composed the series of songs published as the collection *Gitanjali*.

The Tagore political strain reclaimed him now. There had been a time in adolescence when he and his brother Jyotirindranath had belonged to a secret society vowed to destroy India's enemies by force, when sophisticated young Bengalis were full of Mazzini and talk of emulating the Italian Carbonari. But now politics were mature and very serious indeed; Lord Curzon was upon the land. Tagore became the high-priest of swadeshi, battling with the British in print and on platforms, ceremoniously tying the coloured rakhi cord round the wrists of all good men and true to emphasize their brotherhood, helping to run the shops that might break the thraldom of Manchester and Dundee. At the Calcutta Congress of 1911 (which Ramsay MacDonald would have presided over had his wife not just died) the delegates sang Tagore's specially-composed anthem 'Jana Gana Mana Adhinayaka' for the first time, as all Indians were to sing it on national occasions from 1947 onwards. This was, for him, a climactic moment in politics. By 1921 he had started to distrust, with bhadralok aloofness, Gandhi's cotton-spinning culture, and made a series of speeches in the city attacking the Mahatma's anti-intellectualism and narrowness of view. He had already told his good friend, the missionary C. F. Andrews, that 'Our present struggle to alienate our heart and mind from the West is an attempt at spiritual suicide', and he was not to take part in political life again, though he was writing with political awareness until he died in 1941.

Maybe the Nobel prize in 1913 had given Tagore pause to think. It could never have bought him, but it took him to Europe again to mix with a range of thinkers that he could not have encountered in person before. The King of England was to give him a knighthood and Calcutta University was to make him a doctor of literature, but the Nobel committee pushed him into the arms of Croce and Gide, Schweitzer and Russell and many minds like them. In spite of the apparently windy mysticism of the *Gitanjali* (for Tagore, it is said, comes very badly out of translation, and this work, in any case, was intended to be heard with music that few Westerners have ever appreciated) W. B. Yeats was quite overcome with emotion when he read the verses in front of their author at a gathering in Hampstead, and even Ezra Pound, who was also present, said he felt a barbarian before them. Tagore was embraced on all sides as some kind of Messiah from the East and, indeed, he somewhat looked the part for he was deeply bearded and he wore a form of long cassock when abroad; though at a dinner one night George Bernard Shaw, who did not venerate other people easily, inquired of his immediate neighbour whether this guest of honour was old Bluebeard, and wondered how many wives he had. When the triumphal tour was finished Tagore came home to make, a little later, the grandest gesture any man could manage. He returned his knighthood to the King Emperor's Viceroy with a contemptuous letter explaining that he could not tolerate such a bauble from a people who were now clamouring with sympathy and subscribing £26,000 for their poor General Dyer, who had just been removed from his command after massacring 379 Indians at the Jallianwalla Bagh in Amritsar. Then this most distinguished of all the Tagores decided, in his sixties, that he must learn the principles of painting; and proceeded over the next twenty years to produce some of the most celebrated art in modern India, vividly colourful compositions with a touch of Paul Klee about them. At bottom he remained what he had always been, what was equally a caste mark of the bhadralok as a whole, what is perhaps at the heart of a particularly Bengali dilemma. He was a man caught at a cultural crossroads, forswearing one minute what he took to be destructive elements from the West, and at the next, desperately afraid of alienation from them.

He is still a great weight in Calcutta. The Rabindra Bharati University there is dedicated entirely to expounding his philosophy of gentle humanism. Every night, some hall in the city is packed with middle-class people to whom his music means as much as Mozart's means to the citizens of Salzburg. Every day, the pilgrims dawdle round the rambling red brick house of Jorasanko, high up the Chitpore Road, to marvel at those late-flowering paintings, to peer at samples of the elongated English handwriting, to see one photograph after another of Tagore with Einstein, Tagore with Romain Rolland, Tagore with Gandhiji, Tagore with almost everyone who counted for anything in the universal world of culture in the first few decades of the twentieth century. This is part of their heritage and they cannot, will not, forget it. As for the Tagore heritage at large, there is plenty of that in Calcutta as well. There is a Tagore villa up the river, near the Dakhineswar temple, a cross between the Marble Palace and the Tollygunge Club, whose owner some time ago was reported to be thinking of filling the large ornamental pool with Hooghly mud so that he could start farming lobsters. Another Tagore residence has now left the family but it remains as one of

their most priceless monuments, a full-blooded piece of Scottish
Baronial complete with rounded turrets and castellated battlements, built by Jatindsamohan Tagore in 1896, just after he had
been knighted and had decided to exercise his ennobled right to
dwell in his own castle. There is a Tagore Chemical Works up at
Baranagar to maintain the family remnant in funds. There are
twenty-five Tagores listed in the telephone book. And, just to
show that the clan can keep pace with Calcutta wherever she
may go, there is a Tagore commanding a Communist party
which may only have a membership of one; and a Tagore who
not long ago contributed to the Sex Special of a local film magazine ('Boldest Attempt on the Subject Ever Made in India'). She
seems the first female Tagore to have been more than an appen-
dage to a husband.

The most inexplicable thing about the people who have produced the Tagores and so many other outstanding figures in
modern Indian history, is how on earth they could also have
been so outsmarted and outmanoeuvred so many times by so
many other people until they can, with some justification, claim
that they have been almost dispossessed in their own chief city.
For time and again outsiders have remarked on the brightness of
the Bengali; they have discovered that it can be highly unpleasant
to get in the way of his national and regional aspirations. The
Bengali is by no means lacking in self-confidence, he upholds a
perfectly handsome image of himself. Twice within the past few
years, social scientists have set out to discover just what the cosmopolitan peoples of Calcutta think of each other and a synopsis
of the two samples has come to some fascinating conclusions. The
Bengali, it seems, regards the Bihari above all else as shabby. He
looks down on the Assamese as provincial, the Oriya as cowardly
and backward, and the Muslim (for this is exclusively Hindu
sampling) as cruel and quarrelsome. The Marwari is business
minded, selfish, opportunist, greedy and narrowminded in that
order. The Nepali comes out very well as courageous and dutiful
and the South Indian is presentably gentle and progressive. The
Bengali sees himself more than anything as a gentle fellow but
after that he is a literary chap, he is hospitable, he is peace-loving
and he is patriotic.

Curiously, no one else regards him as any of these things. Canvass all the other sub-species of the race in Calcutta, and you find that they all think of the Bengali first and foremost as a man with an inbred craving for an office job, in administration if possible; after that they see him as cowardly, jealous, selfish and quarrelsome. It is widely rumoured that when a businessman in Bombay, Madras or Delhi is told by his employer that he and his family must spend their next few years at the Calcutta office, there are groans in the household at the news, not merely because Calcutta is physically a trying place to live in. It is mostly because they don't much want to get mixed up with the cocky Bengali on his home ground. If only they knew the agonies of this stereotype, as he sits among his friends in the Coffee House off Chittaranjan Avenue, with English phrases like 'political expediency' and 'revolutionary cadres' streaming out of his Bengali torrent across the grubby tables and the slopping tea-cups, while his city and its great nobility decays around him. Only just up the road is a passing but symbolic monument to this moment in Calcutta's history; the house of Keshub Chandra Sen, no less, dilapidated and nearly collapsed, with its frontage raddled by the tattered display of gaudy cinema advertisements.

PEOPLE, PEOPLE

THE time to enjoy the claustrophobic sensations of the most crowded place on earth is during a religious festival. On any day of the week you will encounter more people than you think you can possibly have met before if you go down to Kalighat. It is a hazardous business driving a car along the last few streets before you get there, for they are generally choked with pilgrims, with beggars, with sadhus and with people whose business is to attend to the dozens of slatternly hotels and restaurants that surround the shrine; for there is money attached to religion in India, just as these things go hand in hand anywhere else in the world. In Calcutta, not only are twenty-five new temples illicitly created each year to provide persons unknown with a substantial competence in beggary and alms (according to a Corporation which prefers to licence such places and collect a revenue itself) but at Kalighat there regularly appears a particularly awe-inspiring figure on the mercenary landscape; he puts the better-looking class of pilgrim into a trance under the guise of spiritual exercises, obtains their address and their keys while they are thus preoccupied, and rifles their premises while they are communing with the goddess.

The shrine itself is as intimidating as Kali. This is possibly the only Hindu temple in the city a non-Hindu would never dream of trying to enter. So you stand by the railings and watch the pilgrims climb the steps beneath the brightly painted eaves, brushing past the garlands of marigolds and the strings of tinkling bells as they go, bearing their small gifts of sweetmeats and spices upon fresh green leaves for Kali, gently encircled by the drifting smoke of incense. Then you observe the block in the courtyard, at which each day a goat or a sheep is beheaded in blood sacrifice; and you remember that just occasionally Kali still accepts a human sacrifice – fourteen throughout India since the beginning of 1967, that are officially recorded, though none of them, as it happens, was in West Bengal. So you turn away with a shiver and watch more pilgrims splashing merrily and ducking themselves with religious rhythm in the sand-coloured waters of Tolly's Nullah.

Something like that is going on all the time, at every temple across the city. And all the concentrated fervour, all the press of people, all the spectacular and colourful strangeness of it, all the beggary and the bickering that goes with worship, is magnified by many multitudes on a festival day. West Bengal is very strong on such occasions. There are twenty full public holidays here, ranging from Netaji's birthday in January to the annual closing of bank accounts at the end of December, and on top of them come days when employers must release religious minorities, like Christians and Buddhists, for ceremonies of their own. There are communal occasions like Holi, when people slosh coloured water over each other and hurl bags of coloured powder around the streets and Calcutta becomes very giddy with delight. There is a day when everyone takes time off to celebrate the birth of Guru Nanak, who founded the Sikhs. On Bengali New Year's Day, as many as possible make for the Dakhineswar temple, a rambling shrine set among palm trees by the riverside a mile or so above the Howrah Bridge; and there, businessmen and shop-keepers in particular take their new account books and their little images of Ganesh, who looks after their interests as well as those of writers. There are three days in January when pilgrims from all over India come into the city and sail by steamer for Sagar Island, a few miles beyond Kedgeree, where the Hooghly is fifteen miles wide and rushing into the sea; infants used to be thrown to sharks here, to propitiate the gods, but now there is mass bathing by up to half a million instead, and nothing more terrible than the occasional capsized boat and half a hundred drowned.

Yet none of these festivities compares to the four days each October of the Durga Puja. Durga is Kali's alter ego, a matri-archal figure rather than a terrible one. She had always been there, of course, lurking in the shadows behind the fearsome Kali, she had always been celebrated, but she was not invoked as the object of Bengal's most powerful cult until the composer of *Bande Mataram,* Bankim Chandra Chatterjee, represented her as the image of Motherland at the start of the twentieth century. At almost the same time the Swami Vivekenanda and his closest disciple, Sister Nivedita (who was Irish and known to her family as Margaret Noble), were urging Bengalis to consider the lessons of Kali in a contemporary setting; both were invoked for nationalism, but whereas Durga was for pure symbolism, Kali was for destruction. Kali is by no means a back-number in Calcutta now, but she has been far outstripped by Durga in popular esteem.

All year hundreds of men at Kumartuli have been preparing for Durga Puja in their sheds and workshops. Here, in a few streets alongside the river in North Calcutta, is the district of the idol-makers; there must be many thousands of images in preparation at any time, to Lakshmi, to Ganesh, to Kali and even (unless your eyes deceive you) just here and there among the more homely stuff, to Father Christmas. But by far the biggest quantity is always in the smiling image of Durga; no more than a bundle of straw tightly packed into shape to start with, but then with projections of lath and cane, and then with grey clay added and smoothed most delicately and thickly along the manifold arms and legs. The whole thing is painted in the brightest colours when finished and nothing exhibited at the Blackpool Illuminations or along Regent Street at Christmas was ever half as magnificent as some of Durga's images that come, larger than life could possibly be, from the ramshackle sheds of Kumartuli. People compete to produce the biggest and the most dazzling idol in their part of town, in their street, in their block of flats, so they do not flinch from the cost of bartering with the craftsmen.

As Puja approaches, the shopkeepers of Calcutta go dotty with offers of ten per cent discounts on all purchases, while some people prepare to leave town for a holiday. But most stay, while the Corporation workmen string fairy lights along the outlines of public buildings, illuminate a couple of trams, and make ready to put out the fires when people accidentally set their Durga stalls alight. For the next three days and nights people rush about in funny hats, inspect the Durgas one after another, listen to drummers thumping their way along the exhibits, spend a handful of paise to watch an indigent student sit in a whitewashed garage with twenty-five king cobras, pick each other's pockets, knock each other about when discovered, and generally fall around laughing. There are prizes for the committee which has produced the most sumptuous pandal, with Durga surrounded by other god-figures, perhaps, in which even her consort Siva is consigned to a secondary and admiring role. And while Puja is on, Calcutta will not seem such a desperate place after all, there will be renewal in the fairy-lit air, and the promise of hope and better things to come.

But on Dasami, the fourth day, something perfectly terrible happens. With evening well on its way, it seems as if the entire city has gone down to the river, standing so thickly along Strand Road and upon the ghats that anyone arriving just before dusk will be lucky to catch a glimpse of water. Lorries begin to appear, bringing Durgas from all parts of Calcutta, together with the people who have worked and saved to make their Puja as find and spectacular as the last. Each of these groups take their Durgas down to the water very gently and with reverence, bobbing her smiling face up and down on their shoulders as they go, making her marigold garlands swing and sway in the lamplight. They put her into the Hooghly and give her a push and soon the river is teeming with scores of gaudy goddesses, floating and foundering in the direction of the sea. Eventually the crowds turn away from the Hooghly and this time they are not so gay. The days of rejoicing are over for another year, leaving behind them images of perfection which have been cast away with the everlasting prodigality of India.

Yet however much is colossally wasted in this land, in this city in particular, it is always replenished. However many people die here, there are always many more to take their place. It is said that the very biggest crowd to assemble with a sense of purpose in Calcutta, did so in 1955 when the Russian leaders Bulganin and Khrushchev visited the city. Mr Nehru, the Prime Minister, (an uneasy man that day, for he had a political tightrope to walk between East and West, and Russian technicians in Delhi were coincidentally and ostentatiously offering to build

India a brace of coveted atomic reactors) said that he believed the meeting of welcome on the Maidan was the biggest ever held in the country. The newspapers talked of two million people, and it may have been so. Apart from congregating on the Maidan, they thickly lined a route from Dum Dum to the Raj Bhavan which had been decorated with twenty-four massive ceremonial arches, one every quarter of a mile. Lamp posts had been painted silver, and when the Russians finally reached the city centre they found that every Government building had been freshly colour washed, that the towering Ochterlony Monument had been festooned with lights. They very nearly didn't arrive because of the crowds. Their car was stopped several times after leaving the airport because people were pressing too close, and the enthusiasm was so great that at one stage there were fifteen extra and strictly unofficial passengers aboard. Finally, the long-suffering vehicle broke down under weight of numbers (as many a local bus has done since) and the Russians completed their triumphal entry into Calcutta quite hidden from view inside a police van. After they had taken pan from the Governor, after they had doffed their straw hats to the people once more, and after five hundred pigeons had been released across the Maidan, the rest of the day's programme had to be abandoned, simply because of Calcutta's impossible enthusiasm and its even more impossible numbers.

Its crowds can be much more alarming than that, even when they are infinitely smaller. These are the people who refined Gandhi's technique of passive resistance by numbers beyond a crafty weapon of offence into an instrument of wicked torture called the gherao. The gherao began as a form of industrial action when labour relations had become strained. It meant that if an employer refused to submit to the normal pressures of workmen for the improvement of their wages or conditions they would, quite literally, surround him. Whether he was in his office, walking down a corridor, crossing the factory yard or simply preparing to drive home in his car, a mass of men would appear and stand round him; they might or they might not jeer at him, but they would not touch him; the thing that mattered was that the employer could not budge without their permission or until police could be summoned to get him out of that intimidating mob. The gherao was so effective in obtaining results that it has been extended to cover every situation where one man can yield anything imaginably required of him by a number of men; teachers have been gheraoed by their students, tax collectors by their debtors, bus drivers by their passengers; even a judge has been gheraoed by witnesses at a judicial committee of inquiry. Men have collapsed half-dead from exhaustion and dehydration in Calcutta after being gheraoed in the blazing sun for the best part of a day by perpetually fresh mobs operating a shift system.

It is irrelevant for a brave Westerner to wonder why a man in such a predicament doesn't charge the mob and try to battle his way through them; the man knows perfectly well that they would beat him to death without hesitation with their fists if they had nothing else handy. The only thing you can do if you are ghera-oed is to sit tight with as much calmness as you can manage, and hope for the best. When a newspaper in this city reports that a car, a bus or a lorry knocked someone down in the street the day before, it frequently adds, without explanation, that the driver fled. Every reader in Calcutta knows that a driver in such a mess who doesn't fly, stands an excellent chance of being lynched on the spot. Tram-burning is almost a curricular activity among students in Calcutta; and the trams, like most other public-service vehicles, are increasingly provided with heavy wire mesh round the drivers' cab, to protect him from mob violence. People are quite often found decapitated round here, or stabbed or axed to death.

There are several reasons for the terrible violence of Calcutta. One is the anger of excessive poverty confronted by excessive wealth, and all the complex and sometimes cynical things that follow from it. Another has something to do with the fact that there are so many men without women in this city. Another has traditionally been a clash of religions. Another has come from frictions of cultures and sub-species of people. Even in 1857, Girish Chandra Ghosh was writing that 'Calcutta contains a fusion of races as antagonistic to each other as the tribes of American Indians'. There has been a much greater fusion since then; and much, much more violence. Apart from the violence offered the British in the cause of nationalism, which was considerable and which lasted almost until the Second World War, the most common cause of brutality and bloodshed in Calcutta during the first half of this century was the bitter communal differences between the Muslims and the Hindus. Curzon's partition had given the overwhelmingly Muslim population of East Bengal a sense of freedom they had not felt since the rise of the Hindu bhadralok, and they had deeply resented the Hindu agitation which had led to Partition being revoked. It was thus typical of local feeling that, when a festival procession passed a mosque during Durga Puja in 1924, the Hindus should clap their hands in a mixture of high spirits and provocation. The Muslims attacked the procession at once with ballast from the nearby railway line and six people were wounded, one of them fatally. That sort of thing became so commonplace that it was barely worth reporting. There were more serious communal riots in 1918 and 1926.

In 1926 there was tension on several fronts in Calcutta. There had been years of terrorism directed against the British and the British had reacted vigorously, which is to say brutally as often as not. They had also been playing off Muslim leaders against Hindu leaders, in their efforts to maintain a balance of power themselves. On the Hindu side, the bhadralok had almost totally lost the support of their own lower castes, who quite properly suspected them of self-interest; Chitta Ran jan Das, recently dead, had made notorious use of Calcutta Corporation as a patronage machine during his mayoralty. On the Muslim side, their leader, Sir Abdur Rahmin, had long since decided that Islam came before India and had just told the All-India Muslim League conference that the time had come for an organized fight for Muslim rights. Apart from a few Muslims in the Swaraj Party there were, by now no groups of Muslims and Hindus working together within the legislative body of Bengal. This was the climate when the Hindu Arya Samaj held its annual procession in North Calcutta on 2 April 1926. It was led by a band, it had the usual police escort and it had marched a couple of miles when it reached the Dinu Chamrawalla's mosque in time for azan, the Muslim call to prayer at four p.m. A Muslim ran out of the mosque and asked the band to stop playing till it was out of earshot. The inspector of police with the procession advised the Hindus to do as they were asked. One drummer alone kept up his beat. At once a crowd of worshippers rushed out of the building and began to pelt the procession with garbage. The procession began to hit back. Instantly, Hindus and Muslims from surrounding streets began to pour into the confusion and the fighting spread across that part of the city; mosques and temples alike were desecrated by mobs. For the next fortnight the riots continued throughout Calcutta, shops were looted, places of worship were burned down, fifty people were killed and seven hundred were injured. It took troops with armoured cars to stop the fighting, and even that was only a short relief. Three weeks later a drunken brawl in Central Calcutta started a fresh riot which lasted a fortnight, killing seventy and injuring four hundred. The most frightening thing about these collisions was the suspicion afterwards that they had been deliberately engineered by leaders on both sides. Almost from the start, leaflets had appeared on the streets, exhorting both Hindu and Muslim to combat. One said; 'Moslems Beware! Otherwise the Hindus will eat you up.' Another said 'Rise up, O Hindus! girding up your loins, and stand up steadfast on the arena of the fight. . . Let all the higher and lower castes unite and exhibit the glory of the Hindus.' Yet this, with the intermittent riots which followed during the rest of the year and the ones that occurred in the thirties, was merely a small rehearsal for the horror that came a couple of decades later.

At the turn of the century Muslims had outnumbered Hindus throughout Bengal by ten per cent, and they at least maintained the distance between them in the years ahead. They were always a minority in the towns, though; even in Dacca and Chittagong, in the middle of an enormously Muslim area, Hindus were able to outweigh them. By the end of the war the Muslims formed no more than twenty-three per cent of Calcutta's population, yet they had dominated the political affairs of the city and state for several years (as the Marwaris had started to dominate native commerce) under the patronage of the British, who found them slightly more reliable than the insubordinate Bengali Hindus. The first Muslim Vice-Chancellor of the University had been appointed in 1930 and Fazlul Huq had become the first Muslim mayor in 1935. Since 1927, moreover, successive ministries in Bengal had been headed by Muslims, dependent for existence upon the combined votes of Muslim and British members of the legislative body.

In April 1946, Mr H. S. Suhrawardy – the same Suhrawardy who had underplayed the seriousness of the Bengal famine in 1943 – formed a new Muslim League administration. By this time it was quite clear, though the intention had not yet been officially declared, that British rule had not much longer to go in India. The wrangle was now between Mr Nehru and Mr Jinnah about a division of the country into Hindustan and Pakistan when government was eventually relinquished by the Raj. Stoutly backing up Jinnah from Calcutta, Suhrawardy at once threatened to declare Bengal an independent state if the British eventually handed control of all India to the Hindu Congressmen in Delhi. 'We will see that no revenue is received by such central Government from Bengal,' he said, 'and consider ourselves as a separate state having no connection with the Centre.' July came, with Jinnah and Nehru locked in acrimony and Jinnah calling upon all Muslims to make Friday, 16 August, a Direct Action Day. In Calcutta, one strike after another marked the restlessness there and on 13 August Suhrawardy declared that Friday would be a public holiday; at which all Congressmen in the state assembly promptly walked out. One of Suhrawardy's ministers said the holiday had been declared because the provincial government feared there might be communal troubles that day. It is doubtful whether even he realized what his government had just deliberately let Calcutta in for. Even amidst the atrocious insincerities of local politics at the time, it is not conceivable that the Muslim League could have been prepared for anything on the scale of what followed.

In Bombay, that Thursday, the two national leaders met for over an hour, at the end of which Jinnah said, 'There will be no more meetings between me and Pandit Nehru.' In Calcutta, it was announced that bank employees would demonstrate on Saturday against a police lathi charge that had taken place during a bank strike the day before. Rita Hayworth was appearing in *Gilda* at the Tiger Cinema that week and on Friday the Elite was due to start showing *Intermezzo*, with Leslie Howard and Ingrid Bergman. Marie Desty, French dressmaker, was going to reopen her showroom and make the best of holidaymaking shoppers. The Calcutta Stock Exchange had just had a quiet day. On Friday morning the temperature was 88 degrees, the humidity was 91 per cent. And for the next few days, Calcutta became hell.

It began where trouble has almost always begun in this city, in North Calcutta, with stabbings and lootings and bombs of soda-water being thrown. Mobs made for wine shops and got drunk on the spot. Then they went in search of more plunder and both Hindu and Muslim shopkeepers were clubbed and stabbed to death trying to defend their property. Goods worth Rs 7 million were taken from a store in Dharamtala Street. All this was just a preamble. On Friday afternoon there was a mass meeting of Muslims at the foot of the Ochterlony Monument, part of the Direct Action Day strategy. They streamed in procession from every direction, and when their demonstration was over they streamed off again into streets where men were now rushing about with shouts of 'Jehad' (Holy War). An old man walking down a lane with a small bundle was tripped by one of a gang coming in the opposite direction; as he fell, the lot of them set upon him and beat him with lathis (which are staves of bamboo, usually iron-shod at the tips) until he was still; a moment or two later he stirred, whereupon one of the gang ran back and stabbed him until he would never move again. Four men walking down another street were attacked by another gang and, when they appeared senseless, they were picked up and hurled into an open sewer. A mob surrounded a bustee and, when some of the inhabitants rushed out, these were hacked to death with axes; the mob then set fire to the shanties, and the slum-dwellers who remained in their homes were burnt to death, until nothing of the bustee and its people was left but a pile of ashes.

A curfew was imposed on Friday night, but Calcutta had only just started to tear itself to pieces. At dawn on Saturday, the atrocities were still mounting. The 36 Down Parcel Express train was stopped just outside the city and looted, its crew butchered. Defenceless people were now sheltering together in the hope that this would make them more secure. The families of four houses gathered in one, when a crowd appeared bearing lathis, spears, axes and blazing torches. They battered the doors down and rushed in shouting 'Plunder and kill'. The families took refuge on the roof while the mob ransacked one room after another, taking away everything portable; then they set fire to the rest and one man survived the wreckage to tell what happened. In some parts of the city, where Hindus and Muslims lived close together, pacts were made to keep the peace and to protect each other from mobs. A Muslim family in a predominantly Hindu district on the banks of Tolly's Nullah were saved when a large crowd was marching upon their house; their neighbours hustled them into a boat and got them away down the canal. In a Muslim district, a Hindu family were about to be attacked with iron bars and daggers when three or four Muslim women rushed in, stood between the two groups, and warned the mob that it would be necessary to kill them first.

Just after noon on Saturday the police decided they could no longer contain the massacre and the military were at last called in to help; there had been one Indian, one Gurkha and four British Battalions in the city, together with a few tanks, when Friday began; a week later another battalion from each source had been summoned in reinforcement. For the city was now berserk and the garrison could not at once subdue the madness. By Sunday morning even the politicians were appalled at what they had started and local Muslim and Hindu leaders began peace talks; they proposed a joint procession the following day through Central Calcutta. Both Muslim League and Congress supplied sixty marchers bearing their party flags and white banners, and they met in Dharamtala Street while bystanders clapped and there were cries of 'Hindu Muslim ek ho' (Hindus and Muslims unite). Then the procession stopped, its leaders apparently uncertain which way to go next. Three men shouldered their way into the middle of the procession and hauled one of the marchers out to where five other men were standing. Together, the eight began to beat the marcher until he fell down, while the rest of the procession and the bystanders fled. The beaten man was left on the ground looking dead. One of the goondas suddenly turned round, ran back to him, and was seen to plunge a knife into the body three times. Then another goonda ran back and beat the corpse with a lathi. Not far away, a man who looked as though he had been thrown through a shop window was sitting on the pavement alongside the wreckage, his back streaming with blood, very carefully tying a triangle of broken glass into the cleft of a stick, to make a sort of axe.

The stench of rotting bodies now began to wrap itself around the city. A reporter who went out with a military detachment wrote that 'in an open plot of land surrounded by dwelling houses in Upper Chitpore Road, near Shampukur, about fifty bodies had been thrown haphazardly in two heaps and were being devoured by vultures. Adjoining them was an abandoned lorry containing about a score of corpses ... at the junction of Syed Ameer Ali Avenue and Circus Market Range, the former a main thoroughfare of Park Circus ... beside the burnt and looted remains of a two-storeyed house, lay the bodies of two men and a dog. Vultures had attacked the former, leaving the dog alone'. The British military commander, Brigadier J. D. C. Sixsmith, wanted to burn all corpses where they were found, to prevent the possibility of a cholera epidemic; he was firmly told that neither Hindu or Muslim religious susceptibilities would permit anything less than customary rites in every case.

Refugees were now streaming out of the city, through Howrah Station and by road; a week after the killings started, it was estimated that 110,000 had fled from Calcutta, that another 100,000 had been displaced within the city itself. And still the carnage continued when the ghastly weekend and the Monday of nominal bygones had passed. On Tuesday morning *The Statesman* struggled to find words that would say what had happened to this city, in a leading article: 'When we wrote two days ago, conditions in Calcutta were horrifying. They have passed beyond that since, whatever the appropriate adjective is ... the fire brigade reports four hundred calls and four fires to each call, with a thousand calls that can't be answered ... This is not a riot. It needs a word found in medieval history, a fury ...' A week later, a paragraph of bold type surrounded by heavy black lines on the paper's front page told almost all that it was necessary to add to that. 'Information would be welcome about

those Indian members of *The Statesman* staff in Calcutta who
have not been in the office since 16 August. Would those whom
recent events still preclude from returning to duty please send
news of themselves?'

By then the mobs were sated; temporarily. There were now
45,000 troops in the city and they had managed to impose a kind
of peace by 25 August. Frightened people were still forming
vigilante patrols in their streets at night, their women were still
keeping a lookout from the rooftops, with conch shells and
trumpets which they blew if they saw the slightest suspicion of
hostile movement below. Corpses were still being discovered
where men had been cut down and shoved into sewers. Sometimes people were found there alive. Akbar Ali Molla was
rescued almost dead from a sewer in Ballygunge nine days after
he had been flung into it, bleeding from a knife wound in the
side. As always in Calcutta, it was difficult to count the dead and
the injured. By 27 August 3,468 bodies had certainly been
accounted for, but it is likely that just as many had been thrown
into the Hooghly by their murderers, that they had vanished
beyond any identification. Maybe fifteen thousand had been
injured.

And it was still not over. There were several days without a
reported incident and on 2 September, the Stock Exchange
reopened. But on 6 September a series of stabbings killed three
and wounded a dozen. On 14 September, another eight people
were stabbed in North Calcutta. On 24 September, nine people
were killed and fifty-four were hurt in another riot. Twenty
more had died by the morning of 29 September, when the turf
correspondent of *The Statesman* wrote 'The present uneasiness in
Calcutta was reflected in the poor attendance on the opening day
of the Tollygunge Autumn Meeting. The racing was very enjoy-
able to some and those who lost heavily on such favourites as
Playtime, Sweetheart, Pladda Light and Gypsy Moon, will look
forward to better luck in the near future.' Every few days the
long casualty list was increased until the inevitable happened
and the Mahatma came to see if there was anything he could do
to staunch this apparently interminable flow of blood. He came
on a day at the end of October which had spent another fourteen

lives, and got off his train a few miles outside Howrah, so that he could avoid the vast crowds that were waiting to welcome him. At his prayer meeting that night he said that he had come with a blank mind to do God's will, that God would tell him what the next step should be. He met the Governor of Bengal, Sir Frederick Burrows, for a couple of hours and he had meetings with Mr Suhrawardy and other Indian leaders in the city. He was suffering from a bad cold and he spent most of the next few days nursing it. Then he left Calcutta for East Bengal, where peasants were now behaving with the savagery of the city.

For almost a year the small butchery of Calcutta continued. Occasionally a day or two would pass without a killing, then it would begin again, with two or three deaths on a Tuesday, followed by a dozen on a Wednesday, with another score on the Thursday, declining to eight on the Friday and peace again by Sunday, until two more men were stabbed to death on Wednesday . . . In Delhi, frightened politicians were now at least going through the motions of reconciliation, the British were announcing that they would be leaving Indians to their own devices within fifteen months, they were replacing their penultimate Viceroy with their last one and Lord Mountbatten was charming and pressing everyone in sight into a kind of civilized behaviour, but civil war was breaking out in the Punjab and Muhammad Ali Jinnah was getting his way, and the British were now deciding to shake the dust of this turbulent Empire from their feet by midnight on 14 August 1947. And Calcutta was still savaging itself.

On Saturday, 9 August, Gandhi returned to the city. He spent the whole of his first day there with the Indian ministers of Bengal and the British Governor. He told the people that night that he would gladly give his life if it would slake Calcutta's furious thirst for blood. He had intended going on to Noakhali in East Bengal, where things had been so bad on his last visit, but now he would stay for a little while here instead. He stayed the weekend at an ashram at Sodepore, a few miles outside the city, and on Sunday thousands of people made their way there to see him. On Monday he toured the worst of Calcutta in a car which he never left, while people came up and told him their troubles and the Mahatma quietly made notes. At one place so many thousands were pressed round the car, chanting 'Jai Hind' and 'Gandhiji-ki-Jai', that he plugged his ears with his fingers to shut out the noise. It was his day of silence. For Calcutta it was a day when nine people were murdered and fifty others were hurt. In one of the most devastated parts of the city, a patrol of British troops had been standing by; quietly, they slipped into position close to Gandhi's car and stayed with him for the rest of the day. Next morning it was announced that the Mahatma and Mr Suhrawardy were going to live in a bustee together, in one of the badly mutilated areas. 'Mr Gandhi,' wrote the reporter, 'said he had been warned that Mr Suhrawardy was not to be relied upon. The same thing was said about him also. He was described as the worst enemy of Islam. He was supposed to be a consummate hypocrite. God alone knew what was in men's hearts. He would trust Mr Suhrawardy as he expected to be trusted. Both would live under the same roof and have no secrets from each other.' The two didn't exactly live in a bustee. They took up quarters in a large house standing in its own grounds in Beliaghata, the property of a Muslim businessman. But it was surrounded by bustees, mostly inhabited by Hindus where they hadn't been abandoned in panic.

It was not entirely a popular move. As Gandhi's car swung into the grounds of the house that Wednesday afternoon a couple of hundred people at the gates were shouting 'Go back, Gandhi' and they carried it on for hours in the rain while the British picket stood watchfully by. The Mahatma abandoned his usual prayer meeting and asked a score of the loudest demonstrators to step inside to talk; in the middle of the conversation they got up and walked out, and the crowd outside started to throw stones at the doors and windows. Gandhi looked upset and began to write letters. By eight p.m., with the military picket still standing by for real trouble, the demonstration died down and the people went away. On Thursday there was no hostility at all near the house. Instead, thousands of pilgrims came, and most of them were women. India would be Independent at midnight and the city was suddenly transformed by the prospect. On Friday it was consumed by another kind of madness, in which 'almost unbelievable scenes of fraternity and rejoicing were witnessed in some of the hitherto worst-affected areas – particularly Chittaranjan Avenue, Lower Chitpore Road, Zakaria Street, Harrison Road, Bowbazar Street and Dharamtala Street'. People were now wandering these places with shouts of 'Hindu Muslim ek ho' and 'Jai Hind' and 'Inquilah Zindabad'. They were singing 'Bande Mataram'. Suddenly, they had stopped hurting each other. On Sunday, 75,000 of them were to march on Gandhi's prayer meeting to give thanks with him. But on Independence Day itself they left him rapt in a twenty-four fast at his spinning wheel and his prayers. Mr Suhrawardy fasted with him.

Calcutta began to enjoy a kind of freedom.

FADED GLORY

IT is quite impossible to forget or ignore Calcutta's imperial past, for the city has been pickled in its origins. The chances are, indeed, that the English-speaking visitor will bring with him one of the smaller but more enduring relics of the Raj. No better guide to India and the adjacent countries exists than Murray's Handbook, which was first published in 1859 and which still, in its twenty-first edition of more than a century later, insists on taking travellers back to the great old days, even though in the city now 'all the amenities of civilization such as air-conditioning are available'. Before ever it arrives at the hard stuff of the gazetteer, Murray is full of careful warnings that excessive bodily exertion and consequent fatigue should be avoided by all who are no longer young, and splendid reassurances that the stationmasters in this part of the world are generally civil and obliging. It has advice for the hardy: 'Those who intend to go into camp (as the British-Indian term runs) should be experienced, or have friends who will make arrangements for them . . .' It has tips for the discriminating collector: 'One must not forget the maxim *caveat emptor*, and realize that in bargaining the final figure will always leave the smaller dealer with a margin of profit, which may be considerable.' A man armed with his Murray is well equipped to take the imperial parts of Calcutta as they come.

They come from the moment his plane starts its approach to Dum Dum, with that first ridiculous glimpse of an English village church tower sticking up out of Bengal jungle. After that there is no getting away from the building styles of the British, with their own antecedents deeply embedded in everything from Greek Classical to French Gothic. On the way into the city from the airport you pass the factory of The India Hosiery Mills; the title is wrought upon the iron arch over the main gate, there is a gas lamp hanging from the centre of the curve, and if it were not for the crowd of Indians swirling past that gateway and along the high brick factory wall, the whole composition might just as well be in Rochdale, where the local guardians of industrial archaeology would be wondering already what their chances were of preserving it for posterity in the face of those dreadful modernizers. The industrial parts of Calcutta, indeed, are nothing more nor less than deliberate replicas, grimy red brick upon grimy red brick, of their old competitors in the North of England, and they could quite easily have figured in some of Doré's nineteenth century slumscapes if it were not for the people who go with them. There is even a thoroughfare in this city called Gas Street. Occasionally, these reproductions are so exact that they bring you to a halt with gaping astonishment. Just across the river at Shalimar, a road which has been lined with factories turns sharp right to avoid the goods shed of the South Eastern Railway. At once (give or take 50 degrees or so of heat) you are standing where this little cameo properly belongs – seven thousand miles away in the rundown Ardwick district of Manchester; for not only is that road bumpily surfaced with the same stone setts, but the lettering on the side of the goods shed has come from the same type-book and been cast in the same foundry moulds as the Manchester signs of the old London, Midland and Scottish Railway.

If you look along the outline of most street frontages in Calcutta, it is not at all unlike looking down the sides of Bruegel's Tower of Babel, such is the busy confusion of things one on top of the other – balconies, awnings, wires, washing, belvederes, stanchions, wooden blinds, indistinct projections and leaning people. But if you confront each building separately head-on, you often find yourself goggling at a perfect rhapsody of architecture. There will be a doorway set between Doric columns with 'AD 1879' carved into the pediment above. On either side of this, where there ought to be windows, there will be rooms open to the street instead, with trade going on inside; and pilasters will spring away above, to a wrought iron balcony on the first floor, which will be partly enclosed by Early English arcading and which will also be provided with wooden shutters that neither the early nor the late English ever needed in their climate. Above

this will come another storey, whose window openings have been
carved in a faintly Mogul style; and to top it all off there will be
a stone balustrade with Gothic ogees piercing it so that, from the
other side of the street, you can even see the hoofs of the large
stone horse that is galloping across the roof – or the hem of
Aphrodite's dress as she gracefully bends to pour the contents of
her urn on to the pavement far below. The consistent Classicism
of the Mullick's Marble Palace, and several of its rivals, is really
very unambitious when contrasted with a lot of what has been
built in Calcutta. There is a tall and narrow house on Strand
Bank Road, not far from the river, which rises through four
floors and four building styles that have originated in four separate countries. There is a small thesis to be written by somebody
on Calcutta's rooftop monuments alone; not only horses and
Aphrodites, but lions rampant, hawks stooping, and naked young
ladies reclining rather brazenly as well. These reach their full
height of imagination in the Bengal Baroque fantasy of Jhagra
Kothi in Armenian Street, a building erected for commerce at
the turn of the century which for some unrecorded reason started
a communal riot in the district; possibly because the Muslims in
the mosque opposite thought the architect was engaged in a
parody of their faith rather than their building styles, but conceivably because they found it too much of a good thing when
the collection of angels lining the roof was each provided with an
electric lamp sticking out of his halo.

The most impressive of the imperial remains are all to be
found within a mile or so of the Maidan, which is itself the most
splendid of the lot. Calcutta is not desperately short of public
parks, though most of them are tiny and overrun with garbage,
refugee families and a perpetual feeling of imminent invasion by
anything that cares to stake its claim. Alone, and quite remarkably when you consider what has become of this pullulating city,
the Maidan feels like a very wide open space; and, truly, it might
be a dangerous place for anyone with a touch of agoraphobia.
The Honourable Emily Eden likened it to Regent's Park in London, but it is twice as big as that and only half as exclusive. It is
two square miles of parkland, essentially, though it used to have
more trees until the cyclone of 1864 blew many of them away. It

is crossed by half a dozen thoroughfares and one of these, the Red Road, was laid down especially so that Viceroys and their Emperors could make a very imperial progress towards their Government House at the top. George V and his Queen were carried in state up here to pacify Calcutta after they had dropped that unforgiveable bombshell in 1911. Security ordained that the Maidan should stretch away green and empty on either side of the Red Road that day; and what with the royal carriages, the outriders, the Mogul triumphal arches put up for the occasion, the lining of the route by Highlanders standing at the present, with white pith helmets, red tunics, white blancoed gaiters up to their knees and tartan capes draped in regulation neatness over their left shoulders, it all looked like a cross between the first day at Ascot and the penultimate scene from *Gunga Din*.

The edges and the intersections of these roads were where the British put up the statues to their idols. George V himself was here in bronze and so were Lords Curzon, Kitchener, Roberts, Minto, Northbrook, Canning, and many of their peers who had known Calcutta well, together with men like Sir Robert Peel, whose relationship with the city was more elusive. Two or three were put down in the first few years of Independence because they were occupying sites of more obvious usefulness without them. But it was not until the middle of 1969 that the last sixteen were removed. A few were handled as the museum pieces they had become and were simply parked inside the boundary of the Victoria Memorial at the bottom of the Maidan; two or three were fondly procured by Canada, New Zealand and other parts of the old Empire where they still retain an affection for such things; the rest were unceremoniously dumped in a Corporation yard out at Barrackpore, leaving behind on the Maidan a series of stumpy plinths to keep company with Netaji Subhas Chandra Bose at one end, and with the Mahatma, who is peering down the length of Park Street half way towards the other. And nothing in this highly confusing land is more inconsistently bewildering than the memory of Lord Mayo, still trotting on his horse at a cross roads in the middle of the Maidan, twenty-two years after Independence, above an inscription which read: 'To the honourable and beloved memory of Richard Southwell, 6th

Earl of Mayo, Humane, Courteous, Resolute and Enlightened. Struck down in the midst of a Patriotic and Beneficent career on 18th February 1872 by the treacherous hand of an assassin. The People of India, mourning and indignant, raise this statue.'

The Maidan is much used. It is used by people who like to keep clean and who are forever dhobying themselves or their garments in the three great tanks – the Manohar Das, the General's and the Elliot – which are set one after another down the edge of Chowringhee. Parts of it are stockaded during Durga Puja and other festivities, to become a sort of fairground. One of its roads is lined with tiny bungalows belonging to the Calcutta Kennel Club, the Rajasthan Club, the Armenian Sports Club, the Wari Athletic Club, the Engineers Club, the Calcutta Tramways and Athletic Club and many another organization that likes to build a bunker in a small garden, surrounded by a high thick hedge, in which its members can take refuge and amusement at the weekend. There is a middle section of the Maidan devoted to cricket every Saturday afternoon and every Sunday morning, with a dozen or more pitches heaving with figures in natty white flannels, who are dripping with sweat below their floppy white hats and their gaudy club caps. Indian cricket began on the Maidan indeed, with a two-day match in January 1804 between Old Etonians employed by the Company and 'Calcutta'. Robert Walpole's grandson Richard opened for Calcutta and one of Sir Elijah Impey's sons scored thirteen for the side; but the Etonians won by 152 runs, being fortified by a Vansittart and (inevitably) by a Metcalfe major and a Metcalfe minor – one of the brothers later becoming a Governor-General of India. And on almost the same length of turf now stands the Eden Gardens stadium, where they play Test matches and where the spectators are rather more liable to lay on a riot than the batsmen a century.

People play crown green bowls under floodlights at night on the Maidan. They hold the biggest political rallies on earth on the Maidan. They wander with large flocks of hornless, pimple-headed, flop-eared goats across the Maidan. When they are young and Indian they play hide and seek in the ditch that surrounds the glaring white walls of Fort William on the river side of the Maidan. When they are older and British they go for a constitutional before dusk down at the Racecourse end of the Maidan and, on meeting each other, they exchange a polite good evening without stopping, just as they would on Hampstead Heath. In the terrible heat of high noon, travellers from one end of India to the other shelter beneath their long-distance buses, which are also resting on the edge of the Maidan by Strand Road; and, a mile away across the spinneys and the grass and the ditches, taxi-drivers are doing the same thing beneath the trees which flank Chowringhee, with cardboard cinema posters dangling from their branches; and a handful of idlers are slumped beneath the filigree ironwork shading a fountain there, which was presented to the Municipality in 1884 by Mr Ezra, who had it made (as you can still just make out) by Walter Macfarlane and Co., Glasgow.

The Maidan's biggest old totem is still in place, presumably because it was too big even for a Communist Government to shift into limbo with all the other monuments to the Raj. There are 165 fluted feet of the Ochterlony Monument, which is forty feet less than the Monument to the Great Fire of London. It starts with an Egyptian base, proceeds through a Syrian column, and is topped by a Turkish dome; a confection which is usually passed off as a deference to Sir David Ochterlony's taste for all things Muslim. And conceivably the monument was raised in the first place not only to commemorate Sir David's annexation of Nepal, but also to salute the days when he and his thirteen wives would take the early morning air by the banks of the Hooghly, on one elephant after another; or possibly because he was that very rare bird indeed among the eighteenth century rulers of India, the man who died almost penniless because he had not bothered to graft for a fortune. Ochterlony was half Scots but he was born in Boston, Massachusetts, though this does not explain why Mark Twain was so besotted with the monument when he was in the city, for he seemed unaware of Ochterlony's background. His journal of a trip round the world spent only seven pages on Calcutta, though Benares rated forty, and he spent most of his space ruminating on the 'cloud-kissing monument to one Ochterlony'. Today, the Monument (having been rechristened Sahid Minar, a title unused by anyone but the Communist Minister who insisted on the change) tends to be in the middle of all those colossal rallies at which the name of even a half-American is implicitly considered worse than Hooghly mud. It is also the focal point of those splendid weekend happenings on the Maidan, a Mukta Mela here, a man juggling with spinning things there, someone whirling by his feet from a rope lashed to a tripod round one side, someone else trying to charm a dozy snake from its basket round another; and all these entertainments are watched and applauded by scores of people who are, given the circumstances of the city and their lives, unaccountably merry. The Monument is used by the police as a watchtower during the Maidan rallies and anyone else needs constabulary permission to climb to the top, just in case he should be a Pakistani spy wishing to take a long-distance look at the Howrah Bridge.

From the top you can pick out one by one the other outstanding monuments to the Raj. Almost by your elbow is Chowringhee, which Edward Lear thought a fearful humbug of palaces and distinctly inferior to the Promenade des Anglais at Nice. Bishop Heber took more kindly to it, for he occupied one of the palaces and there he would sit drinking his favourite Bass ale, enjoying the company of his wife, whom he was always loth to leave; whenever he had a prolonged visitation to make upcountry he would write her long love letters, which Mr Gladstone later translated into Latin for amusement and intellectual exercise. Lord Macaulay, who lived almost next door, alongside the rising Bengal Club, agreed with Lear, for 'a lodging up three pairs of stairs in London is better than a palace in a compound of Chowringhee'. He must have been the only titled visitor to the city from the early nineteenth century onwards not to have been mightily impressed by that very self-satisfied road. And if, today, it has no reason at all for self-satisfaction it still has the presence of an international thoroughfare. Once they rise above the scruffy trade of the pavement arcades, its buildings are presentable and gleaming with creamy stucco, as they should be with all the money tucked inside them. Its roadway is wide and sweeping, almost the only one in Central Calcutta where traffic

can usually proceed at the rush, sometimes being thrown into
great confusion when a herd of white Brahmani bulls decides to
advance down the centre lane at the stroll, ten or twenty at a
time, while the taxis and the buses pile up around them.

Chowringhee is nicely counterweighted across the Maidan by
the sprawling octagon of Fort William, which is where the Central Government of Delhi maintains a thoughtful and secure
foothold in this frequently rebellious city. It is almost a small
town, as you can see from the top of the Monument, for it can
garrison ten thousand men, but in all the years since Robert
Clive started it, not one shot has yet been fired in anger from its
battlements, though they are said to be well mounted with guns.
And though the Fort keeps much to itself, a distant and enig-
matic colony on the edge of potential insurrection, just occasionally it yields up an old-fashioned delight to the connoisseur
of the Maidan. For on a Sunday morning you may see, emerging from one of its portals, a troop of cavalry in splendid line
ahead. Delicately the horses pick their way across the grass,
stiffly moving with the animals each trooper rests a hand by his
bucketed sword, chatting with composure are the two officers at
the head. The tone is khaki, not scarlet or blue, but for a moment
or two, until the column disappears down Strand Road for exercise along the river, it is as though the Raj were still firmly in the
saddle here. Five minutes later a lorry swerves round the corner
onto the Red Road, full of young Communists in red berets,
thumping their staves in time to some rousing chorus, on their
way to yet another rally beneath the Monument. And it is as
though the revolution had already broken out.

A vision of white marble dazzles at the bottom of the Maidan.
When W. H. Auden was here in the fifties, some enthusiastic
guide told him that the Victoria Memorial had been designed by
the man who did the Taj Mahal. This is not quite as comical as
you might suppose, for you would certainly swear that it was at
least George Gilbert Scott heavily inspired by the Taj; a sort of
St Pancras by the Hooghly, but Classical not Gothic. Instead, it
was the work of Sir William Emerson, President of the British
Institute of Architects in his day, whose only building in England
worth a moment's attention (if you laboriously investigate the

forty-odd volumes of Pevsner) was the Hamilton House he put up just past King's Bench Walk on the Victoria Embankment in London. The idea of the Memorial was Lord Curzon's, of course; its foundation stone was tapped into place by George V on his princely excursion to Calcutta in 1906, and whatever professional frustrations Sir William may have suffered from at home, he let them all loose in one majestic throw right here. They landed amidst sixty-four acres of lawns, ponds, shrubbery and herbaceous borders and nothing in Calcutta ever had more pleasing or more amply open surroundings. Here, as you walk up one of the drives, past the bronze Victoria on her throne, or the bronze Edward VII on his horse, or the marble Curzon looking very stern and ruly, you behold something which is more palatial than memorial; a great white cliff which in Calcutta's light hurts the eyes, with its vaguely Renaissance sides ending at each corner in a sort of minaret, with its entrance arches soaring through two high storeys, with its entire rambling, derivative, nostalgic and impressive rectangle dominated by a colonnaded dome (the Taj, with concessions to St Paul's Cathedral, maybe) which is itself capped by three tons of bronzed and victorious angel.

It echoes inside, as it was doubtless meant to echo for ever and a day. It echoes most resonantly under the dome, in the Queen's Hall whose walls have been deeply graven with the text of Victoria's proclamation of herself as Empress. But reverberations from those illustrious days pursue the visitor to the Memorial wherever he goes along its galleries, its armouries, and its ennobled chambers. Many of India's old rulers are represented here in stone, quite often dressed in Roman togas, like Warren Hastings and Lord Cornwallis. And where they have not been immortalized with a chisel they have most certainly not been forgotten with a brush and a palette of oils. The Queen herself, quite naturally, comes first in all things. You have her in paint at her coronation, at her marriage, at the baptism of her son and heir, at her first and then her second jubilee celebrations in her cathedral church, at her son's wedding, at her residence of Frogmore, and at exercise with dear old John Brown holding the horse's reins. You have one or two of her possessions: the piano-

forte (that's what the label says) at which she received tuition in
childhood, the writing desk and chair occupied for daily correspondence at Windsor, the last letter she wrote to her people in
India thanking them in person for their sympathy on the loss of
her grandson in the Boer War ('she cannot deny that she feels
a good deal shaken ...'). You make the unexpected discovery
that from her favourite Indian attendant, Abdul Karim, she
learned Hindusthani.

There are portraits of other Great Britons who were in Calcutta at one time or another; Macaulay, of course, and Kipling
and Bishop Heber and William Hickey with the closest of his
sixty-three servants and his little dog. William Makepeace
Thackeray gets his bust in because he was born here and Florence
Nightingale hers because, like the Queen herself, she took a distant interest in India. From time to time an Indian face is displayed without discrimination among these alien images –
Keshub Chandra Sen, poor Michael Madhusudan Datta who was
so nearly an Englishman himself, Rabindranath Tagore and his
enterprising grandfather Dwarkanath. There are documents, including the forgery which had Nuncomar judicially executed.
There are treaties, among them the one Clive made with Siraj-
ud-Daula after he had recaptured the city. The Permanent Settlement is here. So is a model of the battlefield of Plassey. And an
antique musical grandfather clock by Whitehurst of Derby. Yet
nothing that the Victoria Memorial contains is more memorable
than the gallery displaying Mr Finden's Portraits of the Female
Aristocracy of the Court of Queen Victoria – all fifty-six of
them, with the occasional damp stain having intruded upon the
ladies since they were engraved in 1849. Lady Georgina Toler,
Viscountess Canning, Miss Blanche Bury, Caroline Countess of
Mount Edgecumbe, The Lady Ashley, the Honourable Mrs Fox
Manle and the rest – there they all are in two long rows, almost
all of them bonneted, with ringlets, with chins carefully poised on
slender hands and with variously arch expressions; though Lady
Agnes Buller, much the most individual, looks faintly Sultanate
and fingers a harp. And on Sunday afternoons small Indian children, being towed round the premises by elders with a fine sense
of history, pause for a long time before Mr Finden's Portraits

and gaze at them silently with large and wondering eyes; as well they might. For the Victoria Memorial cost Rs 10,500,000 to build and, under the gentle persuasion of Lord Curzon, their great grandparents paid every last anna of it by loyal and dutiful subscription.

Balancing this monumental expenditure of glory a couple of miles away, on the north side of the Maidan, is Raj Bhavan – the Government House in which Viceroys sat and ruled India as though they were Emperors themselves. This was quite the grandest gesture Lord Wellesley made to his subject peoples, Fort William College perhaps being the most careless. Before Wellesley came to Calcutta, a strong-minded dapper little man with a refined taste for Classics, the Governors-General of Bengal and India inhabited a Buckingham House on this site, rented from the local Nawab. Wellesley at once decided that this was insufficient to his position; India, he let it be known, should be ruled from a palace not a counting house, with the ideas of a prince, not with those of a retailer in muslins and indigo. Without bothering to consult the Directors of the East India Company, he summoned architects and began to build, and there was much anguish in Leadenhall Street when the bills began to roll in – £87,000 for the structure, £71,000 for the land, £18,000 for the furnishings and over £3,000 for the two new roads laid alongside; Wellesley could scarcely complain when his flabbergasted Directors, hearing that he had started building a second residence at Barrackpore, stopped its foundations in their tracks. Government House when finished was seen to be almost identical to Kedleston Hall in Derbyshire and, by a noble coincidence, a Curzon of Kedleston was to move out of one into the other within a century.

It was – and is – not exactly like Kedleston. Where Kedleston has only two projecting wings to the main building, two others never having been finished, Government House was given all four to catch every suspicion of breeze that might come its way. Where Kedleston has two floors, Government House has three. Where Kedleston's upper salons are illuminated from above by skylights, Government House gets its light from the sides. Where Kedleston is made of sandstone, Government House was built of brick with colour-washed plaster on top. Otherwise, no one could tell the two places apart, particularly after Lord Curzon himself had placed a row of urns along the roofline, to establish the details just as they were at home. Wellesley had already ordered the busts of twelve Caesars to be situated in the Marble Hall, to conform with the model, and among these each night, it was said, he would sit plotting his moves and counter moves against opponents military and political. His main staircase already terminated in a pair of sphinxes, whose breasts were amputated shortly after installation on the orders of a discreet aide de camp, who thought they might offend his Lordship.

From the moment of its completion, Government House became the scene of such entertainments as Calcutta had never known before, though the most memorable was not held until Curzon mounted a centenary ball at which he set the pace by dressing in the style of Wellesley, and so inspired a guest to write that 'We became our grandparents again, imitating in spirit, language and dress the high-waisted ladies and stately men who danced in these very halls a century ago.' Scarcely a British ruler of India lived here without making his contribution to the place. Lord Hastings imported the finest gravel from Bayswater for the paths. Lord Ellenborough bequeathed a Chinese cannon mounted on a brass dragon for the front terrace. Lord Elgin introduced gas. Lord Northbrook laid on hot water. Lord Curzon provided those urns, experimented with the plasterwork after having the plans of Chatsworth sent out, and put in a lift as flimsy as a bird cage which still works today. Lord Hardinge replaced the front gates when he heard that his King Emperor was coming to town. The ladies of the household were no less interested in their direction of the grounds. According to Emily Eden, it was Lady Amherst who started the splendid garden, though Lady Bentinck, coming close behind her, had everything uprooted within the first week because she thought flowers unwholesome. The Eden sisters recovered this lost territory when their brother Lord Auckland was in command and added a fish pond for good measure. Lady Mayo started planting trees, Lady Lytton installed a swimming pool and, by the time dear Lady Dufferin arrived, there wasn't much left for her to do except to suggest a tennis court.

From this building were sovereign and imperial rights exercised over a people who had grown to 300 millions, a fifth of the world's population, by the start of the twentieth century. The men who exercised that right generally believed that in the whole hierarchy of British Empire they and their position were second only to the imperial monarch, not excepting the British Prime Minister himself. Sir Herbert Kitchener was so cast down when Lord Hardinge got the nod he thought should have been his, that he went into hiding for ten days to conceal his disappointment. Apart from their aspirations and their belief in the rectitude of their rule, they were a mixed bunch of men. They could be as arrogant as Lord Amherst, who never moved from one room of Government House to another without being preceded by a column of mace bearers and who, during morning exercise on the Maidan, would not suffer his wife to approach closer than his horse's backside. They could be as homely as Sir John Lawrence, who used to work stripped to his collarless shirt with slippers on his feet, who preferred rambling through a bazaar to attending the races (he even declined to present the Viceroy's Cup), and who would continue to play croquet on his lawn long after dark, when great crowds would gather to watch him by lamplight through his railings. They could be as genuinely loved by their subjects as Lord Canning, who ruled during the detestable years of the Mutiny and after and of whose departure the normally caustic Girish Chandra Ghosh could even then write: 'If India grieved at the loss of one who had proved himself so worthy to rule, it rejoiced on the other hand at the presence in England of a friend whose mature judgement and intimate acquaintance with local politics, feelings and requirements, would at all times offer Her Majesty's Government a true criterion by which to settle Indian questions.' A Viceroy might be as effectively nonconformist as Lord Lytton, who set up a famine control scheme and who startled the exclusive society of Simla by smoking cigarettes between courses at dinner. Or he might be as thickly imperious as Curzon himself, who wrecked almost every good thing that had preceded him with one insufferable assessment of his situation the moment he arrived, and who was himself startled to discover that guests at his levees would stuff their pockets with his cigars and his cigarettes before bidding him good night. A Viceroy could be as thrifty as Lord Lansdowne, who told his successor Hardinge that he had managed to save £20,000 out of his salary of £16,700 per annum. A Viceroy could eventually be remembered less for what he had done than for the guests he had entertained in Calcutta.

Such is the plight of the banker-Viceroy Lord Northbrook, a Baring who happened to be an old friend of the Queen's former tutor, Edward Lear. Notwithstanding his own imperial connections, Lear shocked British Indian society during his fourteen-month tour round the country because he brought a white man with him as servant (to whom General Palmer politely passed the cake at tea one afternoon, as he did to everyone else at the reception). Lear was not himself much impressed by the British of Calcutta. He mentally divided them into Cummerbundians and non-Cummerbundians, let it be known that he preferred Tolly's Nullah to Chowringhee, thought the main staircase of his lodging and its mutilated sphinxes preposterously magnificent, not to say awful, and immortalized Government House and its contents as Hustlefussabad. People were always dropping in at Government House. Young Winston Churchill spent days on end shut up in a room along the South-east wing, writing *The River War* about the Omdurman Campaign; and, having occasionally ventured forth into this reception or that, he would report back to Mama in London that 'Calcutta is full of supremely uninteresting people endeavouring to assume an air of heartiness suitable to the season'. The visitors continued to come even when Government House had been relegated to provincial status with the departure of the Viceroys to New Delhi. George Mallory stayed here before making his first attempt to climb Everest in 1922. Noël Coward strolled in while he was entertaining troops in Calcutta during the last war; and, having been taken on the obligatory tour of the establishment by his host, paused amidst the Caesars, swept the gallery with an appraising and thoughtful eye, and murmured – only half to himself – 'Pokey place'.

Viceroys and their staffs were always dropping out whenever the weather became too impossible, after Lord Bentinck decided that Simla was a better place for summer imperialism. Gladly they would forsake the Calcutta of Cockle's Pills (for dysentery) and interminable subscriptions (for the sake of appearances) and take to the healthier hills; though Curzon was to reckon that never in his life had he been fitter than during his Viceregal years in spite of a recurrent pain in his leg and an intermittently nagging toothache. But at Simla you could enjoy polo at 8,000 ft, and wander round a perfectly adequate Viceregal Lodge whose rose garden and herbaceous borders had been first organized by Lady Minto. You took your very strict sense of courtesies with you, of course, including all the people involved in the sixty-three official ranks of precedence, which started with the Viceroy, finished with the superintendent of a telegraph workshop, and had the Archdeacon of Calcutta neatly inserted between a brigadier-general and the Tea Controller for India. You also, by and by, had to put up with a great deal of criticism from the British who remained in Calcutta, who believed that the nation's government was not being effectively conducted unless it was being conducted where it could be effectively lobbied. Many a Viceregal heart must have been heavy when the time came each autumn to strike camp in Simla and return to the city, to those awful levees where you had to shake 1,900 hands and make 1,900 little bows before you could even moisten your lips on the first cocktail of the evening, where you had to walk 250 yards to get from your own room to your daughter's, and where you might be required to endure the more pungent parts of Calcutta once or twice a year, like the student hostel attached to the university, because you had scarcely been able to refuse the appointment of Rector when it was obediently offered you.

Most of the Viceroys survived all this well enough to enjoy an authority in the House of Lords and a stately pension in Gloucestershire or elsewhere. But Elgin died here and so did Lady Canning, as well as a couple of Governors of reformed Bengal, while Mayo, whose agricultural policies were among the better Viceregal fingerprints laid on India, was assassinated on a visit to the Andaman Islands. The rest came and went, leaving Government House and its staff to be slightly modified by the whims of the next man. And eventually this too became part of India's legacy, to be translated at once into the Raj Bhavan, but still to be maintained with a staff of liveried flunkeys and to be occupied lately by a Hindu but non-Bengali Governor of West Bengal, whose son was simultaneously presiding over the Union in the University of Cambridge.

Raj Bhavan is not the only building in Calcutta that looks distinctly familiar to a visiting Englishman, who may find himself wondering where he has seen the outline of that large church before, the one just across the road from the Victoria Memorial. The answer is that the church is Calcutta Cathedral (another St Paul's, as it happens) and that the tower is a painstaking copy of the Bell Harry at Canterbury, which the Primate of All England knows so well. The walls, moreover, have something of Norwich Cathedral about them, and there are bits and pieces of decoration (a capital here, a pinnacle there) which might set some vague old ecclesiologist to thinking that perhaps the master masons of York Minster had wandered rather farther afield than he had supposed. There is a West window by Burne-Jones and, indeed, once you get inside Calcutta Cathedral it would be possible to lose yourself in a reverie which persuaded you that you were now meditating in some splendid wool church of the Cotswolds rather than an outpost of God's Empire on the Tropic of Cancer. One thing, however, soon dispels hallucination. For the wide white roof, with its moulded Tudor roses all shining with gilt, is partially obscured by the network of ironmongery necessary for the suspension of forty-six great fans one after the other above the choir and the nave; which has never been known to happen anywhere in the see of Gloucester. There are other churches in the city even more eerily imitative than this. Both St John's and St Andrew's, the first just behind Dalhousie Square, the other on one of its corners, could quite easily have come from the drawing boards of a Wren, a Gibbs, possibly a Hawksmoor; refined and elegant exercises in Anglo-Greek architecture on the outside, they contain galleries, fonts, lecterns and reredoses just like those you have seen only a few weeks ago on the edge of Trafalgar Square or somewhere just past the Bank of England.

The secular has been cribbed as freely as the sacred. The most marvellous bartering place in Calcutta is Sir Stuart Hogg's old New Market, just behind Chowringhee. For almost a century it has been possible to obtain here practically all that imagination could conceivably want to buy. You can get anything between dangling charms from a Tibetan stall and a baby crocodile from the adjacent bird and animal mart – though you need a very strong stomach and preferably no sense of smell if you are going to patronize that. As you approach the New Market you also do well to select the first porter who rushes up to you with a basket, for if you think you can purchase and then carry one packet of liver salts yourself without assistance, you are liable to move around with an entourage of half a dozen basketeers, all negotiating quite fiercely for a temporary position on your payroll. All of this – the demanding porters, the purposeful memsahibs, the small boys who offer you blandishments with their trade – is housed under one long and very rambling roof. Without the local colour, these interminable rows of stalls, this endless maze of small shops, would be scarcely distinguishable from the Grainger Market in Newcastle, the Pannier Market in Barnstaple and the covered daily markets to be found in any self-respecting town from one side of Lancashire to the other of Yorkshire. They even have a clock-tower by the entrance to the New Market which is so completely Northcountry Victorian, with stone buttressed corners, Gothic louvres piercing the red brickwork, a steep slate roof above the dial which is then topped by a lightning conductor surrounded by a small iron fence, that many people have supposed some Anglophile Maharajah transported it once, brick by brick from Huddersfield, like a rich American taking an obscure fancy of his own across the Atlantic. Which is not the case, any more than it happened that someone once brought Calcutta High Court over from Belgium. For that great bastion of Gothic, with its files of pinnacles doing sentry duty along the roof and its columns ornamented with Caen stone capitals, each subtly different from its neighbours, bears such a close resemblance to the Staad-Haus of Ypres that the two buildings are now linked in legendary fashion. It is said that when the Belgians lost their Town Hall by bombardment during the Great War they

immediately sought the plans of Calcutta High Court so that they
might rebuild their original faultlessly – though no one can ever
lead you to the source of this stimulating myth.

There is nothing at all fanciful about the origins of Calcutta's
most suggestive buildings. Most of them were designed as a
military operation, by officers of the Bengal Engineers. Apart
from Emerson's Victoria Memorial the most notable exceptions
are the High Court and the General Post Office, which both
came from Walter Granville, Architect to the Government of
India, and the Writers' Building, whose architect was probably
Thomas Lyon, a former carpenter who had come out to work
on the construction of the new Fort William. It was quite customary for young Sappers to put up the odd public edifice in the
growing years of the Raj, even though their professional equipment was minimal. Permanent buildings were not beginning to
rise in Calcutta until about the last thirty years of the eighteenth
century, and by then the Company as well as the regular Army
was giving its engineers some basic training before leaving for
India. Once in Calcutta, however, they usually had only their
notebooks to guide them, together with a handful of standard
architectural works like *Vitruvius Britannicus, The Antiquities of
Athens* and *A Book of Architecture* which James Gibbs had published in 1728, just after finishing St Martin's-in-the-Fields. It
was this last volume, with its plans of the London church, that
allowed Lieutenant Agg to design St John's as he did half a
century later. Captain Wyatt, who was a nephew of the professional British architect James Wyatt, was able to imitate
Kedleston Hall so well when Wellesley invited ideas (and selected
Wyatt's plans for Government House in preference to those of
the Company's Italian architect Edward Tiretta) because the
architect of Kedleston, James Paine, had published his drawings
in *Plans, elevations and sections of Noblemen's and Gentlemen's
houses* in 1783. Having absorbed this, having copied it carefully,
and having finished his splendid Government House in 1803,
Wyatt went home with money in his purse and became the MP
for Sudbury.

His superior officer Colonel Garstin was by then designing
the Town Hall to Doric specifications, though with rather less

success; shortly after its opening the front portico collapsed, somewhat later the ballroom floor began to spring and the whole structure had to be overhauled, which caused Sir Charles D'Oyly (sometime opium agent up at Patna, always an amateur artist and now gentleman about Chowringhee) to write a mocking little verse that would have come well out of a production much later on by his family's light opera company. Soldiers, however, take these things as they come, and Major Forbes was proceeding with his plans for the Mint, which was so strikingly impressive that he was commissioned to design the Cathedral after it. The Mint, naturally, was a copy as well. Its portico was nothing less than a half-size replica of Minerva's Temple in Athens. Everything in Calcutta was derivative. The gates of Government House were a mixed reproduction of those belonging to Syon House in Middlesex and Wilton in Wiltshire; the Turf Club's frontage could have been seen before by anyone acquainted with West Wycombe Park; many of the handsome town houses now going up carried obvious traces of John Nash and his terraces round Regent's Park; people were even having open fireplaces installed.

What the original artists in the city thought of all this we can only guess from the occasional oblique hint they dropped; the Daniells wrote that 'The streets are spacious, and from the diversity of European and Oriental manners present a scene of inexhaustible variety and amusement'; which perhaps meant buildings as much as people, but it wouldn't do to laugh too loudly in Calcutta's face, for she was a considerable source of patronage to painters at the time; though, curiously, they seem to have vanished by 1836. Emily Eden remarks that by then there is only one professional in town, and he is capable of nothing better than a second-rate sort of sign-post; it was one reason for her own prolific output. The first to discover what a wealth of prospects lay here was Tilly Kettle, who arrived in time to be empanelled on the jury at Nuncomar's trial and whose work is frequently confused with that of Sir Joshua Reynolds.* After him came

---

* Even the National Portrait Gallery in London catalogues a painting of Warren Hastings by Kettle and attributes it on postcards to Reynolds.

William Hodges, recently returned as artist aboard the *Resolution* on Cook's second voyage to the Pacific. It was Hodges who tipped off his old friend John Zoffany to catch the first boat to the Hooghly.

Zoffany was a glittering character who had started life as a cabinet maker in Prague, who called himself Sir John at this stage (with the uncertain permission of George III), who had earlier been dubbed 'the Baron' by Marie Thérèse of Austria, and who had just been making himself a reputation for portraiture in London, particularly among the theatrical acquaintances of David Garrick. As soon as he reached Calcutta in 1783 he found the Nabobs falling over themselves to sit for him. He would rarely paint a solitary individual, for his nose for profit was as sharp as anyone else's in the city and he charged Rs 1,000 for every figure on his canvas, usually finding himself much too busy to oblige anything less than a family group unless someone very important like Impey or Hastings approached him. His paintings are therefore generally well-crowded compositions, and they were sometimes a means of settling scores, for Zoffany was a quarrelsome man. He excelled himself when the Reverend Tally-Ho Johnson and the Vestry of St John's commissioned him to paint The Last Supper to hang behind their altar. Zoffany had lately been bickering with a Mr Paull, a Company official, and now he made him into Judas. A Mr Blaquiere, a police magistrate of effeminate good looks whose hostility to Christianity was notorious in the town, appeared as St John the Divine. Christ was represented by Father Parthenio, a Greek priest of Calcutta, in what seems to have been a mark of approval. The Vestry, after much testy debate, finally settled with Zoffany for Rs 2,500 when the painting was worth at least three times the amount at his current rates.

The Daniells were more assiduous than colourful. Thomas Daniell had been a bricklayer's labourer who learned to varnish carriages when he was later apprenticed to a coach builder. He also learned to paint and by the time he was twenty-three the Royal Academy had accepted one of his flower pieces. When his brother died he agreed to look after nephew William, and thus the famous partnership began. William was only fifteen when the

Daniells received the Company's permission, in 1784, to sail for
India to make engravings of this fabulous land. They arrived two
years later, by way of China, and they at once opened a subscription list in Calcutta for a dozen aquatints of the city by
Thomas. William's part in the enterprise was to fetch and carry,
to operate the camera obscura and to make simple sketches,
though eventually he was to become an artist in his own right;
Thomas was made a Royal Academician in 1799 and William
twenty-three years later. For almost ten years they travelled all
over India, sketching steadily as they went, and they produced
hundreds of landscapes, from the Himalayas to Ceylon. Sometimes they slipped themselves into a composition, riding on a
horse or in a palanquin or sitting by their drawing board while
an Indian servant held a large umbrella over them; but they never
allowed themselves to be more than tiny figures in a landscape, a
device to establish its scale. No other place on the sub-continent
was as thoroughly pictured by them as Calcutta; it is largely because of the Daniells that we know what the city looked like at
the end of the eighteenth century.

Ironically, while men in the Indian capital were building in
the styles of Europe, their counterparts in England were beginning to create follies in the native idioms of India. Sometimes
they had served in the East; invariably they had been stimulated
by the now celebrated Daniell prints; and from time to time they
would ask Thomas Daniell what he thought about this or that
project they were planning. He was consulted by Sir John
Osborne, formerly Colonel of the Nawab of Oudh's Light Infantry Battalion, about a garden temple in honour of Mr Hastings
(who was to be represented as an incarnation of Vishnu) at Mel-
chet Park in Hampshire, and Thomas eventually supplied the
designs. He was consulted by Sir Charles Cockerell, who had
just come home from Calcutta with a fortune after some years
as the Company's Postmaster there, about his new mansion at
Sezincote in Gloucestershire, for which Daniell designed a garden
temple, grottoes, fountains, a bridge and an ornamental pool.
The Prince Regent was so impressed by this work when he
visited Sezincote that he drew the attention of his own architect,
William Porden, to Daniell's prints and designs; a by-product

of this encounter was the Dome at Brighton, and probably the whole of the Royal Pavilion there, though Daniell was unmoved by John Nash's major part in the work.

The Victoria Memorial is well stocked with Daniell prints, and occasionally some lucky fellow manages to unearth one among the secondhand bookshops of College Street. In the High Court you may inspect Zoffany's portrait of Sir Elijah Impey, a portly figure in a red robe, with a blue cummerbund and with his right hand raised in a kind of archiepiscopal blessing. The Vestry of St John's eventually had to shift 'The Last Supper' from behind the altar, where it was being attacked by rising damp, to the Lady Chapel, and there poor Mr Paull still is, fixed forever as Judas, sitting at the front of the table with a hand reflectively on his chin, looking very sinister and plotting. And these are only two of the imperial ghosts that are apt to haunt you at almost every turn in Calcutta.

Cross Dalhousie Square after finding (if you can) the tablet marking the Black Hole, and you run into the Great Eastern Hotel, where the businessmen mustered their unnecessary vigilantes during the non-existent local Mutiny; and where Rudyard Kipling stayed while he sent those despatches back to the *Civil and Military Gazette* about the work of the Hooghly pilots and the night he spent in Calcutta with the police vice squad, when he observed Dainty Iniquity and Fat Vice at their accommodating trade. Go shopping in the New Market: if you take one side street to it off Chowringhee you pass a tailor's shop which still mounts an impressive coat of arms above its doorway 'By appointment to the Marquis of Linlithgow'; if you take the only other approach you pass the Empire Cinema, which may be showing *Blow Hot, Blow Cold!* this week, but which is where Harry Lauder once performed, not to mention Anna Pavlova, Marie Tempest, Matheson Lang and Dame Clara Butt; and where, according to one local historian, 'as a frightened amateur Merle Oberon stared across the footlights'. Follow Chowringhee to its conclusion beyond the Racecourse and you run into the Seth Sukhlal Karnani Memorial Hospital, which was once the Presidency General, where you can see a small pink-washed hut which is now used as a dump for unwanted hospital junk.

Malaria was finally defeated in that hut, when it was a laboratory, and on the hospital gates they have fixed a plaque with the verse that Ronald Ross composed to celebrate his triumph:

> This day relenting God
> Hath placed within my hand
> A wondrous thing; and God
> Be praised, at his command.
> Seeking his secret deeds
> With tears and toiling breath,
> I find thy cunning seeds
> O million-murdering death.
> I know this little thing
> A myriad men will save.
> O death where is thy sting
> And Victory, O grave?

Not half a mile away, just inside the Corinthian portico of the District Magistrate's House on the banks of Tolly's Nullah, a pair of swords are crossed above the front door and there is an inscription on each lintel. The one on the left says 'Sir Philip Francis lived here 1774–1780'. That on the right says 'William Thackeray the novelist also lived here during infancy 1812–15'; and so he did, being sent home to England at the age of six, having been born where the Armenian College now stands, of parents who were married in St John's, of a father who was Secretary to the Board of Revenue.

The most haunted place of all is the old cemetery in Park Street, where ghosts began to accumulate from August 1767, when the sick season of the year was getting under way. Such was the mortality rate of Calcutta, so grandiose the habits of the British, even when they were burying their dead, that it is only just possible for a lugubriously sacred cow to squeeze between the tombs today, to get at the odd tuft of grass – as three or four always seem to be doing, whenever you pass – while mangy dogs nose the rubble and a refugee family cooks a meal in the shade of the first mausoleum on the right. The Old Jewish Cemetery in Prague is probably the only one in the world more congested with corpses than Park Street, for there the grave slabs slope sometimes one on top of the other; here the dead merely lie dust to dust, but the mood of Park Street is one of much greater claustrophobia, for scarcely a grave is without a monument quite four feet tall, and most are higher. Richard Barwell's wife, the entrancing Miss Sanderson that was, lies under the tallest, a twenty-foot pyramid which was copied from the even larger one that marks the end of Caius Cestius at the Porta Paolo in Rome. The whole cemetery is spiky with pyramids. Where there is a gap between pyramids it is filled with a block of masonry whose pedimented roof is level with your head. Or else it is occupied by a temple whose columns rise to twice a man's height. And all with their plastered surfaces flaking off and lying crumbled at your feet, with their slabs lurching tipsily, with weeds prising them apart, sad and heavily decayed relics which are now pie-bald with exposed brickwork and lingering cement.

It is difficult to read the inscriptions on many, so worn and demolished are they by a century or two of Calcutta's weather; but one or two can still be picked out, together with crossed swords, gun-barrels, trumpets, banners, scythes, arrows, torches, hour glasses and other funereal symbols of imperial mortality. Job Charnock is missing, of course; he enjoys an even larger mauso-leum than any here (though nearly as dilapidated) in the church-yard of St John's. But General Clavering was brought to Park Street, after his fruitless plotting against Hastings. So was Colonel Pearse, who was the Governor-General's second in his duel with Francis. So was Lady Anne Monson, of royal blood and high reputation at the whist table, whose coffin was carried to the cemetery gates by Hastings and Francis among others, where it was handed to six ladies of gentle birth, who bore it the rest of its way to the grave. And somewhere among these melan-choly surroundings lie Walter Savage Landor's old sweetheart and William Thackeray's father and Walter Bagehot's father-in-law and Fanny Burney's half-brother and sons of Charles Dickens and Captain Cook. Yet the saddest graves of all in Park Street Cemetery are those of the men and sometimes women who had astonishingly survived half a lifetime in Calcutta, who set sail for England and retirement, who died somewhere just out at sea, and who were brought back by sons and daughters carrying on the family tradition of helping to rule India; or who, if they had got as far as Aden, as happened now and then, were dumped overboard and fondly memoralized with an urn and a tablet in the middle of these rotting pyramids.

Some things the British started here are more deeply embedded in Calcutta than any of their buildings, caste marks that will still be visible when the cemetery as well as its contents is reduced to dust and when the Victoria Memorial is no more than a crumbled ruin. And, alas, no one can say with any certainty that these will include our vaunted rule of law, for that has been oozing out of Calcutta for quite a while now; no one can even be sure that its government by a parliament will endure, for twice within the past few years this has been dissolved by the order of a higher authority. The most lasting legacy of the Raj may well be a stamp which almost every other Bengali in Calcutta carries around with him every day of his life. Bengali names are very often not Bengali names at all, but some dilution of the original made by the first British, who were unable or unwilling to wrap their alien tongues round it. Mukherjee and its thirteen commonplace and Anglicized variants ought properly to be rendered as Mukhopadhyaya when transliterated from its native script; Chatterjee should be Chattopadhyaya (you can see just where that sweating Company man gave up in exasperation and said 'For God's sake, let's call it —jee'). A handful of proud Bengalis insist on the purist version even when they find it necessary – as they so often do in India's linguistic labyrinth – to communicate it in English. There are some nominations to be found in this part of the world much less defensible than those.

No student of British India who gets as far as Calcutta should ever fail to go down to Gopalpur-on-sea. It lies about four hundred miles South on the coast of Orissa, in the country of temples to the Lord Jagannath (which the British, of course, turned into Juggernaut; and, indeed, there is something cumbersomely unstoppable about the great chariot upon which the god is trundled out during his festival each year). To get to Gopalpur-on-sea you take the overnight train to Madras from Howrah Station, and well-wishers beforehand are likely to insist

that you lock your compartment, once safely inside; twelve years
ago, Mummy's cousin forgot to and she was beheaded by dacoits
in the middle of the night. Long before Madras, you reach what
must once have been the most genteel watering place East of
Frinton-on-sea, which in some ways Gopalpur still resembles.
This is where some of the British took their annual hols from
the confinements of the city; Mr Nehru himself used to come
here occasionally, and today rising Indian executives follow in
those imperial footsteps from Calcutta to dear old Gopalpur.
They stay, for the most part, in the posh Palm Beach Hotel, the
only thing in Gopalpur which is not now distinctly sad and
failing. The tourist brochures may insist that Gopalpur is 'set like
a precious stone beside the creamy blue of the sea' but it has
become, except for its short annual holiday season, a ghost town
where fisherfolk barely subsist beside the Bay of Bengal.

Once there were twenty-seven flourishing boarding houses
here, served and waited upon and victualled by 160 Anglo-
Indian families. Now there is only Ocean View, Christopher
Lodge, Colbon House and Sea View, with no more than twenty-
four Anglo-Indians to maintain them. These do their best still to
make the lodgings like a home from home, as every landlady
the British Empire ever produced always has tried to. In Ocean
House there is a typewritten sheet behind a bedroom door which
says 'We are not responsible for anything done without our
knowledge' and 'No anti-social or unlawful things are allowed
here'. In the dining room there is a much larger notice which
says 'Silence', and which you also have to yourself. The street
outside, like all the streets in Gopalpur-on-sea, is adrift with
sand which has blown up from the beach fifty yards away, leaving only a small channel of cracked tarmacadam for pedestrians
in between its shallow banks. The sand has drifted up to and
inside The Anchorage and Wroxham House and all the other
old boarding houses, where the paint has peeled in the blistering
sun and where everything is gently subsiding into the earth from
which it sprang. It whirls in miniature storms round the wreckage of one building whose two marble gateposts, the only things
there not yet collapsed or tottering, bear the inscriptions 'Ralph
N. Moore' and 'Blue Haven 1938'.

The beach still makes all this well worthwhile, however, for it is long and deep and you can laze on it while the Oriya fishermen, wearing curious pointed hats which help them (so they say) to cleave the water more easily when they have to swim, struggle to launch their boats through the surf and the powerful undertow. So strong is the inshore current along this coast that it is usual for swimming boys – who are very full-grown men – to offer their services as lifeguards when they see you proposing to take a dip. At Gopalpur-on-sea, the swimming boy who presses himself most engagingly upon you is in his mid-forties, with a wife and five children. He is very dark, as Oriyas are, he wears a rag round his head, for their sun is desperately fierce, and he brandishes and cracks like a whip the long thin tail of a sting ray he has caught, which he would like to sell you, for he is also very poor. He is a mixture of shyness and eagerness; he is a diffident chatterer. You ask him his name and he grins very widely, bobbing his head to the side as he does. It is, he says, Nancy Boy Number Five. And you can believe him. You can even visualize its conception one night on the verandah of Ocean House, in the mindless inspiration of some imperial manager with his origins in Braintree and his office just behind Dalhousie Square.

Now and then, in Calcutta, the English language can be turned back upon its begetters by Indians who can manipulate it as skilfully as any descendant of Lord Macaulay. You can be watching the documentary film *The Rise and Fall of the Third Reich* in one of Chowringhee's cinemas one night. As that standard shot of Dunkirk comes onto the screen, with the troops wading through the water to get to the boats, after some stirring commentary from the sound track an unmistakably Indian voice in the row behind murmurs 'Good show'; and it is quite impossible to tell, from the inflexion or the tone, whether its owner is identifying himself with the British and their sturdy retreat, or whether he is mocking them as deftly as any young satirist fresh from the Cambridge Footlights.

There are other British caste marks. In spite of the large majority of British names upon the roll of lay officers at St Paul's Cathedral (they dominate the Indian names by thirteen to six) an average congregation there consists of many more Indians than

British. Nevertheless, both Matins and Evensong are otherwise quite indistinguishable from those of the Church equivocal at home. The choir sings the Nunc Dimittis with a tonic harmony that His Grace of York would applaud. As the fans whirr and click overhead, the four Indian sidesmen advance upon the altar with the collection in the same slightly embarrassed, carefully in step, all rolling together manner of the English parish churches. During Lent in 1970 the priest in the cathedral pulpit, who was also Indian, produced a sermon one Sunday of impeccably Anglican felicity. He spoke of marvellous concepts like 'to love is to make the unlovable, lovable'. He did it under a text entitled 'The relevance of Christ's Cross to the Teacher in Calcutta'. Somehow he managed to preach on this theme for twenty minutes without once mentioning either Calcutta or anything that had ever happened there. You can discover many such attitudes, all of them at odds with their situation and some of them slightly sinister. At approximately the same time as that sermon was preached, there was a train crash in Australia which killed fifteen people and injured thirty more. It was reported by *The Statesman* in what journalists call a box or a panel, a setting of bold type to catch the reader's eye better than any surrounding story, and this box was placed high on the front page. It is possible that as many people died on the street of starvation and undernourishment the night before, within a mile of the newspaper's office, though if so the loss was unrecorded. Perhaps nothing other than this can be expected in a city which still includes twenty-three telephone subscribers beginning with the word 'Empire' and another thirty-nine beginning with the word 'Imperial'. Where a few letter boxes may still be caught out with an imperial cipher on them. Whose Ambassador cars and taxis, the only such vehicles produced in India are, beneath their Birla monopoly, to all intents and purposes the 1957 Morris Oxford model. Which runs every year at its Racecourse a Calcutta Derby, a Calcutta St Leger and a Calcutta Oaks. Whose most revolutionary elements frequent a Coffee House which they themselves have nicknamed the House of Lords.

The sponsors of all these manifestations are beleaguered in Calcutta now, but that is because they are rich much more than it is because they are British. They do not have an insulation of Anglo-Indians between them and the natives any more and the Anglo-Indians have totally isolated problems of their own. No longer patronized by their old masters, they are nervous of what they suppose (even when it is not evident) is hostility brewing among their old inferiors. The Bengalis do, in fact, generally call them Firinghi, which means foreigners. And the daughter of a Bengali family which is highly self-conscious in its generally cultivated ways can be heard producing a wicked imitation of an Anglo-Indian girl in her class, the point of which is completely that she is not as others in school are. So the Anglo-Indians tend to sigh at the thought of Auntie, who managed to secure a foothold in Bayswater or Notting Hill Gate before the British decided that not even half-caste chee-chees (or Eurasians, as milord Hastings would more scrupulously have called them) were welcome on their doorstep any more. They wonder what the chances now are of finding sanctuary in Australia, which is said to be allowing a few in. They cling fiercely, where they are able, to the positions of responsibility they managed to retain when the Raj abandoned them; like the police officer whose moustache is waxed to a pair of pinpoints, whose jackboots are burnished with blacking, whose eyes are invisible behind very dark glasses and who tells you that the boot and the baton are the best thing for a lot of these people; by which he means the full-blooded citizens of Calcutta; and he thwacks his own boots smartly with his cane by way of emphasis.

In a city where it is possible to telephone London only between 10.45 in the morning and 9.30 at night, the British must sometimes feel even more beleaguered than they actually are. They have been dwindling in number quite rapidly this past year or two; a large proportion of their post-war, post-Independence population decided to call it a day when the rupee was devalued in 1966; by 1968 only 2,000 of them remained on the books of the High Commission; by the beginning of 1970 these had shrunk to 1,350, though there are possibly a few more than that who have never bothered to sign themselves in. The British are thus reduced to roughly the same number of people as were here a few years before the Black Hole happened.

You get a queer feeling sometimes that they may not have changed very much in those two centuries. A small number swivel round the British Council, decently if rather earnestly interested in Bengali culture. A handful of women take care of everybody's conscience by doing whatever they can to help Mother Teresa in her various works of charity. But these do not represent the general flavour of the British in Calcutta. The general flavour tends towards the pursuit of tigers in the Sundarbans and wild pigs around Meerut for the exceedingly rich, towards golf at Tollygunge for the merely wealthy and towards the Racecourse for almost everyone. It includes the Vintage Car Rally, mounted each year by *The Statesman*, by no means an exclusively British occasion, in which someone's Delauney Belleville from Ballygunge will be competing with a 1914 Humbrette which has lumbered over from Lucknow and a 1913 Model T Ford which has rolled down from Shillong. For those who have been in India since before the war, or who are over forty, it usually means being deeply involved in the meetings and collective attitudes of Calcutta's branch of the United Kingdom Citizens Association.

This started life as the European and Anglo-Indian Defence Association, and under that name it was founded to defend the position of the white and the rather off-white when Lord Ripon's Ilbert Bill threatened to put darker men on equal terms in the courts of law. One of its members will tell you quietly that it really exists to organize the entry of duty-free booze and to speed the passage of remittances to and from England, with an OBE each year almost guaranteed to the chap who's just served as President. A recent President, quite naturally, saw it more importantly as something 'to enable the British community in India to speak with one voice'; to which he added that 'We have a great stake in this country and it is inevitable that for many years yet, British Nationals will continue to come to India, albeit on short-term basis, to supervise the administration resulting from that investment'. Then he went on to tell that attentive audience of compatriots in the Bengal Club of the progress made by their lobby at Westminster and its efforts to obtain some Government relief in the high cost of educating, at British boarding schools, the children of those Great Britons who were spending their working lives in India ('. . . our very sincere appreciation of the terrific amount of work undertaken by both Sir Percival Griffiths and Sir Ridgeby Foster in an endeavour to arrive at a solution to our very pressing problem'). The young expatriates, he sadly noted, were not nearly as interested in the UKCA as the old India hands.

The young expatriates, smart young things in their mid or late twenties who would go down well in South Kensington, are too mobile by far to become involved in anything as static as the UKCA. They belong to British firms whose trading posts are strung across the world, so that they come to Calcutta full of talk about the Sudan, or Rhodesia, where they've already spent three really super years; and before they've been in the city six months they are beginning to wonder what their chances might be of a posting next to Buenos Aires. They are Oxbridge almost to a man and wife, usually with one good Second between them, and their life in Calcutta inclines towards the Rowing Club or the Swimming Club. Even when they are not actually rowing or swimming in these establishments they are holding a dance there, planning or taking part in a revue there.

When one of these young couples are about to leave the city at the end of the Indian tour, they are wont to throw a party on the Hooghly. They hire a small steamer, invite all their friends to share it with them for the day, load it to the gunwhales with booze and stride aboard with much loud merriment at the Swimming Club Jetty on Strand Road. The loudest of them, eye-catching in straw hat, Bermuda shorts, the deepest and most fashionable of sideburns, pauses before stepping off the jetty and assumes the utmost amazement. He is contemplating two or three hundred Indians who are bathing off the adjacent ghats. 'I say,' he shouts to his compatriots, 'look at that bloody crowd.' Then he raises his cine camera and proceeds to shoot the natives. Thereafter he spends his day downing one drink after another, never seeming to become more than slightly unsteady, while he flirts with every woman aboard except his wife. A mile or two downstream, when people have started to peel off their clothing to the decently minimum for sunbathing, three of these young expatriate women, reduced to their bikinis, pretend to begin a strip routine by the rails for the especial benefit of half a dozen Indian boatmen who are just passing close by in a junk; and their gestures are as archly provocative as any that come out of the classier joints of Soho. They are well aware that the boatmen probably haven't had a woman between them since their last visit to their home villages down in Orissa, six months or more ago.

Yet these are not Wog-bashers by any old-fashioned definition of the term. It is just that they have areas of blank incomprehension or indifference. Two nights before, one of the couples have been talking sensitively about the Indians he knows in his work and the ones she patronizes once a week in her expeditions to the New Market; they have been discussing the terrible dilemma of every soft-hearted person in town who finds himself half-wanting to kick the umpteenth beggar child out of his path. Their bearer brings the coffee into the lounge after dinner, the cups rattling because an electric storm has been raging all night and it frightens him. She tells him to leave the washing up till morning, that he can go home now, at a quarter to midnight. You ask how far he has to go. Neither of them has any idea; they have never asked him where he lives. One doesn't, it seems, in Calcutta.

The same curious inconsistency is quite liable to happen in reverse. A pillar of the UKCA, a man of much money with that boarding school problem hanging unbearably upon his purse, behaves very badly indeed to his servants in front of his guests; he bawls at the first like an incompetent sergeant major and attends to the second with the exquisite courtesy of a colonel on ladies night in the mess. A few days later you surprise him at a piece of homework on his desk. He is painstakingly creating a book picturing the birds and animals of Bengal, with simple informative captions to each, which he is going to have printed at his own expense. He is then going to distribute copies at Christmas to the children of his many Indian employees. 'Better they should feed on this,' he says briskly, 'than be stuffed with a load of bloody Communist propaganda.'

People like that man have generally been in India at least

since the war and frequently for a few years before it. They
probably soldiered with the 4/10th Baluchis or some such regiment, and Johnny Gurkha is always a damn good chap to them,
however lowly he might be. Or else they joined their old-estab-
lished family firm in Calcutta after Oxbridge and National Service at the tail end of the war. Their homes are still palatial in
scale and comfort, the residue of a century's healthy profits.
They may, both man and wife in their early forties, be running
to unhealthy bulk themselves, though they ride for exercise
most days and they are particularly keen on shikar, hunting the
Bengal tiger whenever they can get away to their property down
in the Sundarbans along the edge of the delta. Three of their
children are at school in England, the fourth will soon be going,
and the absentees come over to Calcutta whenever there is more
than a week of school holidays to be spent; where the boys, who
will also be gentlemen of substance one day, are called 'darling'
by their father and charged with mixing gins and tonic for the
adults. They see quite a bit of their parents, one way and another,
for Mummy and Daddy always manage to spend a couple of
months each year at Home. It seems a very well settled, enormously rich existence, though Daddy confides that in Calcutta
these days it is very difficult not to be cynical; and you can see
what he means. 'It's virtually impossible,' he says, 'for anyone in
this country to net over £2,000 a year' because of the high Indian
rates of taxation upon the wealthy. Then he goes off to business
in the Mercedes, driven by his liveried chauffeur, leaving behind
in the garage the ageing Jaguar, the recent Fiat and the stout and
knockabout Landrover.

Gone forever are the days when *The Statesman*'s headlines
would include 'Lancashire Fusiliers Survive' – which was no
cause for great alarm, for it meant only that those artisan soldiers
had managed to effect a goal-less draw with Wari Athletic on the
Brigade Ground football pitch; an achievement, in the heat,
quite equal to any regimental battle honours taken from Minden
or Spion Kop. But at least once since Independence the pride of
the British-Indians was restored to the high level of the glorious
years of the Raj. In 1961, the Queen and her consort visited Calcutta. They were preceded, several weeks before, by their Com-

monwealth Secretary, Mr Duncan Sandys, who let it be known
that he thought it an inspiring task to try to improve the conditions of the city's slum dwellers. Mr Sandys had scarcely
removed himself when the city was visited by a cloud of locusts,
five or six miles long in the sky, which was proceeding in roughly
the same direction. The day after that the World Health Organization reported that a major disaster threatened Calcutta unless
there was an immediate solution to its water problem. Then Her
Majesty arrived.

There were twenty-five thousand people waiting when she
flew into Dum-Dum, and though it was never likely that she
would finish her journey in the Black Maria, as Bulganin and
Khrushchev had done six years before, the Chief Minister of
West Bengal kindly remarked when she reached the Raj Bhavan
that he could not remember larger or more disciplined crowds
in Calcutta. That night there was a reception in the former
Government House, which must have been quite like the old
days of Lord Curzon's entertainments. A reporter wrote that 'in
a fairyland setting, 9,200 wide, glistening and intent eyes were
fixed on the Queen, who was in pale blue net with a full skirt
embroidered with silver roses and wearing a sparkling diamond
tiara, a ruby and diamond necklace and a pair of earrings and
bracelet to match'. Indian musicians performed a song by
Tagore, whose first line translates as 'In this world of dust of
ours . . .' Next morning the Queen and her Prince attended a
service in the Cathedral, where the string quartet of the Oxford
Mission out at Behala played 'Sheep may safely graze'. In the
afternoon they watched Pa Bear win the Queen Elizabeth Cup at
25 to 1 on the Racecourse.

The rest of their time in Calcutta was in the same pattern.
They dropped in at the Royal Calcutta Turf Club. They visited
the National Agricultural Fair at Alipore. They met British
children at a special reception for juvenile expatriates in the Raj
Bhavan. They toured the Victoria Memorial, where two men
were arrested for disorderly conduct. The Prince played polo. He
and his wife did not see a jute mill in Howrah, as Bulganin and
Khrushchev most carefully had. They went nowhere near any
of Mr Sandys' inspiring bustees. Six years earlier, never one to

miss an opportunity, Khrushchev had told the people of Calcutta
that there were countries which sucked the blood of other
countries as leeches suck human blood. Her Britannic Majesty
might well have agreed with him, seizing the chance to point out
that such countries were to be found in the East as well as in the
West. But she was Queen Victoria's great grand-daughter and
very well bred, so she merely remarked, on leaving a city
which was, in a highly constitutional and quite remote manner of speaking, still hers: 'We have been highly impressed
by the reception Calcutta gave us. We shall never forget
it.'

There have been few other opportunities for the beleaguered
British to cheer in Calcutta since Independence. They have
suffered the end of Empire and their own supremacy in the city.
They have endured the devaluation of their money, first in
Britain, then in India. They have remained exceedingly wealthy
by anybody's standards in spite of these blows, fabulously rich
in the context of Calcutta. It is not enough for them, it never
has been. They enjoyed the power of their wealth, just as their
ancestors enjoyed it through two and a half centuries before
them. In this city they have had to stand by and watch not only
the power vanish, but the old symbols of that power wither and
shrink.

Even the Bengal Club is now merely a haunted and much
reduced miniature of what it once was. After Macaulay came the
clubmen's carriages, which would trot through the high wrought-
iron gates and pull up on the driveway before a domineering
frontage of high Corinthian columns. The ladies of British Calcutta half a century ago picketed that frontage to collect money
for the subscription fund that had been set up in London to
comfort the wretched General Dyer, who had lately made Indians
crawl on their hands and knees down a street in Amritsar after
shooting nearly four hundred of their countrymen in one of its
squares. They were talking Dyer's language inside the Bengal
Club just after the Mutiny had failed even to scratch them in
Calcutta. And within three years of the Dyer subscriptions being
collected, the men of the Bengal Club were organizing a Citizens
Protection League to supply armed assistance to the police and

subdue the Bengali nationalists. There always have been in Calcutta some Britons at odds with the attitudes of the clubmen.
During the Mutiny there was Canning himself, the Viceroy in
person. At the time of the Citizens Protection League there was
Tagore's great friend and correspondent C. F. Andrews, who
wrote that in Calcutta 'a circle of advanced thinkers and workers
may be found with whom it is a pleasure and a privilege to con-
verse on subjects covering the widest range of thought and life.
They are the men who will mould the future – men of character
as well as intellect, men who have surmounted difficulties such as
we ourselves have never experienced.' But men like Andrews, the
ones who came before him, the ones who came after, have always
been a small minority of the British population here. The majority have always aspired, even when they have not managed to
belong, to the superior and exclusive manipulations of the auto-
crats at 33, Chowringhee Road.

So many of these latter-day Moguls had taken themselves and
their small fortunes back to Britain for good by the end of the
1960s that the Bengal Club had sold off its impressive exterior
and its library and moved in close order and closer confinement
to the back of the building. Early in 1970 came the two mortify-
ing days when the auctioneers disposed of the last remnants of
the power and the glory in the front, and there never was a
gloomier moment in Calcutta's long, long history of the Raj and
its reach-me-downs. For the front rooms of the club had been
reduced to a jumbled heap of junk. On the terrace, with its commanding view across the Maidan, there were thirteen bathtubs
drawn up in line ahead, and they were all very grubby. Beside
them were thirteen lavatory bowls, and heaven knows what de-
graded future lay ahead of them. The corridors were piled with
wicker rocking chairs, springy bedsteads, mahogany tables and
disconnected lamp brackets. The front rooms were buttressed
with wardrobes and chests of drawers, more bedsteads and rolls
of mirzapore carpet. Pictures were stacked in their frames on
top of the drawers – two copies of a print by Stubbs, of *William
Evelyn of St Clere in Kent*, a version of *Man with a Soft Hat* by
Franz Hals, dozens of watery reproductions of boats, among
them Prince Philip's *Bluebottle*. On top of everything there was a

layer of dust. During the hours of viewing before the auction, the occasional British memsahib could be seen and heard bustling around the premises with her bearer dogging behind '... can't find them ... and I haven't got time to mess about today ...' But when they actually auctioned this decrepit residue of the old Bengal Club, practically everything in sight was knocked down cheap to once subservient Indians. Who never, in all Calcutta's history, would have been allowed past those wrought-iron gates for any other reason at all.

The British were merely repeating, on a small and ingrown scale, what they had experienced twenty-three years before at Independence. But that had differently and perversely been a time of hope as well as a time of regret and nostalgia. For there had just been horror in this city, which had seemed bent on destroying itself, and suddenly this had stopped, as though a tap had been turned off. So that when the end of the Raj came, it came in Calcutta rather decently and well, with expressions of goodwill and old comradeship in arms and mutual aid in the years ahead.

The only people hurt in the city that Friday, when imperialism was over and Indians ruled themselves at last, were the ones who fell off overloaded lorries which were rolling round town as mobile grandstands. They had been Independent since five minutes past one in the morning, Calcutta time, when bells had started ringing, conch shells had been blown and people in the streets had started shouting 'Jai Hind' (Glory to India) whether they were Hindu or Muslim. A few hours later Mr Suhrawardy, the Prime Minister of Bengal, returned to Mahatma Gandhi, who was praying and fasting in their house among the bustees, and told him; 'I have just been round Calcutta and I have seen a miracle.' At eight o'clock a salute of seventeen guns boomed from Fort William, the Indian flag was broken for the first time from the masthead there, and half an hour later Mr Fairbairn, secretary of the Bengal Chamber of Commerce, unfurled another brand new flag over the Royal Exchange. Charitable institutions started feeding the endless poor of the city.

Throughout that day there were crowds everywhere, happy for the first time in well over a year; 200,000 surged round

Government House, where the last representative of the Raj was packing his bags. Some of them scaled the gates, got inside the building and pinched some of the gubernatorial crockery as souvenirs; the Mahatma let it be known next morning that he would be glad if every plate and saucer were returned at once. There were even Hindus of the lowest castes ducking each other exuberantly in the swimming pool that Lady Lytton had installed long ago for persons of much higher rank. On the streets, portraits of the Mahatma and Netaji Subhas Chandra Bose were held high by dancing people. Brass bands mounted on some of those lorries played the British and the Indian national anthems alternately, with 'Tipperary' and 'Pack up your Troubles' on the side. The Grand Hotel had thought fit to announce beforehand that Scotch and beer would be available on this occasion in its Palm Court, for there had been much austerity since the war and during the year of terror. The Golden Slipper Club held a dinner-dance that night at which evening dress was essential. The Empire Cinema was showing Robert Young and Susan Hayward in *They Won't Believe Me*.

For the British the day was overloaded with sentimentality, as it was almost bound to be. The BBC was giving them their daily dose of that everlasting serial radio diary, 'The Robinsons', on its long-wave broadcast from London at breakfast time, with 'Music While You Work' and 'Those were the Days' to follow later. Listeners could see from their morning paper that Queen of the South had just beaten St Mirren 8–0 at home in Scotland. They could also see that in England there were people with the same sharp trading instincts that had been sending them and their ancestors to Calcutta since 1690. The Dormy House Hotel in Westward Ho, the Montpelier Hotel in Budleigh Salterton and sixteen other hotels in the West Country were all anxiously enquiring 'Are you leaving for England?' and offering a refuge if they were, for a consideration. Miss Grove, of The Garden School at Gulmarj in Kashmir, was offering to escort children to their final destinations in England in exchange for the part-payment of her own fare home. The British, in fact, were coming excellently up to scratch. Burmah-Shell was giving its employees an Independence Day bonus. *The Statesman*, which was still owned in London, was bubbling with proper pride. 'The speed with which, during this final, brilliant Viceroyalty, less than five months in duration, the transfer of power has been achieved, is almost stupefying,' it said that morning. 'Nothing of comparable magnitude or such spontaneous generosity has been effected in the annals of mankind.'

There was a letter in the paper a few days later from an Englishman which caught far better than any editorial what many of his compatriots in Calcutta were doubtless thinking and feeling, though few of them would have cared to show this, because to be British in this great imperial city had always meant that at the very best, you never unbuttoned yourself too much in front of the natives, however friendly you might have become. 'Yesterday,' wrote this Mr Stephens, 'for the first time, and from the heart, much to my surprise, I said "Jai Hind". In itself, for its bigger meaning, I have always liked the term, as I like India. But its recent historical associations are most obnoxious. It stuck in my throat. My whole energies and idealism as a civilian had been put into helping to win World War II for what I thought was righteousness. Like other British folk in India, I at that time underwent bitter personal suffering, in long separations and in loss of dear friends and relations, also of my home, and scarcely more than two years ago "Jai Hind" was still being shouted on the Burma front against those fine men, British and Indian, fighting on my side, the right side as I believe, by those others – traitors to my thinking – who had joined Subhas Bose and the Japanese. I was not, until yesterday, able to forget these things.

' "Jai Hind" was also shouted at British people here in Calcutta with plainly insulting intent, during the cold-weather riots of '45/'46; and forgetfulness of insults is not easy. Even last Friday, Independence Day, it sometimes seemed to be meant more in challenge than friendship. In general, however, that was a wonderfully friendly day, our harried, hatred-filled Calcutta was transformed, and I felt happy too, so I smiled and waved in answer to the shoutings; but I could not bring myself actually to utter the phrase. It was one for which I felt perhaps almost as much repugnance as Muslims themselves have for parts of

"Bande Mataram". Yesterday, the day of Id, in Chowringhee, next to me in a traffic block, was one of Calcutta's countless lorry-loads of jubilant, slogan-shouting people, Hindus and Muslims intermixed. They waved and smiled, shouting "Jai Hind" and I waved back. Seated nearest to me, on the wooden footboard, was a young Muslim in colourful fresh clothing for the Id. He had evidently noticed that, though smiling too, I had carefully avoided answering. He bent forward. "Please say it, sir," he pleaded. "We didn't like it either, but we do now. We have forgotten about quarrels."

'I said it at once, without reflection, readily, from the heart; and I do not think I will have further difficulty.'

The moment when every Englishman would have to swallow his pride and the insults it attracted, when he would have to get out of India with a sore but rather soft heart, had been a long time coming, but it had been prepared some years before it actually happened. It was certainly within the scheme of things maturing in the collective mind of Mr Attlee's Labour Government which, two years before, had appointed the gentleman who was packing his bags in one part of Government House while the jubilant citizens of Calcutta were removing his cups and saucers from another. Sir Frederick Burrows, in fact, departed in some confusion. In order to catch the flying boat from the river at Bally to England at the appointed hour, his bodyguard had to hustle him and his lady wife through the crowds so unceremoniously that there was no time to say goodbye to his civil and military officers or to any of the leading citizens. Thus did Calcutta see off the last British Governor of Bengal. It would never have done for Queen Victoria, or even for Lord Curzon, who had also represented the mightly Raj here.

But, then, Sir Frederick Burrows, GGSI, GCIE, DL, had never been quite as other men usually were when appointed to sit in Government House at Calcutta, in spite of his various decorations. In the place of men who had never, during their own military service, been much less than a captain of Lancers or a lieutenant of Dragoons, here was one who had been but a company sergeant major in the Grenadier Guards. And where Wellesley, Hastings, Amherst, Auckland, Hardinge, Bentinck, Ronaldshay and most of his other predecessors in that splendid palace had been peers of the realm, Sir Frederick, on stepping into their shoes, had just completed several industrious years as President of the National Union of Railwaymen.

9

THE PETRIFYING JUNGLE

THE Western world began to take notice of Calcutta's now celebrated plight fourteen years after Independence. Many people were well aware of it before then, but only if they had been in professional contact with it, or if they had actually seen it developing themselves. In the spring of 1960, however, the World Bank sent a mission to India to review the progress of the republic's economic development during its First and Second Five-Year Plans, and to investigate the prospects of the Third Plan which was due to come into operation the following year. The mission was shocked by what it found in Calcutta and said so in its report. At almost the same time, the Indian Prime Minister was quoted in the international press on the same subject. 'Calcutta,' said Mr Nehru, 'is the biggest city in the country, its problems are national problems, quite apart from problems of West Bengal, and it is necessary that something special should be done. If the whole city went to pieces, it would be a tremendous tragedy.' From that moment Calcutta became news, for here were clearly the makings of disaster, which always has provided the most stimulating news, mankind being never more lively than when he can respond to the dreadful with a twinge of horror and a spasm of compassion.

A handful of mankind from the world outside became involved. Some went to Calcutta to see what could be done, they usually returned and they heightened the sense of impending catastrophe by what they had to tell. A typical excursion was that of Professor Colin Buchanan and eight other Anglo-American town planners, who in 1967 reported: 'A city in a state of crisis. We have not seen human degradation on a comparable scale in any other city in the world. This is one of the greatest urban concentrations in existence rapidly approaching the point of breakdown in its economy, housing, sanitation, transport and the essential humanities of life. If the final breakdown were to take place it would be a disaster for mankind of a more sinister sort than any disaster of flood or famine.' Which stimulated more journalists and television crews to fly into Dum Dum to collect more copy and more film. Meanwhile, the great cities of the West, New York in particular, began to have faint and uneasy intimations that what they were hearing about Calcutta might indeed be in store for them one day. The metropolitans of Europe and the United States are now quite frantically certain that it is possible for a city to strangle itself in its own traffic, to poison itself with its own pollutions, to tear itself to pieces by the hand of its own people; and they no longer need the example of Calcutta to convince them that this is so. So they struggle with themselves and, spasmodically, they cast a glance over their shoulders to see how the forthcoming disaster is proceeding in the first city in the world scheduled to perish of its private misfortunes. They continue to send their emissaries from time to time, with their notebooks and their cameras, and Calcutta has become so weary of these visitations, which have brought little but expressions of sympathy so far, that a man with a camera is now very likely to have it smashed in anger and resentment, and a man who flaps his notebook too obviously may swiftly be surrounded by a mob who will not question him gently.

A city does not suddenly break down. A metropolitan collapse has not yet happened in the modern world, but if Calcutta should provide the first example then the ultimate civic disaster is clearly preceded by a long and gradual process of neglect and decay which undermines the city's foundations to a point at which a very small push will send the whole structure tumbling into ruins. This process can take just as long as the process of a city's growth to maturity and supremacy. The two can even be seen. passing the years in tandem, one of the city's parts thriving and becoming grand while the other becomes increasingly wasted and diseased. This is manifestly so in Calcutta's case. Almost from the moment there was something more than a collection of straggling mud huts by the Hooghly here, proud and imperial voices have proclaimed the glories of this city, and they have been well heard in the heart of Empire and beyond. Yet every time boasts were made, there was someone pointing out other things that were nothing to boast about. Just occasionally, someone cried shame in the same tongue and with the same breeding as the boasters; and, generally, he seems to have gone quite unheard by his fellows, his message lost maybe in the historically well-known difficulties of communication.

Lord Valentia, an early tourist, was one of the best-known scrutineers of Calcutta in its early period of magnificence. He came just ten years after Sir John Shore was appointed Governor-General with that ringing and Biblical assurance of service to every native of India, whatever his situation might be. Lord Valentia seems to have been the first man to remark on the palatial grandeur of the city, particularly of Chowringhee. He also took the trouble to investigate the native quarters and was honest enough to report that 'The Black Town is as complete a contrast to this as can well be conceived. Its streets are narrow and dirty; the houses, of two storeys, occasionally of brick, but generally mud and thatched, perfectly resembling the cabins of the poorest class in Ireland.' In 1803, no literate Englishman could be expected to imagine greater human wretchedness than that. Throughout the nineteenth century the developing picture is one of a burgeoning European city, accommodating a small proportion of acceptably wealthy natives, surrounded by a swelling cantonment of helots; and while the first progressively equips itself with all the amenities of civilization as they become available to it, the second is more or less left to its own resources, or at best provided with one or two spare parts of urban equipment long after the needs of the masters have been attended to. In 1836, the Chief Magistrate, Mr Farran, was noting that 'The only broad streets in the native part of the town are Amherst Street and the Central Road, the former unfinished and neither of them considered thoroughfares. The Chitpore Road is the great thoroughfare, but it is narrow, winding, dirty and encroached upon, while the cross-ways are all lanes, very narrow, very filthy and bounded generally by deep open ditches.' Sixteen years before that, the British had started metalling the roads of *their* Calcutta.

It was the perpetually watchful and usually caustic Girish

Chandra Ghosh who remarked on another disparity between the
two communities a couple of decades later, almost on the eve
of the Mutiny. 'Calcutta is flatly getting too rich for poor people
to abide in it ... as we see from the last meeting of the Legislative
Council in the debate on the report of the select committee on
the proposition for lighting the St James portion of Calcutta
with gas ... The Gas Company is not a philanthropic body
whose mission to India owes its origins to a Christian desire of
rescuing the people of the country from eternal night and blessing them with a light equal in radiance to that of the God of day
– free of charge! ... we are obtuse enough not to perceive how
the comfort and convenience of men who inhabit hovels and
breathe the contaminated air of cess pools can be augmented by
their European neighbours revelling in a light which is seventeen
times more bright than candlelight . . .' It was Mr Strachey, the
sanitary commissioner for Bengal, who in 1864 pointed out a
hazard to local health that not even the British could have escaped
very easily, unless they took the most stringent domestic pre-
cautions. 'More than 5,000 corpses have been thrown from Calcutta into the river,' he wrote, 'which supplies the greatest part
of its inhabitants with water for all domestic purposes and which
for several miles is covered as thickly with shipping as almost
anywhere in the world. One thousand five hundred corpses have
actually been thrown into the river in one year from the General
Hospital alone.'

At about this time, Florence Nightingale was writing from
England to Sir Bartle Frere, who had served in Calcutta and had
then become Governor of Bombay. That city, she remarked, 'has
a lower death-rate on the last two years than London, the healthiest city in Europe. This is entirely your doing. If we do not take
care, Bombay will outstrip us in the sanitary race. People will be
ordered for the benefit of their health to Bombay . . .' This was
not a thing that anyone could ever have said of Calcutta. There
was another difference between the two cities and Girish Chandra
Ghosh had inevitably picked it up. The same debate that had
produced the gas-lighting proposals had produced a reference
to the taxation of wheel-and-horse traffic. 'These taxes exist in
Bombay,' wrote Ghosh, 'and it was a great mistake to have with-

drawn them after Calcutta had begun to be accustomed to the new imposition. The horse and carriage tax is a tax on luxury and its operation is not therefore grievously felt by those who come under it, whereas a general tax to the benefit of particular classes is a never-ending source of discontent.' The tax had been withdrawn in Calcutta, as many other things unwelcome to the British community there were frequently altered to suit them, because they had the Imperial Government cornered where they wanted it, and could press it into an acceptable shape. 'In India,' wrote Ghosh in 1863, 'there are two interests. There is firstly the government interest, which rightly employed is identical with the interest of justice and native interests ... and secondly, there is the non-official English interest, claiming special immunities and consideration by right of conquest, superior intelligence, energy and power of consideration. This gives birth to an antagonism by no means unnatural ... It is injurious only to the interest which assumes that India is a family preserve of the fifth-rate men of England – not even of the classes which supply the Civil Service – which claims the privilege of obtaining land under conditions only slightly removed from those of an absolute gift, which clamours for a contract law calculated to enslave the native population, and demands immunity from the criminal jurisdiction of the established courts of the country.'

A few months later, he logged his own progress report on the physical state of Calcutta. 'The Imperial city in the middle of the rains is a sight worth the enthusiasm of the tourist. Perhaps no other chief city in the world presents variations of road scenery so great or so interesting. The traveller who lands at Chandpal Ghat, fresh from the atmosphere of European civilization, is regaled with the view of a splendid metropolis, with church steeples reaching up to the clouds, rows of palaces on each hand, streets smooth as bowling greens – wide, dustless and dry – the very perfection of macadamization. He drives into Chowringhee through all its by-lanes and larger thoroughfares, and his heart cannot wish for higher displays of municipal talent and conservancy genius and activity than those before him. Everything except Dhurmtollah Bazar is neat, clean and tidy; even the lamp posts wear an appearance suggestive of the idea of being weekly varnished ... But should business or curiosity call him to the native town ... he will see or rather feel by the jolt of his carriage, streets than which the natural paths of the forest are better fitted for travelling. He will have his nose assailed by the stench of drains which have not felt the ministering hand of man ever since the last rains, his affrighted horse will obstinately back from pits in the thoroughfares wide enough to bury all the rubbish in the adjoining houses, his carriage wheels will stick resolutely into ruts from which release is possible only by the aid of half a dozen men and as many bamboo poles ... After a heavy shower of rain he will in some places deem it more pleasant and advantageous to hire a boat than swim his horse.'

By the time Kipling came to Calcutta, twenty years later, it was notorious in some circles as the City of Stinks as well as palaces. This was at the bottom of his abiding dislike of it and 'in spite of that stink, they allow, they even encourage natives to look after the place! The damp, drainage-soaked soil is sick with the teeming life of a hundred years, and the Municipal Board list is choked with the names of natives – men of the breed born in and raised off this surfeited muck-heap.' He took the view that an efficient municipal government in England would have made short work of Calcutta's obnoxious problems; they wanted shovels, not sentiments, in this part of the world. Which was slightly beside the point, even though Indians by then had a loud voice in municipal affairs. In 1876 the Bengal Government had created Calcutta Corporation largely, though by no means completely, on an electoral basis. Its Bengali councillors could not have been much encouraged by the condescending patronage of their masters in the provincial government, let alone that of the even more superior beings of the imperial ruling body. When the Entally drainage system was opened in 1896, the Lieutenant-Governor of Bengal, Sir Alexander Mackenzie, told them what he thought of their struggling efforts in self-administration in the roundest terms. 'You have, gentlemen, no doubt,' he said, 'been hampered in the task of improving Calcutta by many things, and perhaps by nothing so much as by your own constitution. The marvel is that with such an impracticable organization so much good work should have been done. You have a constitution borrowed *en bloc* from the most advanced models in England, and without any reference to the utterly different circumstances of an Oriental city, and a very mixed community. It seems to have been supposed that because Birmingham, for instance (which I know well), is admirably managed by an elected Council of 72, Calcutta could be equally well managed by a council of 75, of whom 50 are elected. But in Birmingham, to begin with, the population is homogeneous and accustomed for generations to managing its own affairs on lines as to which all parties are agreed. The council there is composed entirely of shrewd, capable men of business, manufacturers, merchants, tradesmen and the like, whose one object is to treat every question before them not as an opportunity for speech-making, but as a matter to be settled as promptly as may be in the most practical way . . . Now I think everybody in Calcutta outside the Corporation, and a good many people inside it, will admit that there is here far too much speaking for the sake of speech . . .'

A great deal of Calcutta's problems, clearly, arose from the enormous migration of Indians to the city, which had occurred almost from the moment of Charnock's first settlement. At the time of the Black Hole the population was estimated at 400,000 or so, and no more than a couple of thousand could have been Europeans then. By Kipling's day there was something approaching a million people here. They had not been driven to Calcutta to provide some kind of slave labour for European masters (although the *Bengal Chronicle* in 1831 was remarking on a slave market in the city then, and the practice throughout India was not effectively outlawed until 1845) even if the conditions of their employment might sometimes be indistinguishable from those of slavery. They had poured down the Hooghly in search of wealth, just as the Englishmen had sailed up it for the same purpose, and they had been incited to do this, as likely as not, by their own people. In 1823, Bhabanicharan Bannerji had written a book called *Kalikata Kamalaylay*, which can be translated as 'Calcutta; dwelling place of the goddess of fortune', which described the city as a 'bottomless ocean of wealth' and which was intended as a guide to countrymen arriving in the metropolis for the first time.

There is an indictment of the British to be made out of the relative living and other conditions of Calcutta, but it is not one of brutality and deliberate degradation of the native population; the indictment is the same one which has stood from start to finish of the British connection with the city, of indifference and incomprehension by all but a comparatively small handful of exceptions who felt some moral obligation (especially in those self-consciously Christian times) to be much more than indifferent. It was the British, after all, who started this place in order to tap the wealth of this land. The fact is, of course, that until the last quarter of the nineteenth century the relative conditions of rich and poor in Calcutta were not vastly different from those of Britain; it is scarcely surprising that men who had been unconcerned about them at home should not notice or care about them here; it is approximately from 1875 onwards that the developing conscience of the rich in London becomes the more conspicuous by its almost total absence in Calcutta.

Lord Curzon well knew what Calcutta stood for, and he put it all into one noble paragraph when he was addressing the businessmen of the city in 1903. 'To me, Calcutta is the capital, not merely of a province, great as that province is, but of the Indian Empire. As such, it appears to me fitly to symbolize the work that the English have done, and are doing, in this country. For though, of the enormous population of over 1,100,000 souls that make up the city on both banks of the river, not much more than 30,000 are returned as Europeans and Eurasians, yet a glance at the buildings of the town, at the river and the roar and the smoke, is sufficient to show that Calcutta is in reality a European city set down upon Asiatic soil, and that it is a monument – in my opinion one of the most striking extant monuments, for it is the second city to London in the entire British Empire – to the energy and achievements of our race.' Within twelve months, the local historian H. E. A. Cotton had written that 'Ten minutes walk from Dalhousie Square will land the seeker after sensation in a labyrinth of narrow, unpaved winding lanes, polluted with odours that put those of Cologne to shame and swarming with humanity, where the scavenging carts are the rarest of visitors and the ghostly glimmer of an occasional and inadequate gas lamp furnishes the solitary illumination. Not a thousand yards from Government House, troops of jackals may be heard after sunset sweeping through the deserted street and making the night hideous with their fearsome howls.'

One reason for the excessive anger of the local British community when they heard that the imperial capital was to move to Delhi, was that a Calcutta Improvement Trust had just been set up, which had involved a certain amount of expenditure even though it had not yet started to yield results. It was established by an Act of 1911, which sought to improve and expand the city 'by opening up congested areas, laying out or altering streets, providing open spaces for purposes of ventilation or recreation and ... the rehousing of the poorer and working-classes displaced by the execution of improvement schemes ...' A member of the Institute of Civil Engineers and the Town Planning Institute in Britain, Mr E. P. Richards, was appointed Chief Engineer of the Trust six months after the Viceroy's flag had been removed from Government House. He subsequently had a breakdown, which caused him to return to England before he could actually engineer any changes in Calcutta. But in 1914 he produced a report for the Improvement Trust, based upon his investigations while he was in the city. He had been consulted in Calcutta, among other things, about the possibility of replacing the single bridge across the Hooghly and he had agreed that this matter was extremely urgent and of paramount importance, but it had become very clear to him 'that the proposed new bridge as tendered for would be too narrow even from the first day it was opened to traffic'. And so the tender was withdrawn, and the proposal was quietly forgotten, and although a second Hooghly bridge was put across the river six miles upstream at Bally in 1931, the main crossing to Howrah remained as a contraption of pontoons until 1943, when it was replaced by the present towering structure. Although work had started on the Howrah Bridge in 1937, it might have still been building if the military had not required a proper crossing at that point for fighting their war against the Japanese.

Quite apart from the incompetence imputed to the bridge planners by Richards, his report would have fallen as a piece of

anarchy upon the ears of Lord Curzon for one. 'The writer' –
Richards generally referred to himself in the third person – 'The
writer found that very many Europeans who lived in Calcutta
possessed little or no knowledge of the dense back blocks that
compose three quarters of the city ... Most of us have had no
occasion to go about anywhere except in the Dalhousie Square,
Old Court House Street, Chowringhee and Park Street area,
which make a mere fringe along only half the West side of the
built-up mass of Calcutta ... One can walk day after day for
hours in the lanes of North Calcutta without meeting a single
European ... the general public of Calcutta are not conscious
of the state of their city; it has never been put before them
forcibly and clearly ... we have all heard Calcutta described
glowingly and quite sincerely as the fairest city in the East ...
but the speakers are plainly unaware of the real conditions ...
Reform measures are looked upon with suspicion, indifference or
with a positive and powerful hostility. It should be made
thoroughly known that the city is in a most serious condition,
and that only prompt, big and concerted action will maintain our
commercial supremacy and save Calcutta and Howrah from becoming the largest slum in the world.'

This is a very angry man writing. He has found the housing
conditions of the city 'scandalously bad. An acute housing
famine prevails and increases. It has prevailed during the last
thirty years and nothing has been done to remedy it ... Rents
are tremendous and the accommodation given is all too small and
far too crowded. Comfortable, wholesome family life is being
pushed right out of existence in Calcutta. It has already vanished
to the extent of forty-five per cent ... infant mortality and tuberculosis stand at world records.' Richards estimated that at least
800 acres of 2,500 acres in central Calcutta must be classified as
'rank slum'; at least 250,000 people were living in houses that,
under any ordinary by-laws, would be condemned and closed as
unfit for human habitation. 'Nearly all the working-class families
can afford but a single room in which they have to live, eat,
sleep, propagate their species and die. It is seldom a room of
decent size and usually it is ill-lit and badly ventilated and is in
a slum or chawl. Often two families exist in one room. Men –

most especially in India where family life and early marriage rules are so potent – would certainly bring their families to Calcutta if accommodation for them existed ... 900,000 people live in 45,000 houses; i.e. the average number of people per house is twenty. The average Indian house contains twice as many rooms as an English house, so that for genuine comparison, the Calcutta housing squeeze is equal to about ten people per house in Great Britain.' And there, at that time, the average content of a house was just over five people.

As for town planning, it was virtually non-existent. 'A casual glance at the Calcutta plans shows instantly that the city, as a whole, actually possesses no streets. There are but two small areas in Calcutta having the normal street system which is found throughout the whole area of almost every city in the world ...' The mass of lanes shown on most of the survey maps available were, Richards had discovered in · those lonely rambles of his, fictitiously broad, having been represented on paper wider than they were on the ground so that the draughtsmen could get the names printed along them. 'Urban, built-up Calcutta has no street system; 2,500 acres are provided only with highly irregular lanes and passages. It would require the creation of ·110 miles of ordinary 30–40 ft streets to bring Calcutta into line with even the old built-up sections of European cities.' Since 1875, a British public health act had forbidden the building of any street less than 36 ft wide in the United Kingdom and most British towns insisted on a minimum of between 40 and 50 feet. In the second city of the British Empire, where there were roads at all, they were scarcely ever more than 20 ft wide and more frequently they were only 10 ft from wall to wall; and not one road in the entire city, British or native quarters, started in the middle and ran out into the surrounding country.

For the two hundred and fifty or so pages of his report, Richards enumerated one defect after another. The tramways of Calcutta did not belong to the city, but to a limited liability company and there were no tram tracks at all across the Hooghly; Richards called this unprecedented, and pointed out that it was one reason why North Calcutta, on the East bank, was so fearfully congested. He suggested that one cause of overcrowded dwellings in Calcutta was a habit of settling litigation which happened neither in Bombay nor Madras. It was called the 'partition suit' and it meant that when two or more brothers quarrelled over an inherited property and took their quarrel to court, the court usually ordered that the house should be divided by partitions into separate habitations for the warring factions and their families; elsewhere, judges usually ruled that the property should be sold, if no agreement could be reached, with the money divided between the brothers. The former Chief Engineer pointed out that the dock sills at Kidderpore were not deep enough to take vessels of six thousand tons and above unless they had been partly unloaded first. He also strongly advised the city fathers to look to their accounts, for no great headway with their enormous problems could be made unless they substantially increased their revenue. He even compiled a table of towns and cities in India and Great Britain, so that Calcutta could compare its financial position with communities that were something less than second in the whole Empire. Part of it showed these figures:

City	Population	Rateable Value	Debt	Average Rate
Calcutta	896,867*	£2,478,000	£2,951,294	12s. 9½d.
Bombay	979,445	£3,217,000	£2,796,510	14s. 6½d.
Birkenhead	131,000	£679,000	£2,227,000	39s. 6d.
Bolton	182,000	£852,000	£3,852,056	31s. 11½d.
Dundee	170,000	£975,000	—	37s. 4d.
Manchester	720,000	£4,657,000	—	54s. 10½d.

Throughout his report, Richards was taking Lord Curzon's proud estimation of Calcutta at its face value. It was indeed the second city of the whole British Empire, and not merely in population. By the time Curzon's former aide-de-camp Ronaldshay became Governor of Bengal in 1917, the seaborne trade out of Calcutta was running at £175 million a year. Richards was therefore insisting on comparisons in keeping with its substance

* This excluded the population of Howrah across the river which, except for purely municipal purposes, is usually included as part of Calcutta in every count. All figures in the table are for the fiscal year 1911–12.

and its status. He pointed out that, a few years earlier, Chicago had felt itself degenerating into a mess but that with a firm sense of purpose (and a population twice that of Calcutta's) it had pulled itself together and become proud with reason again. He even ended his report with a series of helpful suggestions for making Calcutta more handsome after it had been made more habitable, with models taken from a number of great European cities. There was a picture of the Beethoven Square in Vienna, with its trained creepers, and Richards thought that eventually Dalhousie Square might look quite becoming with something similar. There was an illustration of the 'tank' in the Parc Monceau in Paris – 'a good example of the artistic treatment of small artificial ponds'. Calcutta, he well knew, had a long way to go before it could afford to think of embellishing itself like that. He had found only one thing to applaud from start to finish of his report. With the largest water tank in the world, the city could, by 1914, be proud of its water supply.

It is impossible to judge from his report whether Richards was extremely naïve, or whether he was writing with his tongue jammed into his cheek, when he challenged the British of Calcutta in their proudest assumptions about their city. Curzon's claim clearly invited comparison at an international level, yet there is no sign that he or any of his local peers measured their second city of the Empire in any terms other than those of population statistics, trading returns and sovereignty over an enormous territory. Richards really was baying at the moon if he seriously thought that the Bengal Chamber of Commerce or the membership of the Bengal Club would lift a finger to prettify a water tank that no Englishman need ever go near from the moment he came to Calcutta to the moment he left. Nevertheless, in the next few years, certain of his submissions were taken up. A great widening of streets and cutting of roads occurred, and something approaching £5 million was spent in the process, though Calcutta still waits for the thoroughfare that will start in the city centre and finish up in the country.

When the 1921 census was taken, the author of the official report on Calcutta's progress in the previous decade remarked that 'The city may have lost a few officials from the changes that have been made' (with the shift of capital) 'but otherwise it has been little affected.' He also spoke of 'the crying need for better communications, whether by tram, tube, electric railway or other means between the business quarters of the city and its immediate suburbs'. He further remarked that 'In the localities of Barabazar, Bowbazar, Bentinck Street and Dharamtala, the Marwari community, the Chinese, Anglo-Indians and others live under conditions of overcrowding unimaginable until they have been witnessed, and are rack-rented to an extent far exceeding that to which the Bengali population or the better-class European population is obliged to submit.' No. 10 Gas Street, he noticed, was a bustee with several hundred huts pitched behind its street front and a population of three thousand. Nor was this by any means unique. 'It may be taken as a fact ... that the accommodation offered in Calcutta to its population is about 1·8 rooms per family.' At almost the same time a committee on the increasing industrial unrest in Bengal was reporting that between June 1920 and March 1921 there had been 137 strikes in and around the city; 74 of them totally concerned with grievances about pay, another 36 pressing for higher wages and other things simultaneously. In 1930, a report on the standard of living among jute mill workers in Calcutta showed that, judging by samples taken from six mills, 76 per cent of the working families were in debt by an average of more than two and a half times their monthly income, even though labourers were putting in a sixty-hour week.

By the time the penultimate British Governor of Bengal arrived in Calcutta in 1944, both province and city were in chaos. There was, of course, a war on, though Calcutta curiously missed any direct enemy action apart from a few light air raids which did little damage. On top of this, the famine had only just receded, and there had been half a century of civil disorder. But these events did not explain everything that Mr R. G. (later Lord) Casey found when he reached the city and was welcomed by leading articles which wondered whether the Bengalis had now become a colony of Australia. Anyone as close as he had been to the ultimately Sir Robert Menzies in an administration run from Canberra, was perfectly capable of caricaturing British ruling attitudes in some respects; but at least he had the gift of bluntness and didn't much mind whose feet he trod on below the level of sovereign. Casey found that he had inherited a machine that 'was bankrupt, as far as any government can be said to be bankrupt ... For the last fifty years the Government of Bengal had been starved of money. The policy had been to keep taxation down to the minimum, with the result that the provincial revenue was wholly inadequate.' The administration of the province and city, moreover, had evolved without any apparent design over a century or so. It had been originated to administer law, to maintain the public peace, to collect land revenue. 'Bits and pieces had been tacked on to the system from time to time to keep pace with the increasing functions of government, but frequently the new bits had been attached to the wrong parts. Thus I found one department administering the strange alliance of Forestry and Excise under a secretary who had a full-time job in another department; another department dealt simultaneously with Education and Land Registration, also under a secretary with preoccupations in another department.'

Casey, unlike most men in his position before him, toured the bustee areas of the city and was appalled, as perhaps only an Australian (or a Swiss, or a Scandinavian) could be appalled by slum dwellings. He told an entourage of newspapermen 'I have seen something of the way in which hundreds of thousands of the citizens of Calcutta are obliged to live. Human beings cannot allow other human beings to exist under these conditions ... My only interest is that these conditions should be improved, and neither politics nor vested interests should be allowed to stand in the way. The people of Calcutta have the right to ask in six months time what has been done about it.' What Casey himself did was to write a memorandum to Lord Wavell, such a document of candour as Viceroys had rarely been accustomed to receiving. 'At some time in the past,' it said, 'the British administration evidently decided that Bengal should be run on the minimum possible expenditure of public monies, very low taxation, and no expediture of loan monies for development purposes ... Quite apart from any specific war-time burdens which have been thrown on the Bengal administration, there is the fact that the

functions of government have changed very rapidly in recent
years. In Bengal, the administration for generations has traditionally been concerned with law and order and revenue. It is
only recently, and relatively suddenly, that they have been called
upon to adjust themselves to coping with the full range of
matters that concern a modern government, for which their previous training and tradition have ill-fitted them. In consequence,
they are making rather a poor fist of things. This last criticism,
I believe, applies perhaps with special force to the European
members of the ICS on whom, in my opinion, the major responsibility for the administration of Bengal still rests ... the risk is
that if things go on as they are going on at present, we may well
see the situation degenerate into something quite unpleasant,
which we shall all regret ... as near a breakdown as no matter.'

Just below this ramshackle apparatus of the Raj, and of necessity beholden to it at all times, was the even more suspect appli-
ance of Calcutta Corporation, which by now was completely
officered by Indians, even though a proportion of its councillors
remained British. Six months after Independence was proclaimed, the new Government of West Bengal's Biswas Commission began to investigate the Corporation and its workings,
and eventually produced a report that was so damning to almost
everyone who had come under scrutiny that it was never actually
published. It had discovered, among many other things, that 'the
powers of delegation varied from time to time according to the
whims and caprices of the Councillors, and reduced the Chief
Executive Officer to a position of complete subservience, so much
so that even in matters in which the Chief Executive Officer had
statutory powers, individual Councillors had their way'. It outlined the history of Calcutta's water supply, which even E. P.
Richards had thought a matter of pride, but which was now a
potential source of disaster and typical of every part of the municipal machine. Until 1820, British Calcutta had received its
water from the bags of its bheesties, who had drawn from the
Great Tank, Loll Diggy, in what was eventually named Dalhousie Square. The native community, of course, then fended for
itself in the Hooghly or wherever else it might find water. But in
1820 Messrs Jessop and Co. had installed a small pumping plant

at Chandpal Ghat, for lifting water from the river and into aqueducts which would serve the British quarter for seven hours a day, eight months in the year; in the remaining four months the Europeans, like everyone else, collected much safer rainwater. Filtered water was supplied from 1870, along cast-iron main pipes with a life expectation of a hundred years, and at the beginning it was designed to provide six million gallons a day for a population of 400,000; which was considerably larger than the European population of the city, substantially less than the total number of people there when it was installed. Twice this filtered supply had been extended or improved, in 1903 and again in 1923. The last extension had been made with an expectation of 1,300,000 people living in Calcutta by 1941; in fact, by then 2,100,000 were in the city and twelve months later the figure had risen to 3,000,000.

For what, only six months previously, had been the second city of the British Empire, this was not, therefore, a particularly well provided place. Nor was it a particularly luminous place, with only 9,000 electric lights, 19,000 gas lamps and 350 oil lamps. It was not a particularly wholesome place, with 4,371 bustees inhabited by more than one million people. It was not a very promising place, either, for the Biswas inquiry was to reveal about the Corporation more or less what R. G. Casey had discovered only four years earlier about provincial government, that 'the finances are in a bad state and the administration full of abuses due to neglect of duty, corruption and wilful violations of the law. It would not be an exaggeration to say that financially the Corporation is heading for a disaster, and is unable to meet its necessary expenses. This inability is largely, though not entirely, due to maladministration ...' In spite of its vast built-in wealth, Calcutta was not – one way and another – the most splendid bequest the British might have made to their residuary legatees by the Hooghly.

It is all much worse now, twenty-five years later. Things are so bad in almost every respect that it is not at all uncommon in Calcutta today to encounter an Indian, by no means a wealthy man, who affectionately remembers the years when the British were here, when the city was not quite such a frightful place and when some things appeared to work with a modicum of efficiency. He is not being quite just to his own administrators when he takes this charming view of old imperial relations, however, for part of this crumbling structure is the result of events over which they have had no control. The largest of these is the flow of refugees from East Pakistan, which began at Partition and which has continued with intermittent pauses ever since. Just over four million refugees came into the country in the first decade and threequarters of them came to West Bengal, perhaps a million to Calcutta itself, which is only thirty-five miles from the border. The city was so totally unprepared to receive this inundation on top of its already swamping mass of people that until 1956 there were nearly five hundred refugee families permanently encamped upon the platforms of Sealdah Station in the middle of the city; 244 of them were then shifted into some unemployed film studios in Tollygunge, another 217 into the godown of a disused jute mill at Cossipore – and there they all remained for another decade. Another horde at once turned four of the city's mosques into massive and communal doss houses. The flow was reduced to a trickle until a second great wave came from the East during the Indo-Pakistani war, and since then an average of 300 refugees a day have crossed into West Bengal, with occasionally larger numbers as some slight imbalance in Pakistani politics or religious sensitivity tipped more than usual on the road to Calcutta. In the middle of 1970 for a while there were up to a couple of thousand a day coming over, and it is possible that 60,000 entered West Bengal in the first five months of the year. Most of them came on foot, some poled themselves by boat down the Ichamati River, one of the larger watercourses in that muddy, swampy endlessness of the Ganga delta. A great number camped exhausted at Hasnabad in the 24 Parganas, where the railway platform, like the one in the city, has perpetually been lined with makeshift shelters to protect these people from the sun.

The Government in Delhi has committed itself to helping them by giving a small dole of money as soon as they have crossed its borders, by providing three blankets for each family, by finding milk for the children and the sick, by eventually producing a grant of cash so that the new citizens can rehabilitate themselves. But there has never been enough of anything to go properly round. Early in 1969 there were 1,300,000 refugees in West Bengal still waiting for their rehabilitation grants. For those who were still coming, the ones who survived the periodic outbreaks of cholera in the places where they first encamped on Indian soil, the ones who didn't quietly die of exhaustion or lack of food in the same spots, there was very often nothing better to look forward to than the beggary of Calcutta's already overpopulated streets. So many refugees have now come to this city from East Pakistan that students of Bengali have observed that the standard provincial argot of the streets has been slightly modified by their presence, with a fresh word here, a new phrase there, a subtle change in pronunciation throughout the vocabulary. Being Bengalis themselves, they have inevitably brought poets with them and one of these, Samsher Anwar, has written his own epitaph to the years of precarious sanctuary:

> Under the frost-bitten, rain-marred lamp-post
> I have stood here, deserted, for the last twenty years of my life,
> Looking slantingly I have been watching the criss-cross game of
>   sorrow.
> I fear, having stood thus for such a long time, one day I will be
>   murdered while asleep.
>
> If one calls this fated picture History, then I accept History.
> The creation and civilization that has grown beyond my existence
>   has no meaning for me at all.
> If I ever attach any meaning to a truth then it is
> This Calcutta and my lonely bed.

Always there has been the prospect of more refugees flowing in one direction from East to West; for nothing like the exchange of Muslims and Hindus across the boundaries of the Punjab and West Pakistan at the time of Partition, which virtually cancelled each other out, ever happened here to any significant degree. And apart from the refugees, there has been the steady migration of those other hordes enticed by the basilisk wealth of Calcutta – in the ten years up to 1961 there were 24,000 of

these from Western India alone, 5,000 from Assam, 16,000 from
South India, 33,000 from Orissa, 71,000 from Uttar Pradesh,
183,000 from Bihar, 168,000 from elsewhere in West Bengal.
Even if none of these people had reproduced themselves several
times over, Calcutta would by now be in an awful mess. As it
is, the city faces catastrophe partly because of their deadly lack
of birth control.

The Indian Government over the past few years has invested
enormous sums in its birth control programme, and there are
calculating men in Delhi who will assure you that at last it is
beginning to have an appreciable effect. There has been an
engaging campaign of propaganda throughout the republic to
persuade people that two children are respectable but that three
are a menace. Elephants have paraded with the message. It has
been displayed on the backs of buses. All over the country, the
inverted red triangle and its beaming family of four has sym-
bolized moderation even to the illiterate; you see this sign in
gigantic poster form above the ghats at Benares, and half the
trees in Orissa have been placarded with it. All forms of control
have been advocated from time to time, so that a commuter with
a civic conscience has been able to drop in for a vasectomy at a
clinic on Bombay railway station *en route* to the office, while a
pair of newly-weds in Kerala have been liable to receive the
nation's gift parcel of 144 condoms neatly packed among all
their other presents. In West Bengal, it is said that 433,000 men
were sterilised in a couple of years recently. Yet it is typical of
Calcutta's awful capacity for wasting its resources that, although
the red triangle may well be displayed on some of its walls, the
symbol's most noticeable appearance is on the back of the local
telephone directory, where it can only engage the attention of
those least in need of its message. A gloomy man might well
think that even at its most effective the birth control programme,
which didn't start until 1967, has come far too late to save Calcutta from itself and its people. The city's population had already trebled between 1921 and 1961 and nothing that a state
pledging itself to democracy can do is going to prevent more
people arriving, even if they don't reproduce when they settle
here. The lack of homes was bad enough in 1952 for judges to be

tut-tutting when they had to pick their way between the five hundred or so employees who by then were permanently living in the corridors and upon the verandahs of the High Court, with their belongings scattered all round that Gothic monument. Even at that stage, two decades ago, they could have hoped for nothing better.

Any one of those five hundred men would presumably have been glad to occupy something in the area which 'consists of two rows of houses with a street seven yards wide between them; each row consists of what are styled back and front houses – that is, two houses placed back to back. There are no yards or out-conveniences; the privies are in the centre of each row, about a yard wide; over them there is part of a sleeping room; there is no ventilation in the bedrooms; each house contains two rooms, viz. a living place and a sleeping room above; each room is about three yards wide and four feet long. In one of these houses there are nine persons belonging to one family and the mother on the eve of her confinement. There are forty-four houses in the two rows ... in the centre of which is the common gutter, or more properly sink, into which all sorts of refuse is thrown; it is a foot in depth. Thus there is always a quantity of putrefying matter contaminating the air.'

The first sentence betrays the origin of that description, which is far removed from Calcutta. It comes from the pen of William Rayner, medical officer for Heaton Norris, Stockport, and it is part of Edwin Chadwick's report on the sanitary conditions of the labouring population of Great Britain, which was presented to Parliament in 1842. From start to finish, if it is stripped of purely local terminology like references to 'back and front houses', Chadwick's report can be read as a document on the living conditions of the labouring population of Calcutta and district in 1970. Consider, for example, Mr Howell on the London parish of St Giles in 1842: '. . . upon passing through the passage of the first house, I found the yard covered with night-soil, from the overflowing of the privy, to the depth of nearly six inches, and bricks were placed to enable the inmates to get across dry-shod; in addition to this, there was an accumulation of filth piled up against the walls, of the most objectionable nature; the interior of the house partook something of the same character, and discovering, upon examination, that the other houses were nearly similar, I found a detailed survey impracticable, and was obliged to content myself with making general observations ... I am constantly shocked beyond all endurance at the filth and misery in which a large part of our population are permitted to drag on a diseased and miserable existence. I consider a large portion, if not the whole, of this accumulation of dirt and filth is caused by the bad and insufficient sewerage of the metropolis.' All that might have been said with almost perfect accuracy of Howrah today, with its population of half a million and not a sewer between them.

Nor is the menace of the bustees, and the disease that comes from them, a threat only to Calcutta and its people. When experts from the World Health Organization were here in 1959, after a particularly bad outbreak of cholera, they discovered that although only just over a quarter of the population lived in bustees, something approaching half the cases of cholera in the city occurred in these slums. When they wrote their report they went on to remark that 'the Calcutta area still forms the starting point for a long-distance spread of cholera. In the central part of this area (situated along the banks of the Hooghly River and the two canals arising from it) are located the terminals of the two principal railway systems which connect Calcutta with the rest of the country, and it is along their routes that the spread of the infection appears to occur ... In India, the region of endemic cholera falls within the State of West Bengal with its nucleus in Greater Calcutta and dominantly in the bustee population, ill provided with even elementary sanitary facilities. The cholera situation has great significance not only to West Bengal and all of India, but to the world at large.'

The Hooghly itself bedevils Calcutta here, almost as much as the city's primitive sanitation. The WHO report pointed out how alarmingly it had declined over the years as a source of water that was both drinkable and safe. The earliest pumping station at Chandpal Ghat was supplemented forty years later by a larger plant at Palta further upstream. At approximately the same time, the Ganga began its notorious change of current

towards the River Padma and the sea, and a by-product of this
was the gradual creation of a sandbank between the mainstream
and the River Bhagirathi, which itself flows into the Hooghly. It
meant, eventually, that fresh water from the Ganga slopped
over the top of the sandbank and downstream towards Calcutta
only for the four monsoon months of the year when all the
watercourses of Bengal were swollen with rains. It has effectively
reduced the Hooghly almost to the condition of a long trench,
blocked at one end by the sandbank, open at the other to the sea,
with its contents merely sloshing backwards and forwards for
two thirds of the year. The result is that sea water is gradually
creeping higher and higher up the river. By 1940 the salt content
of the water pumped out of the Hooghly at Palta had risen to
380 parts per million of chlorides (the generally acceptable level
for drinking water being 250 parts per million). By 1959 it had
gone far beyond the tolerable limit for human consumption, to
2,480 parts per million. This was not a consistent level; it depended upon the state of tides. But even when they were
juggling with tidetables and pumping plant, the engineers at
Palta in 1959 were unable to supply Calcutta with water at any
time containing less than 800 parts of salt.

Like everything else connected with this city, the situation has
deteriorated since then. For a couple of years in the late sixties,
indeed, all improvement works came to a standstill because the
fifty-five members of the Calcutta Metropolitan Water Supply
and Sanitation authority were locked in political combat. And
the building of the Farakka barrage, one hundred and sixty miles
away North up the Ganga, to divert fresh water into the Hooghly
among other things, has been miserably slow since it was first
planned in 1954 because of hostility between India and Pakistan
– which also has a stake in the Mother of the World. A scheme
such as this was contemplated by Sir Arthur Cotton, the great
irrigator of Madras, who foresaw grave dangers to the Port of
Calcutta in 1858, when the Ganga was on the turn, who could
see what a boon a great dam on the river might be; as it will.
When the squabbling is done and Farakka is finished, whenever
that may be, the intolerable salinity of the Hooghly will be

squirted safely downstream beyond the shipping at Garden Reach. Then there will only be sanitation to worry about.

The shipping is having a hard time in the Hooghly these days, and Calcutta as always is suffering on account of both. The same reduced flow of the sacred Ganga that lets the salt water in, also prevents the silt from running out. Millions of tons each year come rolling down from the river sources and none of it now reaches the mouth, as it once did, spreading and helping to create the delta. Instead it lies in the Hooghly and, below Calcutta, has to be expensively dredged every day of the year and even then inadequately. So much now lies in the Hooghly bed that not only have those sixteen sandbanks between city and sea arisen, but the river is generally so shallow that the tidal bores rush upstream every third day, where once they came only two or three times a year; and even in 1947 they were experienced on only seventy days in a twelve-month, which is almost exactly half their present rate. The result is that a vessel proceeding into the Port of Calcutta up 125 miles of river, through the Lord Jim jungle, past the 76 lighted buoys, the 30 unlighted buoys, the 119 lighted shore marks, the three manned lightships and the two which have no crews, the lighthouse and the countless semaphore signals on either bank, will take 24 hours about it; and when it returns to the sea it will take anything between 36 and 44 hours, depending upon its draft and the nerve of the pilot. It will only be able to move downstream at high tide, which comes in so fiercely that the vessel will have to move slowly and it will have to drop anchor between tides in deep water *en route* at Uluberia, Diamond Harbour, Kalpi or off Sagar. And no ship of ten thousand tons or above can now get anywhere near Calcutta. Even those around the maximum permitted draft must plan their voyages to this part of the world with more meticulous care than any tramping company has ever been trained to, so that they can move in on each spring tide just after each new moon and each full moon. If they miss one of these, then there they are, stuck at anchor just offshore, for over a week at least.

More and more traffic is thus being diverted from the once mighty Port of Calcutta. The sugar exporters now find it more economical to ship their cargoes out of Bombay or, just to the

North, from Kandla in Cutch. Oilcake, rice bran, minerals and
ores are increasingly being trucked or railed half way to Madras
to be put aboard ship at Vishakapatnam, where they have deep
water in the harbour, with comparatively placid labour on the
wharves into the bargain. Calcutta, this past few years, has been
going the way of Patna and Satgaon, which were themselves
once mighty ports upstream. If only the city can hang on a little
longer, its maritime health may well be restored. For, forty-five
miles below the docks at Kidderpore, a new port is being slowly
and laboriously constructed at Haldia. It is planned to take vessels of up to forty-five thousand tons and its wharves will be girt
about with a complex of industry, including an oil refinery and
a fertilizer factory which are to be set up by the Government in
Delhi. No one expects it to function for years yet, but when it
does, and when the Ganga again pours into the Hooghly along
a canal much longer than the Suez Canal, it is possible that a
great tide will have turned in the fortunes of Calcutta.

Some people wonder if Calcutta can possibly live to see that
day. Their nightmare is that before very long the management
of this city will simply stop under the awful weight of humanity
pressing its moving parts into the ground. There is a sense in
which all the alarming words and images now generally applied
to Calcutta, like disintegration, collapse, and breakdown, are
somewhat misleading. These are things that could conceivably
happen, that are visibly starting to happen, to society here; the
possible fate of the urban structure itself is something much
more akin to petrifaction, the end of a process similar to that
which transforms once flourishing vegetation into solid coal
under extreme pressure. If you look at Calcutta's transport system today you can see, in the most obvious way, not only how
this might happen, but some of the elements that are making
it possible to happen. The preposterously sketchy communication lines between the divided halves of this elongated metropolis
provide the clearest example of all. Here is a collection of thirty-
five municipalities bordering the Hooghly, with over five and a
half million people on the East bank and more than a couple of
million more on the West. Almost every one of those thirty-five
sub-centres of people marks the spot where in the nineteenth

century a jute mill was built with a village and then a township swelling around it until the whole became fused into the solid mass of Greater Calcutta, stretching 30-odd miles along the river, from Bansberia in the North to Budge Budge in the South. There are still only two bridges crossing the Hooghly, to pull these two sprawling sides together; and the only one carrying railway lines is the one built forty years ago six miles upstream of the Howrah Bridge, though Howrah has one of the two main railway stations at the foot of its western approach and the other terminus a mile or so in a straight line from its eastern end.

There is no riverside city in the world so badly off for river crossings. London, with a population only half a million or so greater than Calcutta's, has sixteen bridges over the Thames; New York has sixteen bridges to serve a population approaching eleven millions. There are other cities even better off. Pittsburgh has sixteen bridges for 2,403,000 people, Rome has sixteen for 2,160,000, Frankfurt has eleven for a population of only 671,624. To stand on the Howrah Bridge at any time is to feel that you are in the middle of some colossal refugee movement struggling to make headway against an impending doom; and these refugees are so bewildered by their plight that they are attempting to move in both directions at once. In 1947 it was estimated that 12,000 motor vehicles alone crossed the bridge every day; by 1964 the figure had risen to 34,000; today it will be something over 40,000. On top of the motor traffic there is the traffic in bullock carts, handcarts, tramcars, bicycles and simply the endless stream of people; there are half a million pedestrians pushing and heaving their way over Howrah Bridge every day. Very often everything just locks into a solid jam in which nothing can move for hours. It is now not unknown for the multitudinous traffic of Howrah Bridge to seize up before noon and to stay that way until late in the evening, by which time the police have been called out not only to disentangle everything, but to charge with their lathis and their shields, to put down the riots that have broken out where there is enough room for civil disturbance at each end of the bridge. The traffic in this city is now so overwhelmingly beyond Calcutta's capacities that even on the widest arterial roads the average peak-hour speeds are down to something between nine and fourteen miles per hour. And even at these crawling rates the number of accidents, particularly fatal accidents, rose by twenty per cent between 1960 and 1965.

Of all Calcutta's traffic, the public transport vehicles are in the very worst condition. If you stand by the platform gates at the two main railway stations at Howrah and Sealdah during the incoming commuter hours, you see something that makes the rush hours at Waterloo, at Victoria or at any of the other London termini seem no more than rather invigorating exercises in mass movement. The trains of Calcutta come in with their passengers immovable inside the carriages, hanging to the outsides of carriages, and squatting upon most of the carriage roofs as well. Some of these commuters have been travelling thus for anything up to a couple of hours and the lucky ones are those on the outside; those inside can have become so maddened by the suffocating conditions of a compartment whose temperature has risen to 120 degrees or so, that their journey into town has been punctuated by a series of claustrophobic knife fights, with the odd corpse left for the station staff to remove at the end of the line. The survivors have then to face a journey by tram or bus, as often as not, and conditions there are scarcely any better.

If you detach yourself from the implications of what you are seeing, one of the more splendidly memorable sights of Calcutta is of any double-decker bus charging down Chowringhee with a battered durability that must be both a grief and a pride to British Leyland, who have made it. The bus will be driven madly, for Chowringhee is one of the few places in this city where a man can put his foot hard down on the accelerator, as the bus drivers invariably do in relief from the rest of the frustrating day. Its bodywork will be heavily bashed with indentations of gleaming metal pocking the grimy red paintwork. Passengers will be standing hard up against each other on both top and bottom decks, and so many will be packed onto the platform that it will sway and surf only an inch or two above the roadway; half a dozen will have no more than a toehold on the platform's rim, clasping each other's shoulders to maintain position, disaster certain if the three men with a grip on the bus itself should be prised loose. Occasionally the conductor has abandoned his own place in the vehicle and taken a seat on the nearside mudguard alongside his driver, from which position he enters into the spirit of the journey, waving his free arm in a gesture of attack, his money-bag streaming in the wind, uttering cavalry cries of exuberance or insanity. And from the back of this rollicking, swaying, dangerously canting museum piece, comes a long and billowing jet of thick black fumes. More frequently it will be obliged to proceed round the city at a jerking pedestrian pace and the black smoke from its exhaust will be aesthetically balanced by the white plume of steam from its radiator. Quite often, it will subside into immobility because of the totally unscheduled demands that have been made upon it. The Calcutta State Transport Corporation, which runs the double-deck buses, has 600 vehicles at its disposal; every day, between 150 and 180 of them break down. This is partly because of age – 350 of the buses are a dozen years old or more – but at bottom it is because they are always overloaded, their engines strained far beyond their designed limits. The average load of a Calcutta bus, from the first one in the morning to the last one at night, is eighty-five passengers; if the number of vehicles were almost doubled this would merely bring down the average load to seventy passengers. The average load of a London bus is precisely seventeen people.

The trams are scarcely in a better position. There are 360 of these belonging to the Calcutta Tramways Co. Ltd, still administered by a British manager, and between them they carry three-quarters of a million passengers a day in circumstances not greatly different from those of the buses. In four months of 1969 there were 930 derailments because tracks had fractured and shifted out of line, or because the rims of tram wheels had worn down so much that the whole vehicle would swerve off into the road. There is never enough money, of course, to provide anything like the servicing of equipment that would be vital if even what Calcutta possesses were to be kept in effective condition. An impossible circle has developed in which the transport system is so overloaded that only a proportion of the revenue from fares can be collected, in which there is not enough revenue to help to reduce the loads. It has been estimated that more than six thousand people come and go through Howrah Station every day without having bought a railway ticket, and no ticket inspector on earth could possibly scrutinize everyone among the hordes who bear down on the gates as each train arrives; and conditions aboard the buses are such that it is remarkable when the conductors manage to collect any fares at all. The Tramways deficit was thought to be about Rs 10 million in 1969. The state bus undertaking was so beggared by the end of that year that not only was it running into a monthly deficit of Rs 2 million, but it was fast approaching the stage at which it would not be able to pay its men their wages; it was deeply in debt to the Indian Oil Corporation for fuel and lubricants, and it was going cap in hand to a provincial Government that was itself on the edge of collapse, for enough money to obtain a consignment of spare parts that had been held up at the docks until payment was forthcoming. The Government, for devious political reasons of its own as well as for any proper considerations of consequent hardship, was meanwhile refusing the bus authority permission to increase fares.

Political factors, as we shall see, have played their own calculating part in adding to the chaos of Calcutta; they are deep in the middle of those interminable strikes of recent years which amounted, in West Bengal as a whole, to 60 per cent of all the man hours lost by industrial action in 1969 throughout India. They are therefore partly responsible for the decline in traffic from the Port of Calcutta by approximately 30 per cent between 1965 and 1969, by which time it was functioning at only half its potential capacity. They are similarly culpable in the ominous run-down of West Bengal industry as a whole, whose income between 1961 and 1968 grew by only 2·6 per cent against a national average of 3·7 per cent, and where employment in factories fell from 840,000 to 817,000 between 1966 and 1968 although the national average trend showed an increase of 10 per cent. Politics have doubtless even something to answer for in the case of the 3,219 trains which were abruptly brought to a standstill in the Calcutta district during February 1969 because persons unknown had decided to pull their communication cords.

But even where political action is clearly responsible for some further movement towards the ultimate petrifaction of the city, it is itself merely a response to an intolerable situation which has slowly developed over a long period and which has been generally shaped by other agencies.

The contemporary politics of Calcutta and West Bengal can scarcely be held responsible for conditions at the R. G. Kar Hospital, where patients lie on the floor because there are not enough beds, where dogs and goats are sometimes to be seen roaming through the wards, and where a casualty block whose foundation stone was laid in 1963 had still made no further progress towards completion by the end of the decade. They cannot be held responsible for a water supply which by 1965 was supplying no more than twenty-eight filtered gallons per head of population each day, whereas in 1931 it had managed to produce 52.3 gallons for every person in the city. They cannot be held responsible for the lack of proper educational facilities which allows only sixty per cent of all children between the ages of six and eleven to attend school. They cannot be held responsible for the hopeless confusion which generally results from such a simple thing as trying to locate a particular address in a given street. Heaven knows how the postmen ever manage to deliver mail to its intended destinations along Lower Chitpore Road, for example, which is otherwise known as Rabindra Sarani. For along that frenetic thoroughfare No. 18 is found next door to No. 242, which then gives way to No. 156, which is succeeded by No. 45, which is followed by No. 260 – all on the same side of the road, which proceeds in the same haphazard fashion throughout its entire length.

The truth is that years before Calcutta's multitude of Communist parties began to make their own devastating contribution to this city, the signs of its decline from supremacy were perfectly visible. Between 1951 and 1960 the average daily employment in West Bengal's registered factories increased by less than 5 per cent; in Maharashtra it grew by 45 per cent and in Gujerat by 13 per cent. The number of scrips quoted on Calcutta Stock Exchange between 1947 and 1962 increased by 12½ per cent, while in both Bombay and Madras the increase was about 100 per cent.

West Bengal, moreover, has been consistently starved of materials allocated to the Indian provinces by the Central Government in Delhi. In 1963 it received only 11·5 per cent of its assessed annual requirement of copper, only 7 per cent of its zinc assessment, only 17·5 per cent of its tin requirements, only 2·3 per cent of its lead allocation; both Maharashtra and Gujerat did substantially better in each case. Aid from Delhi has become such a nefarious thing that when, at the end of 1969, there was news that Rs 400 millions might be allocated from Central funds for the relief of Calcutta alone under the national Fourth Plan, it was printed as a comparatively short story down the pages of the local newspapers, which had heard so many marvellous rumours of a similar kind so many times before that they presumably assumed this one, too, was far too good to come to anything.

On top of financial and other forms of starvation regulated by Delhi, the city still suffers from its deeply traditional aversion to taxing its own wealth intelligently. In the financial year 1963–4, Bombay was levying Rs 54 for every man, woman and child in the city; Calcutta was collecting only Rs 20 that year. Since then, Bombay has been spending an average of Rs 35 millions each year on capital improvements; Calcutta has managed a bare Rs 15 millions. Yet in all the statistics that can be mustered to demonstrate and to measure the predicament of this city, the most telling one is that which shows how growth has diminished, how petrifaction has become an ultimate prospect. In the thirty years between 1931 and 1961, Bombay grew by 218 per cent, Delhi by 424 per cent, Madras by 167 per cent, Bangalore by 288 per cent. In the same period, in spite of the vast numbers still heading for this overburdened stretch of the Hooghly, in spite of the threefold increase of people in Greater Calcutta, the city itself grew only 140 per cent. It was moving towards stasis a decade ago – or something else, just as dreadful. It cannot, in truth, take very much more of anything now.

There has been very little to relieve Calcutta's distress. Whatever good intentions and determined efforts may have come from Delhi, from the Government of West Bengal or from the Corporation over the past few years, there is not much to show for the combination. The most chronic miseries of its people have more often than not been left to the totally inadequate concern of charitable organizations, in which the city is well endowed. Hinduism has spawned a great number of bodies like Siva Sakti Seva Samiti, whose members distribute drinking water in bustees or among the crowds attending festivities, who run schools, who arrange the cremation of corpses belonging to families too poor to purchase the necessary wood. Its various sects maintain a score or so of rest houses for pilgrims to the temples (the Muslims have half a dozen for their own faithful). It has produced the institute for student welfare and accommodation dedicated to Ramakrishna Paramahansa, who was a nineteenth century Brahmin given to ecstatic visions, a Franciscan figure whose most notable disciple was the Swami Vivekenanda, that rabble-rouser of the swadeshi days. From time to time secular relief organizations have appeared, like Mahanagar Parishad, which was started by an idealistic chartered accountant inspired by the American New Frontier, which for three years manned dispensaries and bustee night schools, lobbied officialdom for mechanical necessities of life, and tried to teach poor people some elements of self-help; and which finally died of exhaustion itself. It seems perverse to single out the most alien body of all as an example of what charity has done where government has so far failed; except that Mother Teresa's Missionaries of Charity have almost certainly been more effective than any other welfare organization in Calcutta, and that this is one of the only two points at which the conscience of the Western rich has been tapped to any noticeable degree in an effort to relieve the worst of the poverty.

Mother Teresa had been quietly grafting away in the city long before Malcolm Muggeridge (who once worked here as a journalist for *The Statesman*) introduced her to the television audiences of Britain. She is an Albanian who came to Calcutta in 1928, when she was eighteen and known as Agnes Gonxha Bojaxhiu, to join the Irish Loreto Sisters in their teaching convent off Park Street. By 1950 she had concluded that prayer and catechism were simply not enough for any nun to be offering to her

God and her pupils in this bedevilled place and so she started her own order after picking up a woman from the pavement who had been attacked by rats. Twenty years later she commanded what was by then probably the most flourishing religious order in Christendom. At a time when convents and monasteries throughout the world were becoming alarmed not only at the small trickle of people coming in to test their vocations but at the increasing flow of religious who were simply abandoning their vows and walking out, the Missionaries of Charity numbered 246 fully professed sisters, 130 novices who had tasted the life and were waiting to take their final vows, 90 postulants who were waiting to commit themselves to the novitiate and another 59 aspiring young women simply waiting to get in when the order could afford to have them – recruiting figures that would turn any Benedictine Abbess or any other missionary superior puce with envy. Apart from the base camp in Calcutta, there were twenty-four branch houses spread across India and another four already established in other countries; and the order has continued to expand since then. The twentieth century has seen only one comparable phenomenon, significantly inspired by much the same variety of Christian philosophy, and that was the much earlier foundation and growth of Charles de Foucauld's Little Brothers and Sisters of Jesus.

The convent stands on Lower Circular Road, not far from that series of shops and pavement trading posts whose commerce is almost completely in bits and pieces of motor bikes and kindred ironmongery. In any light half as intense as Calcutta's it would be pretty bleak-looking, for it is a drab grey on the outside, pierced by small square windows, and the only decoration is the hammer and sickle someone has whitewashed on the wall next to a slogan left over from the last election – 'Vote for UF. Stop lockout and automation'. Visitors go down the narrow passage alongside, pull a piece of string dangling by the door, a tin can rattles, and instantly the door is opened by a girl who sits there and does nothing else all day. In a courtyard, twenty or thirty nuns are dhobying linen in a row of buckets. From a row of windows along one side of the yard you can hear the voice of Sister Joseph, soon to fly to Venezuela to take charge of the house there, but for the moment instructing a classroom of novices in the peculiar philosophy of these surroundings. 'Let the poor eat you up, is Mother's motto', she is telling them. She used to be an accounting clerk and a piano teacher in Southampton, herself, before she gave it up for this. There are maybe a dozen or so women who have come out from Europe to join the missionaries here. The rest are Indians. None of them can have an expectation of life much greater than those of the people who live in Calcutta's bustees. They are exposed to every disease in the city, they work preposterous hours, they are not encouraged to spare themselves. The German doctor-sister at the dispensary down the road, who has been drugging, inoculating and plastering for most of a sweltering day without benefit of fans, is soaked in sweat and pasty with fatigue. Not one of the Europeans looks very healthy. The Indians merely look placid, but they succumb, too; they buried one a few days ago, after it had been discovered too late that the playful puppy which nipped her in a bustee was rabid.

Mother Teresa herself looks a bit shrunken, a small person with an olive face much wrinkled like a nutmeg. She has dark brown eyes which can twinkle disarmingly and nothing about her suggests the toughness that is there, or the will-power which no founder of a religious order has yet been known to manage without. She may well be a woman of whim on close acquaintance; you can drop in unexpectedly one day and discover upon the anteroom table, alongside the thumping hidebound Bible, a paperback volume entitled 'Fun Lover's Guide to Surprising Amsterdam'. She smiles when provoked to it, but she is mostly very serious, very quiet and there is no energy in her handshake. She says 'Thank God' a lot, as the Irish do, by way of breaking up her sentences rather than in pious reflection: 'It's a lovely day, thank God, and you've just arrived, thank God, and very soon I shall have to leave you and be off, thank God ...' There is nothing at all pious about her. She simply recites the details of the convent's work, talks about the condition of the poor, all of it nearly in a monotone with a sad little nod of the head when she comes to some particularly frightful incident. She becomes a little frosty if anyone inquires what the conversion rate is among the people she works for. She tries to convey as delicately as possible, beneath a dutiful colour print of the Pope, that the conversion of souls in any orthodox sense determined by the Vatican is rather beside the point she is attempting to make.

The point is clear enough in the shed at Nirmal Hriday, where people are dying in a scrap of dignity, surrounded by much care and attention; it is evident out at Dhapa, where the lepers are encouraged to struggle on with their mutilations, to hope for something that might eventually matter more to them than the ostracisms of society. At the dispensary just down the road from the convent, the point seems to be that a lot of sick people are being inoculated, cajoled into taking medicines of which they may be suspicious, occasionally scolded for failing to take pills as prescribed, because that is what you do when you have some medical training and a few resources and when you are confronted with sick people. There are always long queues waiting by the dispensary gates; Hindus one day, Muslims the next, Christians after that, rotated in segregated groups so that there is a little order in all the city's chaos, and to reduce the risk of a sister perpetrating some unthinking religious offence upon a patient. At the orphanage the point of the exercise appears to be that if you hear the mew of a kitten upon a garbage heap one day and, on investigating, discover that it is not a kitten but a very new baby shaped and sized like a wizened rat, you bring it back and try to rear it out of pre-natal malnutrition so that it will be strong enough to face existence in Calcutta, rather than let it perish almost quietly within the hour. Mother Teresa's sisters wouldn't understand if anyone asked why. They probably wouldn't be shocked, either, for Calcutta can immunize a human being against some conditions just as steadily as it can infect him with others.

It is difficult to judge how Calcutta regards Mother Teresa and her missionaries. They are reported warmly and respectfully in *The Statesman* from time to time but civic leaders ignore them almost completely. Some years ago there was a great fuss and considerable cries of outrage because on one of her trips to Europe Mother Teresa had seemed to imply that there were more

unmarried mothers in the city than Calcutta wished to acknow-
ledge. The missionaries acquired Nirmal Hriday with something
approaching the blessing of Kalighat next door because, when a
couple of the Kalighat priests became destitute and half dead
themselves, Mother Teresa was the only person in sight who took
any notice of them; but at the beginning of 1970 there was
angry talk in the neighbourhood about a house of pestilence on
its collective doorstep and the nuns were told that the sooner
they found premises elsewhere in Calcutta, the sooner the
Kalighat quarter of the city would be pleased. But the nuns have
never been molested. Even alongside Kali's most sacred temple,
which might be the most unpleasant place here for any Christian
flaunting his own faith, these unmistakable women in the blue-
trimmed white saris come and go in their truck or on foot, with
only the inescapable band of beggars occasionally approaching
them. Perhaps the word has gone further round Calcutta than
anyone might think, that they really are almost as poor as anyone. No sister possesses anything but two saris and one bucket.
She is materially very much better off than anyone in a bustee
only insofar as her own compound is spotless, and properly
drained, and in her assurance that her ration of gruel and rice
and fish will come to her every day.

Quite remarkable sums of money are now raised in the West,
together with ambulances (which the Indian Government makes
a curiously longwinded fuss about before allowing the vehicles
into the country). Most of it comes from Mother Teresa Com-
mittees scattered across the Catholic communities of the wealthy
world; the British supporters alone raised £33,000 in 1969. It is
all deployed with calculating thrift. The convent on Lower
Circular Road and its outposts around the city may well be the
only places in Calcutta where absolutely nothing is wasted.
People who have made contact with the sisters are apt to turn
every item of junk over to them before leaving for England, as
well as their spare enterovioform and aspirin, for they have been
given clearly to understand that these women can find a use for
anything at all; empty bottles are invaluable for storing boiled
and therefore decontaminated water and old matchboxes are
splendid for issuing pills to outpatients. There were 111,000 of

those at the dispensary in 1969; another statistic from Calcutta, to be added to 143 abandoned children in the orphanage, the 13,000 lepers, the 1,250 wrecks who had passed through Nirmal Hriday. And this city needs much more than charity.

It has something more than that in the Calcutta Metropolitan Planning Organization. For the past few years this has been the one excuse for hope that Calcutta might just avoid its ultimate civic disaster without a political upheaval that would almost surely be accompanied by a massacre as frightful as the one of 1946, or even worse. The origins of the CMPO lie in that mission from the World Bank and the earlier exploration of water supplies and sanitation by the World Health Organization. The mission was highly critical of Delhi's failure to appreciate Calcutta's predicament even in the Third Five Year Plan, which had not then been put into operation. Its report said that 'it is essential, first, that the Central Government should accept a direct and special financial responsibility for the improvement of conditions in the city, and second, that the provincial and municipal authorities should co-operate in establishing an effective body to carry through an enlarged programme of municipal reconstruction and improvement.' Very tactfully, the mission said that 'the Corporation of Calcutta has neither the power nor the financial resources to cope with the staggering problems of the city. The annual municipal revenue is restricted to the paltry sum of about Rs 85 millions – a good deal less than Bombay, which is a smaller city. The Government of India tends to regard this problem as wholly the concern of the Government of West Bengal which, in turn, is struggling with many other difficulties and must respond to a legislature that inadequately represents the interests of the urban areas. The very magnitude of the challenge that Calcutta presents to the conscience and political commonsense of those in authority no doubt in part explains the inadequacy of the response. Everybody admits that more ought to be done about it. Nobody is ready to do it.'

That was the CMPO's charter. Before the World Bank reported, a scheme had already been prepared for the reclamation of three and a half square miles of salt marsh on the city's eastern edge, where between fifty thousand and a hundred thousand families might eventually be rehoused; a very sketchy start had been made to the construction of a new highway from Howrah to industrial Durgapur. Apart from those two things, every thoughtful step forward that has been taken in Calcutta since 1961 has been taken by the CMPO. It is a cosmopolitan organization more than it is a metropolitan one. It is administered entirely by Indians, very largely staffed by Indians, most of them Bengalis, but it has also relied heavily from the start upon a number of foreign consultants. It has been supplied with funds from the Central Government in Delhi and the West Bengal Government in Calcutta, but it has also been supported by the Ford Foundation, which by 1969 had contributed five million dollars as well as recruiting some of the best available experts from the United States and Europe to come and work in Calcutta. Their numbers have varied from time to time for several reasons. At one stage there were twenty-one of them in the city, at another only five. Either the money was running out of the current budget or the provincial Communist government was campaigning against the Ford Foundation or an individual now and then simply became discouraged by the terrible inertia of the official machinery of India, by the almost total lack of progress anywhere except on paper.

The ones who have stayed have developed a very fierce loyalty to the city, marvelling at the patience of its people, scorning outsiders who dismiss it as an appalling mess beyond redemption, doggedly determined to see the thing through to whatever the end might be. They have been working in what would be regarded as quite intolerable circumstances anywhere else in the world. Their offices just off Lower Chitpore Road, situated where they cannot possibly forget the magnitude and the nature of Calcutta's basic problems, are as bare and totally functional as a military command post just behind the trenches. They have been gheraoed, even knocked about once or twice by mobs. Their families have been badly frightened by political violence on the way home from school, on the way to the cinema, even sitting at home in the evening. Not one of them has shown the slightest bitterness in return. They have instead acquired the most painfully developed conscience of the rich in all Calcutta. They very nearly draw lots now if there is a new visitor to be guided through his first bustee, for they do not care to parade themselves yet again before people whose circumstances are no better than they were years ago, when the planners first came to their aid; and the guided tour of Calcutta's slums is just a little bit like turning over a stone in a stagnant pond to see what is wriggling underneath. They write memoranda to Ford, suggesting that conventional American automobiles might well be replaced with something more modest, like Volkswagen, because the Oldsmobile does invite unpleasant attention and because it has begun to seem offensive to the planners themselves.

There is scarcely anything on the ground to show for almost a decade of the CMPO, nothing to suggest that the necessary miracle is at last being wrought in this city. The highway has proceeded on its unsteady way towards Durgapur and, beyond the penitentiary housing blocks of Maniktala, the grey wasteland of the reclamation which you observe from incoming aircraft, still stretches away in an almost empty plateau of compressed refuse towards the eastern swamps, signposted on its edges as Salt Lake City. The major achievement of the CMPO is its Basic Development Plan, the blueprint for a miracle which was finished in 1966 and which has been awaiting measurable action ever since.

The prospect it held out for Calcutta was exciting. It foresaw the day when there could be a genuine linear city stretching along both banks of the Hooghly here, in place of the sprawling mess which is almost totally devoid of services along most of its length today (for no jute mill owner dreamed of laying drainpipes in the nineteenth century when he started the nucleus of a township). There would be two anchorholds for the people of this vast community. One would be the existing twins of Calcutta city and Howrah themselves; the other would be to the North, where the townships of Bansberia and Kalyani would be developed and joined into one urban centre supporting as many people as now live in Copenhagen, Chungking or Naples. Even today the makings of this vision can be seen in Kalyani, for uniquely it is a recent township built around textiles, engineering, paper-making and distilling; it has a planned road system and, marvellously, it has space. To the North of the linear city, express motorways and improved railways would sweep away to the Indian Ruhr around Durgapur, Asansol and the other heavy engineering towns. To the South, modern lines of communication would flow down to the new port of Haldia. In between Kalyani and Haldia, those two exemplary visions of the future, Greater Calcutta would very gradually be made endurable for all its people.

This was not a document produced by dreamers. It was in the first place an exact measurement of every problem in sight. It calculated to the last half gallon just how much unfiltered water the slum dwellers of Cossipore were getting in 1961 compared with 1931. It was the CMPO plan which produced the famous projection of twelve million people living here by 1986. At the outset it stated that 'The extreme urgency of the present situation of Calcutta and its region is such ... that the search for new ideas and new techniques must be tempered by the need for immediate action. Calcutta cannot wait for a perfect plan.' So the CMPO produced a strategy to be put into action by stages over two decades, well aware of the fact that towards the end of any twenty-year period in Calcutta a great number of early calculations would be demonstrably unrealistic. Its emphasis from start to finish was on flexibility, making no large assumptions about what any government would or would not do, but developing a machinery for application in the field under any political philosophy. It was rigid only in its selection of early priorities. And, overwhelming as some of the earliest tasks would appear to anybody preparing to tackle them, the planners were confident enough to suggest that 'with the combined and concentrated efforts of Government, private industry and commerce, and of voluntary organizations, a steady progressive improvement in the situation can be accomplished, leading to cumulative and dramatic change in the urban environment of Calcutta within a generation.'

The very first priority was to stop things getting even worse than they were when the CMPO was devised. The planners pointed out that it would be completely unrealistic to assume that the bustee dwellers could be rehoused in decent, safe and sanitary pukka buildings within a decade, except in very limited numbers. Before they could be rehoused, there would have to be space in which to rehouse them, and space is the rarest thing of all in Calcutta. The first step must therefore be reform of land-use, beginning with the compulsory purchase of all bustee lands. Once the civic authorities or the government took possession of the bustees, the slum improvement agency would then move in and provide the minimally acceptable requirements in the way of water supply, drainage and lighting. And there the bustee dwellers would remain for quite a while longer, still shockingly over-crowded but at least living in approximately healthy conditions for the first time since they were born. The planners proposed that simultaneously the authorities should seize any vacant land that became available and merely furnish it with a network of services; after that, they should allow people to move in and build their own makeshift dwellings as so many of them have had to do ever since they came to the city, without benefit of any services at all. The CMPO plan estimated that if these suggestions were promptly carried out in 1966, half a million people in Calcutta and Howrah would by 1971 be provided with paving, lighting, sewerage, safe water points and communal bathhouses for one sixteenth of what it would cost to mount an orthodox slum clearance programme. Meanwhile, the authorities could spend the bulk of their available funds where they were most needed, in the improvement of the existing water supply for the entire community to a tolerable safety level, in the beginning of three new townships to siphon some of the population from the most congested areas, in the conversion of the ghastly service privies to sanitary latrines, in the first steps towards a rapid transit system to prevent Calcutta from choking itself with its own traffic.

Scarcely a brick has been shifted. The bustees remain more or less as they were when the CMPO plan was composed. There was a time in 1962 when it took a thousand men of the National Volunteer Force, together with a hundred five-ton lorries a month to help the regular Corporation cleansing staff remove accumulated garbage from the streets of Calcutta; in November 1970, it took a hundred and sixty five-ton lorries the whole of one night, from dusk to breakfast, to remove the accumulated garbage from just one stretch of Strand Road by the Old Mint. That is a measurement of progress in Calcutta. At the beginning of 1969 the men of the CMPO were convinced that at last some of their plans might shortly be put into practice. It had just been announced that a new budget had been concocted, producing Rs 800 millions from the combined resources of the Central Government, the West Bengal Government and the local business community, who were prepared to advance one quarter of the total sum at the unprecedented interest rate of a mere five per cent. Nothing ever came of it, partly because the businessmen took fright at the election of a chiefly Communist West Bengal Government and withdrew their offer. There was subsequently much talk of a start being made on the CMPO's rapid transit plan for a circular railway round the centre of the city. A few months later, it was announced that this plan had been abandoned once and for all, and that instead Calcutta was going to have an Underground railway. This idea had been toyed with once before. In 1949 a French firm had investigated the possibility and decided that it was impracticable, largely because of Calcutta's notoriously soggy foundations. Finnish engineers, however, had now advised that an Underground was possible, a contract had been signed with a team of Russian experts to render further assistance and it was promised that soon there would be Underground stations at Kalighat, at Sealdah railway terminus and in Dalhousie Square. Moreover, tenders might soon be called for the construction of another crossing of the Hooghly not far from the Howrah Bridge.

None of this has been in accordance with the priorities of a development plan which produced some credible solutions to an incredible situation. The planners have continued to draft their more detailed steering orders for Calcutta. They have flown to Delhi every few months to lobby the authorities there; they have returned to lobby authorities in the Writers' Building or in the Raj Bhavan almost every other day. They have devised simplified equipment that peasant workmen might use effectively to rebuild this city, they have demonstrated it to the people in whose hands the rebuilding really lies; and these people have sat in rows in bleak sheds on blazing days, nodding gravely, murmuring encouragement, applauding warmly, departing calmly with fresh sheaves of documents which they will possibly never read. Nothing has really changed. No one who has seen what has not been accomplished since the CMPO was created can easily share its most splendidly visionary moments now. 'The rebirth of Calcutta,' wrote the authors of the plan some years ago, 'and the emergence of a flourishing new river metropolis demand a heroic effort. But the potential reward is great, for this is a metropolis that can become one of the world's foremost urban centres.'

A kind of heroic effort, in fact, was just gaining momentum as the plan was being shuffled together. Men who had grown weary of waiting for Calcutta to become merely tolerable were even given an opportunity to accomplish the vision. They promoted fear more than anything else.

THE ROAD TO REVOLUTION

THE origins of Communism in India are scarcely more than a quarter of a century behind those of Europe. At least one commentator has seen a strike of Bombay textile workers in 1908 as deriving from the doctrines of Karl Marx, though it was not for another decade that the British could be absolutely certain that this pernicious new philosophy had spread to their Indian Empire. The Communist Party of India was founded in Tashkent in 1920 by expatriates who had usually struggled on foot across some of the bleakest country on earth to get away from the strictures of British rule. One of the early leaders, Muzzafar Ahmad – ancient, ailing, almost bedbound in Ballygunge, and clearly *en route* to his place in the great Bengali pantheon – remembers one such group slogging over the Hindu Kush mountains to Tirmiz in Soviet Tadzhikistan, where a military band of the Red Army played them aboard a train for Tashkent and its new Indian Military School, which specialized in teaching political philosophy and the mechanics of the machine gun. At home that year, the All India Trade Union Congress was founded with a strong and militant left wing, and from then on Communism became a very active ingredient in the turbulence of British India. Within twelve months it had inspired an industrial strike. In 1927 it brought the Bombay textile workers out for eight months. In 1930 it produced a serious riot in Calcutta after a railway strike there. It was seen to be at the bottom of the Meerut conspiracy case, which sent twenty-two men to prison after a long trial. By 1933 the exasperated British had decided to outlaw the CPI and it remained underground until 1942, when its leaders were released from gaol after agreeing to make common cause against fascism.

What they did next partly explains why Communism has made comparatively little headway in India, which many outsiders find remarkable in view of the country's appalling and endemic poverty alongside its grotesque and overwhelming examples of wealth. The British had sent Stafford Cripps to India in 1942 to parley with its Congress leaders in an effort to get the country wholly behind the war effort against the Japanese. Cripps, who was virtually repeating an offer made a couple of years previously, proposed greater Indian representation on the Viceroy's executive council after the war, together with a local voice in the organization of the war effort. Congress, bent on post-war independence and nothing less, turned it down. The CPI leaders not only supported Cripps and refused to touch the Quit India campaign of Congress, but had the satisfaction of watching Mr Gandhi and his colleagues restored to prison cells which they themselves had only just vacated.

They were to pay for this treachery. From the moment of Independence they began to fight the new Indian Government for pandering to Anglo-American imperialism, and they were responsible for outbreaks of terrorism in West Bengal, in Madras, in Uttar Pradesh and in Bombay. In February 1948, they played host in Calcutta to what was described as a South-East Asia Youth Conference under the auspices of such bodies as the World Federation of Democratic Youth, which turned out to be nothing less than the final and joint planning operation for the Communist uprisings shortly to begin in Burma, Malaya, and Indonesia. By April, the CPI was outlawed for a second time and its leaders remained in totally Indian prisons until 1950 at least, though the detainees in Bengal were not released until the following year, after a ruling by the Calcutta High Court. With terrorism added to treachery and with leaders cut off from their supporters, the party membership throughout India fell from ninety thousand in 1948 to twenty thousand a couple of years later. Yet by 1957 the CPI had revived enough to win an election in Kerala; twenty months later its government was dismissed by Delhi, in accordance with the Indian Constitution, for being unable to maintain law and order in the state. Given the all-Indian factors weighted against the success of Communism, even a fairly short reign was a triumph.

No other land and people can offer such difficult ground as

this one for anyone demanding unity and solidarity of effort from his supporters. Always, and however you examine India and its people, there are infinite conflicts of loyalty, of belief, of life style, of regional and self-interest; they all go very deep and they all run fiercely strong. Nothing could be more discouraging or shocking to a good international Communist than the effect of Indian linguistic antagonisms, for example, on the communications of Indian Communism. When the CPI organized its national peasant congress at Barasat, in 1970, every speech made by delegates from Bihar, Bombay, Rajasthan, Kerala, the Punjab and all other corners of the republic, was made first of all in English which, according to the literature of the congress, was the language of notorious despots and merchant-pirates. The speech was then translated several times over. When asked why the first version was not delivered in Hindi, which a majority of delegates would have understood as well as they understand English, and possibly better, shrewd party men said that if Hindi had been made the official language of the congress, the South Indian delegates would have walked out in protest against the implicit insult offered their own Tamil.

The fact that India has always been fundamentally a peasant society and is still predominantly a peasant nation, is yet another counterpoise to the advance of Communism which, until fairly recently, concentrated its efforts among industrial workers. Yet in Calcutta, the party made much slower progress than anyone with a knowledge of conditions there would think possible. It suffered, paradoxically, because its local leaders were Bengalis and inevitably conducted themselves as such. Not only did they fight against the partition of their province at Independence on the traditional grounds of Bengali nationalism, but they rooted their organization within the local trade unions among Bengalis, which meant that they were basing themselves upon a minority of the labour force; only one sixth of the dock workers in Calcutta, for example, are Bengalis. Apart from disbanding, they could not have done very much more to help Congress to rule without a break for the first two decades of Independence.

First there was the Government of B. C. Roy, once a brilliant surgeon who entered politics under the patronage of C. R. Das and his Swaraj Party in the 1920s; then there was the Government of P. C. Sen, who once advised people to eat green bananas if they could not obtain rice, which would have been rather less helpful to them than Marie Antoinette's cake. But throughout those twenty years there was, above all, always in the background the lurking figure of Atulya Ghosh, a Bengali Tammany boss with a picturesque black eyepatch (legacy of a disease contracted in a British Indian prison) who, when not manipulating people and politics in city and state, was frequently to be found camouflaged behind his current subscription copy of the *Times Literary Supplement*. Between them, these three Congress leaders and their henchmen gradually made it inevitable that Communism, its own enormous handicaps notwithstanding, would run Calcutta and West Bengal according to any prescriptions it cared to offer.

Apart from the hopeless poverty and the nauseating wealth, together with a certain incompetence in administration, there was the corruption. Governor Casey had confessed himself 'appalled by the hold which bribery and corruption had taken on the public, and on the subordinate ranks of the administration', not long before the British left. There was an occasion in 1945 when the Government of Bengal was beaten by a snap vote during a budget debate 'by reason of twenty Government supporters crossing the floor, a manoeuvre engineered by a Muslim with ambitions to get into the Ministry. A lot of money was said to have passed and it was clear beyond doubt that it had. The individual who engineered it was frank enough to let it be known that he would repeat the performance the next day unless he were told that he would be given a place in the Ministry.'

The Biswas Commission, which looked into the workings of Calcutta Corporation shortly after Independence, reported in 1950 that instances of corruption were to be discovered throughout the municipal organization. So many people appeared to be involved, or under some obligation to those who were involved, that the members of the commission found fewer witnesses prepared to give them evidence than they expected. All the same, they compiled a dossier so damaging to men of influence that it is perhaps not surprising the authorities shrank from publishing it in the end. Late in 1947, for example, the Government had ordered a sample survey to be made of rating assessments in the city. The commissioners found that, generally, assessments had been undervalued by half and in some cases by up to eighty per cent. 'A well-known house in Calcutta, for instance, was in the occupation of the Secretary of State for India in Council. He occupied a part on Rs 3,000 a month, and the remainder was in the occupation of a limited company. Rs 2,000 a month was the actual rent, and the annual value was computed on that footing. There is no doubt that if, on the average, half the actual rent was taken as the actual value, described as based on the actual rent, the Assessing Inspector assisted in the undervaluation and he could not have done so unless someone made it worth his while to do so. The Assessing Inspector draws a salary of Rs 60 rising to Rs 185. We have seen no case in which the figure he had put down as the annual figure was increased.'

The commission found that 'No Assessing Inspector has ever been punished for dishonest assessment, even when this was manifest. The flats at 6, Bishop Lefroy Road, have an interesting feature. In respect of these flats the tenants mentioned the rents. In each case a lesser figure was adopted as annual value, apparently because the owner was a Councillor, not on the theory of reasonable rent.' There were even instances of reduction in assessment, such as that in the case of a garden house in Buttokristo Pal Lane. 'In the first quarter of 1944–5, the Assessor valued the building at old rates and valued the land at Rs 2,250 per kottah, and allowed thirty-six per cent as depreciation on the value of the buildings estimated at the old rate, all obviously intended to reach as low a figure as possible. . . The Deputy Executive Officer 11 reduced it to Rs 1,275 as Lump Sum reduction (which means a reduction on no special ground). The owner is an influential Councillor.'

The commission was suspicious of the public health department, too. 'In May 1948, Food Inspector Dr Daud sent thirty samples to the laboratory and against only two the result noted is "adulterated". Against the rest the column was blank and on the day of his examination he put down the word "good" in each of the blanks as though all the samples were good and only two bad. If that was so, the true position would seem to be that Dr Daud is an adept at securing "good" samples, and everyone who lives in Calcutta knows that out of the articles from which he has taken the samples (milk, dahi, butter, ghee, mustard oil etc.) it would be hard to find a single one in Calcutta that is not adulterated.' There was another racket in the New Market. 'On 5 March 1946 the Public Utilities and Markets Committee sanctioned settlement of what was called the Chhota Chandney at the South-west corner of the Vegetable Chandney with Sheik Amjadali for the opening of a hotel. The Chhota Chandney, with four doors and measuring 1,636 sq. ft., was numbered as stall No. 40 of Block H. There were seventeen applicants for the stall, which was put to auction. The settlement was made with Sheik Amjadali for an initial rent of Rs 17,000 and a daily rent of Rs 30, calculated on the basis of the usual rate of Rs 50 per 100 sq. ft. of floor space per month plus ten per cent increase as per resolution of the committee meeting dated 17 March 1945. On 26 March 1946, without any application from the party and without calling for any report from the department, the committee, on the motion of Councillor Mr Md Rafique, reduced the daily rent from Rs 30 to Rs 15.'

The report continues along those lines for six chapters before it begins to analyse the merely inadequate though not necessarily dishonest workings of the Corporation. It reviews the racket run by the councillor who was trying to get stallholders evicted from one market to another, where they would become his tenants; it notes the curious reappearance of thirty-five cases of tinned butter after reaching the District Health Inspector for destruction because they were judged unfit for consumption; it remarks upon the workings of a Law Department which allowed some very rich people to remain unsummoned for arrears of rates a full fifteen years after the summonses had actually been drawn up ready for serving; it reviews many similar things besides.

And while the Biswas Commission was investigating a Corporation dominated by Congress councillors, other abuses were mounting in the name of the Congress Ministers of West Bengal and their supporters. These were not to become public knowledge until 1967, when the Communists at last gained power in the state and swiftly opened the accounts as a piece of highly effective propaganda. Quite apart from the nepotism that had been obvious to many people for a couple of decades, there had been financial swindling on a gigantic scale in the year preceding the election; something over Rs 43 millions was involved. This was the amount that had been budgeted for the relief of the poor and distressed in the 24 Parganas, in the Bankura, Purulia and Midnapore districts of West Bengal that year. It had been spent through local government bodies whose chairmen and vice-chairmen were in each case Congressmen. Nominally it had been used on sanctioned schemes of relief, but not once had the spending been first reviewed by the local finance standing committee, as required under law. Where work had been done, it bore no relation to the payments made; account books had not been kept for months and sometimes didn't even balance. In the 24 Parganas, Rs 850,000 were never accounted for even after the Communists had sent their men in to investigate. In Bankura the sanctioned funds had risen from Rs 2 millions in 1965 to Rs 7·5 millions in the following pre-election year; Rs 84,000 was unaccounted for and relief had apparently been distributed to people who did not exist. In Purulia, three of the paymasters appointed by the local government chiefs were fictitious. All this was merely the tally for one year. In addition, the Government had been allotting Rs 20 millions annually for fifteen years previously for relief and rehabilitation work and, bearing in mind the refugees who spent nine years on the platforms of Sealdah Station and another ten in the decrepitude of a disused jute mill godown, a distinctly non-Communist observer might well remark that 'one comes to the conclusion, on the evidence, that if all the money allotted had been used for the purpose intended, the problem would have been solved long ago.'

The last years of Congress rule over Calcutta and surrounding district had become so unpopular that P. C. Sen and his Ministers were unable to address public meetings or move anywhere without very large police escorts. Congress had moreover, suffered a serious internal dispute. Although its effective commander in chief was Atulya Ghosh, its President in West Bengal was Ajoy Mukherjee, and the two had become such bad enemies by September 1965 that Mukherjee was expelled from office; whereupon he publicly denounced corruption among his old colleagues and formed his own party, the Bangla (Bengal) Congress. When the 1967 elections arrived it joined forces with an already shambling collection of political units opposing the Ministry of P. C. Sen. This opposition's backbone consisted of the original Communist Party of India and the rival Communist Party of India (Marxist). Communism had itself split in 1964 on the issue of Sino-Soviet differences .The CPI broadly maintained its allegiance to Moscow while the CPI (M) was created by those who found themselves much more in sympathy with Peking, and in West Bengal these had now become a loud majority of local Communists.

A result of this rivalry was that the 1967 elections were contested, roughly speaking, by three political cohorts. One consisted of P. C. Sen's ruling Congress. A second was called People's United Left Front and was a combination of Bangla Congress, Communist Party of India, Praja Socialist Party, Bolshevik Party, Gorkha League, Forward Bloc and Lok Sevak Sangha. The third called itself United Left Front and included Communist Party of India (Marxist), Forward Bloc (Marxist), Revolutionary Socialist Party, Revolutionary Communist Party of India, Workers Party of India, Socialist Unity Centre and Samyukta Socialist Party. In some constituencies the two popular fronts fought each other, but always they opposed Congress and between them they brought it down. In the 1962 elections, the undivided Communists in West Bengal had collected 50 seats in an Assembly of 280. In 1967 the CPI (M) took 43 seats, the CPI took 16 seats, Bangla Congress took 34 seats and Forward Bloc took 13 seats; the rest of the popular front parties could number their elected representatives in ones and twos. Against this combination of 140 new members of the Legislative Assembly, Congress now had 127. Numerically it was, therefore, quite a close-run thing. Psychologically, it was a crushing blow. Almost all the senior Congress Ministers had been defeated. A former Finance Minister of the Central Government in Delhi had been put out by a nephew of Subhas Chandra Bose. Atulya Ghosh had been ejected by an unknown trade unionist. P. C. Sen had been toppled by Ajoy Mukherjee.

There was a rapid settling of differences between the bits and pieces of popular frontage and a United Front emerged, with Ajoy Mukherjee as the new Chief Minister of West Bengal, largely in grace and favour for personally removing the previous incumbent. Mukherjee was an elderly man who had built his political life on the philosophy of Mahatma Gandhi, which he has since topped off with some notably Gandhian mannerisms. He has been seen as little more than a respectable figurehead and, while this probably does him rather less than justice, he has quite clearly been bewildered by many of the subsequent events with which he has been politically associated. From the moment he obtained office it was obvious that the real power in his Government resided immediately in the person of the Deputy Chief Minister, Jyoti Basu, of the CPI (M).

Basu is the kind of man from whom Bengali legends are created. He was a doctor's son and he was first educated by the nuns of the same Loreto Convent to which Mother Teresa belonged when she came to Calcutta from Albania. After that, the Jesuits of St Xavier's College had him until he spent time at university before going to London to read law. It was there, in the late thirties and early forties, that he picked up his political training at the hands of the British Communist Palme Dutt. He returned home in time to be put into prison for his politics by an Indian Government and after that he was never anything but a full-time politician, particularly responsible for organizing activity among the railway workers of Calcutta. Like many a Bengali before him, he is idolized by people with whom he has apparently little in common. He is a neat, fastidious-looking man in his early fifties and it is quite impossible to tell whether his bearing and his mannerisms come naturally or whether they are carefully cultivated to fulfil a role. He is never known to smile in public and it is widely believed among the rank and file of party workers that he is a totally ascetic man who has never in his life touched drink; which certainly isn't true. The point is that he looks ascetic, striding purposefully from the public platform, his hair carefully oiled in an impeccable quiff, his dhoti always immaculately white, his eyes forever hooded by their upper lids.

There is a tension in him that he never conveys in public. Catch him behind a Ministerial desk, or in an armchair at home, and the foot of his crossed leg never stops moving up and down. Yet on a public platform he stands out from every other Communist leader merely by virtue of his control; he has none of the rhetorical tricks, he does not harangue, he is generally thought slightly dull as a speechmaker in Bengal. But there is no questioning his power. And there is little doubt that the exercise of power satisfies him. Before you are half across his threshold his greeting is 'Yes?; the impatient gesture of the headmaster who has just been disturbed in his study by some lowly fourth former. He never melts. Every reply he makes is brisk and brief. He gives absolutely nothing away. He makes you feel that you are unforgivably interrupting the world's work upon which he alone is engaged. Ajoy Mukherjee rambles on for half an hour in reply to just one question, without ever coming within a mile of its point. Jyoti Basu answers fifteen in ten minutes flat and, before you know where you are, you are down the stairs and out into the yard of his thoroughly unpretentious little house, where half a dozen stout party workers are lounging as watchfully as the guardians of Birla Park. You have barely been given time to notice the three plaster ducks flying across the living room wall, or the tubular chrome armchair that would look very nice in the front room of a semi in Enfield.

This new Government of fourteen political parties began with a sense of flair. It announced that the police would no longer be required to protect the Ministers of West Bengal. It reduced the Chief Minister's salary from Rs 1,150 a month to Rs 700 and the salaries going with every other portfolio were cut from Rs 900 to Rs 500. It let Calcutta know that air-conditioning would now be shut down in the Writer's Building, the Government secretariat, as a gesture of solidarity with the poor people. At a mass rally on the Maidan shortly after taking office, it sought and obtained something it called 'formal approval' from its supporters for an 18-point programme. According to this document, high on the United Front's list of priorities were particular attention to the plight of the peasants and to land reform generally, educational reforms and a liberation of the forces of freedom and progress.

Within a month, the Central Committee of the CPI (M) had produced its own April Resolution on the new situation in West Bengal. This was curiously at odds with the Government's 18 points. 'The particular immediate task,' it decided, 'is that of educating, reorganizing, rebuilding, consolidating and expanding the Party organization ... of proper selection, promotion and grading of cadres and their proper deployment in different class and mass fronts ...' It was, nevertheless, highly conscious of the party role in Government. 'Our Ministers, without either undue illusions about giving relief in a big way or courting despair that nothing can be done under the present set-up, should always bear in mind that they are the Party's representatives, should strive to tender our bona-fides to the people. Any failure on this score compromises the Party's political line ... will not help us to resist and overcome the vacillations, wobblings and sometimes even possible backsliding of some democratic parties in the United Front ... In a word, the UF Governments that we now have * are to be treated and understood as instruments of struggle in the hands of our people, more than as Governments that actually possess adequate power, that can materially and substantially give relief to the people. In clear class-terms, our Party's participation in such Governments is one specific form of struggle to win more and more people, and more and more allies, in the cause of People's Democracy and at a later stage for Socialism.'

There was much novel activity in the first few weeks of the United Front. Calcutta Corporation was instructed to reduce the tax on bustees and to raise it on buildings with an annual valuation of Rs 15,000. The State Transport Corporation was ordered to reinstate over six hundred workers who had been dismissed for sabotage, violence or theft during the previous few years. The police budget was cut by Rs 4.8 millions and the Commissioner of Police in Calcutta was informed that in future, when a gherao of management by workers was reported, it should be referred to the Labour Minister before any other police action was taken. The refugee families who had spent the best

* There was another similar Government in Kerala.

part of twenty years in appalling conditions on Sealdah Station and elsewhere, were finally rehabilitated. And a start was made on a reform of the land question. This was to lead to yet another division within the Communist ranks and to what may be the most crucial political event in India since Independence.

The average size of land-holding in West Bengal at this time was 3·88 acres, a smaller area than anything else in the country, with the exception of Kerala. There were, nevertheless, 53,000 holdings of between 15 and 30 acres and another 3,000 holdings of more than 30 acres, although an early statute of the new republic had declared that no one could legally own more than 25 acres. That figure is, in effect, a nonsense, for it has been possible to inflate it by dividing a large holding among innumerable members of a family. The system of cultivation, moreover, has scarcely changed in West Bengal since the Permanent Settlement. A petty landlord, or jotedar, leases ground to a bargadar on a crop-sharing basis. If the jotedar provides seed, bullock, plough and manure he takes half the crop; if he provides only land he takes forty per cent of the crop. It is a primevally miserable arrangement, inviting dishonesty on both sides and offering no security at all to the bargadar. This was the territory into which the United Front swiftly took an important step under a manifesto composed by the Land Minister, Hare Krishna Konar, a senior member of the CPI (M). 'The primary task,' this declared, 'is abolition of large-scale landholding and distribution of land to the landless. The next step would be for the Government to explain to the peasants the disadvantages of cultivating small holdings. The peasants will then voluntarily take to collective farming. Private ownership of land will then be done away with.'

The method used to abolish the large landholdings was quite simple. Landless peasants were encouraged to march on selected jotedars. A procession would stream upon its target behind a red banner, its members armed with lathis, spears, bows and arrows. They frequently shouted 'Mao Tse Tung Zindabad' as they went. On reaching their objective they marked its four corners with red flags, declared it forthwith to be in the possession of their citizen's committee and, as often as not, looted whatever grains or other crops were in store. If the jotedar was brave enough to get in the way, he was beaten up and sometimes killed. At first, the police took steps to intervene in this procedure, but they were instructed by the Government in Calcutta that this was legitimate and democratic struggle and must not be interfered with. Inside six months the CPI (M) found that its peasant membership had risen by 450,000 in West Bengal. Then Naxalbari happened, and the issue was no longer a simple and straightforward struggle for possession between landless and landed peasants.

Naxalbari is a police district lying in the narrow strip of West Bengal that is enclosed by Nepal on one side and East Pakistan on the other; Tibet and the Chinese are only eighty miles away. This is tea garden and jungle hill country, perfect for guerrilla warfare and admirable for infiltration by anyone so inclined; there are no towns, scarcely a village containing more than one thousand people. Its population consists almost entirely of tribespeople and, never having been nourished with fertilizers which are monopolized by the tea gardens, the yield from their various efforts in cultivation is approximately a third of the average for West Bengal. There has been a long history of peasant militancy in the district. The hill country flowing away from Darjeeling, of which this is part, was almost permanently unsettled when the British were here. There was an uprising in the Naxalbari area in 1939, another in 1959; and on the second occasion it was largely an insurrection against the fraudulent conversion of land to family holdings when the Indian Government had established its limit of twenty-five acres. A few months before the United Front took office in Calcutta in February 1967, the local wing of the CPI (M) had told the Central Committee that it was not very happy with the party's new taste for parliamentary procedures. For the next three months this was to be the scene of West Bengal's most vigorous redistribution of lands. There is some reason to believe, from subsequent events, that the new Government itself by the middle of May thought the situation up there was getting a little out of control. On 17 May, Hare Krishna Konar went up-country to meet local party leaders. As he arrived at the nearest railhead in Siliguri, he was met with a huge poster which read 'This movement can only succeed by the armed struggle and resistance of the working class. Resistance is meaningless without guns – let the working class collect guns and be vanguards in the struggle.'

On 23 May a police inspector was murdered in an ambush. The police heard that an attack might be expected on the Naxalbari police station and a force of twenty constables, a sergeant and an officer set off from Siliguri to intercept it. Two days later they reached Prasadjote, where there was a small bustee, a tea stall and a railway ganger's hut by the level crossing. A crowd appeared on the road ahead of them. At the back were men shouting revolutionary slogans; at the front were women and children, and a subsequent enquiry established that at least one woman had been forced to stand in the front row or else have her baby strangled. While the two groups were eyeing each other at a standstill, a man at the tea stall signalled to the police that another crowd had now appeared to cut off their retreat. An arrow hit the sergeant in the arm. The police stood back to back and the officer ordered both crowds to disperse. When this had no effect he ordered his men to fire. Ten rounds went into one crowd and thirteen into the other. Several people were killed and most of them were women and children. Almost a month later, on 19 June, the West Bengal Committee of the CPI (M) met in Calcutta to review the peasant warfare and particularly to take stock of the Naxalbari affair. It noted that there were extremists in the party who had 'already organized themselves into anti-Party groups' and it expelled nineteen members of the Naxalbari cell; the West Bengal party secretary, Promode Dasgupta, even alleged that the American CIA had infiltrated the Naxalbari group in order to create discord. Discord, in fact, was already being initiated from another direction.

For on 5 June, although the United Front Government was still telling its police headquarters in the Darjeeling district to keep out of disturbed areas as far as possible and to avoid action, the *Peking People's Daily* had accused the 'so-called non-Congress Government of West Bengal' of 'bloody suppression of the revolutionary peasants'. On 28 June, the party expulsions having been announced, Peking Radio made its own summary of the Indian situation. 'Under the leadership of the revolutionaries of the Indian Communist Party (Marxist) the tens of thousands of local peasants, who have small pieces of land or have no land at all and suffer the cruel exploitation of landlords and plantation-owners, began to arm themselves. They established their own political power and organized peasant societies, thus rebelling against the reactionary Indian Government and the landlord class. Defying laws, human and divine, and trampling under-foot the reactionary Government's law which protects landlords, plantation-owners, and the reactionary Government, they ploughed the land, drove away the plantation owners, used force to harvest the paddy in the fields of the landlords, seized grain, guns and ammunition from the homes of the big landlords, collected money and grain from the landlords and eliminated hoarding and speculation. They established people's courts to put on trial and punish the stubborn local bullies ... The emergence of this struggle in India ... signifies a new state in the Indian people's surging struggle against reactionary rule. This forecasts the approach of a great people's revolution in India with armed struggle as its major force ... The Indian people must proceed along the path pointed out by Chairman Mao ... this is the road of armed revolution, to oppose armed counter-revolution, the establishment of rural bases, the concentration of forces in the villages, using the villages to encircle the cities and finally taking over the cities.'

If this was intended as some kind of olive branch to Jyoti Basu and his immediate colleagues, it was already too late. That same day, the expelled Communists tried to seize the party news-paper, but were prevented by police. A week later they added yet another publication to West Bengal's already respectable tally of 1,024 newspapers and periodicals, with the first issue of their own journal. Its first editorial declared that 'Our Party, which was born out of the struggle against revisionism, is sought to be captured again by the revisionists. The Party, which is not the personal property of the leaders, must be saved from their hands.' From now on, peasants on the march against jotedars had an-other slogan to add to their collection of chants; 'Naxalbari Lal Salaam [Red Salute to Naxalbari]'. And from now on, the vocabulary of Communism could include the word Naxalite im-mediately after Bolshevik and Red Guard.

The revolutionary mood was just as evident in Calcutta as it was in the countryside, particularly among the industrial workers. The gherao was not unknown in West Bengal before the United Front took power. Every autumn it was customary for workers to lobby managements for a bonus on the eve of Durga Puja and frequently this led to demonstrations; occasionally it resulted in the police being called to free an employer and his executives who had been confined to their rooms in a genuine gherao. But there had never been anything approaching the scale of the gherao movement that broke out from the moment the new Government instructed the police to stay put after such an emergency call until the Labour Minister himself had cleared them for action. By September, no fewer than 1,016 gheraos had been staged in the state, for a wide variety of reasons. They were held to force the reinstatement of workers who had accepted a scheme of voluntary retirement and who had already collected compensation. They were held to support a demand for recruitment of more staff when management held that there were already too many staff; to back a demand for wages during unauthorized absence; to force the dropping of an inquiry into theft by workmen; to demand the promotion of certain people and the removal of others; to demand the reinstatement of workers who had been dismissed for misconduct two-and-a-half years previously after an official enquiry. There were gheraos laid on to demand an improvement in the statutory bonus of four per cent payable even when a firm does not make a profit in any year; the Labour Minister himself let it be known that, although the matter was in Delhi's hands and not his, the figure should be eight per cent; but gheraos backed demands for anything up to twenty per cent.

Gheraos were now not only much more common; they lasted longer. Two or three hours had previously been a general limit. But now, the manager of a factory just behind Park Street was forced to stand in the sun for seven hours without any water and without being allowed to use the lavatory, while the girl on the switchboard was threatened with violence if she tried to call the police. The manager of a jute mill and his assistant were made to stand in their yard for twelve hours, and kept fainting.

The longest recorded gherao had a manager confined to his office for seven days. The Labour Minister, Subodh Banerjee, was perfectly clear about what was now generally happening in industrial West Bengal. On 19 June he told trade unionists in Rourkela that 'I have allowed a duel between the employees and employers in West Bengal and the police have been taken out of the picture so that the strength of each other may be known.' There was some indication that the whole apparatus of law enforcement had been pressed to get out of the picture. Without the police to help them, managements began to look to magistrates for aid and, sometimes finding them less beneficial than they might have hoped, took their complaints to the High Court. It was there that Mr Justice Das was severely critical of the Sub-divisional magistrate in Alipore, who had refused an application for relief from a gherao after the police had also declined to intervene. His order, said the Judge, 'betrays a lack of understanding of the seriousness of the allegations made affecting personal liberty'. Then he added,' I wonder if the learned magistrate was aiding and abetting the commission of offences likely to lead to lawlessness.'

The situation had become so bad by the end of summer that the High Court had a number of applications before it for injunctions against the Government's instructions to the police. Chief Justice Sinha created a Special Bench of himself and four colleagues to hear the evidence; and while they were sitting, the High Court itself was one day subjected to the gherao, which was lifted only when the Chief Justice telephoned Ajoy Mukherjee and threatened to suspend the courts of West Bengal *sine die* if the police did not move in and shift the culprits. On 29 September, he issued the High Court's judgement. It quoted a variety of English lawyers on industrial action, from Lord Hewart to Lord Denning. It also distinguished carefully between English law that was still applicable by legacy in India and that which was no longer valid in the republic. The heart of the judgement was that the Government instructions were invalid and therefore quashed. It went on to say that 'There can be little doubt that encouragement from high quarters has resulted in a small group of militant trade unionists creating for themselves an enviable notoriety which they would otherwise not have achieved. Emboldened by such encouragement, they have become successful in rendering the forces of law and order ineffective, so that they could with impunity use violent methods against the management and terrorize them into submission. Thus, a small group of determined and violent men are holding up the whole industrial world to ransom. There is no doubt in my mind that the Labour Minister has deliberately assisted in the spread of this evil in the industrial world, and the two impugned circulars are in aid of it.' The Chief Justice had one more quotation to offer before his judgement finished. It was from a Tagore Law Lecture that had been delivered in Calcutta sometime earlier by the American Justice Douglas, who had said; 'The judiciary is in a high sense the guardian of the conscience of the people as well as of the law of the land ...' Almost the last words in Chief Justice Sinha's eighty-seven pages of ruling were: 'It is this public conscience that we have proceeded to exercise in this judgement of ours, hoping that it will contribute to the restoration of peace in West Bengal. In the gathering darkness I hope its voice shall be heard and obeyed.'

Within a few days, the Labour Minister retired to hospital, to be treated for the early stages of leukaemia, having left behind a substantial wreckage in industry. By then, 43,947 workers had been laid off in West Bengal since the beginning of the year because production had been disrupted by gheraos and strikes; another 4,314 had been made unemployed because their factories had decided to close down altogether. It was estimated that Rs 2,500 millions in capital had been withdrawn from the state during those first seven months of the United Front. These were only a few shades of Chief Justice Sinha's gathering darkness. Between March and October, 147 murders had taken place in which the motive was reckoned to be chiefly political; eighteen of the victims were active trade union leaders.

At this point the first signs of strain within the United Front became obvious. The Communist members of the Cabinet had lately taken to public criticism of the non-Communist members. Ajoy Mukherjee actually devised a code of conduct to inhibit his Ministers from speaking harshly of each other before the electorate. He also discovered that on more than one occasion his own authority had been bypassed by Jyoti Basu or by someone even lower in the hierarchy. He therefore decided to resign on Gandhi's birthday, 2 October. Later he was to give four reasons for this; there was widespread discontent and sometimes inhuman treatment in industry, too much force was being used to settle the land question, lawlessness generally was dislocating life in West Bengal and 'A wing of a political party is openly inviting China to help the party in bringing about an armed revolution, starting in West Bengal. Such a tendency should be nipped in the bud.' Ajoy Mukherjee was not, in fact, proposing to vanish into political obscurity. He still had contact with many of his old Congress colleagues and he was proposing to form a new Government with their aid, provided that his old enemy Atulya Ghosh could be kept out of it. Unfortunately for the Chief Minister, his political skill remained far inferior to that of Ghosh. He was outmanoeuvred behind the scenes, the plan was stillborn and the resignation never took place. Instead, there was a public reconciliation between the disjointed parts of the United Front at yet another rally on the Maidan.

No sooner had the cheers died down after that, than the Chief Minister was once more discovered in a sidelong shuffle away from his Communist colleagues. One of his Bangla Congress supporters had initiated a new national party consisting of all moderate men who had been disillusioned by the excesses of both Congress and Communism. It was to be entitled Bharatya Kranti Dal and it now held an inaugural session at Indore. This was attended by Ajoy Mukherjee and his supporters, together with another group from West Bengal, which had become disaffected from the Bangla Congress and its increasingly indecisive leader. And a memorable meeting it was, when 350 more Bengali delegates than the allotted number turned up, stormed the conference hall and came to blows. Almost as much confusion was now reigning politically in Calcutta. The Minister of Food, an Independent, decided to resign and took sixteen United Front supporters into Opposition with him.

It was now early November and the Governor of West Bengal, Dharma Vira, moved onto the fringes of a scene he was to occupy alone before very long. The legislative Assembly, which had not sat since mid-summer, was not due to meet again until February, but the Governor asked for a new session to start without delay, in order that the balance of power in West Bengal, if nothing else, might be decided. The United Front said that this would be impossible before mid-December. The Governor insisted that it should be much earlier. The United Front then asked the President of India in Delhi to define the Governor's powers through a judgement of the Supreme Court. Ajoy Mukherjee hastened to Delhi to add his personal weight, such as it was by then, to the United Front's request. He was told that his Government stood in peril of dismissal and, backed by his Cabinet, he suggested that if this happened there might well be a bloody revolution in West Bengal. Delhi was in no mood to accept threats from Calcutta. Within a few days the United Front was dismissed and a conglomeration of Congressmen and United Front defectors was pressed into service in its place. For a few tumultuous weeks it seemed likely that Ajoy Mukherjee's threat might just materialize, until the makeshift Government died of its own incapacities and Delhi stepped in once more. West Bengal was placed under President's Rule, which meant that Governor Dharma Vira, sitting where Lord Curzon had once sat, now administered the state alone with the authority of the whole republic behind him.

Just 371 days later, the United Front was back in office. With a police force in full commission, the year of President's Rule had been marked by gradually diminishing violence, though the loud cries of political outrage against Delhi's impositions continued. Otherwise nothing had changed. Nothing had been done to remedy the fundamental ills of Calcutta. When Delhi announced that in February 1969, West Bengal might share mid-term elections with the Punjab, Uttar Pradesh and Bihar, it was almost inevitable that the voters should restore the dismissed Government; very few of them, after all, had been on the receiving end of gheraos and other unpleasant manifestations of Communist rule. They restored their Government with an overwhelming majority this time. Where Congress had 127 seats in the previous Assembly, now it had only 55; where the CPI (M) had first enjoyed power with 43 seats, now it was swollen with 80; where the CPI had made do with 16 seats, now it advanced to 30; the Forward Bloc rose from 13 to 21, and of the major parties only the Bangla Congress stood virtually still with 33 seats, one fewer than before. Almost the same collection of men took office a second time. Ajoy Mukherjee reappeared as Chief Minister and Jyoti Basu as his deputy; but this time it was Basu and not Mukherjee who took possession of the Home portfolio, and with it control of the police.

Once again it was announced that the air-conditioning would not be required in the Writers' Building. Once again there was an inaugural rally on the Maidan; a million people turned out to hear the two leaders warn industrialists and big landlords to take note of the changed political situation and act accordingly if they did not want the Government helping the workers and the peasants in their struggle. Someone on the platform also suggested that Governor Dharma Vira had conspired to remove the United Front. The Government proceeded to settle its score with him when it drafted the inaugural address that he was obliged to read to the new Assembly. The Governor, however, could be as bloody-minded as anyone in the United Front and he coolly skipped two paragraphs that were quite pointedly offensive to his person and to the part he had played in the dying days of the first United Front. At which there was great uproar and a demand that he should be removed from office immediately. Within a month, Delhi took the hint and Dharma Vira left for a post in more tranquil surroundings.

There were other flourishes to celebrate the restoration. Jyoti Basu lodged a High Court claim for Rs 200,000 damages against the State of West Bengal, in compensation for illegal detention during the days of Congress administration twenty years previously. The Maidan statutes immortalizing the Raj were finally removed and a Martyrs' Memorial to local party heroes was put up across the road from the Writers' Building. There was a great renaming of streets, which has always been a regular pastime of people with any kind of municipal power in Calcutta. In the twenties, C.R.Das and Subhas Chandra Bose rechristened several thoroughfares in response to this or that episode in Bengali nationalism. After Independence, Harrison Road became Mahatma Gandhi Road and the upper part of Chowringhee was changed to Jawaharlal Nehru Road. At some stage or other Lower Chitpore Road was translated into Rabindra Sarani, though most people still use the first name. The United Front now ordained that Dalhousie Square should become Benoy-Badal-Dinesh Bagh, that Dharamtala Street should be called Lenin Sarani, that the Ochterlony Monument should be known as Sahid Minar. With a playful sense of humour, it changed Harrington Street (which contains the United States Consulate) into Ho Chi Minh Street, and surpassed even this masterstroke a little later when the Russians offered Calcutta a bronze statue of Lenin to celebrate the centenary of his birth. It cost the city Rs 40,000 to mount alongside the tram terminus at the top of the Maidan, but there it now stands, gazing down the new Lenin Sarani, upon a plinth which was placed in the centre of the small public garden dedicated to Lord Curzon.

Delhi was clearly not going out of its way to ease West Bengal's predicament, whatever form that might take under its second United Front. Communists were not the only people in Calcutta who were arguing for improved financial aid from the Central Government. The United Front had scarcely been elected when the President of the Bengal Chamber of Commerce, Mr J. M. Parsons, told his annual meeting that if the state was to be properly rehabilitated it would require 'a liberal measure of sympathy and assistance from the Central Government'. Within a month of re-election, the two United Front leaders had gone to Delhi to plead for a redistribution of resources between the Centre and the states, which received only a quarter of the income and corporation taxes collected in their area; West Bengal, with its comparatively huge contribution to the national economy on both these counts, obviously had a better claim than most states to a larger share in the final disbursement. The Central Finance Minister, that deeply conservative old Congressman, Morarji Desai, who was shortly to find his Prime Minister Mrs Gandhi too far to the Left for comfort, flatly refused to tolerate any review of finances. The Centre had already committed itself to

expenditure on a third Hooghly Bridge (whenever that might
be built) and it had also been persuaded to put up the money for
a circular railway in Calcutta (soon to be abandoned); more than
that it was not prepared to do. For the rest of 1969 there was to
be a running battle between the United Front and the Congress
Centre, between Calcutta and Delhi, about this apportionment
of money, and by the end of the year Delhi had still not yielded
another rupee.

By then, there was again chaos within the province of the
United Front. There had never really been anything else. There
was the chaos of sheer frustrated exuberance, for example, that
had nothing to do with politics in any sense that a political
scientist would immediately recognize. Just after the election, a
couple of Bengalis had arrived in the Andaman Islands after
rowing all the way from Calcutta and half way down the Bay
of Bengal. When they flew home, thousands turned out at Dum
Dum to hail them as heroes. On the way to the airport a small
boy clinging to an overloaded bus fell off and was killed; there
was a riot and the bus was stoned by a crowd. At the airport, a
crowd poured across the tarmac before the oarsmen's plane had
pulled up, surrounded it so thickly that the gangway couldn't
be placed in position for twenty minutes, and started throwing
shoes at the plane in impatience at the delay. For three hours a
mob overran Dum Dum. Some people tried to climb onto the
tail of an international jet that was hoping to take off. Others
roamed the aviation fuel stores, smoking as they went. Three
aircraft of Indian Airlines were chased as they were taxied to the
safety of hangars. A number of international airlines later threatened to boycott Calcutta unless security could be improved at
Dum Dum.

There was the chaos of frustrated bitterness by students well
aware that the degrees they were acquiring at Calcutta and
Jadavpore Universities were almost useless to them as means to
qualified employment and a standard of living that most university students throughout the world have some reason to expect.
In September 1969, no fewer than one thousand graduates applied for jobs as peons with Calcutta Corporation, though there
was not a single vacancy even for this lowliest municipal occupa-

tion of fetching and carrying. Months before that, sixteen professors of Calcutta University were gheraoed in their rooms for seventeen hours by students demanding that they should not be required to attend as many as half their lectures in order to be eligible for examination; the professors were allowed no food during the gherao, and a pitcher of water in one of their rooms was flung out when it began. The Vice-Chancellor of Calcutta was gheraoed so frequently by students abusing him as a CIA agent or something equally unpopular with them, that the newspapers were eventually reporting each incident as a commonplace worth no more than two or three inches of their space. By June, a conference of headmasters was claiming that its members had already suffered more than one hundred gheraos in the first six months of the year.

There was the chaos of things just breaking down under the strain of being Calcutta. Very early in the first session of the new Assembly, a Budget debate had to be carried on by candlelight because the electricity supply in the city had failed; and even when the electricity supply was working, the city gradually became dimmer and dimmer at night because so many bulbs on street lamps were smashed and so much wire was stolen. Garbage accumulated on the streets in mounds that were massive even by Calcutta's standards because people living near the Corporation's dumping grounds blockaded the entrances and refused to allow more lorries in; they complained that, because of the potholed roads, too much refuse spilled off the lorries and landed on their doorsteps. During the monsoon, five municipal wards in North Calcutta became completely awash for days because the manholes were blocked with silt. No sooner had the monsoon departed than the city endured a water crisis, when four-fifths of the filtered supply was cut off for a week because a short circuit had badly damaged the main pumping station; and it was the best part of two months before water flowed normally again.

The United Front's performance was only more confidently different from its first year in office. It began by moving to abolish the upper house in West Bengal's legislature. It followed this soon afterwards by declaring a one-day strike of absolutely everything without exception in the state. There had been a riot

at the Cossipore Gun and Shell Factory, which was controlled
by the Central Government in Delhi. Some six thousand workers
had demonstrated outside the gate, before starting the morning
shift, for the reinstatement of fifty-four men who had been
sacked during the period of President's Rule. The security officers
had lost their nerve and opened fire on the demonstrators, killing
four of them. At once, the Politbureau of the CPI (M) demanded
that the security officers should be handed over to the West
Bengal police. Delhi replied that it preferred to conduct its own
enquiry into the conduct of its own men. So the United Front
declared a strike. For twenty-four hours West Bengal was at a
standstill. Trains came to a halt wherever they happened to be
inside the state boundaries at four o'clock in the morning. Four
international jet flights landed at Dum Dum and there they
remained until the twenty-four hours were up. Otherwise, nothing moved in Calcutta. Even the telephone service was almost
completely cut off. In Delhi, the Indian Home Minister, Mr
Chavan, called this a 'deliberate effort to bring the functioning
of the economic system to a standstill'. In Calcutta, Jyoti Basu,
speaking as he was to speak more and more frequently for the
Government nominally led by Ajoy Mukherjee, said 'We are
happy at the justified and peaceful protest by the people.' It
hadn't, in fact, been entirely peaceful. At Kanchrapara, in the
24 Parganas, a group of men turned up for duty at the railway
workshops and began to fight the pickets there. Bombs were
flung, huts and shops were set on fire, and when the police
arrived they were bombed too.

The United Front pressed on with its unfinished business on
the land. Three bills were passed through the Assembly, one of
them exempting families with less than three acres from the payment of revenue, the other two aiming to protect tenants against
eviction. Meanwhile, the landless peasants were again marching
round the countryside with their red flags, staking out their
claims. Six months after regaining his Land Ministry, Hare
Krishna Konar was saying that another 200,000 acres had been
retrieved by the poor of West Bengal in addition to the 150,000
acres they had taken possession of under the patronage of the
first United Front; and, with the paddy harvest shortly to come,

he gave warning that his peasants 'would resist any onslaught that might come from the jotedars, which would lead to a blood bath'.

The Government could see nothing like the same progress in industry, even though four months of hard bargaining were to produce a twenty per cent wage increase for 200,000 engineering workmen. There were businessmen in Calcutta at the time who publicly declared themselves confident of being able to work with the United Front; who, indeed, expressed relief at the prospect of what they were pleased to call the restoration of stable government in the state. The fact is that from the moment the United Front returned to office nothing more was heard of the proposed share to be borne by the business community in a joint financial venture with the state and national Governments for the relief of Calcutta. And, immediately, the United Front had to deal with the by no means unique problem presented by the British firm of Westinghouse Saxby Farmer Ltd. This had been established in Calcutta since 1906; it manufactured railway equipment and it employed 1,700 men. It had expanded until 1965, when a recession occurred and it ceased to make a profit. In October 1968, while West Bengal was under President's Rule, one of its senior directors flew to India and offered to sell the entire works to the Central Government for the sum of one rupee; the offer had not been accepted and the London directors had therefore decided to close the firm on 26 March 1969. There was no chance of getting them to change their mind, particularly as National and Grindlays Bank (which is perhaps the most substantial bank in the city) was refusing to grant an overdraft though the bank's chairman, Lord Earlington, did fly to Calcutta to meet Jyoti Basu. It was Basu who wrote to the London directors of Westinghouse, asking them at least to defer the closure, which they did for a month, and it was Basu who lobbied Mrs Gandhi for the Centre to take on what it clearly regarded as a liability. In the end, it was the United Front which had to accept the running of Westinghouse at a loss; by which time, two or three other concerns in similar predicaments were all asking the state Government to control them.

Whatever constructive industrial policy the Government might have had, it lay in ruins by the end of the year. In August there was an eight-day strike in the jute industry which cost £4·5 millions in lost production. In September there was a fortnight's strike in the tea gardens which cost £1,390,000 in lost foreign exchange. In October the Dunlop factory laid off 6,000 workers and Hindustan Motors declared a lock-out of 13,000 workers. In 1967 there had been 438 industrial disputes in West Bengal, involving 165,000 workers and a loss of 5 million man-hours. In 1968 there had been 417 disputes involving 263,000 workers and 6·7 million man-hours. In 1969 there were 710 disputes, involving 645,000 workers and 8·5 million man-hours. The strikes and disputes surged from one end of the state to another and not even the most vital enterprises, such as the steel works of Durgapur or the rising dam at Farraka, were left out of the turbulence. Firms had started to answer workers in some of their own currency. Not far from a long and whitewashed wall slogan inviting everyone to 'Stand by the side of struggling Birla workers', it was possible to find another one which said 'Don't believe false propaganda by dismissed workers', under the imprint of Jusla Drinks, Winners of the All-India Mango Competition. Some organizations began to buy newspaper space to put their point of view in advertisements. The West Bengal Business Convention asked readers of *The Statesman* one morning to 'CONSIDER FOR A MOMENT ... Consumer trade is facing disruption. Essential commodities are becoming scarce. Retail market is threatened with non-availability of goods. With mounting wharfage, railway yards and transport depots are piled up with goods not being cleared. Before long, day to day business will come to a stand-still. A section of porters have stopped work. Others are being deprived of their daily earnings through intimidation. There is organized obstruction of movement of goods. Goods are being secured for ransom and penalties realized under duress. Threatening demonstrations and general lawlessness are prevailing in the vital trade centres. Feeling of panic and insecurity is assuming serious proportions. All this because a section of porters in wholesale and retail business centres have started an agitation demanding Bonus ... Is this agitation really justified? Where will all this lead to? What will happen when the consumer trade virtually collapses? Who will provide the solution?'

The feeling of panic, at least, was no piece of commercial propaganda by then. There had been one demonstration after another since the Cossipore riot and, like the gheraos, they had become increasingly vicious. People squatted on railway lines to stop trains from running and they placed barricades of stones across roads to bring buses and trams to a standstill. Two hundred headmasters held a demonstration throughout one night to protest against being gheraoed by their students and fifteen thousand jute growers marched on the Writers' Building one day to demand a fair price for their crops. There was a pitched battle at the National Medical College and Hospital between employees striking for the removal of the hospital superintendent and volunteers of the CPI (M) and the Revolutionary Socialist Party; twenty-two hospital patients were injured when bombs began to explode in some of the wards and a group of tubercular patients were almost suffocated when the police arrived and lobbed tear-gas in their direction by mistake. There was a riot at Eden Gardens, during a Test match between India and Australia, and six people lay dead at the end of the day's play. There was even a riot by policemen inside the state Assembly. Two of their colleagues had been killed in street battles a couple of days earlier and *esprit de corps* had turned to maddened resentment against the politicians. First, a handful of them wrecked the office of their superintendent and then marched upon the Assembly, where they smashed more furniture and knocked two or three politicians about before being placed under close arrest by a larger body of more orderly policemen. They had uttered threats against Jyoti Basu, and he responded with more threats a few days later at a rally of United Front supporters on the Maidan. His Government, he said (and by now Jyoti Basu was invariably speaking of the United Front as a personal possession), would be making a political enquiry into the conspiracy behind the police raid and such terrorism would be totally uprooted. At the same time he warned his vast army of supporters that 'acts of vengeance against us' might follow the dismissal of some policemen. Tactfully – for he was, after all, Minister in charge of police affairs, as well as much else – he told the crowd that they must not take law and order into their own hands, that they must help the police to perform their duty. And the crowd, responding to the mood of the leaders on the platform, shouted back 'No pardon for the conspiring policemen, ordinary policemen need not fear.'

It was only the beginning of August, yet there was already much to fear. If there was no one else to frighten a law-abiding citizen in Calcutta by then, there were certainly the Naxalites. On May Day they had come in force to the city and there they had held their own rally beneath the Ochterlony Monument. The purpose of this meeting was to announce the formation of yet another arm to the Left-wing body politic. This one was called the Communist Party of India (Marxist-Leninist) and it had been born thus a week before, on Lenin's birthday, some-where in the jungle of West Bengal. The Maidan meeting, how-ever, offered a rare chance for wellwishers to clap eyes on one of the two Naxalites-in-chief, Kanu Sanyal, a landless man who had been involved in the 1967 struggles around Naxalbari, al-though he did not come from that area. There were apologies for the absence of Charu Mazumdar, who carried even more weight in the new party, a veteran of the pre-war struggles in the hill country, who lives in Siliguri when he is not away in hiding from authority; a landed peasant who, according to the whispers of political enemies, owns rather more land than he is strictly entitled to in law. Sanyal told the May Day rally that Mazumdar was to be compared to Mao Tse Tung in his revolutionary wis-dom, that under his leadership it was important for the Naxalites to take part in revolutionary peasants' struggles in this 'semi-colonial, semi-feudal country'. The Naxalbari movement had been 'a successful application of Mao's teaching in a specific case', and people could now look to a bright future, provided they shunned the 'petty-bourgeois revolution-mongering' of Jyoti Basu and his comrades. The Naxalites proposed to differ from existing forms of Indian Communism not only in fine philo-sophical distinctions but in their organization; they would head-quarter themselves in the village, not the city, and they would have no permanent stronghold; they would shift their bases in accordance with the needs of the revolutionary struggle. Already, said Kanyal, their fire was to be seen blazing beyond West Bengal. And it was. There had been much Naxalite activity in the hill country of the Srikakulam district of Andhra Pradesh, far to the South. By December there were to be 3,500 policemen combing those hills in search of Naxalite guerrillas who were becoming uncomfortably popular with their mixture of terrorism and redemption. Peasants were warming to them because they were in the habit of publicly burning mortgage deeds and promissory notes in village squares; landlords and moneylenders were, one by one, being decapitated before a not particularly mournful populace.

The same sort of savagery had now been occurring in West Bengal for the best part of two and a half years. And the most terrible retribution was apt to fall not upon landlords and moneylenders, but upon those who had left the Naxalite cause for some other form of political action. There was a man called Kamakhya Banerjee, a peasant farmer in a small way, who had once been a member of CPI (M) but who had later joined the Naxalites and become a district leader near Siliguri. He subsequently rejoined the CPI (M) and one day in December 1969 he disappeared while he was harvesting his paddy. His body was later found by the railway line just outside Naxalbari; they had tied him to a bamboo pole and they had disembowelled him before cutting his throat. In Calcutta the Naxalites were now said to be responsible for many of the killings with bomb and with knife that were increasing in the city. It was very difficult to prove this, usually. There were so many people with other allegiances using the same tactics and in a city where it has always been comparatively easy to hit and then run into the crowd, more often than not a culprit was not caught. Eventually, more and more of the violence in Calcutta was to be blamed upon the Naxalites, partly through police incapacity to track down those responsible, partly because there were good political reasons for placing the blame in their quarter even when it did not justly belong there.

Openly they demonstrated whenever they had a good excuse. Frequently they would converge upon the Soviet Consulate or the Soviet Information Centre, bearing their placards of Mao Tse Tung, shouting their slogans which lumped Russian and

American imperialism together. When Durga Puja arrived, they set up their propaganda stalls among all the other pandals around the Maidan and hoisted portraits of Mao alongside posters advising the people to take the path of armed struggle. In College Square, near the University, it was a little difficult to decide whether the Naxalites or the CPI (M) or one of the other parties in the United Front were responsible for the portraits of Ho Chi Minh and Lenin, for the posters displaying comments on the Vietnam war by Bertrand Russell and U Thant, for the banners telling how obscene books sponsored by the CIA, together with American films and bourgeois newspapers, had so corrupted the immaculate youth of Calcutta that people were actually dancing in a Western manner during the Puja. But if, at any time, portraits of Mr Kosygin, Mr Nixon and Mrs Gandhi were publicly burned together, then you could be fairly sure it was the Naxalites who had put torches to them. The police were fairly sure that it was Naxalites who smeared the statue of Mahatma Gandhi with tar one night in October, such a desecration that an armed guard cordoned that hallowed corner of the Maidan for several days afterwards; and this was only a hint of what was to come. Within a month or two many other statues in Calcutta had been attacked, not even Netaji Subhas Chandra Bose was spared, and from time to time the citizens would wake up in the morning to discover that yet another Bengali hero had lost his stone or metal head, which was later dredged out of the nearest water tank.

There was a brisk circulation of the Naxalite journal *Liberation*, with its regular articles by Charu Mazumdar, and one issue in the New Year was to be a manual of guerrilla tactics. It advocated secrecy in the formation of units, which must never consist of more than seven men. 'The unit should be kept secret from those among the local people whose vigilance has not yet reached the required level, and even from those party units which have not yet fully mastered the methods and discipline required for illegal work. The method of forming a guerrilla unit has to be wholly conspiratorial. No inkling of such conspiracy should be given out even in the meetings of the political units of the party. This conspiracy should be between individuals and on a personal basis. The petty bourgeois intellectual comrade must take the initiative in this respect as far as possible. He should approach the poor peasant who, in his opinion, has the most revolutionary potentiality, and whisper in his ears 'Don't you think it a good thing to finish off such and such a jotedar?' This is the way the people must be roused and emphasis must be put on liberating their own villages ...' The condescending author of this advice (presumably neither 'petty' bourgeois nor poor peasant) suggested that the guerrillas should not rely on firearms at this stage in their campaign; the use of spears, javelins, sickles and choppers would do very well for their purposes at present. 'The petty bourgeois intellectual cadres and those leaders who have to travel far and wide may, however, carry small pistols with them to frighten away, disperse or kill the enemy if they find themselves suddenly surrounded by him. But we should never give unnecessary importance to it, because that might encourage us to put our reliance not on the people, but on weapons, which is dangerous.' As for the slightly more than short-term aims, *Liberation* had this advice to offer. 'We must never be impatient or hasty, especially so in case of the first attack, which has the greatest importance. We should rather be prepared to make several attempts than make a hasty attack and fail. It may be difficult, in the first few actions, to raid the house of the class enemy and confiscate his moveable property. So, it would be better to lay more stress only on killing him. Later, when the masses are roused and take part in various kinds of work and the attacks become regular, easier and more powerful, the enemy can be killed even in his stronghold and his property confiscated. The conditions will gradually become so favourable that after carrying out a guerrilla action, the guerrillas themselves will be able to address the masses, explain before them the importance of such actions, and with arms in their hands, even inspire the masses by making fiery speeches.'

The police in Calcutta were not quite helpless in the face of such incitement to violence, but by mid-summer they were rapidly becoming demoralized. They could scarcely be expected to know whether they were coming or going in any direction, given the behaviour and the utterances of the Minister in charge of police affairs. While the state and civic constabulary lumbered around the city in their heavily meshed trucks, with steel helmets on their heads and floppy shinpads on their legs, with their shields, their lathis, their tear-gas and their rifles at the ready for the next fatal riot, Jyoti Basu continued icily to wield his portfolio with some indifference to the disturbance it was causing. Occasionally his personal intervention caused a gherao to be lifted, as happened one day in October after the Shipping Master in the Port of Calcutta had been confined for seven hours by some seamen. But only a few weeks before that, Basu had calmly announced that, since March, 1,010 criminal cases had been withdrawn on the Government's instructions because it was felt that the situation would improve if thousands arrested during 'democratic movements' were released; and he was candid enough to add that political considerations alone had been taken into account. He seemed to be in complete control of the Government, and the United Front as a whole was almost reduced to announcing collectively that West Bengal would observe a holiday to mourn the death of Ho Chi Minh in September. In fact, the Government had been riddled with internal dissent for some time and it was now on the threshold of disintegration again.

There had been occasional straws in the wind. In April a fight had broken out in one of the ministerial rooms in the Writers' Building, between supporters of the Bolshevik Party and members of the Socialist Unity Centre, both of which were part of the United Front, over policy on the rehabilitation of refugees. In August, while the CPI (M) leaders were in Delhi for a meeting of their Politbureau, a number of their partners in the Government demanded that there should be a redistribution of portfolios, of which the CPI (M) had held the biggest share since the election. But there had been nothing to prepare city and state for what followed on 8 October. The Bangla Congress, with Chief Minister Ajoy Mukherjee presiding, passed a resolution which stated that inter-party clashes in the field, gheraos, repressive measures in educational institutions, forcible occupation of land, police inaction, a general deterioration of law and order, activities of anti-social elements protected by various political parties, indignities suffered by women and the indifference of the administration had all combined to create a deep sense of insecurity and uncertainty among the people. The resolution named no names, but everyone in Calcutta knew which politician and which party the Bangla Congress and its remarkable president had in mind.

Mukherjee and Basu met shortly afterwards and declined to say what had passed between them for ninety minutes. Next day the entire United Front held a meeting (which a headline in *The Statesman* described as 'Infructuous') at which virtually every other party in the Government accused the CPI (M) of being at the bottom of West Bengal's current troubles. The general secretary of the Bangla Congress produced a list of relevant incidents; according to this there had been 378 murders since the Government was elected, in September alone there had been 40 inter-party riots, 36 head teachers had been forced to resign after persistent gheraos, and in 292 cases of riot the police had remained conspicuously inactive. The leader of the CPI said that the CPI (M) wanted to annihilate other parties. To all charges Jyoti Basu replied that the Bangla Congress figures were a fabrication, though he conceded police inaction, this being partly because he had been waiting for the United Front to draw up a code which would facilitate his own work.

For a month there was an uneasy peace round the Writers' Building. The new Governor of West Bengal, S. S. Dhavan, lately Indian High Commissioner in London, was at this stage telling the Indian Institute of Management at Barrackpore that those who counselled the working class to wait for better days did not even have the merit of practicability; for himself, 'I hate to be a Governor of a State of slaves'; and he wondered how anyone could expect Communism to be halted under the existing state of affairs in West Bengal. At almost the same moment, the friends of the British Council in Calcutta were carrying, by thirty-one votes to twenty-one, a motion regretting the disappearance of the gentleman from their society; a fact observable, some of them suggested, from the scarcity of males who now opened the door for females, or offered their seats to women on public transport. Ajoy Mukherjee had gone to Delhi, where he was telling a press conference that although there was a feeling of insecurity to life and property in West Bengal, he was in no position to relieve Jyoti Basu of the Home portfolio and its control of the police. Nor was he willing to invite intervention by the Central Government. As for the possibility of resigning himself, he said, 'I do not like that the Government should fall just now.' He had one positive announcement to make. Together with 42,000 Bangla Congress supporters in his state, he would shortly be taking part in a satyagraha, a peaceful demonstration with fasting, in the grandest tradition of Mahatma Gandhi.

The three-day public fast began on 1 December at 104 different places in West Bengal. The Chief Minister held his own in an elaborate tent in Curzon Park, where Lenin's statue was shortly to be placed. He had the telephone installed and he brought his ministerial work with him from the Writers' Building, as the Minister of Industries did in the canvas compartment alongside him. Thus fortified with Government files, with blankets, pillows, mosquito nets and buckets, the most distinguished part of the state-wide satyagraha began at eight o'clock in the morning, to the chanting of Vedic hymns and recitations from the Koran. It was not a peaceful demonstration at all. Thousands turned up to file respectfully past the Chief Minister, to garland him with flowers and to make their dutiful bobs to him. A journalist who went along reported that 'The Chief Minister was at times seen disposing of office files.' But at noon a mob arrived, cut the telephone lines, smashed tables and chairs, tore down curtains and flung a variety of missiles around, two of which hit the Chief Minister in the face, before police came and peace was restored. There was more violence outside the tent the next day and Ajoy Mukherjee told a crowd of friendly demonstrators that the police in the state who were not in the good books of the administration were either being transferred or dismissed. On the third day in Curzon Park, when it was reckoned that 800,000 had visited the ministerial tent, Mukherjee told a great gathering at dusk that 'If the people of West Bengal think that the present state of lawlessness should continue we shall silently bid them farewell. We shall quit. We shall never be a party to the prevailing barbarism.' As Chief Minister, he said, he had tried his best to resolve the differences at various levels, within the

Cabinet and within the United Front. Again and again it had been pointed out that the United Front image was being tarnished. There had been prolonged discussions and pious resolutions on resolving the inter-party disputes. But the agreement was looked upon as a scrap of paper to be thrown into the dustbin. It had turned out to be a great hoax. The police were made inactive and then violence was let loose. 'I could have appreciated their guts,' he said, 'if they had confronted the police while launching their campaign. Let the people judge if the charge of barbarism made by me is correct or not.'

For the next few weeks the Chief Minister was busy touring the country around Calcutta, making the same points again, with a number of embellishments. In Krishnagar he said he had been reduced to the role of silent onlooker in Government, that neither the police nor the district magistrates would obey his orders. In Durgapur he said that fifth-grade CPI(M) workers were dictating orders to policemen. In Howrah he invited Jyoti Basu and his party to sue for defamation. Basu, meanwhile, was keeping his own counsel for the most part. He told his constituents that any attempt to form an alternative Government without the CPI(M), which had just happened in Kerala on the subsidence of another United Front for superficially different reasons from those now plaguing West Bengal, would have serious consequences. He thought that in the Bangla Congress's concern for law and order could be heard 'the voices of the jotedars and the big bourgeoisie'. Curiously, almost nothing was heard from any of the other political leaders in Calcutta, although the Congress leader P. C. Sen had artfully tried to make some capital out of the satyagraha by congratulating the Chief Minister on his 'purificatory fast' while observing that he could scarcely shirk responsibility for the failure of law and order in the state. But from a dozen party bosses in the United Front there was silence now. It was as though they were waiting to see what outcome there might be between two gladiators, the ineffectual politician who could bank on considerable moral support from the public in the land of Gandhi, and the supremely skilful politician who in this jungle stood or fell in the end upon the strength of his own political machine.

If some kind of truce had been implicitly called, it had not much farther to go. But before it ended there was a moment which in any other context would have been glorious farce. The state Assembly was due to sit again, after its mid-winter break, for a Budget session in the third week of January. It was proposed that the week before there should be an informal meeting of the United Front for the settling of differences. The CPI leader had insisted that, as a matter of party prestige, the meeting should be held at the CPI offices. Several hours before it was due to begin, some party leaders decided that it should be held at the offices of the Lok Sevak Sangha party instead, and instructed the convenors to see to the change of plan. Unfortunately the message never got right round the United Front; it had rather a long way to travel, after all. Five o'clock came with Ajoy Mukherjee and representatives of the Gorkha League, the Forward Bloc and the Socialist Unity Centre sitting with their hosts of the CPI, while Jyoti Basu, together with members of the Revolutionary Socialist Party, the Workers' Party of India and the LSS, were gathering in another building at the other side of the city. A handful of Bolsheviks, members of the Samyukta Socialist Party, Revolutionary Communist Party of India and Forward Bloc (Marxist) had managed to distribute themselves in roughly equal proportions at both meetings. And there, for the next hour or so, the two groups sat, looking at their watches, wondering what new plot had now been hatched, consuming tea and toast (at the CPI office) or more seasonable Bengali delicacies (on the premises of the LSS).

There was to be no more fun and games in Calcutta for a long time, now. The Budget session began with the Chief Minister having to fight his way along the corridors of the Assembly, through a mob demonstrating against police interference in a riot at a school in Beliaghata the night before. It had scarcely started to debate West Bengal's collapsing economy than Mukherjee and Basu were making public two long letters they had written to each other, extraordinary documents of perhaps ten thousand words apiece, in which a variety of British politicians from Winston Churchill to Harold Wilson were cited. Mukherjee's share in this correspondence was first into the public prints, accusing Basu of giving away state secrets about a recent intervention in police affairs by the Chief Minister, who had cancelled an order made by the Home Department for the withdrawal of eight criminal cases and for the transfer of a police officer. Basu's reply was that it had been necessary to make public some facts because of the Chief Minister's objectionable propaganda and that 'Your dissertation on the provisions of the Constitution will do much credit to a schoolboy.'

No hope remained of healing the breach between the two leaders after this windy exchange or, by extension, of saving the United Front. Mukherjee's response to Basu's letter was to warn him of the legal consequences that could follow the violation of a ministerial oath of secrecy. A week later, in the Assembly, the Chief Minister repeated that his Government was now uncivilized and barbarous, and when a member of the CPI (M) jeered at him he turned in his temper and thrust an old Congress grudge at the Communists. 'Don't you feel ashamed?' he shouted. 'I was in politics before you were born. When we fought for freedom, you were acting as agents for the British.' Somehow, the Assembly stumbled onto even harsher facts of life in Calcutta and West Bengal. Mukherjee himself was obliged to announce that the Budget Estimates showed a deficit of Rs 405 millions. The United Front had inherited a deficit of Rs 250 millions twelve months before but now, he said, unless production in the state could somehow be increased, 'we shall have little to distribute except poverty'.

And terror. For the Chief Minister had not exaggerated in the least during his eccentric denunciations of the lawlessness flowing from his Government. Violence had been there throughout the year, but since 1946 Calcutta had not known greater violence than that which raged through the city from the start of 1970, during the last few weeks of the United Front. Before then, there had been the customary violence of Calcutta – a rickshaw runner strangled for refusing to subscribe ten paise to a collection for an impromptu concert in the street at Dum Dum, three people killed when 10,000 rioted in Burrabazar, barricaded the roads with handcarts and tar boilers and set fire to cars and a fire engine. There had been a spate of bank robberies with gun play during 1969 and early in the New Year there was another one in Park Street, which led to the arrest of Ananta Singh, who had been a great Bengali hero in the Chittagong Armoury Raid against the British forty years before. More dreadful things than bank raids began to happen now.

Almost every day brought massive riots, which the police could no longer control even with firearms because they were outnumbered. On one night, seven cinemas were bombed simultaneously, one of them was set on fire, and everybody blamed the Naxalites. From time to time there would be an explosion in a house and rescuers rushing into the wreckage would discover the mangled bodies of youths who had been making bombs. An ambulance which picked up an injured man after a street battle was mobbed and its drivers were held at the point of pistols and knives while their patient was dragged out and stabbed. Couples coming out of cinemas to their cars were surrounded and stripped of their clothing. Women had their jewellery taken by men threatening them with knives; occasionally they were raped into the bargain. At the Racecourse one afternoon in January a crowd suddenly turned on the stands, the weighing rooms, the restaurants and the offices of the Royal Calcutta Turf Club and started to wreck and set fire to them. And, for the first time since the most violent years of the Raj, Europeans were now being attacked in Calcutta. At the Racecourse riot the wife of an official in the British High Commission had her necklace torn off by a man who reached to grab it through her open car window, while the wife of the West German Consul was injured when her car was surrounded by a mob carrying burning timbers. A week later, the wife of the French Consul was hacked to death in her bed one night, and her badly injured husband survived only because their son rushed into the room with a sword and frightened the three goondas away. The streets of Central Calcutta now became deserted after dusk by people too frightened to move out of their homes. And when, on 9 March, Ajoy Mukherjee announced that he and his Bangla Congress supporters would be resigning from the Government a week later, there was such a panic that, within hours, every forthcoming flight by Indian Airlines from Calcutta to Bombay, Delhi and elsewhere in the land, was completely booked up by businessmen and their families fearful of a greater wrath to come.

The statement of resignation said what had been said time and time again for months now. 'The 32-point programme which was pledged before the electorate on the eve of mid-term election has not been implemented as it should have been because of the atrocious, aggressive, high-handed and fascist activities of the CPI (M). . . In spite of some spectacular achievements in some spheres, the number of unemployed in the state is on the increase. During the rule of the United Front, unbridled chaos and disturbances have taken place all over the state. The state machinery has become the pathetic onlooker in almost all activities of vandalism and barbarism. In fact, a reign of terror has been established by the CPI (M) in different parts of the state, including the metropolitan city of Calcutta.' There was an attempt to cobble up an alternative Government after this, but it was a pointless exercise, as everyone well knew who took part in it. Even Jyoti Basu, standing before another huge Maidan rally the day before Mukherjee abandoned his seals of office, was making no more than a rhetorical gesture when he told his followers that the CPI (M) had a right to lead Government in these circumstances.

Next morning, the Governor of West Bengal advised New Delhi that there had been a breakdown of the Constitutional machinery in his state and suspended the Assembly. That afternon, long convoys of military began to roll down Chowringhee to take up positions around the city. The sight of them lightened many hearts but, in truth, they meant only that the darkness of Calcutta was gathering more thickly still.

ZINDABAD

THE bickering, of course, did not end with the dissolution. A few weeks later it was Lenin's birthday again, and for this hundredth anniversary Calcutta mounted a perfect cameo of the more attractive side to its political life. There stood the great god figure, bronzed and flatfooted upon his plinth, dominating what had been Curzon Park until he moved in and caused it to become Lenin Square. There was Governor Dhavan to unveil him, with Ajoy Mukherjee and Jyoti Basu and many other old comrades to applaud him, and there was the Russian Consul-General trying to look paternal and filial at one and the same time. Naxalites were preparing to march somewhere in the vicinity, for it was their birthday too. The Governor declared that Lenin had been a great friend to India and for his pains was told, five minutes later by a speaker from the CPI (M), that he represented the class of which Lenin was the sworn enemy. Ajoy Mukherjee narrated the whole of Lenin's life, from birth to death, and when he had at last run out of breath was told by Jyoti Basu that he and his cohorts had better abandon their fruitless attempts to destroy Marxist Communism. A Mr Gupta of the CPI aired his views on the CPI (M)'s disruptive influence, and was asked why he was taking part in a function at which capitalists were trying to create confusion in the people's minds at the expense of Lenin. The Russian Consul-General was told by someone else that he had no business to be there either, representing as he did the forces of revisionism. Everyone spared a slanderous thought for the Naxalites, who were just then mustering by the Birla Planetarium.

There wasn't much else to laugh about in Calcutta. The day President's Rule was declared, the city was once more quiet and empty with the menace of a total strike. Within a fortnight, an attempt was made on Jyoti Basu's life in Patna, the bullet killing the man next to him as he was being greeted by local party workers on the railway station. Had it hit Basu, there is little doubt that Calcutta would have been visited by another medieval fury of retribution, for party passions were then at their highest, their internecine animosities inflamed even more by the bitterness of lost power. As it was, the customary violence merely continued for months, after a short breathing space imposed by the presence of troops in the city, who were withdrawn as soon as Delhi felt that the first hot wave of resentment against outside control had passed. In November, the Indian Parliament was told that there had been 313 murders in West Bengal in the previous quarter alone, of which more than half were reckoned to be political; and since the United Front collapsed there had been 526 attacks on policemen, with fatalities increasing at an unprecedented rate. The police had begun to respond in kind. The Naxalites threatened everyone more than ever before and their strategy changed to bombing and killing in the city rather than in the country. Their student mobs became particularly vicious in their antipathy to Gandhi, to Tagore and to anything connected with those two gentle ghosts. They attacked the Gandhi Study Centre at Jadavpore one day and burned all its literature; and things became so impossible at the university that in May it was closed indefinitely.

A few days later, a young teacher from Essex called Mary Taylor was captured with a band of Naxalites in the jungle near Jamshedpur, which seemed to astonish people much more than it should have done; what the Naxalites are fighting for is, after all, not substantially different from what students on campuses across Europe and the United States have been demonstrating and rioting for in the past year or two. And in India, as elsewhere, forces even more sinister were being marshalled ready to strike back and smash when the opportunity occurred. General Cariappa, sometime Indian High Commissioner in Australasia and former Commander-in-chief of the Army, could be heard advocating President's Rule for the entire nation. The powerful men of Jana Sangh and Shiv Sena, purveyors of religious and racial bigotry, were beginning to press their policies ever more closely upon Mrs Gandhi, when she was already hemmed in by a cordon of Congressmen including Morarji Desai and Atulya Ghosh, who had divided the party and stood off to the Right.

The gheraos went on, and the most mindless gheraos of all were now being conducted against the Commissioner of Calcutta Corporation, M. G. Kutty. He had been Director of the CMPO until the United Front persuaded him to use his considerable and incorruptible skills upon that organism in the city which stood most in need of them. By the time the monsoon came he had been knocked about so often, he had been so frequently abused by mobs as he sat at his desk and tried to work, that he was almost broken upon the wheel of Calcutta's poverty-stricken and uncomprehending rage. Yet gheraos were not even the worst of what had happened there, any more than the violence was. The worst of it was the sixty-five factories which had closed in the state during January and February after factories had been closing one after the other for a year, and the seventeen state undertakings that were running at a loss both before and after the United Front, and the capital investment that had dropped from Rs 209 millions in 1966–7 to Rs 90 millions in 1968–9 with the end not yet in sight.

It is the easiest thing in the world to come close to despair in Calcutta. Every statistic that you tear out of the place reeks of doom. Every half mile can produce something that is guaranteed to turn a newcomer's stomach with fear or disgust or a sense of hopelessness. It must be a generation at least since anyone stayed here for more than a day or two unless he was obliged to, or had a phenomenal sense of vocation, or a pathological degree of curiosity. Yet for anyone with the wilful staying power to remain through that first awful week when Calcutta is driving him away with shock and nausea, with resentment and with plain gut-rotting funk, a splendid truth about this city slowly dawns upon his perceptions and his understanding. It is that although he will surely never before have encountered so much that is deadly in any one place, he has never been confronted with so much life, either. It pulsates and churns around him wherever he goes, it swirls in every direction. Though it marches angrily and viciously, it also laughs idiotically and infectiously. While it is staggering miserably it is also wandering thoughtfully. It is reproducing itself minute by minute, it is thriving and proudly brandishing itself. It dominates.

Bruegel would have been at home here. He would have settled down at the top of Chowringhee, on the corner of Lenin's new Sarani, where the unhappy policeman is battling with the traffic before another bout with the citizenry, or he would have opened his sketchbook at the bottom of Chitpore Road, where it swerves off in such palpitating confusion towards the high pink bastion of the Nakhoda Mosque; and there, unless some fool hove a couple of bricks at him because he was about to record something that local pride preferred to keep uncomfortably to itself, he would have started to draw for his life. He would eventually have produced one of his peasant masterpieces crammed with people. Not (let us hope) *The Triumph of Death*, but maybe something like *The Battle Between Carnival and Lent*. He would have found that the mutilations and the beggary of indigence had not changed a bit across four centuries. The mosque would have done for his church, with people praying and thieving, without much distinction between the two, right under its eaves. That pot-bellied babu would go well astride a carnival hogshead, and the sadhu with his holy mud and his trident could preach him lenten mortifications. The buildings here might not have slops emptied from their upper windows (though you can be sure of little in this city) but they would make up for that with the garbage in their gutters. There might not be children here, each flailing at a top with a whip in his hand, but there would be many small boys possibly carrying other weapons of offence. And everywhere the artist looked, he would see people negotiating the business of small trade, just as they were conducting it in 1559, down to the seasonal preponderance of fish; for the Hooghly is just down the road and it is a-swarm with hilsa.

Even when Calcutta is at its most alarming and its most distasteful, it can warm you with some vivid expression of its humanity if you can shed your inhibitions, or at least move them aside for an instant, enough to take this in. The city is now decorated from one end to the other with the slogans and the symbols of what promises to be a brutal revolution if it breaks out properly. Exhortations to action and representations of Mao

Tse Tung are now splattered across half the walls standing between Bansberia in the North and Budge Budge in the South. Some of this is poetry. There are commonplace lines of prose by the hundred, parrotted from the chapbooks of Peking, like 'Make the seventies the decade of liberation' and 'Political power grows out of the barrel of a gun'. But then, one day, you turn a corner in Ballygunge and find yourself face to face with 'Awaken from your slumber, ye sons of Bengal, and give out a Leonine roar' alongside a most engaging stencilled portrait of Mao in delicate light blue wash, as carefully and fondly drawn as the work of the most dedicated pavement artist who is out to secure your appreciation as much as your money.

Or slip into National and Grindlay's Bank on Chowringhee, to change some of the money that has made this place what it has terribly become. Just round the corner in Park Street, a gang of men have been marching behind a red banner, shouting 'Zinda-bad' for the long life of some cause or person, or 'Biplab' for the revolution that will shorten many lives. Outside the bank a row of beggars squats and leans against the wall, not beseeching fiercely as so many beggars in Calcutta do, but each man and woman merely holding one arm out, gazing vacantly at the Maidan across the road, taking not the slightest notice of one another, petrified by the wasting inertia of their situation; for begging outside a bank is the emptiest beggary of all. Inside, all is crisply air-conditioned security. Two or three men in khaki lounge or stroll watchfully with rifles at the sloppy trail. Peons queue listlessly at counters, awaiting the disbursement of their employers' funds, which suggests either shocking arrogance or a superb faith in human nature on someone's part, for these men are not very much better off than the beggars outside. Visiting Europeans sit with glossy magazines in plastic leather easy chairs, nervously eyeing the rifles while they await the call of solvency. Local businessmen pad away to the glass doors and the street, pausing on the threshold to tuck briefcases even more firmly under their arms, for many hazards now await the rich man in this city when he leaves the protection of his stockades. Otherwise, the atmosphere of National and Grindlay's on Chowringhee is simply invested with all the calculated balance between service and self-interest that has put the bankers of London and the gnomes of Zürich so firmly in their place. It is equally depressing. But it lightens wonderfully when you actually transact your modest business in travellers' cheques. For the clerk sits you in a cane chair by his side while he flicks through his variety of triplicated forms and tots up his columns of numbers with the same mannered absorption of his distant colleagues in Cornhill. He offers you a glass of water while you wait. He exchanges polite simplicities about the weather. He hands you a little brass disc which you must carry to the counter over there to recover your money. And when you ask him if you might please have your cash in so many ten-rupee notes, so many fivers and so many singles, he at once transforms National and Grindlay's into something bigger and better than an institution with his reply. 'Ah, yes, yes', he says, scarcely looking up from his accounts, 'if you'll just wait till I have finished this and then go over there with this, you shall have everything you need exactly in accordance with all your own sweet wishes.'

Nowhere do you feel the oppressiveness of Calcutta more than at one of those interminable rallies on the Maidan organized by the CPI (M). They generally start about teatime, they rarely finish before nine o'clock, and some of the hours between can drag heavily when you do not understand Bengali. But they are masterly exhibitions of organization. An entrance has been created along the Red Road by lashing tall saplings together into a fence with an open gateway, and a corduroy path has been laid from this to the platform fifty yards away, so that the leaders shall not get their feet damp. The platform is high, so that everyone on it will be visible at a great distance, and it is large enough to accommodate twenty or thirty if they sit as close together as good comrades should. It is illuminated with spotlights, it flutters with red flags, and it has a huge red backcloth upon which Lenin is straining resolutely forward from a thicket of banners. Everything is perfectly under control. There is a posse of young party bloods guarding the gateway and two lines of them flanking the path to the platform. They are all exceedingly neat in khaki drill trousers, with white shirts and carefully rolled-up sleeves, with standard army webbing belts blancoed in

khaki green No. 3, and with the large red party roundel pinned
on their chests – which makes them look a bit like a lot of very
well disciplined football supporters. Some of them wear boots
and many of them wear the kepi, as fashionably introduced by
Fidel Castro. They look alert, tough and extremely supple. Every
one of them bears a wrist watch. These boys are nowhere near
the bottom of Calcutta's pile. Not many people in the enormous
crowd seem to be utterly poor either; at least, not the ones near
the front. As they sit there upon the ground, row after attentive
row of them, a brigade of young women to the fore, they seem
mostly to be the clerks and the educated workers of the city together with many, many students. But, distantly across the
Maidan, people have climbed trees and others are packed standing on top of the Esplanade tram shelters, and goodness knows
where they come in the scale of things. There must be a hundred
thousand here altogether. The most distant ones have their own
background in glaring red; a neon sign at the top of Chowringhee
with its message of 'Life Insurance For Security'.

The leaders come through the guard of honour to the platform,
men in white dhotis with their heads held high and not a party
badge between them. Jyoti Basu speaks first and in the terms of
Western oratory his would be an impassioned speech, but with
the passion kept finely under control. Privately he thinks that
there will be several more United Fronts here, broken by periods
of President's Rule, until one party comes out of an election with
enough votes to rule alone; but he is not saying this to his audience. He is telling them to beware of revisionism, that their enemies must beware if there is to be no bloodshed, that all who are
not with them are against them. And his audience follows him
closely but quietly, punctuating his hour at the loudspeaker with
occasional surges of handclapping. It is only when he has sat
down, when Promode Dasgupta and Hare Krishna Konar are
having their say, that you see why Bengalis think Basu at his
worst in public speech. For theirs is the oratory that sends men
delirious with dreams, that can set a rabble to a march of destruction. Basu has his rising moments and his dying falls, his left
hand confidently on his hip while his right hand presents an in-
disputable point. But Dasgupta and Konar are magnetic.

They pace themselves as artfully as Billy Graham once did. They begin quietly, almost stealthily, and they will toss away a joke casually to play their people into humour. Gradually their pace quickens, their intonation rises, the crowd's excitement mounting with it, until they shut everything off with a gesture. Silence. Then they start again, but not quite so far down the scale this time, and now they drive on until they are trembling with the passion of their speech, until their voices have risen to a new and more fervent pitch than ever before, until one hand is raised high with its fingers curved and outstretched as though it were about to bring a mighty chorus into a crashing paean of exultation. From start to finish they move this crowd as Jyoti Basu has never moved it for one instant. They have people roaring with laughter, with acclaim, with anger. They have men leaping to their feet and shaking their fists agreeably in return. They have everybody in that hundred thousand of followers prepared to follow them to the death. When the speeches are done, the leaders begin to sing the Internationale. At once, something happens that fixes the contradictory parts of this monstrous but marvellous city. All over that crowd, torches are swiftly lit and held high in flaring salute. There is something horribly lynch-eery about that moment; but at the same time you know that this is a turning point in history perversely like those few blessed days in Prague, when the people went out on the streets and signed that manifesto to stiffen Alexander Dubcek and his colleagues against the browbeating of the Russian Politbureau at Cierna Nad Tisou.

These are not robots, although they can perhaps be made to behave as such. For four and a half long-winded hours, small boys were roaming through that crowd, selling sweets out of glass jars and tea out of kettles, giggling even with the rich European intruder as they went. While Dasgupta and Konar were invoking the most awful penalties against capitalism, a stout party member was threading his way through their audience, assiduously collecting money for the revolutionary funds. Twice he came past the rich European and asked him, comrade, to subscribe with everybody else. On his third circuit he wonderfully forgot just where he was and where the pair of you relatively stood, and called you 'Sahib' instead.

To point out and enjoy these things is not to ignore the real horrors of this city, or in some obscure way to plead mitigation of them. The poverty of Calcutta is an affront to the dignity of mankind and a mocking tell-tale against the achievement of nations. We must be rid of it. But before we can start to do that we must come to terms with it; we must clear ourselves of the temptation to pass it by on the other side because it is too awful to behold. It is not. Yet there can now be very little time left before something which we may call disaster happens to this city. Perhaps it will be the disaster foreseen and feared by the town planners, in which case we can only guess at its course. Possibly this will begin with some plague on a medieval scale, for the water pipes which the heirs of Messrs Jessop and Co. laid a century ago have just passed their cast-iron expectation of life and they are surrounded by earth soaked in sewage, whose moistures will flow into the pipes when they finally burst with age. While some people are counting their rising piles of dead, others will have become so maddened by their loss and by their fury at the fates, that they will set out to destroy. They will rage through this city with torches, with knives, with bombs, with pistols, with axes and with bare hands. They will burn everything that can be put to the torch and they will smash everything that cannot be burned and they will kill and terribly mutilate anyone who gets in their way and even those who flee. The destruction will be such that Calcutta will cut itself off from the world outside as, in a small way, it has already twice cut itself off in recent times; the telephone lines will be severed, the roads will be blocked, the railway lines will be blown apart and, at Dum Dum, aircraft which come in to land will be set upon by swarming mobs and destroyed, their passengers massacred. Nothing will be heard from Calcutta for days and the world will wonder what has at last become of it. When the world finally lumbers down to the Hooghly, past the refugees who will be streaming away in hundreds of thousands and possibly millions, it will discover a city of smoking ruins with a handful of savages who are beginning to destroy one another. And writers will struggle for the words to describe what has happened, as they struggled once before.

Perhaps there will be another kind of disaster before Calcutta is left to its plague, though this one threatens only the rich in their nightmares. In this haunting horror, the night comes when every poor man in the city rises from his pavement and his sqalid bustee and at last dispossesses the rich with crazy ferocity. The arsenals of the rich will be no protection against this onslaught in the close confinements of Calcutta, for there are so many millions of poor here and only a few thousand of rich, and life is very cheaply lived upon a pavement and in a bustee. The poor shadows will come quietly out of their deeper darkness and they will pick off the first few rich in small handfuls, hauling them out of their cars and butchering them on the spot; and when the rich reach for their defences they will be overwhelmed and buried by the numbers of the poor. There will be a signal for this nightmare to become reality and it will be given by the rickshaw men who have pulled so many rich people around Calcutta like animals all their lives. They will begin to pass it on when darkness falls, as the rich move away to their homes and their pleasures. All over the city and along the Hooghly there will be the sound of bells being tapped one after another against the shafts of motionless rickshaws or upon the sides of lamp posts. As any rich man walks the streets that night he will be followed wherever he goes, from one pool of light to the next, by this dull anvil ring of rickshaw bells. Tap-tap-tap, the signal will pursue him mysteriously down each street; and there will be no shaking it off. It will tell him that his time has come.

The time for compassion will be past.

BIBLIOGRAPHY

THIS covers all the books I have drawn on, but not the various reports, pamphlets, newspaper articles and other documentation I have made use of. These are referred to where relevant in the source notes. Anyone making a study of Calcutta is recommended to start by getting hold of two exhaustive bibliographies, which were invaluable to me. One of them, *Calcutta 1690–1900*, was compiled by the National Library there in 1967. The other curiously appears in English in a book whose text is otherwise in Bengali, *Tin Sataker Kolkaka* by Nakul Chaterji, who is himself on the staff of the National Library. It contains a list of relevant publications during the first half of this century.

Ahmad, Muzzafar; *The Communist Party of India and its Formation Abroad*, Calcutta 1969.

Ahmad, Saiyid Amin; *The Black Hole of Calcutta*, Patna 1935.

Andrews, C. F.; *The Renaissance in India*, Church Missionary Society 1912.

Bose, Nirmal Kumar; *Calcutta; a Social Survey*, Calcutta 1968.

Broomfield, J. H.; *Elite Conflict in a Plural Society*, University of California 1968.

Burman, Debajyoti; *T T K and Birla House*, Calcutta 1957.

Buckland, C. E.; *Bengal under the Lieutenant Governors*, Calcutta 1901.

Busteed, H. E.; *Echoes From Old Calcutta*, Calcutta 1897.

Casey, Lord; *Personal Experiences*, Constable 1962.

Chaudhuri, Nirad C.; *Autobiography of an Unknown Indian*, Macmillan 1951.

Churchill, Randolph S.; *Winston S. Churchill*, vol. 1, *Youth: 1874–1900*, Heinemann 1966.

Cotton, H. E. A.; *Calcutta; Old and New*, Calcutta 1907.

Curzon, Lord; *British Government in India*, Cassell 1925.

Das, Tarak Chandra; *Bengal Famine 1943*, Calcutta 1949.

Dilks, David; *Curzon in India*, Hart-Davis 1969.

Doig, Desmond; *Calcutta; an artist's impression*, Calcutta 1969.

Eden, Emily; *Letters from India*, London 1872.

Fay, Eliza; *Original Letters from India*, Hogarth Press 1925.

Feiling, K.; *Warren Hastings*, Macmillan 1966.

Ganguly, N.; *Calcutta Cricket Club, its origins and development*, Calcutta 1936.

Ghosh, Girish Chandra; *The Writings of*, Calcutta 1912.

Gupta, Atulchandra, ed.; *Studies in the Bengal Renaissance*, Calcutta 1958.

Hamilton, Captain Alexander; *A New Account of the East Indies*, London 1710.

Hardinge, Lord; *My Indian Years*, Murray 1948.

Harrison, Selig S.; *India, the most dangerous decades*, Princeton 1960.

Hickey, William; *Memoirs*, ed. Peter Quennell, Hutchinson 1960.

Hopkins, Harry; *New World Arising*, Hamilton 1952.

Holwell, J. Z.; *A genuine narrative of the deplorable deaths of the English Gentlemen and Others, who were suffocated in the Black-Hole in Fort William, at Calcutta, in the Kingdom of Bengal; in the Night succeeding the 20th Day of June, 1756*, London 1758.

Hunter, Sir W. W.; *The Thackerays in India*, London 1897.

Irani, C. R.; *Bengal; the Communist Challenge*, Calcutta 1968.

Kennedy, M. D.; *A short history of Communism in Asia*, Weidenfeld 1957.

Kincaid, Denis; *British Social Life in India*, Routledge 1938.

Kipling, Rudyard; *The City of Dreadful Night*, Sampson Low Marston 1891.

Kopf, David; *British Orientalism and the Bengal Renaissance*, Calcutta 1969.

Lear, Edward; *Indian Journal*, ed. Ray Murphy, Jarrolds 1953.

Macaulay, Lord; *Historical Essays*.

Manners, Lady Victoria; *John Zoffany*, London 1920.

Massey, Montague; *Recollections of Calcutta*, Calcutta 1918.

Nehru, Jawaharlal; *Autobiography*, Bodley Head 1936.

Nilsson, Sten; *European Architecture in India*, Faber 1968.

Ronaldshay, Lord; *Essayez*, Murray 1956.

Roy, B. V.; *Old Calcutta Cameos*, Calcutta 1946.

Seth, Mesroub Jacob; *Armenians in India*, Calcutta 1937.

Sherry, Norman; *Conrad's Eastern World*, Cambridge 1966.

Singh, S. B.; *European Agency Houses in Bengal*, Calcutta 1966.

Smith, George; *Bishop Heber*, Murray 1895.

Stewart, Charles; *History of Bengal*, Calcutta 1812.

Symons, N. V. H.; *The Story of Government House*, Bengal Govt 1935.

Toye, H.; *The Springing Tiger*, Cassell 1959.

Trevelyan, G. O.; *Letters of a Competition Wallah*, London 1864.

Tripathi, A.; *Trade and Finance in the Bengal Presidency*, Longman 1956.

Twain, Mark; *Following the Equator*, American Pub. Co. 1897.

Tyson, G. W.; *The Bengal Chamber of Commerce 1853–1953*, Calcutta 1953.

Valentia, Lord; *Voyages and Travels to India, Ceylon, the Red Sea, Abyssinia and Egypt*, London 1809.

Woodruff, Philip; *The Men Who Ruled India*, Cape 1953.

SOURCE NOTES

A NUMBER of sources have been much harder worked than others in the construction of this book. Utterly indispensable has been the *Basic Development Plan for the Calcutta Metropolitan District 1966–1986* (CMPO 1966) for an understanding of what is structurally happening to the city; and all statistical information is taken from there, unless otherwise noted. The files of *The Statesman* newspaper have yielded the basic material from which the following episodes have been written: the local reaction to George V's announcement in 1911 that the Imperial capital would be moved to Delhi, the Bengal famine of 1943, the massacre of 1946, Independence in 1947 and the period since the United Front Government took office for the second time at the start of 1969, together with the sketches of such passing moments as the visits of Bulganin and Khrushchev in 1955 and Queen Elizabeth in 1961; and anything else that took my fancy as I was wrestling with those disintegrating tomes in Calcutta. Broomfield's work was invaluable to me in navigating the intricacies of Bengali politics after Curzon, as Kopf's was on those fruitful decades just before the Mutiny; and, as Broomfield is a New Zealander and Kopf an American, these books have the additional merit of a detachment no Englishman could possibly manage when he writes about India. The essays on the Bengal Renaissance edited by Gupta need a great deal of staying power but are worth the effort to understand the Bengali attitude both then and now, though Girish Chandra Ghosh presents that with outstanding clarity in his own period and is a pleasure to read into the bargain. As for general histories of India with a British outlook, I don't suppose one could find a more comprehensive background to a study of Calcutta (short of tackling the enormous Cambridge History itself) than the two volumes by Philip Woodruff; certainly nothing more superbly entertaining or full of instinct for its subject. It is as well to bear in mind when approaching Woodruff, though, that he was a distinguished member of the Indian Civil Service himself, and that he is therefore as generously and scrupulously partial as that might imply.

CHAPTER 1. ULTIMATE EXPERIENCE

Page

18 line 3	Trevelyn, p. 199
18 line 13	Quoted Kincaid, p. 79
18 line 19	ibid., p. 180
18 line 29	Churchill, p. 297
18 line 38	Twain, p. 518

19 line 6   Maybe Lenin is doomed to association with this sentence forever. Mr Ved Mehta is the latest in a long line of writers to perpetuate the fallacy. Kennedy provides what seems the hottest tip with this quotation as an introduction to his book on Communism in Asia: 'There is no doubt that the road to World Revolution lies through the East rather than through the West', which he attributes to Zinoviev in 1925 without, alas, offering his source. My own money, however, goes on Mr E. H. Carr, who tells me that the substantial origin of the misquotation lies in Lenin's last published article, 'Better Less But Better', in which he writes that the East 'has entered finally into the revolutionary movement . . . and been finally drawn into the horizon of the world revolutionary movement.' My thanks

26 line 7   O. H. K. Spate, *India and Pakistan; a General and Regional Geography*, London 1957, p. 524

CHAPTER 2. IMPERIAL CITY

Page

27 line 9	Quoted *Howrah Census Handbook 1951*, p. ix
28 line 14	Quoted Woodruff, vol. 1, p. 19
28 line 34	Stewart, p. 143
30 line 18	ibid., p. 210
31 line 5	*East India Company Letter Book 1690*
31 line 13	Kipling, *A Tale of Two Cities*
31 line 27	Hamilton, *cap.* XXIII
32 line 17	ibid.
33 line 1	ibid.
33 line 5	ibid.
33 line 13	ibid.
33 line 31	ibid.
35 line 17	Seth, p. 421

35 line 25   ibid., p. 422
37 line 10   Woodruff, vol 1, p. 103
38 line 19   Quoted Kincaid, p. 180
38 line 26   Quoted Woodruff, vol 1, p. 106
39 line 36   Macaulay, Essay on Lord Clive
42 line 21   Quoted Busteed, p. 11
43 line 28   Busteed, p. 23
44 line 4   ibid., p. 25
44 line 22   Holwell, p. 21
45 line 4   Even Woodruff appears to accept Holwell's own evalu-
              ation of the Black Hole incident without question. The
              most careful analysis of all available sources, conclud-
              ing that Holwell was certainly exaggerating, has been
              made by Brijen K. Gupta in *Journal of Asiatic Studies*,
              Vol xix, No. 1, November 1959
46 line 13   Spear, *A History of India*, Penguin 1965, p. 84
46 line 36   Quoted Woodruff, vol 1, p. 112
48 line 35   Quoted Feiling, p. 83
50 line 10   Quoted Kincaid, p. 60
52 line 25   Quoted Busteed, p. 147
53 line 4   ibid., p. 60
56 line 2   ibid., p. 97
57 line 17   Ibid, p. 104
58 line 19   Hickey, p. 239
59 line 6   Fay, pp. 181–2
60 line 4   Quoted Kincaid, p. 163
66 line 31   Quoted by R. C. Majumdar, *Glimpses of Bengal in
              the 19th Century*, Calcutta 1960, p. 8
66 line 36   Quoted Woodruff, vol 1, p. 149
67 line 26   Minute on the Foundation of a College at Fort
              William 10 July 1800
68 line 27   Quoted Kopf, p. 63, from *Calcutta Journal* 1 New
              Series, 3 January 1822
69 line 32   Quoted Kopf, p. 161
70 line 10   ibid., p. 184
70 line 32   Quoted Gupta, p. 29
72 line 8   ibid., 144
73 line 28   Valentia, vol 1, p. 236
73 line 38   Quoted Smith, p. 165
76 line 10   Ghosh, p. 424
77 line 6   Quoted Cotton, p. 193
77 line 26   Ghosh, p. 264

78 line 11 Quoted Kincaid, p. 152

79 line 2 Quoted Woodruff, vol II, p. 38

80 line 17 Quoted E. G. B. Reynolds, *The Lee-Enfield Rifle*, London 1960, p. 52. See also article by F. G. Aylott in *Bulletin of the Military Historical Society*, November 1966

80 line 26 Quoted Gupta, p. 3

81 line 33 *The Englishman*, 16 July 1884

83 line 4 *Government of India, Home Education*, file A34–42, Feb. 1904

85 line 10 Chaudhuri, Jaico edition 1969, p. 298

88 line 10 *Statesman*, 15 December 1911

89 line 32 Mary Carmichael, *Lord Carmichael of Skirling, a Memoir*, London 1929, p. 151

CHAPTER 3. POVERTY

Page

95 line 3 *Statesman* 19 November 1969

97 line 1 International Association of Co-Workers of Mother Teresa, annual report, 1969

97 line 19 Mother Teresa's estimate

98 line 22 *New Society*, 20 May 1970

99 line 13 *Bustee Improvement Programme; Calcutta and Howrah*, CMPO and Govt of W. Bengal, 1967 rev. edition, p. 13

99 line 34 Personal inquiry on the spot

100 line 36 ibid.

105 line 15 Dixshit Sinha, 'Life in a Calcutta Slum' (paper given at seminar of Indian Anthropological Society, 22–3 January 1970)

112 line 27 Macaulay, Essay on Lord Clive

113 line 37 'The World of Goondas in Calcutta' (paper given by Sabyasachi Mukherjee of the Central Detective Training School at IAS seminar)

117 line 36 *Statesman*, 14 April 1970

121 line 6 Kali Charan Ghosh, *Famines in Bengal 1770–1943*, Calcutta 1944, p. 20

121 line 30 Das, p. 4

123 line 36 *Hansard*, 8 July 1943

124 line 3 Das, p. 98

124 line 25 *Associated Press*, 25 October 1943

124 line 33 *Hansard*, 15 October 1943

124 line 36   *Statesman,* 16 October 1943
126 line 11   Quoted Das, p. 114
126 line 21   *Times of India,* 16 November 1943
126 line 26   Radio broadcast 1 April 1944
128 line 28   See *Indian Journals* by Allen Ginsberg, Dave Haselwood Books/City Lights Books, San Francisco 1970
128 line 36   *Statesman,* 14 April 1970
129 line 23   ibid., 12 September 1969

CHAPTER 4. WEALTH

Page
133 line 3   *Statesman,* 1 April 1969 and 30 March 1970
133 line 20   A. K. Guha, statistical officer, Calcutta Port Commissioners, *Statesman,* 12 October 1970
133 line 23   *et seq, West Bengal, A Panorama,* Indian Chamber of Commerce 1964
133 line 32   Stewart, p. vi
136 line 4   *Howrah Handbook,* 1969 census, p. ii–iii
140 line 26   Sherry, p. 89
145 line 31   *West Bengal, A Panorama*
146 line 14   Ronaldshay, p. 23
146 line 20   Kincaid, p. 67
146 line 31   Nehru, p. 188
147 line 18   *Statesman,* 29 October 1970
153 line 4   Hopkins, p. 281
153 line 19   Burman, p. 43
154 line 8   Hopkins, p. 282
155 line 2   Edward Rice, *Clipper International,* March 1970
162 line 13   Gauranga Chattopadhyahya, Indian Institute of Management (paper on 'The Culture of Business Executives', given to I A S seminar)

CHAPTER 5. MIGRANTS

Page
168 line 20   Kipling, *The Song of the Cities* (A Song of the English)
176 line 13   M. K. A. Saddiqui, 'Caste among the Muslims of Calcutta' (paper given to I A S seminar)
183 line 22   Bose, p. 62
183 line 25   *Calcutta Handbook,* 1921 census, p. 32
184 line 17   Ronaldshay, p. 80
185 line 22   Hopkins, p. 282

CHAPTER 6. BENGALIS

Page

186 line 23   *The Listener,* 24 September 1970
187 line 10   Woodruff, vol 1, p. 245
187 line 16   Casey, p. 182
187 line 19   Stewart, p. vii
187 line 28   Chaudhuri, Jaico edition, p. 369
187 line 33   Bose, p. 89
189 line 21   *Bengal District Administration Committee 1913–14
               Report,* Calcutta 1915, p. 176
189 line 22   Quoted Broomfield, p. 163 from *Dainik Chandrika,*
               30 December 1914
189 line 30   Sunanda K Datta-Ray, the *Observer,* 11 October 1970
191 line 7   *Statesman,* 21 February 1969
191 line 20   Bijoy Bhattacharya, *Derozio, the maker of Young
               Bengal,* Well-Print Publications 1968
192 line 24   Gupta, pp. 153–4
193 line 11   Benoy Ghose, 'Changing *Élites* of Bengal' (paper given
               to I A S seminar)
194 line 13   Quoted Gupta, p. 263
194 line 21   ibid., pp. 88–9
195 line 13   Quoted Broomfield, p. 66, from *A Native in Making,*
               London 1925, p. 32
195 line 31   ibid., p. 67, Minto to Morley, 19 March 1907
195 line 36   Quoted Woodruff, vol II, p. 171
196 line 10   Quoted Toye, p. 18
199 line 27   *Statesman,* 24 January 1970; meeting of Azad Hind
               Fauj Association, presided over by Mr G. S. Dhillon
201 line 2   Quoted Gupta, p. 205
203 line 21   Letter to Indira Devi Chaudharani 1894. Quoted by
               Alokeran Dasgupta in 'The Social and Cultural World
               of the Men of Literature in Calcutta' (paper to I A S
               seminar)
204 line 13   Tagore, *Letters to a Friend,* London 1928, p. 136
206 line 12   *Film Industry,* January 1970
206 line 27   S. C. Panchbhai, 'Intergroup Stereotypes and Attitudes
               in Calcutta' (paper given to I A S seminar)

CHAPTER 7. PEOPLE, PEOPLE

Page

200 line 1   *Statesman,* 14 October 1970

211 line 35   ibid., 30 November 1955
213 line 34   Ghosh, p. 271
215 line 19   Quoted Broomfield, p. 277
216 line 16   ibid., p. 312
216 line 33   *Statesman*, 16 August 1946
219 line 9   ibid., 21 August 1946
219 line 30   ibid., 20 August 1946
220 line 17   ibid., 28 August 1946
222 line 11   ibid., 13 August 1947
222 line 38   ibid., 15 August 1947

CHAPTER 8. FADED GLORY

Page
224 line 5   *A Handbook to India, Pakistan, Burma, Ceylon*, ed. Professor L. F. Rushbrook Williams, C.B.E., Murray 1968
224 line 9   ibid., p. 88
224 line 15   ibid., p. xix
224 line 18   ibid., p. xxi
229 line 37   Twain, p. 517
230 line 28   Macaulay, Essay on Warren Hastings
235 line 18   Quoted Kincaid, p. 236
236 line 9   Hardinge, p. 4
236 line 28   Ghosh, p. 442
237 line 27   Churchill, p. 297
237 line 38   Casey, p. 225
242 line 23   Quoted Doig from *A Picturesque Voyage to India by Way of China*, by the Daniells, London 1810
243 line 32   *et seq* – There is an informative essay on the Daniells by Mildred Archer in the *RIBA Journal* September 1960
245 line 33   Roy, p. 89
253 line 30   *The Monthly Review* (Journal of the UKCA) January 1969
256 line 30   *Statesman*, 13 July 1926
257 line 18   ibid., 29 February 1961
258 line 9   ibid., 2 March 1961
259 line 6   Andrews, p. 15
260 line 30   *Statesman*, 15 August 1947
262 line 1   ibid., 17 August 1947
262 line 13   ibid., 20 August 1947

CHAPTER 9. THE PETRIFYING JUNGLE

Page

265 line 12   Quoted, *inter alia*, CMPO Plan, p. ix
265 line 27   *Guardian*, 11 February 1967
267 line 15   Valentia, vol 1, p. 236
267 line 29   Quoted Roy, p. 44
268 line 3   Ghosh, p. 202
268 line 19   Quoted Roy, p. 48
268 line 28   Quoted Woodruff, vol. II, p. 39
268 line 37   Ghosh, p. 202
269 line 9   ibid., p. 452
269 line 25   ibid., p. 543
270 line 15   Kipling, p. 6
270 line 34   Buckland, vol II, p. 979
272 line 20   Speech at 50th anniversary banquet of Bengal Cham-
              ber of Commerce 1903; *Lord Curzon in India, A
              Selection of his Speeches*, London 1906
272 line 34   Cotton, p. 242
273 line 10   Report to the Calcutta Improvement Trust 1914, by
              E. P. Richards M I C E, Member of the Town Planning
              Institute, p. xiii
273 line 26   ibid., p. xiv
274 line 1   ibid., p. 77
274 line 23   ibid., p. 29
274 line 34   ibid., p. 31
275 line 10   ibid., p. 21
275 line 19   ibid., p. 35
276 line 31   Ronaldshay, p. 23
277 line 38   *Calcutta Handbook*, 1921 census, p. 5
278 line 2   ibid., p. 7
278 line 5   ibid., p. 11
278 line 14   ibid., p. 15
278 line 17   Report of Committee on Industrial Unrest, Bengal
              Govt 1921
278 line 21   Report on an Enquiry into the Standard of Living of
              Jute Mill Workers in Bengal, Bengal Govt 1930
279 line 4   Casey, p. 183
279 line 11   ibid, p. 196
279 line 23   ibid., p. 205
279 line 33   ibid., p. 210

280 line 24   Report of the Corporation of Calcutta Investigation
              Commission, The Biswas Report, vol II, Part I, par. 24
281 line 25   ibid., Chapter xxv, par. 2
282 line 16   Irani. p. 48
282 line 19   Bose, p. 66
282 line 28   *Statesman*, 19 June 1970
283 line 4   ibid., 7 May 1969
283 line 19   Quoted Dasgupta, *op. cit.*
284 line 25   *Statesman*, 2 May 1969
284 line 38   Mr (later Chief) Justice Sinha in *The High Court of
              Calcutta 1862–1962*, a centenary monograph by him-
              self and others
285 line 8   Report on an Inquiry into the Sanitary Conditions of
              the Labouring Population of Great Britain, HMSO
              1842, p. 17
285 line 33   ibid., p. 45
286 line 20   Assignment Report on Water Supply and Sewerage
              Disposal, Greater Calcutta WHO Project; India 170
287 line 26   G. K. Bhagat, President of Indian Chamber of Com-
              merce, at Calcutta conference on civic crisis, 11
              December 1968
292 line 24   Figure supplied by London Transport, October, 1970
292 line 30   *Statesman*, 3 September 1969
293 line 1   ibid., 15 March 1969
293 line 8   ibid., 6 April 1969
293 line 10   ibid., 4 December 1969
293 line 24   ibid., 17 October 1970
293 line 28   ibid.
293 line 37   ibid., 13 March 1969
294 line 8   ibid., 27 April 1969
297 line 10   Co-workers of Mother Teresa Report 1969
301 line 2   ibid.
301 line 15   Assignment Report of World Bank, India 1960, p. 54
301 line 21   ibid., p 152
304 line 15   CMPO Basic Development Plan, p. 5
304 line 29   ibid., p. 6
306 line 17   *Statesman*, 12 April 1970
307 line 6   CMPO Basic Development Plan. p. 58

CHAPTER 10. THE ROAD TO REVOLUTION

Page

308 line 3   Kennedy, p. 22

308 line 15 Muzzafar Ahmad, p. 65
311 line 2   Irani, p. 50
311 line 18 Casey, p. 197
311 line 23 ibid., p. 216
312 line 5   Biswas, *op. cit.* Chapter III, par. 20 (iv)
312 line 17 ibid., par. 26
312 line 25 ibid., par. 45
312 line 34 ibid., Chapter IX, par. 8
313 line 7   ibid., Chapter XI, par. 19
314 line 5   Irani, pp. 48–9
314 line 29 ibid., p. 48
318 line 4   Quoted Irani, p. 7
319 line 7   Irani, p. 17
319 line 24 *Mainstream*, 29 July 1967
322 line 30 *Deshabrati*, 6 July 1967
324 line 16 Quoted Irani, p. 82
324 line 36 Quoted in full Irani, Appendix 7; High Court Matter
             No. 343, 1967
325 line 23 Irani, p. 69
325 line 31 ibid., p. 77
326 line 4   *Statesman*, 16 October 1967
328 line 23 For missing paragraphs see *Statesman*, 7 March 1969
328 line 30 *Statesman*, 4 April 1969
329 line 15 ibid., 7 February 1970
329 line 26 ibid., 22 February 1969
330 line 36 ibid., 21 September 1969
332 line 18 ibid., 12 April 1969
333 line 1   ibid., 11 October 1969
333 line 24 The end of the offer was marked *Statesman* 27 March
             1969
334 lines 2–11 Reuters assessment, 30 June 1970
334 line 23 *Statesman*, 21 November 1969
336 line 3   ibid., 6 August 1969
336 line 28 ibid., 3 May 1969
337 line 23 ibid., 4 December 1969
338 line 31 *Liberation*, March 1970
340 line 11 *Statesman*, 5 August 1969
340 line 25 ibid., 12 April 1969
340 line 33 ibid., 8 October 1969
341 line 9   ibid., 17 October 1969
341 line 26 ibid., 14 October 1969
341 line 33 ibid., 27 September 1969

342 line 5   ibid., 30 November 1969
342 line 34   ibid., 4 December 1969
343 line 25   ibid., 24 November 1969
343 line 29   ibid., 2 December 1969
344 line 3   ibid., 15 January 1970
345 line 1   ibid., 23 January 1970
345 line 7   ibid., 25 January 1970
345 line 25   ibid., 21 February 1970
345 line 32   ibid., 19 December 1969
347 line 4   ibid., 17 March 1970

CHAPTER II. ZINDABAD

Page
348 line 24   *Statesman*, 23 April 1970
349 line 11   ibid., 28 November 1970
349 line 34   ibid., 18 May 1970
350 line 14   Assessment by Dr Nabagopal Das, *Statesman*, 20
              May 1970

INDEX

advertising, 91, 106, 130, 169, 176
Afghanistan, Afghans, 35, 180, 197
Afridi, 80
Agra, 28, 30, 35, 36, 48
agriculture, 119–21, 238, 257, *see also* land reform; peasants
Ahmad, Muzaffar, 167, 308
Ahmedabad, 103
Akbar, Emperor, 35
Alipore, 50, 56, 97, 113, 129, 139, 154, 155, 185, 257, 324
All-Indian Muslim League, 214
All Indian Trade Union Congress, 308
Amery, L. S., 123, 124–5
Amherst, Lady, 235
Amherst, Lord, 236, 263
Amherst Street, 267
Amrita Bazaar Patrika, 84
Amritsar, 205, 258
Andaman Islands, 238, 330
Andrews, C. F., 204, 259
Anglo-Indians, 85–6, 194, 252, 278
Anthropological Survey of India, 105
architecture, 74, 224–6, 231–2, 234–5, 239–42, 244–5, *see also* mosques; palaces; temples
Arcot, 40
Armenian Church, 35, 36, 182
Armenian College, 246

Armenian Street, 182
Armenians, 33, 34, 35–6, 42, 74, 176, 182
army, East India Company's, 29–30, 31, 35, 40–42, 45, 46, 58, 76–7; Mogul, 30, 42–3; 45; Dutch, 34; French, 40, 45; British, 77–8, 87, 140, 218, 220, 222, 256; Indian, 231, 347, 349, *see also* Indian Mutiny; Indian National Army; Second World War
arson, 217–18, 219, 332, 337, 345, 346
art, 191, 202, 205, 242–4
Asansol, 134, 304
Asiatic Society, 51, 157, 202
Assam, Assamese, 83, 134, 142, 206, 284
atheism, 70
Attlee, Clement, 197, 263
Auden, W. H., 231
Auckland, Lord, 235, 263
Aurangzeb, Emperor, 30, 33, 36, 39
ayahs, 61, 62, 104

Baker, Sir Robert, 49
Ballasore, 29
Ballygunge, 130, 220, 308
Banerjea, Surendranath, 84, 88, 194–5
Banerjee, Hilderam, 188
Banerjee, Kamakhya, 337

Banerjee, Subodh, 324, 325
Bannerji, Bhabanicharan, 271
Bangalore, 295
Bangla Congress, 315, 326, 327,
   340–42, 343, 346
banks, banking, 133, 144, 148,
   188, 200, 209, 333, 352–3
Bankshall Street, 59
Bankura, 314
Bansberia, 303, 352
Baptists, 68, 196
Barasat, 142–3, 310
Barauni, 134
bargadar, 319, see also peasants
Barnagar, 100
Barnagul, 33
Barrackpore, 76, 227, 234,
   341
Barwell, Richard, 49–50, 52, 53,
   55, 62
Basar Gopinathpur, 122
Basic Development Plan, see
   Calcutta Metropolitan
   Planning Organization
Basu, Jyoti, background of,
   316–17; popularity of, 316;
   appearance of, 316–17;
   character, 316–17; as an
   orator, 317, 354–5; and party
   struggles, 322; and struggle
   with Mukherjee, 326, 341,
   343–5, 348; as Minister for
   Home Affairs, 328, 332, 335,
   340–41, 354; claims for illegal
   detention, 328; power of, 332,
   335, 340; resignation of, 347;
   attempted assassination of,
   348–9
Bay of Bengal, 26, 30, 136, 140,
   330
Beercool, 52
beggars, 93–4, 110, 116, 131,
   160–61, 164, 170, 172, 174,
   208, 209, 255, 298
Beliaghata, 222
Belvedere Garden, 56, 57, 155
Benares, 50, 63, 128, 132, 135,
   152, 184, 201, 229, 284
Bengal, European settlements in,
   27–8, 34–5; insurrections in,
   82; administration in, 78, 83,
   85, 192–3, 215, 216, 278–80;
   partition of, 83–4, 86, 214;
   terrorism in, 84–5;
   reunification of, 86–8; race
   riots in, 215; finances of,
   279–80, see also East Bengal;
   East Indian Company; West
   Bengal
Bengal Chamber of Commerce,
   74, 79, 147, 188, 260, 277,
   329
Bengal Chronicle, 271
Bengal Club, 87, 253, 258–60
Bengal Destitute Persons
   (Repatriation and Relief)
   Ordinance, 124, 131
Bengal Engineers, 241
Bengal Gazette, 58, 62
Bengal Herald, 200
Bengal Renaissance, 70–72
The Bengalee, 84
Bengali language, 50–51, 68, 69,
   71, 80, 84, 171, 174, 176,
   195
Bengalis, occupations of, 64,
   75–6, 82, 188–9, 193, 310;
   urban population of, 142;
   rural population, 142;
   characteristics of, 186–7;
   character of, 187–8, 206–7;
   and the British, 187, 189,
   193–5, 200–201; and
   education, 189–90, 193; and

the arts, 190–92, 193, 194, 283; patriotism of, 187, 192–3, 194, 195, 206, 310

Behoy-Badal-Dinesh Bagh, 329

Bentham, Jeremy, 72

Bentinck, Lady, 235

Bentinck, Lord William, 18, 72–3, 200, 238, 263

Bentinck Street, 95, 111, 177, 278

Bepin Behary Ganguly Street, 95

betel, 38, 58, 170

bhadralok, 80, 83, 108, 189, 193, 195, 201, 204, 214

Bhagirathi, River, 287

Bhawani, *see* Kali

Bihar, Biharis, 21–2, 47, 83, 105, 107, 134, 142–3, 178, 186, 206, 310

Bihor, 170, 284

Bikaner State, 183

birds, 21–2, 23, 91, 95, 116, 126, 129, 180, 219

Birla Education Trust, 152

Birla family, 151–4, 251

Birla Industrial and Technological Museum, 152

Birla Park, 154, 317

birth control, 284

Biswas Commission, 280–81, 311–12

Black Hole incident, 19, 42, 44–5, 47, 57, 197, 245, 271

boats, boating, 60, 138–9, 180, *see also* shipping

Bolshevik Party, 315, 340, 344

Bombay, administration in, 51, 78; commerce in, 79, 138, 288, 294; wealth of, 142; health in, 268; taxation in, 268–9, 276, 295; population of, 276; strikes in, 308; terrorism in,

309; mentioned, 88, 153, 207, 310

bombing, 114, 217, 332, 346

Bonaparte, Napoleon, 34, 63, 77

books, 190, *and see* printers; publishers

Bose, Netaji Subhas Chandra, 119, 196–9, 227, 261, 262, 338

Boughton, Dr Gabriel, 28–9, 39

Bowbazar, 63, 179, 278

Brabourne Road, 163

Brahma the Creator, 20, 135

Brahmaputra River, 26

Brahmins, Brahminism, 108, 183, 184, 201, 296

Brahmo Samaj, 71–2, 201

bridges *see* Hoogly River, crossings

Britain, British, population in Calcutta, 32, 252; death rate of, 32, 246–7; development of Calcutta, 39–40, 266–82; *see also* architecture; social life, 39, 49–50, 58–63, 64–5, 75; orientalists, 51; commercial interests, 74–5, 79–81, 146–50, 185, 333–4; administration of, 78–9, 81–90, 119–27, 218–22, 308–9; expatriates in India, 252–60; and Independence Day, 260–64; *see also* army; East Indian Company

British Council, 156, 253, 341

British Indian Association, 133, 195

Buchanan, Professor Colin, 265–6

Buddhism, 183, 209

Buckingham House, 234

Budge Budge, 53, 99, 352

building, 50, 88–9, 179, 183,

building – *cont'd.*
241–2, *see also* architecture; housing
Bulganin, 211, 257
bullocks, bulls, 92, 134, 161, 172, 178, 231, 290
Burdwan, 62, 124
Burdwan Maharajadhiraja of Burdwan, 132–3, 165
Burma, 21, 113, 119–20, 199, 309
Burra Bazar, 171, 184
Burrows, Sir Frederick, 221, 263
buses, 91–2, 291–3, 335
Busteed, H. E., 43
bustees, numbers in, 98–9, 278; definition of, 99–100; rents of, 99; conditions in, 99–100, 102, 105–8, 180, 279; CMPO and, 302–3, 304–5; mentioned, 113, 154, 156, 165, 217, 222, 296
Bux, Mahomed, 80, 192
Byramjee, Dorabjee, 75

Calcutta Cathedral, 239, 242, 257
Calcutta Chamber of Commerce, 75, 86
Calcutta Club, 36, 87, 164, 165
Calcutta Congress (1911), 204
Calcutta Corporation, creation of, 81, 270–71; under Curzon, 82–3, 84, 194; sanitation, 102, 305, 331; street lighting, 109, 281; housing, 179; controlled by Swaraj party, 196; finances of, 208, 301; nepotism in, 214; water supply, 280; mentioned, 171, 210, *see also* Biswas Commission
Calcutta Development Trust, 183

Calcutta Electric Supply Corporation, 148–9, 169
Calcutta Gazette, 64, 75
Calcutta High Court, 240, 241, 285
Calcutta Improvement Trust, 183, 273
Calcutta Metropolitan Planning Organization, 301–7, 350
Calcutta Mint, 70, 242, 306
Calcutta Rotary Club, 108
Calcutta School Society, 69
Calcutta Stock Exchange, 217, 294
Calcutta University, 22, 67, 76, 85, 119, 189–90, 192, 201, 204, 215, 238, 330
Camac Street, 155
canals, 91, 218, 286
cannabis *see* bhang, ganja
Canning, Lady, 238
Canning, Lord, 78, 227, 236, 259
Capital, 86
cards, 60, 101, 106, 166
cars, car production, 152, 178, 181, 183, 251, 303
Casey, R. G., 126, 187, 278–9, 311
caste, 108, 189, 214
Cawnpore, 78, 192
Central Intelligence Agency, 321, 331, 338
Central Road, 267
Ceylon, 244
Chanda Sahab, 40
Chandernagore, 35, 40, 45, 62
Chandpal Ghat, 49, 53, 269, 281, 286
charity, 23, 122–3, 127, 149, 153, 260, 295–300; *see also* Mother Teresa
Charles II, King, 52

Charnock, Job, 17, 26, 29–32, 36, 37, 41, 57, 90, 96, 113, 247
Charnock, Maria, 29
Charnock, Mary, 31
Chatterjee, Mr, 109
Chatterjee, Bankim Chandra, 200, 210
chemical industry, 147, 206
Chhatawallah Gully, 179
chhentai, 111
Chiang Kai-shek, 143
China, 36, 48, 79, 113, 244, 315, 319, 320, 321–2, 326
Chinese, 170, 179, 308
Chinsurah, 34, 44, 47, 56, 76, 99
Chitpore Bridge, 63
Chitpore Road, 202, 205, 267
Chittagong, 52, 215
Chitteranjan Avenue, 21, 179, 223
cholera, 71, 102, 125, 219, 283, 286
Chor Bagan, 21
Chota Nagpur, 83
Chowdhury, Subarna Roy, 189
Chowringhee, British in, 61, 63, 77; opinions on, 73, 230, 237, 267; street-sleepers in, 94–5; entertainments in, 110, 229; shops in, 129–30, 136, 169–73, 231; mentioned, 24, 105, 113, 157, 175, 177
Chowringhee Square, 150
Christianity, Christians, 68, 77, 176, 194, 201, 209, 272; see also Mother Teresa
Churchill, Major-General C. H., 140
Churchill, Sir Winston, 18, 24, 237
Chuttanuty, 31
cigarettes see tobacco industry

cinema, 24, 111, 169, 190–91, 206, 216–17, 245, 261, 338
Citizens Protection League, 258–9
Civil and Military Gazette, 245
class distinction, 107–8, 189
Clavering, General, 52, 53, 54, 55, 247
climate, 17, 18, 22, 24–6, 59–60, 120, 136
Clive, Robert, 34, 37, 38, 40–41, 45–7, 51, 53, 66, 200, 231, 233
Clive Row, 151
Clive Street, 41
clothes, 24, 32, 61–2, 80, 118, 151, 162, 170–71, 180
clothing industry, 133, 140
clubs, clubmen, 163–7, 205, 228, 253, 254, 257, 258, see also Bengal Club; Calcutta Club
Cockerell, Sir Charles, 244
coal, coal mining, 79, 134, 188
Colebrooke, Henry, 51, 68, 76, 157
College Square, 88, 195, 338
College Street, 245
Commerce, 86
commerce, under Moguls, 27, 35–6, 38–9, 46–7; British interest, 74–5, 78–81, 146–50, 185, 333; exports, 133; imports, 133; foreign interests, 147; Indian, 151–3, 183–5, 188; decline in, 288–9, 293–5, 350; effect of industrial action, 323, 333–5, see also East India Company; industry
Committee of Public Instruction, 76
Communism, 114, 119, 169, 178, 186, 206, 231, 294, 302, 306, 308

Communist Party of India, peasants' congress, 142–3, 310; outlawed by British, 308–9; foundation of, 308–9; and Congress, 309, 310–11, 313–14; in Kerala, 309; membership of, 309; split in, 315; in 1962 elections, 1969 elections, 327–8; and CPI (M), 344, 345, *see also* United Front

Communist Party of India (Marxist), political rallies of, 168, 348, 352–6; formation of, 315; in 1962 elections, 315–16; April Resolution of, 318; land reform and, 319–20; and Naxalbari incident, 320; in 1969 elections, 327–8; struggle with Delhi, 332; industrial action and, 335–6, 341; and terrorism, 337, 341, 347; and clash with Bangla Congress, 340–41, 343, 346–7, *see also* Basu, Jyoti; 'United Front'

Communist Party of India (Marxist-Leninist), and CPI, 345

Congress Party, 84, 153, 196, 197, 218, 309, 313–15, 327, 330, 343, *see also* United Front

Contai, 124

Cooch Behar, Maharajah of, 132

cooks, cook-bearer, 65, 104

coolies, 178–9

Cornwallis, Lord, 35, 65–7, 232

Cornwallis Street, 123

Cossimbazar, Maharajah of, 133, 134

Cossipore, 282, 304, 335

Cossitollah, 77

cottage industries, 177–8

cows, 21, 92, 116, 184, 246

credit societies, 144

cremation, 97, 124, 128, 135, 137–8, 296, *see also* suttee

Crewe, Lord, 86, 88, 89–90

Cripps, Sir Stafford, 197, 309

culture, 162–3, 190–92, 204–5

Curzon, Lord, and his monument to Black Hole, 45, 197; and Calcutta Corporation, 82–3, 194; and Calcutta University, 83, 117; and partition of Bengal, 83, 84, 86, 184; memorial to, 227; and Victoria Memorial, 232, 235; character of, 236–7; on Calcutta, 272–3, 276, *see also* Government House; mentioned, 203, 238, 257, 263

Curzon Park, 342, 348

Dacca, 63, 109, 125, 215

dacoits, 63–4, 113

Dakineshwar temple, 205, 209

Dalhousie Square, 76, 145, 150, 163, 177, 239, 306, *and see* Behoy-Badal-Dinesh Bagh

Daniells family, 242

Daniells, Thomas, 243–5

Darjeeling, 25, 79

Das, Chittaranjan, 196, 214, 310, 328

Dasgupta, Promode, 321, 354, 355

Datta, Michael Madhusudan, 194, 203, 233

death penalty, 64, 139

deaths, European, in Calcutta, 32, 60, 246–7; Indian, in streets, 95, 118; Indian, in

Nirmal Hriday, 96–7; from
cholera, 102; and disposal of
corpses in Hooghly, 138, 268;
infant mortality in Calcutta,
274; *see also* cremation;
famine, murder; race riots
Deccan, 35
Delhi, as Mogul capital, 30, 36,
39, 47, 50, 86; Armenians in,
36; Indian Mutiny in, 78, 192;
capital removed to, 86–8, 146,
189; population of, 103;
wealth of, 142; relations with
West Bengal, 295–6, 301, 306,
327, 329; mentioned, 121, 125,
152, 153, 207
Denmark, Danes, 35, 49, 68
DeRozio, Henry Louis Vivian,
70–71, 201
Desai, Morarji, 329, 350
desertion, 107, 122
de Valera, Eamon, 197
Dey, Ram Dollal, (Ramdnlal),
75, 188
Dhakuria Lake, 109
Dhapa leper colony, 97–8, 128,
299
Dharamtala Street, 169, 217,
218, 223, 278
Dhavan, S. S., 341, 348
dhobies, 64, 104, *see also* water
supply
Dhurmtollar Bazaar, 269
Diamond Harbour, 136, 288
Dinu Chamrawalla's mosque,
214
Direct Action Day, 217–18
District Magistrate's House, 246
docks, dockyards, 34, 74, 133,
136–7, 140, 178, 276, 288
doctors, 102, 165
dogs, 102, 116, 123, 126, 138,
219, 294, 298
Drake, Roger, 41, 43, 168
drinking, 59, 70, 158, 161, 162,
165, 166, 254, 261
Dum Dum, small arms factory
at, 80; airport, 91, 117, 157,
163, 212, 224, 257, 330, 356
leopards near, 136; riot at,
330; mentioned, 142
Dupleix, 34, 40
Durbar, King George VI's, 87,
88
Durga, *see* Kali
Durga Puja, 209–11, 214, 323,
338
Durgapur, 134, 302, 303, 304,
343
durwans, 64, 104, 172
Dutta Industrial Licensing
Committee, 153
Dyer, General, 205, 258
dysentery, 122, 238

East Bengal, 83, 85, 115–17,
135, 214, 221; *see also*, Bengal
East Indian Company, formation
of, 28; and Mogul Empire,
28–9, 33, 41–7; and
exploitation of India, 33, 37–9,
45–7, 112–13; expansion of,
33, 37, 40, 73–4, 189; and the
French, 40, 45; financial
difficulties of, 50–51; Indian
Mutiny and, 76–7; liquidation
of, 78; mentioned, 145, 176,
188, 200, 244; *see also*
Charnock, Job; Clive, Robert;
Cornwallis, Lord; Hastings,
Warren; Wellesley, Lord
East Pakistan, 105, 109, 282, 320
Eden, Hon. Emily, 58, 226, 235,
242

education, in nineteenth century, 69–70, 192–3; and nationalism, 84; labour market and, 117, 144; Bengali attitude to, 189–90, 193; Tagore family and, 201–4; of British children, 253–4, 256, 261; mentioned, 108; *see also* illiteracy; schools, students

Edward VII, King, 232

electricity, lack of, in bustees, 99, 106; failure of supply of, 331

Electricity (Supply) Act 1948, 148

Elgin, Lord, 235, 238

Elizabeth I, Queen, 28

Elizabeth II, Queen, 257–8

Ellenborough, Lord, 235

Elphinstone, Mountstuart, 187

Emerson, Sir William, 231, 241

engineering industry, 134, 147, 151, 303

The Englishman, 78, 81, 86, 200

Entally, 97

entertainment, 162–3, 230, 235–6, 237–8, 252–3, 254–5, *see also* cinema

Esplanade, 60, 64, 169

Eyre, Sir Charles, 31, 37

factories, closures, 147, 325, 333, 350; employment in, 293, 294, 334; industrial action in, 323–4, 325, 334; mentioned, 91, 134, 140, 224–5; *see also* commerce; industry; jute mills

factories (warehouses), 28, 29–30, 38

family hospitality, 107

family life, 106–8, 121–2, 274–5

family separation, 101

famine, 49, 51, 118–26, 168,

198–9, 237, 278

Farraka barrage, 287, 334

Farrer, Thomas, 65, 166

fasts, 184, 223, 342

Fay, Mrs, 58, 59

fish, fishing, 32, 120, 138

film industry, 282, *see also* cinema

First World War, 146

food, Indian, 104, 111, 118–19, 143–4, 172

food prices, 118

food taboos, 123

Ford Foundation, 302

Formosa, 199

Fort Gustavus, 34

Fort St George, 54

Fort William, size of, 42; taken by Siraj-ud-Daula, 42–4; deterioration of, 49; rebuilding of, 50, 200, 241; under Hastings, 53; during Indian Mutiny, 76–7; used by Indian Government, 231; mentioned, 37, 56, 63, 87, 141, 182, 228

Fort William College, 67–8, 69, 71, 72–3, 234

Forward Bloc, 315, 328, 344

Forward Bloc (Marxist), 344

47th Native Infantry, 76

Foster, Sir Ridgeby, 254

Foucauld, Charles de, 297

Fourteenth Army, 119, 199

France, French, 34–5, 39, 44, 70

Francis, Philip, 52, 53–7, 60, 62–3, 140, 246

Freemasons, 39, 41

Frere, Sir Bartle, 79, 126. 268

French East Indian Company, 40

French Revolution, 68, 70, 72

gambling, 49, 53, 60, 101

games, exercise, 60, 81, 137, 187, 228–9, 235, 236, 254, 256, 335

Gandhi, Mrs Indira, 155, 329, 333, 338, 349–50

Gandhi, Mahatma, Congress and, 115; Birla family and, 152; Marwaris and, 185; Bose and, 196, 197; non-violence and, 196, 212, 316, 342; Tagore and, 204; and Calcutta race riots, 220–23; memorial in Calcutta to, 227, 338; and Independence Day, 260; imprisonment of, 309; influence of, 316; reaction against, 338, 349; mentioned, 326, 338

Ganesh, 19, 209

Ganga River, 26, 27, 63, 128, 132, 135, 282, 286–8

Garden Reach, 79, 288

gardens, 21, 140, 155, 157, 235, 238, 244, 329

garlands, 98, 137, 161, 208, 211, 342

Garrick, David, 61, 248

Garstin, Colonel, 241–2

gas industry, lighting, 151, 268

Gas Street, 225, 278

George III, King, 35, 52, 243

George IV, King, 244

George V, King, 86–8, 89, 195, 227, 232

George VI, King, 119

Germany, Germans, 197–8, 346

ghats see cremation

ghee, 64, 183–4, 313

gherao, 212–13, 302, 318, 323–5, 331, 335, 339–41, 350

Ghosh, Atulya, 311, 312, 314–15, 326, 350

Ghosh, Girish Chandra, 76, 77, 213, 236, 267–70

Goa, Goanese, 27, 144

goats, 294

Goonda Act (1923), 113

gondas, 112, 114–15, 218–19, 346

Gopalpur-on-sea, 163, 248–50

Gorkha League, 315, 344

Government House, built by Wellesley, 68, 234–5, 241; Hastings in, 68–9, 235; Canning in, 78, 236; social life in, 89–90, 235, 237–8, 257; Curzon in, 234–5, 236–7, 238; cost of, 234; Ellenborough in, 235; Elgin in, 235, 238; Northbrook in, 235, 237; Hardinge in, 235, 236; gardens of, 235–6, 238; Amherst in, 236, Lawrence in, 236; Lytton in, 236; Bentinck in, 238; Mayo in, 238; on Independence Day, 260–61; Burrows in, 261, 263–4; mentioned, 227, 306

Govindpur, 30

Grande, Madame, Catherine, 62–3

Grand Opera House, 87

Grand Hotel, 93, 170, 171–2, 261

Grand Trunk Road, 160

Grant, Captain, 42, 43

Granville, Walter, 241

Great Eastern Hotel, 77, 245

Griffiths, Sir Percival, 254

Gujeratis, 180, 295–6

Gupta, Iswarchandra, 192

Gurkhas, 218

gurus, 72

Gwalior Monument, 140

Haldia, 289, 304
Halhed, Nathaniel, 51
Hamilton, Captain Alexander, 31–3, 57
Hardinge, Lord, 85, 86, 88, 89, 235, 236, 237, 263
Harmonic House, 65
Hasnabad, 282
Hastings, Marquis of, 66, 68–9, 139, 235
Hastings, Marian, 54, 56, 62
Hastings, Warren, as a Junior Writer, 41, 47; background, 47; during Black Hole incident, 47; marriages of, 47, 53–4, 62; financial dealings of, 48; in recapture of Calcutta, 48; as Governor, 48, 50–51; character of, 48–9; and Nuncomar's trial, 48–9, 54–5; scholasticism and, 49–50, 72; as Governor-General, 51–7, 65; memorials to, 232, 244; Kettle's portrait of, 242n.; mentioned, 67, 90, 140, 247
Hastings, Mrs Warren, 47
Harrington Street, 156
Harrison Road, 223
hawkers, 169, see also traders
Heber, Reginald, Bishop of Calcutta, 18, 73, 92, 140, 230, 233
Hickey, William, 58, 60, 62, 63, 65, 233
Hicky, Augustus, 62, 64
Hijili island, 30
Himalayas, 134, 135, 244
Hindi language, 65, 171
Hindu Arya Samaj, 214–15
Hindu College, 69–70, 201
Hindu Mela, 202
Hindustan Standard, 125

Hindustan Times, 151
Hinduism, festivals, 75, 189; food taboos, 123, 179, 184, 208–11; mentioned, 19–20, 22
Hindoostanee Press, 70
Hitler, Adolf, 197, 198
Hodnet, 74
Holi festival, 189, 209
Holland, Dutch, 33, 34, 44, 47
Holwell, John Zephaniah, 41, 42, 43–5, 47
Ho Chi Minh, 338, 340
Ho Chi Minh Street, 156, 329
Hooghly (village of), 28, 29, 30, 36, 40, 54, 79
Hooghly, River, navigational difficulties of, 34, 135–6, 287–9; boating on, 60; industry bordering, 75, 140; activities on, 137–41, 173, 209; corpses thrown in, 138, 220, 268; sacredness of, 135, 137, 139, 184, 209, 211; Durga Puja and, 209, 210–11; contamination of, 268, 286–7; river crossings, 273, 290, 306, 330; as source of drinking water, 286–8; improvements to, 288–90; mentioned, 37, 76, 98, 124, 230
hooka, 48, 61
horseracing, 60, 147, 165, 220, 236, 251, 257
hospitals, 33, 70, 80, 102, 124, 245–6, 294
hotels, 164, 170, 183, 208, 261, see also Grand Hotel; Great Eastern Hotel
housing, European, 42, 50, 59–60, 64–5, 73–4; rural, 91, 143; flats, 92; overcrowding, 103, 142, 145, 274–5; of rich

Indians, 153–4, 155, 156;
planning and development,
179, 301, 303, 305; Richard's
report on, 273–5; partition
suits and, 276; see also
bustees; kothabaris; slums
Howrah, 33, 39, 79, 99, 102,
122, 136, 137, 343
Howrah Bridge, 24, 109, 129,
137, 138, 141, 209, 230, 273,
290
Howrah Station, 95, 248, 290,
293
L'Humanité, 85
hunger strikes, 197, see also fasts
hunting, 170, 253
Hungerford Street, 156
Huq, Fazlul, 121, 215

Ice House, 59
Ichamati river, 282
Ilbert Bill, 81, 253
illiteracy, 103, 171, 294
immigrants, 105, 108–9, 115–16,
121–3, 145, 282–4, see also
refugees
Impey, Sir Elijah, 52, 54–5, 62,
157, 166, 228, 243, 245
Imphal, 199
incense, 173, 208
Income Tax Investigation
Commission, 154
India, Europeans in, 27–8, 34–6,
40; Independence in, 74–5,
146, 222–3, 260–62; Partition,
105, 115, 176, 282, 283; trade
and economy, 133, 145, 152,
265; see also Bengal; Delhi;
Mogul Empire; West Bengal
India Act, 65
India Gazette, 200
Indian Association, 195

Indian Civil Service, 18, 78,
80–81, 189, 195, 196, 200,
202, 280
Indian Councils Act, 85
Indian Independence Week, 198
Indian Institute of Management,
341
Indian Mutiny, 76–8, 87, 113,
143, 192, 236, 258
Indian National Army, 119, 198,
199–200
indigo industry, 81, 82, 143, 200
Indo-Pakistani War, 282
Indo-Portuguese, 42
industry, 17, 19, 133–4, 147–9,
151, 154, 200–201, 225,
294–5, 299, 304–5, 331–5, 350
insurance, 148, 150, 201
insurrections, 76, 82, 143; see
also Indian Mutiny;
Naxalbari; race riots
iron, 134, 152
Isfahan, 36
Islam, 180, 214, 222
Italy, Italians, 15, 197–8, 203

jackals, 124, 126, 273
Jadavpore, 107
Jadavpore, University, 99, 330,
349
Jagannath, Lord, 248
Jain Temple, 185
Jains, 183, 184
Jaipur State, 152, 183
Jallianwalla Bagh massacre, 205
Jamshedpur, 134, 152
Japan, Japanese, 119, 198–9,
262, 273
Jayakar, M. R., 126
Jemdawee, 64
Jemedars, 62
jewellery, jewellers, 166, 185

Jha, Sibsankar, 143–4
Jinnah, Muhammad Ali, 216, 221
Jodpur State, 183
John Bull see *The Englishman*
Johnson, 'Begum', 41, 42, 44
Johnson, Reverend William, 41, 48, 54, 243
Jones, William, 51, 76, 157
jotedar, 319–20, 333
justice *see* law
jute industry, 75, 100, 103, 133, 144–6, 257, 278, 290, 334

Kabul, 197
Kali the Terrible, 19–20, 70, 84, 88, 96, 98, 137, 139, 169, 208–10, 300
Kalighat, 70, 88, 136, 208, 300, 306
Kalikata, 20, 30, 36, 134, 186, 200
Kalpi, 288
Kalwars, 188
Kalyani, 303–4
Kamartuli, 210
Kanchrapara, 99, 332
Kandla, 289
Kangali, 110–12
Kanarese, 68
Karachi, 88
Karim, Abdul, 233
Kashmir, Kashmiris, 163, 180, 261
Kasim, Mir, 38
Kasimbazar, 41, 47, 48
Kerala, 284, 309, 310, 318, 319, 343,
khatal, 99–100, 180
Khrushchev, Nikita, 211, 257–8
Kidderpore Docks, 136, 140, 178, 276, 289

Kipling, Rudyard, 18, 31, 168, 233, 245, 270
knifing 114, 217, 218–19, 220, 221, 337, 346, *see also* riots
Konar, Hari Krishna, 319, 320, 332, 354, 355
kothabari, 106, 107–8
Krishnagar, 343
Kulti, 134
Kurawas, 86
Kweiyang, 143

Lahore, 18, 139
Lakshmi Narain Hindu Temple, 153
Lalbazar, 64, 65
Lamb, Charles, 60
land-holding and redistribution, 66, 188, 319–22, 332, 336–7, 340
Landor, Walter Savage, 60, 247
Landowners' Association, 200
languages, 175–6, 310
Lansdowne, Lord, 237
La Poésie, 35
law, 52, 54–5, 63–4, 81, 85, 154, 166, 290 312–14, 324–5, 327, 340; *see also* police force
lawyers, 83, 201
Lenin Sarani, 329
Lenin, V. I., 19, 143, 338, 342, 348
Lear, Edward, 230, 237
Lebedeff, Herassim, 61
leprosy, 97–8, 128, 299, 300
Liberation, 338–9
libraries, 24, 49, 156
Lipton, Sir Thomas, 147–8
literature, 69, 71, 73, 190, *see also* Tagore, Rabindranath
Little Brothers and Sisters of Jesus, 296

Liverpool, Lord, 41
locusts, 257
Lok Sevak Sangha party, 344
locomotive works, 134, *see also*
    railway wagon
Loll Diggy, 64, 150, 189, 280
London, 17, 18, 24, 62
London Tavern, 60, 65
looting, 114, 215, 216, 217–18
Loreto Sisters, 296–7, 316
Lottery Committee, 73
Lower Chitpore Road, 111, 177,
    178–81, 185, 223, 294, 302
Lower Circular Road, 95, 121,
    157–8, 176, 297
Lucknow, 75
Lyon, Thomas, 241
Lyons Range, 151
Lytton, Lady, 235, 261
Lytton, Lord, 236

Macaulay, Lord, 39–40, 73, 76,
    112, 230, 233, 250, 258
MacDonald, Ramsay, 204
Mackenzie, Sir Alexander, 270
Madras, East India Company in,
    30, 52; Clive in, 37, 38, 45;
    Indians in presidential
    assembly, 79; economy of, 289,
    294, 295; terrorism in, 309;
    mentioned, 207, 248–9, 287
Mahabat Jang, Nawab, 41
Maharajahs, 87
Mahangar Parishad, 296
Maharashtra, 295
Mahatma Gandhi Road, 178
Mahesh Yogi, Maharishi, 135
Mahratta Ditch, 40, 42
Mahrattas, 55, 67, 187
Mahtab, Sir Uday Chand, 133
Maidan, political rallies on, 167,
    229, 326, 353–6; activities on,

172, 190, 228, 236; size of,
    173, 226–7; monuments on,
    199, 227–8, 229–30
Maisonneuve, 17
Malabar, 55
malaria, 26, 80, 125, 192, 246
managing agencies, 74–5, 154
Manasa, 19
Mandalay, 196
Maniktala, 178, 303
Manohar Das tank, 228
Mao Tse Tung, Maoism, 17,
    336, 337, 351–2
Marathi, 68
Marble Palace, 20–24, 155, 205,
    226
marriage, 107, 275
marriage market, European, 61
The Marriage of St Catherine, 22
The Martyrdom of St Sebastian,
    22–3
Martyrs Memorial, 328
Marwari Association, 184
Marwaris, 183–6, 206, 215, 278
Marx, Karl, 308
Mary, Queen, 86–7, 227
Master, Streynsham, 136
Mayo, Lady, 235
Mayo, Lord, 227–8
Mayurbhanj, Maharajah of, 132
Mazumdar, Charu, 336, 338
Mecca, 30
Medical and Relief Society, 153
medicine, 70, 80, 81, 98, 166,
    192, 238, 298–9, 300
Meerut, 76, 78, 253, 308
Melancholy Point, 34
middens, 97, 111, 285, 305–6
Midnapore, 120, 134
migrants, 271, *see also*
    immigrants
Mill, James, 72

mineral resources, 134, 152, 289, 294

Minerva giving the loving cup to Apollo, 23

Minto, Lady, 238

Minto, Lord, 84, 85, 195, 227

Mir Jafar, 45–6, 48

Mir Kasim, 46

Misser, Sepoy Juggernauth, 140

Mission Press, 68

Mission Row, 79

missionaries, 68, 201, 204

Mogul Empire, 23, 27, 35, 39–47, 50–51, 64, 66, 86, 188–9

Molla, Akbar Ali, 220

money-lenders, 71, 144, 183, 337

Monson, Lady Anne, 52, 55, 60, 247

Monson, Colonel, 52, 53, 54–5

Montesquieu, 72

Moscow, 18, 73–4, 92, 142, 197, 315, 337, *see also* Russia

mosques, 180, 181, 182, 214–15, 282, 351

Mountbatten, Earl, 119, 221

Muggeridge, Malcolm, 296

Mukherjee, Ajoy, as President of Congress, 314–15; and relations with Ghosh, 315, 326; and Bangla Congress, 315, 340; as Chief Minister, 316, 325, 326, 327, 332, 340–47; character, 316–17; and Basu, 316, 326, 332, 340–41, 343–5, 348; resignation of, 346–7

Mussoorie, 154

Mukta Mela, 190

Mullick family, 23, 155, *see also* Marble Palace

Mumtaz, 28

Munny Begum, 48

Muharram, 181

murder, 123, 213, 325, 337, 345–6, 349

Murillo, 22

Murray's Handbook, 224

Murshidabad, 41, 45, 47, 63, 181

Mother Teresa's Missionaries of Charity, 96–8, 153, 253, 296–300

museums, 132, 152

music, 190, 199–200, 202, 204, 205, 210

Muslims, land-law, 66; in East Bengal, 83, 214; 1946 race riots, 84, 216–22; food taboos and, 123, 184; Hindi speakers, 176; Partition and, 176; occupations of, 180; festivals, 180–81, 193; dislike of Marwaris by, 184–5; education of, 193; Bengali (Hindu) opinion of, 206; 1926 race riots, 214–15; political activities of, 214–15, 216; numbers of, 215; mentioned, 86, 296; *see also* Mogul Empire

Muslim League, 216–17, 218

Mussolini, Benito, 197

Mymensingh, 126

Nadia, Lady Maharini Bahaduri, 132

Nainital, 154

Nakhoda Mosque, 180, 181, 182, 351

Naogaon, 125

National Library, 156

National Medical College and Hospital, 335

National Volunteer Force, 305

nationalism, 80–81, 84, 184, 194, 195–6, 201–2, 213–14
Nattore, Maharaja of, 132
Naxalbari, 320–22, 336
Naxalites, 336–8, 344, 348, 349
Nehru, Jawaharlal, 146, 197, 211, 216, 249, 265
Nepal, Nepali, 105, 206, 229, 320
Netaji Subhas Road, 150
Netaji Week, 198
New Delhi, 157, 237, see also Delhi
New Market, 240, 245, 255, 313
New Year's Day, Bengali, 209
New York, 17, 103, 266, 290
newspapers, English, 58, 62, 75, 88, 127; Bengali, 84; opposition to partition by, 84–5; during the famine, 124; Dwarkanath Tagore's ownership of, 200
Nicholson, Admiral, 29–30
night-clubs, 110, 158–9
Nightingale, Florence, 233, 268
Nimtallah ghat, 128
Normal Hriday, 96–7, 128, 129, 299, 300
Noakhali, 221
Nobel Prize, 192, 200, 204
North, Lord, 51, 52, 53
Northbrooke, Lord, 227, 235, 237
Numcomar, 49, 54–5, 65, 233, 242

oil industry, 134, 293
Old Court House, Street, 166
opium, 38, 48, 49, 179, 201, 242
ordinance factories, 80, 120, 332
Orientalists, Orientalism, 50–51, 69, 70, 71–3

Orissa, 47, 83, 105, 134, 142, 179, 196, 248, 284
Oriya, Oriyas, 68, 82, 206, 250
Oriya language, 175
Osborne, Sir John, 244
Ochterlony, Sir David, 229
Ochterlony Monument, 70, 72, 212, 217, 229–30
Oudh, 53
Oudh, Nawab of, 41, 180, 244

Padavali of Bhanu Singa see Tagore, Rabindranath
Padma, 135
Padma, River, 203, 287
Pakistan, 135, 145, 287, see also East Pakistan
palaces, 132, 133, 136, 178, see also Marble Palace
palanquins, 63, 132, 244
Palmer, General, 237
Palta, 286–7
Panchanan, 193
Pandava Princes, 86
paper, paper products, 134, 154, 303
Paramahansa, Ramakrishna, 296
Paris, 22, 63, 84
Park Street, 94, 110, 118, 130–31, 158–62, 163, 171, 183, 185, 228
Park Street cemetery, 157, 176, 247–8
parks, 111, 155, 226, 232
'partition suit', 276
Patna, 29, 63, 134, 242, 289, 349
Paull, Mr 243, 245
Pearse, Colonel, 56–7, 247
peasants, 114, 120, 142–4, 310, 319–20, 328, 332–3, 336–7, see also famine; land-holding and redistribution

Peel, Sir Robert, 227
Peking, 19, *see also* China
Peking Daily News, 321
Peninsular and Oriental
    Steamship Company, 79, 138,
    146
peons, 64, *see also* peasants
People's United Left Front,
    315
Permanent Settlement, 66, 71,
    233
Persia, 35, 36, 39, 50–51, 182
pilgrims, 136, 208–9, 222–3, 296
Pillani, 152
Pillani University, 152
Pitt, William, 65
planetarian, 152
Plassey, battle of, 45, 46, 51,
    200, 233
poetry, 190, 192, 194, *see also*
    Tagore, Rabindranath
police force, on traffic duty, 24,
    170, 290; on goondas, 113–14;
    during 1946 race riots, 218;
    vice squad of, 245; attitude of,
    252; and riots 290, 332,
    339–40, 344, 346; under
    Mukherjee, 317, 318–24; and
    murder of officers, 321, 349;
    under Basu, 328, 332, 335–6,
    338, 339, 341–4, 346; riot of,
    335–6
polo, 165, 257
population (of Calcutta), British,
    85, 252; Anglo-Indian, 87;
    increase, 98, 271, 272, 276,
    281, 295; of bustee dwellers,
    99; in Howrah, 102; density
    of, 103, 295; urban, in West
    Bengal, 142; of Marwaris,
    183; of Muslims, 215; forecast
    for 1986, 304

Portugal, Portuguese, 27–8, 35,
    42, 60, 74
Portuguese language, 176
Poshman, Bheddari, 103–4
post office, 86, 150, 171, 241, 294
Praja Socialist Party, 315
Prasadjote, 321
Presbyterians, 33
Presidency General Hospital, 80,
    192, 245, 268
Presidency College, 196
Prinsep Ghat, 139
printing, printers, 51, 68, 69, 85,
    193
prisons, 113–14, 196–7, 308,
    309, 310, 316
processions, 174, 180–81, *see also*
    Durga Puja
Provisional Indian Government,
    121
Provisional Indian Government
    (in exile), 119
protection, 114–15
Publick Advertiser, 52
Puja, 338
Punjab, Punjabis, 18, 180, 221,
    283, 310, 327

Rabindra Bharati University, 205
Rabindra Sarani *see* Lower
    Chitpore Road
Racecourse *see* horseracing
race riots, 84, 216–22
Radical Humanist, 191
Raj Bhayan *see* Government
    House
Rahmin, Sir Abdur, 214
railway equipment, construction
    of, 133, 333, *see also*
    locomotive works
railways, development of, 79,
    289; Anglo-Indian service on,

86; bustees adjoining, 99; and
refugees, 121, 282; and spread
of infection, 286;
overcrowding on, 291, 293;
future planning of, 304; union
activity and, 316; industrial
disputes and, 335; mentioned,
218, 225

Raj Bhavan *see* Government
House

Rajas, 87

Rajasthan, 152, 183, 184, 310

Ranchi, 134

Rangoon, 199

Raniganj, 79

Rashbehari Avenue, 105

Rashtrapati Bhavan, 153

rates, 276–7, *see also* taxation

Rawdon Street, 156

Red Road, 179, 227, 231

refugees, 115–16, 219, 282–4,
314, 318–19, 340, *see also*
immigrants

Regulating Act 1772, 51

Rejasthan, 180, 184

rents, 64, 105–6, 274, 312, 313

Reserve Bank of India, 128

restaurants, 25, 118, 146, 159,
160, 163, 172, 179, 208

The Return of Ulysses, 23

Revolutionary Communist Party
of India, 315, 344

Revolutionary Socialist Party,
315, 335, 344

Reynolds, Sir Joshua, 22

R. G. Kar Hospital, 294

Ribbentrop, 197

rice, 38, 111, 118, 120–21, 125,
126, 143

Richards, E. P., 273–7, 280

rickshaws, 21, 25, 92, 103–4,
116, 128, 160, 169, 174–5

riots, 290, 330–33, 334–6,
339–40, 345–6, 348–9, *see also*
race riots

Ripon, Lord, 81, 82, 253

Rishikesh, 135

roads, 91–2, 151, 183, 233, 267,
272–3, 275, 301, 303–4,
328–9

robbery, 113, 114, 345–6, *see also*
riots

Rohillas, 53

Rome, 17, 21, 133, 290

Ronaldshay, Lord, 184, 263, 276

Ross, Surgeon-Major (Sir)
Ronald, 80, 192, 246

Rourkela, 134

Roy, Rammohan, 71–2, 193–4,
201

Royal Exchange, 150, 151, 154,
260

Rubens, 22–3

Rudd, 81

Russell, Bertrand, 204, 338

Russia, 71, 197, 199, 211–12,
306, 308, 315, 329, 337

sacrifice, 73, 208–9

sadhus, 172, 351

Sagar Island, 209

St Andrew's Church, 239

St Anne's Church, 39, 49

St Helena, 63

St John's Church, 41, 54, 239,
241, 248, 245, 247

St Xavier's College, 202, 316

Samyukta Socialist Party, 315,
344

Sarkerchak, 122

saltpetre, 29, 34, 49, 59

Sandhya, 84

Sandys, Duncan, 257

sanitation, 92, 96, 101, 102,

sanitation – *cont'd*.
105–6, 173, 266, 270, 273,
285–7, 301, 305–6
Sanskrit, 19, 51, 73, 202
Sanskrit, College, 70
Santiniketan, 203
Sanyal, Kanu, 336–7
Sarasvati, 19
Sarhad, Khojah Israel, 36
Satanuti, 36
Satgaon, 27, 289
Satkhira, 124
scavengers, 111–12, 122–3,
125–6
schools, 183, 202–3, 296, 331,
335, *see also* education
Schweitzer, Albert, 204
Scotland, Scots, 74, 100, 146,
147
Sea Ip Temple, 179
Sealdah Station, 96, 129, 282,
306, 319
Second World War, 113, 119,
197–9, 214, 237, 262, 274,
278
Sen, Gurucharam, 188
Sen Keshub Chandra, 194, 207,
233
Sen, P. C., 311, 314–15, 343
Sen, Ram Camul, 193
Sena, Shev, 349
Serampore, 35, 68, 69, 201
servants, 64–70, 75, 104–5,
112–13
Seth, Mesroub Jacob, 36
Seth Sukhlal Memorial Hospital
see Presidency General
Hospital
sexual relations, 107–8
Sèvres, 22
Shah Jehan, Emperor, 28, 29, 30,
139

Shakespeare Sarani, 155
Shalimar, 139
Shampukur, 219
Shanghai, 19
Shaw, George Bernard, 204
Shia, sect, 180
Shillong, 253
shipbuilding, shipping, 34, 137,
188, 200, 288, 293, *see also*
boats; docks
shoeshine boys, 110–11, 174
Shore, Sir John, 67, 267
Sikhs, 116, 170, 175, 178, 180,
209
Silaida, 203
Siliguri, 134, 320, 336, 337
Simla, 81, 238
Singapore, 198, 199
Singh, Naick Runmust, 140
Sinha, Chief Justice, 324–5
Siraj-ud-Daula, Nawab, 41–5,
47, 49, 54, 61, 233
Siret, M., 61
Sitala, 19
Sira Sakti, Samati, 296
sitar, 114, 190
Sixsmith, Brigadier J. D. C.,
219
slavery, 42, 271–2
Slim, Field-Marshal, 119, 199
Siva the Destroyer, 20
slums, 95–6, 99, 101–102,
109–10, 130–31, 136, 145,
257, 285–6, *see also* bustees
smallpox, 19, 102
Smith, Conran, 123
snake-charming, 15, 230
snuff, 61, 63
Socialist Unity Centre, 315, 340,
344
Society for the Promotion of
National Feeling among the

Educated Native of Bengal, 80–81, 202
Sodepore, 221
Sonepur State, Maharajah Ruler of, 132
South India, Hinduism in, 19
South-East Asia Youth Conference, 309
Soviet Information Service, 156
starvation *see* famine
State Tourist Board, 117
Statesman, letters in, 86, 89, 262–3; on removal of the capital, 89–90, on the famine, 124–5; advertising in, 147, 151; contributors to, 165, 296; on race riots, 219–20; and Vintage Car Rally, 253; and Mother Teresa, 299–300; on United Party split, 341; mentioned, 169, 251, 256
steel, steel products, 133, 134, 152, 334
Stewart, Charles, 29, 30, 187
Strand Road, 110, 139, 140, 211, 229, 231, 306
street lighting, 101, 105–6, 108, 281, 305, 331
street-sleepers, 95, 111, 130, 156–7, 174
strikes, 278, 293, 306, 325–6, 331–2, 333–5
students, 213, 238, 296, 330–31, 335, 349
sugar cane, 143, 172
Suhrawardy H. S., 121, 123, 124, 216, 221, 222, 223, 260
Sumatra, 34, 198
Sundarbans, 253
Sunni sect, 180
Surat, 28
Sutanuti, 30, 36, 37, 200

suttee, 33, 71, 72
swadeshi movement, 84, 184,
Swaraj Party, 196, 214, 311 202, 203–4,, 296
sweepers, 102, 104
synagogues, 176

Tagore, Babendranath, 202
Tagore, Debendranath, 201, 202
Tagore, Dwarkanath, 200–201, 202, 233
Tagore, Dwijendranath, 202
Tagore, Jatinsamohan, 206
Tagore, Jnanendramhohan, 201
Tagore, Jyotirindranath, 203
Tagore, Prassanakumar, 201–2
Tagore, Rabindranath, 192, 200, 202–5, 233, 257, 259
Tagore, Satyendrath, 200, 202
Taj Mahal, 28, 231
Talleyrand, Prince, 63
Talleyrand, Princess, *see* Grande, Madame
Tamil, Tamils, 68, 175, 180, 310
Tank Square, 59, 72, 150
Tashkent, 308
Tata family, 152
taxation, 99, 132, 133, 149, 151, 154, 256, 268–9, 279, 280, 295, 318
taxis, 21, 92, 173–4, 178, 183
Taylor, Mary, 349
Taylor, William, 69
tea industry, 79, 134, 320, 334
Telegu, 68, 175
temples, 41, 152, 179, 185, 205, 208–9, 214–15, 249, 296
terrorism, 84–5, 88, 214, 303, 309, *see also* riots
textile industry, 32, 80, 151, 153, 180, 303, 308

Thackeray, William Makepeace, 233, 246, 247
theatre, 39, 61, 87, 190, 194, 201, 245
Thiers, 72
thika tenants, 99, 109
thieves, 65, 112, 208
Thompson, George, 201
Thugs, 20, 72
Tibet, 35, 320
tigers, 147, 253, 256
timber, 134
The Times of India, 126
Tipu Sultan Mosque, 169
Tirmiz, 308
Titian, 22
tobacco industry, 38, 111, 147, 180
Tokyo, 17, 133, 198, 199
Tollygunge, 253, 282
Tolly's Nullah, 139, 209, 218, 237
Toltalah Bazar, 64
trade *see* commerce
trade unions, 307, 324–5
traders, 27, 36, 64, 75–6, 79, 88–9, 107, 150, 171, 176–8, 180; *see also* commerce; East Indian Company
trams, 79–80, 92, 148, 177–8, 213, 275, 291, 292, 335
traffic, 24, 25, 92, 133, 151, 152, 173–4, 178, 181, 231, 289–93, 335
tuberculosis, 102, 275
Twain, Mark, 18–19, 229
24 Parganas, 45, 118, 122, 282, 314, 332

U Thant, 338
Udaipur State, 183
Uluberia, 288

unemployment, 293, 325, 333, 346, *see also* factories, closures
unemployment benefit, 101
United Front, 316, 317–19, 322–3, 325–33, 335, 338, 344–5, 347, 350, 354
Unitarians, 72
United Kingdom Citizens Association, 253–4, 255
US Information Service, 156
Upper Chitpore Road, 219
Urdu, 50, 68, 171, 175, 176
Uttar Pradesh, 105, 178, 284, 309, 327

Valentia, Lord, 73, 267
Vansittart Row, 60
Varadachariar, Mr Justice, 154
Vedas, 201
Viceregal Lodge, 238
Victoria, Queen, 22, 78, 82, 113, 232–3, 237, 258, 263
Victoria Memorial, 227, 231–4, 239, 241, 245, 257
Vietnam, 143
Vira, Dharma, 326, 328
Vishakapatnam, 289
Vishnu the Preserver, 20, 135, 172, 244
Vivekenanda, Swami, 210, 296
Volunteer Guards, 76, 77

wages, 101, 103–5, 106, 117–18, 151, 166, 278, 333
water supply, under East India Company, 63, 149, 280; standpipes for, 95, 96, 99–100, 131, 156; in bustees, 99, 105–6, 296; impurity of, 100, 116, 268, 286–7; in tanks, 173, 228, 277; World Health Organization's warning, 257;

shortage of filtered, 280–81, 294, 301, 322; CMPO plan and, 305
Watson, Colonel, 56–7, 140
Watts, W., 41, 42, 47
Wavell, Field-Marshal Lord, 120, 279
weapons, 114, 132, 217, 218, 339
Weldon, Commissioner, 30, 33
William IV, King, 33, 34, 176
Wellesley, Richard, Lord, 67–8, 72, 73, 234, 235, 263
Wellesley, Arthur, Duke of Wellington, 67
West Bengal, industrial action in, 293–4, 321–4, 331–3, 334–6; relations with Delhi, 295; United Front rule in, 306; terrorism in, 309; poor relief in, 314; 1962 elections in, 315; 1967 elections in, 315–16; 1970 elections in, 315–16; unemployment in, 325, 334; President's rule in, 327, 332, 333; and partition, 83–4; and reunification, 86–8; lack of hospital beds in, 102; industry in, 133–4, 145–6, 294–5, 333–4, 350; population of,

142; income in, 142; administration in, 150; immigrants in, 282–3; cholera in, 286; see also Bengal; Calcutta, riots; United Front
West Bengal Business Convention, 334
West Pakistan, 283
wheat, 120, 123, 125
Wilson, Horace, 70, 76, 193
Wood Street, 156
Workers' Party of India, 344
working hours, 60, 101, 278
World Bank, 265, 301
World Federation of Democratic Youth, 309
World Health Organization, 257, 287, 301
Wyatt, Captain, 241

Yeats, W. B., 204
Yorkshire Regiment, 80
Young Bengal Movement, 70–71, 72, 194

Zakaria Street, 223
zamindars, 39, 46, 65–6, 71, 115, 133, 136, 200
Zoffany, John, 243, 245

FOR THE BEST IN PAPERBACKS, LOOK FOR THE 🐧

In every corner of the world, on every subject under the sun, Penguin represents quality and variety – the very best in publishing today.

For complete information about books available from Penguin – including Puffins, Penguin Classics and Arkana – and how to order them, write to us at the appropriate address below. Please note that for copyright reasons the selection of books varies from country to country.

In the United Kingdom: Please write to *Dept E.P., Penguin Books Ltd, Harmondsworth, Middlesex, UB7 0DA*.

If you have any difficulty in obtaining a title, please send your order with the correct money, plus ten per cent for postage and packaging, to *PO Box No 11, West Drayton, Middlesex*

In the United States: Please write to *Dept BA, Penguin, 299 Murray Hill Parkway, East Rutherford, New Jersey 07073*

In Canada: Please write to *Penguin Books Canada Ltd, 2801 John Street, Markham, Ontario L3R 1B4*

In Australia: Please write to the *Marketing Department, Penguin Books Australia Ltd, P.O. Box 257, Ringwood, Victoria 3134*

In New Zealand: Please write to the *Marketing Department, Penguin Books (NZ) Ltd, Private Bag, Takapuna, Auckland 9*

In India: Please write to *Penguin Overseas Ltd, 706 Eros Apartments, 56 Nehru Place, New Delhi, 110019*

In the Netherlands: Please write to *Penguin Books Netherlands B.V., Postbus 3507, 1001 AH, Amsterdam*

In West Germany: Please write to *Penguin Books Ltd, Friedrichstrasse 10–12, D–6000 Frankfurt/Main 1*

In Spain: Please write to *Alhambra Longman S.A., Fernandez de la Hoz 9, E–28010 Madrid*

In Italy: Please write to *Penguin Italia s.r.l., Via Como 4, I-20096 Pioltello (Milano)*

In France: Please write to *Penguin Books Ltd, 39 Rue de Montmorency, F-75003 Paris*

In Japan: Please write to *Longman Penguin Japan Co Ltd, Yamaguchi Building, 2–12–9 Kanda Jimbocho, Chiyoda-Ku, Tokyo 101*

A CHOICE OF PENGUINS

Riding the Iron Rooster Paul Theroux

An eye-opening and entertaining account of travels in old and new China, from the author of *The Great Railway Bazaar*. 'Mr Theroux cannot write badly ... in the course of a year there was almost no train in the vast Chinese rail network on which he did not travel' – Ludovic Kennedy

The Life of Graham Greene Norman Sherry
Volume One 1904–1939

'Probably the best biography ever of a living author' – Philip French in the *Listener*. Graham Greene has always maintained a discreet distance from his reading public. This volume reconstructs his first thirty-five years to create one of the most revealing literary biographies of the decade.

The Chinese David Bonavia

'I can think of no other work which so urbanely and entertainingly succeeds in introducing the general Western reader to China' – *Sunday Telegraph*

All the Wrong Places James Fenton

Who else but James Fenton could have played a Bach prelude on the presidential piano – and stolen one of Imelda's towels – on the very day Marcos left his palace in Manila? 'He is the most professional of amateur war correspondents, a true though unusual journo, top of the trade. When he arrives in town, prudent dictators pack their bags and quit' – *The Times*

Voices of the Old Sea Norman Lewis

'Limpidly and lovingly, Norman Lewis has caught the helpless, unwitting, often foolish, but always hopeful village in its dying summers, and saved the tragedy with sublime comedy' – *Observer*

Ninety-Two Days Evelyn Waugh

With characteristic honesty, Evelyn Waugh here debunks the romantic notions attached to rough travelling. His journey in Guiana and Brazil is difficult, dangerous and extremely uncomfortable, and his account of it is witty and unquestionably compelling.

FOR THE BEST IN PAPERBACKS, LOOK FOR THE 🐧

A CHOICE OF PENGUINS

The Russian Album   Michael Ignatieff

Michael Ignatieff movingly comes to terms with the meaning of his own family's memories and histories, in a book that is both an extraordinary account of the search for roots and a dramatic and poignant chronicle of four generations of a Russian family.

Beyond the Blue Horizon   Alexander Frater

The romance and excitement of the legendary Imperial Airways East-bound Empire service – the world's longest and most adventurous scheduled air route – relived fifty years later in one of the most original travel books of the decade. 'The find of the year' – *Today*

Getting to Know the General   Graham Greene

'In August 1981 my bag was packed for my fifth visit to Panama when the news came to me over the telephone of the death of General Omar Torrijos Herrera, my friend and host...' 'Vigorous, deeply felt, at times funny, and for Greene surprisingly frank' – *Sunday Times*

The Time of My Life   Denis Healey

'Denis Healey's memoirs have been rightly hailed for their intelligence, wit and charm ... *The Time of My Life* should be read, certainly for pleasure, but also for profit ... he bestrides the post-war world, a Colossus of a kind' – *Independent*

Arabian Sands   Wilfred Thesiger

'In the tradition of Burton, Doughty, Lawrence, Philby and Thomas, it is, very likely, the book about Arabia to end all books about Arabia' – *Daily Telegraph*

Adieux: A Farewell to Sartre   Simone de Beauvoir

A devastatingly frank account of the last years of Sartre's life, and his death, by the woman who for more than half a century shared that life. 'A true labour of love, there is about it a touching sadness, a mingling of the personal with the impersonal and timeless which Sartre himself would surely have liked and understood' – *Listener*

A CHOICE OF PENGUINS

The Assassination of Federico García Lorca   Ian Gibson

Lorca's 'crime' was his antipathy to pomposity, conformity and intolerance. His punishment was murder. Ian Gibson – author of the acclaimed new biography of Lorca – reveals the truth about his death and the atmosphere in Spain that allowed it to happen.

Between the Woods and the Water   Patrick Leigh Fermor

Patrick Leigh Fermor continues his celebrated account – begun in *A Time of Gifts* – of his journey on foot from the Hook of Holland to Constantinople. 'Even better than everyone says it is' – Peter Levi. 'Indescribably rich and beautiful' – *Guardian*

The Time Out Film Guide   Edited by Tom Milne

The definitive, up-to-the-minute directory of 9,000 films – world cinema from classics and silent epics to reissues and the latest releases – assessed by two decades of *Time Out* reviewers. 'In my opinion the best and most comprehensive' – Barry Norman

Metamagical Themas   Douglas R. Hofstadter

This astonishing sequel to the bestselling, Pulitzer Prize-winning *Gödel, Escher, Bach* swarms with 'extraordinary ideas, brilliant fables, deep philosophical questions and Carrollian word play' – Martin Gardner

Into the Heart of Borneo   Redmond O'Hanlon

'Perceptive, hilarious and at the same time a serious natural-history journey into one of the last remaining unspoilt paradises' – *New Statesman*. 'Consistently exciting, often funny and erudite without ever being overwhelming' – *Punch*

When the Wind Blows   Raymond Briggs

'A visual parable against nuclear war: all the more chilling for being in the form of a strip cartoon' – *Sunday Times*. 'The most eloquent anti-Bomb statement you are likely to read' – *Daily Mail*

FOR THE BEST IN PAPERBACKS, LOOK FOR THE 🐧

A CHOICE OF PENGUINS

Brian Epstein: The Man Who Made the Beatles Ray Coleman

'An excellent biography of Brian Epstein, the lonely, gifted man whose artistic faith and bond with the Beatles never wavered – and whose recognition of genius created a cultural era, even though it destroyed him' – *Mail on Sunday*

A Thief in the Night John Cornwell

A veil of suspicion and secrecy surrounds the last hours of Pope John Paul I, whose thirty-three day reign ended in a reported heart attack on the night of 28 September 1978. Award-winning crime writer John Cornwell was invited by the Vatican to investigate. 'The best detective story you will ever read' – *Daily Mail*

Among the Russians Colin Thubron

One man's solitary journey by car across Russia provides an enthralling and revealing account of the habits and idiosyncrasies of a fascinating people. 'He sees things with the freshness of an innocent and the erudition of a scholar' – *Daily Telegraph*

Higher than Hope Fatima Meer

The authorized biography of Nelson Mandela. 'An astonishing read ... the most complete, authoritative and moving tribute thus far' – *Time Out*

Stones of Aran: Pilgrimage Tim Robinson

Arainn is the largest of the three Aran Islands, and one of the world's oldest landscapes. This 'wholly irresistible' (*Observer*) and uncategoriz-able book charts a sunwise journey around its coast – and explores an open secret, teasing out the paradoxes of a terrain at once bare and densely inscribed.

Bernard Shaw Michael Holroyd
Volume I 1856–1898: The Search for Love

'In every sense, a spectacular piece of work ... A feat of style as much as of research, which will surely make it a flamboyant new landmark in modern English life-writing' – Richard Holmes in *The Times*

FOR THE BEST IN PAPERBACKS, LOOK FOR THE 🐧

A CHOICE OF PENGUINS

Return to the Marshes Gavin Young

His remarkable portrait of the remote and beautiful world of the Marsh Arabs, whose centuries-old existence is now threatened with extinction by twentieth-century warfare.

The Big Red Train Ride Eric Newby

From Moscow to the Pacific on the Trans-Siberian Railway is an eight-day journey of nearly six thousand miles through seven time zones. In 1977 Eric Newby set out with his wife, an official guide and a photographer on this journey.

Warhol Victor Bockris

'This is the kind of book I like: it tells me the things I want to know about the artist, what he ate, what he wore, who he knew (in his case ... everybody), at what time he went to bed and with whom, and, most important of all, his work habits' – *Independent*

1001 Ways to Save the Planet Bernadette Vallely

There are 1001 changes that *everyone* can make in their lives *today* to bring about a greener environment – whether at home or at work, on holiday or away on business. Action that you can take *now*, and that you won't find too difficult to take. This practical guide shows you how.

Bitter Fame Anne Stevenson
A Life of Sylvia Plath

'A sobering and salutary attempt to estimate what Plath was, what she achieved and what it cost her ... This is the only portrait which answers Ted Hughes's image of the poet as Ariel, not the ethereal bright pure roving sprite, but Ariel trapped in Prospero's pine and raging to be free' – *Sunday Telegraph*

The Venetian Empire Jan Morris

For six centuries the Republic of Venice was a maritime empire of coasts, islands and fortresses. Jan Morris reconstructs this glittering dominion in the form of a sea voyage along the historic Venetian trade routes from Venice itself to Greece, Crete and Cyprus.

THE PENGUIN TRAVEL LIBRARY – A SELECTION

Hindoo Holiday J. R. Ackerley
The Flight of Ikaros Kevin Andrews
A Desert Dies Michael Asher
The Innocent Anthropologist Nigel Barley
The Deer Cry Pavilion Pat Barr
The Path to Rome Hilaire Belloc
Looking for Dilmun Geoffrey Bibby
First Russia, Then Tibet Robert Byron
Granite Island Dorothy Carrington
An Indian Summer James Cameron
Siren Land Norman Douglas
Brazilian Adventure Peter Fleming
Caucasian Journey Negley Farson
The Hill of Devi E. M. Forster
Journey to Kars Philip Glazebrook
Pattern of Islands Arthur Grimble
Writings from Japan Lafcadio Hearn
A Little Tour in France Henry James
Mornings in Mexico D. H. Lawrence
The Stones of Florence and **Venice Observed** Mary McCarthy
They Went to Portugal Rose Macaulay
The Colossus of Maroussi Henry Miller
Calcutta Geoffrey Moorhouse
Spain Jan Morris
The Big Red Train Ride Eric Newby
The Other Nile Charlie Pye-Smith
The Marsh Arabs Wilfred Thesiger
Journey into Cyprus Colin Thubron
Ninety-Two Days Evelyn Waugh
Maiden Voyage Denton Welch